NEW JERSEY IN THE
AMERICAN REVOLUTION

★ ★ ★

NEW JERSEY *in* *the* AMERICAN REVOLUTION

Edited by Barbara J. Mitnick

Rivergate Books

AN IMPRINT OF RUTGERS UNIVERSITY PRESS

New Brunswick, New Jersey & London

LIBRARY OF CONGRESS CATALOGING-IN-PUBLICATION DATA

New Jersey in the American Revolution / edited by Barbara J. Mitnick.
p.   cm.
Includes bibliographical references and index.
ISBN 0–8135–3602–2 (hardcover : alk. paper)
1. New Jersey—History—Revolution, 1775–1783. I. Mitnick, Barbara J.
E263.N5N715 2005
973.3'09749—dc22   2004020839

A British Cataloging-in-Publication record is available for this book from the British Library.

The publication of this book was made possible, in part, by grants from the New Jersey Council for
the Humanities, the New Jersey Historical Commission, and the Pheasant Hill Foundation.

Manufactured in the United States of America

Contents

Foreword

FOR MORE THAN a century and a quarter, the Washington Association of New Jersey has served the state and nation by preserving important aspects of New Jersey's Revolutionary War history. The association's sponsorship of *New Jersey in the American Revolution* is yet another example of its magnificent historical public-spiritedness.

In Benjamin Franklin's legendary opinion, New Jersey may very well have been just "a barrel tapped at both ends," but without a doubt it was at the center of the American Revolution. Whether the people of this state or the American people in general know this fact, however, is an open question. The Task Force on New Jersey History reported in 1997 that New Jersey ranked dead last among the thirteen original states in the number of historical publications related to state population.

The goal of this book as envisioned by the Washington Association, Rutgers University Press, and others who have been involved in supporting and funding the project is to help educate the public, especially young people, about New Jersey's central role in the Revolution. The exciting essays that editor Barbara J. Mitnick has assembled touch on various aspects of life in the last third of eighteenth-century New Jersey, including a review of general social and economic conditions, the state's central location as a military theater, the radical nature of the state's first constitution, the role of women and African Americans, as well as analyses of the literature, arts, architecture, geography, and archaeology that existed here. What an impressive group of topics for us and our descendants to read; what an inspiring group from which we might further understand the life and times of Revolutionary New Jersey.

Moreover, the essays are based on important new historical research by distinguished scholars. Educators will have an exciting new source of information from which to teach the rising generation, which is particularly important now that the legislature has required new curriculum standards in our schools. The general public, not only here but in other states as well, will be able to appreciate better New Jersey's importance in the founding of the nation.

The Washington Association of New Jersey and Rutgers University Press should be immensely proud of this important addition to the historical literature of the state. We honor those who helped create the new nation two and a quarter centuries ago by this publication; we also honor New Jersey, the state we love in no small measure for the critical part it played in the American Revolution.

— LEONARD LANCE,
NEW JERSEY STATE SENATOR

Preface and Acknowledgements

LEGEND TELLS US that in the eighteenth century, New Jersey was thought of as "a barrel tapped at both ends" by the major nearby cities of Philadelphia and New York and the rather uninteresting corridor through which travelers to other colonies would have to pass. Even today, remnants of this reputation unfortunately persist; the derogatory question "What exit?" [of the New Jersey Turnpike] more often than not follows the announcement of one's New Jersey residence. But those of us who live here know better, for despite the fact that the state is the most densely populated in the Union, its residents enjoy beautiful landscapes and open space. Although New Jersey is sandwiched between two major American cities, the artistic creativity of many of its citizens is well understood; and although many consider Virginia, Massachusetts, and Pennsylvania to be the preeminent locations of America's eighteenth-century past, it is clear that more Revolutionary War history took place in New Jersey than in any other state.

At the same time, it is ironic that many New Jerseyans do not have an adequate knowledge of their own history, even though a modicum of information is provided in the state's schools. Responses (or lack of responses) to some of the most basic questions are surprising. For example, how many know that more Revolutionary War battles and skirmishes were fought in New Jersey than in any other state? How many know that the true "Crossroads of the American Revolution" was in New Jersey and that the first turning points of the war for independence occurred in Trenton and Princeton? How many know that New Jersey passed its first constitution even before the adoption of the Declaration of Independence by America's Second Continental Congress? How many know about the state's extensive archaeological sites and numerous extant historic buildings? How many know that some of America's finest artists came to New Jersey to visually document significant Revolutionary War events and battles? How many have knowledge of the social and economic conditions existing in eighteenth-century New

Jersey, its literature and architecture, as well as the plight of women, blacks, and American Indians? And how many of us can truly comprehend what it was like to live in New Jersey during the first successful revolution in history against a mother country?

These are some of the questions that were posed in early 2001 when New Jersey's 225th Anniversary of the Revolution Celebration Commission was established by former New Jersey governor Christine Todd Whitman. From the beginning, it was clear that commission members were concerned about these serious problems, for in 1997 the state's Task Force on New Jersey History had accurately examined and then quantified a severe lack of knowledge of New Jersey's participation in the American Revolution as well as the state's history in general. Thus it was agreed that one of the major legacies of the work of the 225th Commission would be to address New Jersey's need for more textbooks and other sources of information. The mission was clear; we would create an anthology of essays by major writers to include the most up-to-date scholarship.

We began our work, and within a short time, Morristown's Washington Association of New Jersey resolved to become a cosponsor of the publication. As the congressionally legislated advisory body for Morristown National Historical Park and longtime guardian of the memory of George Washington and his two Revolutionary War encampments in Morristown, the association clearly recognized the importance of this work. Carefully selected specialists in the various areas to be addressed were invited to present essays, which, taken together, have created a picture of eighteenth-century New Jersey as not only a theater of war but as a place where people lived, worked, wrote, fought, created, and, in the process, added immeasurably to the development of America's distinctive heritage.

New Jersey in the American Revolution would not have been possible without the financial support of the New Jersey Historical Commission, the Pheasant Hill Foundation, and the New Jersey Council for the Humanities. Special thanks are due to State Senator Leonard Lance for his contribution of the book's foreword, his leadership of the 225th Commission, and his continuing support for New Jersey history. I am grateful to Marlie Wasserman, director of the Rutgers University Press, who quickly recognized the value and potential of this publication and has worked diligently to make it a reality. Michele Gisbert, Marilyn Campbell, and Alison Hack of the Rutgers University Press staff also were enormously helpful, as were copyeditor Robert Burchfield and picture editor Sharon Hazard. Most of all, I offer my sincere gratitude to my coauthors Thomas Fleming, David J. Fowler, Maxine N. Lurie, Mark Edward Lender, Harriette C. Hawkins, Lorraine E. Williams, Giles R. Wright, Delight W. Dodyk, Merrill Maguire Skaggs, Richard W. Hunter, and Ian C. G. Burrow for their stellar contributions, which will surely stand the test of time.

— BARBARA J. MITNICK
MORRISTOWN, NEW JERSEY

NEW JERSEY IN THE
AMERICAN REVOLUTION

★ ★ ★

CROSSROADS OF THE
AMERICAN REVOLUTION

★ ★ ★

THOMAS FLEMING

REVOLUTIONARY NEW JERSEY was a society with remarkably contemporary overtones. It was a diverse mix of religions, from the Dutch Reformed in Bergen County to the Quakers along the Delaware to the Anglicans in Elizabethtown to the Presbyterians in Newark, Princeton, and many other places. Its politics were frequently passionate and often violent and occasionally radical. There were Quakers and other thoughtful men of God, such as the Reverend Jacob Green (fig. 1), who were deeply troubled by slavery in their midst. The state's inner spirit was already democratic with a small d. Philip Fithian, a young minister, noted the way New Jersey "gentlemen of the first rank" associated freely with "the laborious part of men"—those who worked with their hands—and considered them "the strength and honor of the colony." The explanation, Fithian thought, was "the near approach of an equality of wealth among the inhabitants."[1]

What does all this mean? Liberty and its fruits, prosperity and a sense of independent self-worth, were not some future hope for the New Jerseyans of 1776. They had a lot to defend in their contest with the so-called mother country—and a lot to lose. They knew how ruthlessly the British had suppressed rebellions in Ireland and Scotland. No one put it better than William Livingston (color plate 1), the man who became the Revolution's leader in New Jersey. "Whoever draws his sword against his prince must fling away the scabbard," he said. "We have passed the Rubicon. Whoever attempts to recross it will be knocked in the head by one or the other party on the opposite banks."[2]

New Jersey was the first state to discover just how serious the British were about suppressing the rebellion by massive force. On July 1, 1776, militiamen standing guard on Sandy Hook noticed a startling number of ships on the horizon. Within a

FIG. I *Unknown*, The Reverend
Jacob Green, *late eighteenth century.*
Silhouette. University Archives, Depart-
ment of Rare Books and Special Collections,
Princeton University Library.

few hours a huge British fleet approached the coast. There was little doubt that it
carried a very large British army—eventually totaling more than 30,000 men. It was
the largest force Britain had ever sent from its shores. They soon landed unopposed
on Staten Island.

Lieutenant Colonel Nathaniel Scudder of Monmouth County mounted his
horse at 11 P.M. on the night of July 1 and galloped through the darkness to Burlington to warn the New Jersey Provincial Congress. He burst into the deliberations
of the state's founders early on July 2, thereby staking a claim to the title of New
Jersey's Paul Revere. The Provincial Congress rushed the news to the Continental
Congress in Philadelphia. That group of worthies was locked in a ferocious debate
about declaring independence. Scudder's message made it clear that it was a choice
fraught with peril.

That day, the Continental Congress, with New York abstaining, voted to take the
plunge and approve Thomas Jefferson's world-transforming Declaration of Independence. On that same July 2 in Burlington, the New Jersey Provincial Congress ratified
a constitution—their own version of a statement of independence. But the impact
of Scudder's message was starkly visible in the way the delegates voted. No less than
thirty abstained. The decision was carried by an unimpressive twenty-six to nine. A
clause in the document stated that "if a reconciliation between Great Britain and these
colonies should take place . . . this charter shall be null and void."[3]

FIG. 2 *Mather Brown (attrib.)*, William Franklin: Last Royal Governor of New Jersey, *n.d. Oil on canvas. Private collection. Photo courtesy Frick Art Reference Library.*

For New Jersey, the road to independence was not nearly as clear-cut as it had been for the combative Yankees of Massachusetts. There was no gunfire on Lexington green, no dead bodies in the ditches and fields along the road from Concord to Boston. The news of that April 19, 1775, carnage had excited outrage in some New Jerseyans. But it stirred disgust in a substantial number of others who, regarded the quarrelsome New Englanders with suspicion and dislike.

New Jersey's attitude was complicated by a royal governor who was an American with a famous name: William Franklin (fig. 2). This handsome, gifted man stunned his father, Benjamin, and many others by deciding to remain loyal to the king. Around Franklin's gubernatorial mansion in Perth Amboy lived a circle of wealthy fellow loyalists known as "The Group." Mostly heirs of the state's seventeenth-century founders, they owned about a million acres of land in New Jersey, which they sold or leased at a pace steady enough to guarantee many of them an income of 1,200 pounds a year—the equivalent of at least 100,000 of our inflated dollars.

With that kind of wealth and William Franklin's popularity and political skills, it was not difficult to stir doubts about independence in minds and hearts throughout New Jersey. In a move that almost unraveled the Revolution, Governor Franklin had called an emergency session of the legislature late in 1775 and announced that George III was ready to grant New Jersey many special favors, such as the right to print paper money—the answer to every debtor's prayer. All the legislators had to do was petition the king "for a restoration of peace and harmony." The words would implicitly pledge their allegiance to the crown.[4]

The Continental Congress was so alarmed they rushed three of their best speakers to Burlington. The orators warned that Governor Franklin's proposal would turn the shaky American union into a "rope of sand." The assembly withdrew the petition, and New Jersey's independence men, recognizing Franklin as a dangerous man, ordered a regiment of militia to arrest the governor early in 1776.[5]

Into the struggle for hearts and minds now hurtled *Common Sense*, a pamphlet by Thomas Paine (fig. 3) urging Americans to rid themselves of kings and aristocrats once and for all. According to William Franklin, *Common Sense* (see fig. 47) had a backlash effect in New Jersey because it opened the eyes of people "of sense and property" to the real intentions of the independence party.

Soon New Jersey had its own Tom Paine—the Reverend Jacob Green of Hanover, who aimed his *Observations on the Reconciliation of Great Britain and the Colonies* at these doubters. After declaring reconciliation a vain hope, Green, like Paine, repeated arguments that would return to haunt the independence men. The clergyman maintained that Great Britain could not support an army and fleet in America without going bankrupt. Even if the British managed this feat, the Americans could raise an army five times bigger. The next six sanguinary years would prove both Paine and Green inept financial and military prophets.[6]

Meanwhile, some of New Jersey's best soldiers were fighting and dying far from home, in the Continental Congress's campaign to add Canada to the American union. Poorly supplied and led by amateurish generals from New England, in the spring of 1776 the Americans were routed by a reinforced British army. In their headlong retreat, they died by the hundreds from rampaging smallpox and other fevers that often attacked armies in the eighteenth century.[7]

In the fall of 1776, Colonel Scudder's report of the huge fleet and enormous army swelled to nightmare proportions throughout New Jersey. George Washington's Continental army was mauled unmercifully in a series of battles in and around New York. In the first of these clashes, on Long Island, New Jersey's leading soldier, General William Alexander (fig. 4), displayed combat heroism that even the British were forced to admire. With the American army in headlong retreat, Alexander rallied 250 Maryland troops and led a counterattack against 10,000 oncoming British regulars. The bold move checked the British long enough to let most of the fleeing Americans escape. Only Alexander and a handful of those "brave fellows," as Washington called the Marylanders, survived. But from that day, Alexander had Washington's trust and admiration.[8]

With New England's militiamen deserting by the thousands and the morale of his regulars sinking, Washington wrote Congress a letter that transformed the struggle. The politicians in Philadelphia, as well as Tom Paine, Jacob Green, and similar thinkers, had envisioned a short war, ending in a decisive all-out battle—what the eighteenth century called "a general action." In this climactic clash, they were sure the Americans' superior numbers would overwhelm the small British army.

After a month of being battered by a large British army, Washington told Congress that from now on, the Americans would "avoid a general action." Instead, they would "protract the war." The brilliance of this stroke of strategic genius was not immediately apparent. As far as anyone could see, contraction rather than protraction seemed to be the destiny of the war. The end seemed to be looming—in the shape of total American demoralization and defeat—with New Jersey the stage on which the final act of the brief drama would take place.[9]

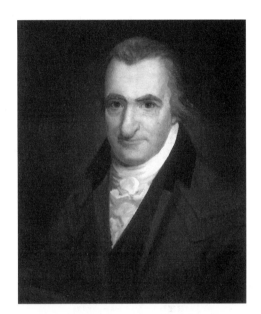

Leaving two-thirds of his dwindling army in Westchester County to block a possible British lunge into New England, Washington retreated into New Jersey and requested Governor William Livingston to call out the 17,000 militiamen on the state's rolls. The response of these part-time soldiers was discouraging. Only about 1,000 proponents of independence turned out. Not a single unit except a company of artillery reported to its assigned place of assembly.[10]

Washington had only one option—retreat and the seeming abandonment of New Jersey (color plate 3). One of his New England generals wrote the commander in chief a discouraging letter, denouncing New Jerseyans for their lack of patriotism. Washington's reply was as historically important as his decision to protract the war. "The defection of the people . . . has been as much owing to the want of an army to look the enemy in the face as to any other cause."[11]

FIG. 3 (TOP) *John Wesley Jarvis,* Thomas Paine, *ca. 1806/1807. Oil on canvas. National Gallery of Art, Washington, D.C. Gift of Marian B. Maurice 1950.15.1.*

FIG. 4 (BOTTOM) *Unknown artist,* William Alexander "Lord Stirling," *n.d. Oil on canvas. From the Collections of the New Jersey Historical Society.*

An army to look the enemy in face became the other cornerstone of Washington's strategy—and the key to New Jersey's survival for the next six exhausting years of protracted war. A supreme realist, Washington saw that militiamen were amateur soldiers with little or no training, no bayonets on their muskets, and no artillery worth mentioning. They could not be expected to stand up to the best professional army in the world, superbly equipped and ready to execute sophisticated battlefield maneuvers, unless there was a regular American army with the same equipment and training to confront the enemy host.

This second cornerstone of Washington's strategy was equally invisible in the chaotic closing weeks of 1776. Retreating across the Delaware with only a remnant of his regulars, Washington apparently abandoned a prostrate New Jersey to the triumphant British. With the red-coated battalions came a swarm of civilians, many of them New Jersey loyalists who had fled to British protection in New York. They went to work on turning New Jersey into the first loyal colony.

By this time, Governor William Franklin had been deported to house arrest in Wallingford, Connecticut. But British agents had no trouble reaching him there. The governor was soon signing pardons to be issued to former rebels if they took an oath of allegiance and promised to remain "in peaceable obedience to his Majesty." In a few weeks, thousands of people took this oath and received a promise of protection.[12]

Other less forgiving loyalists hunted leading rebels through the snowy woods. The president of the Provincial Congress, Samuel Tucker, surrendered to the British in a vain attempt to save his fine house from being looted. Richard Stockton, a signer of the Declaration of Independence and owner of an equally fine house (fig. 5), was captured on the run in Monmouth County. After brutal treatment in a British prison, Stockton signed a loyalty oath and withdrew from the war.

On the Pennsylvania side of the Delaware, Washington soon realized what was at stake in New Jersey. If the British succeeded in making it the first loyal colony, a surge of similar loyalist sentiment could swing Pennsylvania and New York and possibly Delaware in the same defeatist direction. To contest this slide into surrender, the American commander encouraged General William Heath to invade northern New Jersey from the Hudson Highlands, seize arms, and intimidate the many loyalists the British had encouraged to come out of hiding there. He gave General Alexander McDougall three Continental regiments to support a fairly good turnout of militia in Morris County. Finally, on Christmas night, Washington led his 2,500 ragged regulars across the ice-choked Delaware River to kill or capture two-thirds of the garrison of German troops the British had stationed at Trenton (color plate 4).

Ten days later, Washington, his ranks bolstered by Pennsylvania militia, out-maneuvered and outfought a British army at Princeton (color plate 6) and forced the king's men to evacuate most of New Jersey, except for a small enclave along the Raritan River. Reinvigorated New Jersey militiamen began shooting up British patrols. Elsewhere, in the words of one disgruntled Briton who was marooned in Virginia, Americans "went liberty mad again."[13]

The Revolutionary struggle for New Jersey by no means ended with those crucial victories. For the next five years, the conflict remained an often brutal civil war. Cortlandt Skinner, former Speaker of the New Jersey Assembly, became a British brigadier general and recruited a regiment of loyalists, the New Jersey Volunteers. Abraham van Buskirk of Bergen County became commander of another loyalist regiment almost entirely recruited in New Jersey. The same was true of the Queen's Rangers, commanded by the British professional soldier John Graves Simcoe. At the midpoint of the war, there were more New Jerseyans serving in the British army than Washington had in New Jersey's Continental brigade.

Loyalist guerillas remained active throughout the state. Midnight terrorism became a part of every patriot New Jersey family's life, especially along the eastern shore. Farms were burned and looted, and patriot leaders were murdered or kidnapped to British prisons in New York. New Jersey patriots retaliated with equal savagery against the loyalists on Staten Island and within their home state. Perhaps the best view of this little recognized struggle is in the 287 closely printed pages of the minutes of Governor William Livingston's Council of Safety. Each page is jammed with names of New Jerseyans who resisted the Revolution and were

FIG. 5 *Morven, as restored in 2000. Photograph by Dan Dragan for Historic Morven, Inc.*

dragged before this semijudicial body during the war. They received jail sentences and sometimes death sentences for loyalty to George III.

Even grimmer was the way the Revolutionary government used the courts to recruit men for the five regiments of the New Jersey Brigade in the Continental army. At the beginning of the war, patriotic fervor had inspired a turnout that easily filled the ranks. Not many of these men stayed in the army after the disasters of 1776. The New Jersey Brigade had numbered over 2,000 in that pivotal year. Thereafter, its numbers seldom exceeded 1,500, and barely 20 percent were the "free yeoman" the legislature hoped would fight the war. Most soldiers were recruited from drifters and the landless lower classes.[14]

With enlistment quotas unfilled, Livingston's Council of Safety and other courts began offering loyalists condemned to death a choice between the noose and enlistment. One Morristown court sentenced thirty-five Tories to hang; at the gallows, after two died, the rest volunteered for the army. In another case in 1779, similar treatment persuaded all but two of a seventy-five-member loyalist group to join up.[15]

The travails of the New Jersey Brigade were only complicated by this solution to the shortage of soldiers. Desertion of such unlikely recruits was a constant problem. Almost as frustrating was the state's failure to pay and equip the regulars decently. Outspoken Brigadier General "Scotch Willie" Maxwell, commander of the brigade, wrote several letters condemning the ineptitude and penny pinching of the Provincial Congress that would clear the sinuses of any politician in the country today.

Meanwhile, Washington clung stubbornly to his strategy of protracting the war—and making sure that New Jerseyans had an army to look the enemy in the face. When the British tried to advance across New Jersey in the summer of 1777 to assault Philadelphia, they found Washington on high ground in the center of the state, waiting to pounce on them—and absolutely declining to come down from the hills to give all-out battle. A disgusted General William Howe abandoned the stunned loyalists of East Jersey and marched his men to Perth Amboy to sail them down the coast and up Chesapeake Bay to attack Philadelphia in roundabout fashion.

Howe captured Philadelphia, and guerilla war erupted in West Jersey, as the proximity of a British army encouraged loyalists to come out of hiding. For several weeks in the winter of 1777–1778, a loyalist regiment, the West Jersey Volunteers, occupied Billingsport and controlled the surrounding area.

British foraging parties ravaged the farms along the Delaware, fighting off often fierce resistance from patriot militia. One of the most savage clashes took place at Salem in mid-March 1778. Colonel Charles Mawhood's regiment ambushed 300 militiamen at nearby Quinton's Bridge, inflicting heavy losses. Other militia under Colonel Elijah Hand of Cumberland County joined the fray, and the British threw in the Queen's Rangers. As more militia charged into the battle, the British were forced to retreat into Salem, where they threatened to burn the houses of selected patriots if the militia did not cease and desist. Colonel Hand promised awful retaliation on the homes of loyalists, and the British dropped the idea.

That night, Mawhood, hoping to outflank the Americans, attacked Hancock's Bridge, a few miles south of Salem. The regulars bayoneted most of the twenty-man guard, along with Judge William Hancock and his brother, in whose house the militia were posted. Both Hancocks were loyalists. The triumphant British rushed to assault the American flank, only to discover that the militia had vanished. The next day, the royal foragers sailed back to Philadelphia with their booty. The affair was typical of the confused violence engulfing West Jersey.[16]

Violence on a far larger scale erupted on June 15, 1778, when the British army of 11,000 soldiers abandoned Philadelphia and began a march across New Jersey to New York. The news of the French alliance with the American rebels and the transformation of the colonial revolt into a global war forced this decision on the king's forces. Washington, even more determined to avoid a general action when the possibility of an early peace seemed promising, ordered General Philemon Dickinson, commander of New Jersey's militia, to harass the British line of march. Washington sent 4,000 regulars under the command of the Marquis de Lafayette to join the Jerseymen with similar orders. The goal was to give the impression of the British fleeing before the triumphant Americans.

The militia skirmished briskly on the flanks and rear of the British column. They burned bridges in the Royal Army's path and removed ropes and buckets from wells, making their supply of fresh water precarious. The swarming Jerseymen, whose numbers varied from 1,000 to 1,500, were joined by the 1,500 regulars of the New Jersey Brigade and 600 Virginia riflemen under Colonel Daniel Morgan. They made the British march miserable. Captain Johann Ewald, who commanded a company of jaegers (riflemen) screening the head of the column, wrote in his diary: "The whole province was in arms. . . . Each step cost human blood."[17]

On June 27, near Freehold, Washington thought he saw a chance to attack the British rear guard of about 2,000 men. He ordered General Charles Lee, the American second in command, to take the militia and the Continentals under Lafayette and launch the assault. But the British commander, Sir Henry Clinton, quickly recalled 5,500 men from the main army and launched an attack of his own. The panicky Lee retreated, and Washington angrily relieved him from command and ordered the rest of his army into position to repel the oncoming British.

In 96-degree heat, the Battle of Monmouth raged from 10 A.M. until sundown (color plate 8). Many men on both sides dropped dead from heatstroke. But the Continentals, confident that they were the British equals thanks to the long hours of training at Valley Forge under the Prussian drillmaster Baron von Steuben, fought with an élan and competence that left the British and their German allies stunned. "Today the Americans showed much boldness and resolution during their attacks,"

Captain Ewald glumly informed his diary. At 10 P.M. that night, the Royal Army abandoned the battlefield, enabling Washington to claim the victory.[18]

The American commander congratulated the New Jersey militia for the "noble spirit" they displayed during the Monmouth campaign. He estimated that they and his Continentals had cost the British 2,000 of their best troops. The experience confirmed his conviction that the militia would turn out and fight well if there was a Continental army around to look the British in the face.[19]

The war was far from over. The French alliance proved a dolorous disappointment, and Washington's army was not strong enough to attack the British in New York. Guerilla raids and foraging parties continued to ravage New Jersey. Although Washington detached regiments to fight the British invasion of South Carolina in 1780 (as earlier he detached men to oppose the invasion of northern New York in 1777), New Jersey remained the "Cockpit of the Revolution" for him. In three out of the five years of the war after 1777, he made his winter quarters in the state. In the other two years, the ones he spent at Valley Forge, Pennsylvania, and Newburgh, New York, he was never more than a day's march away.

The payoff for this determination to keep a regular army in or near New Jersey came in June 1780, when the British, buoyed by a major victory in the South, the surrender of Charleston, and the capture of over 5,000 regulars, launched a knock-out blow at Washington's reduced army in Morristown. Swarms of New Jersey militiamen turned out to join 3,500 Continentals in stopping the 7,000-man invading army. After two bloody collisions at Connecticut Farms and Springfield, the British withdrew. One of Washington's officers, praising the militia's performance in this forgotten victory, said: "It was Lexington repeated."[20]

In the aftermath of those clashes, one young New Jerseyman experienced a moment of illumination that sums up good deal of New Jersey's Revolutionary story. Ashbel Green was a sixteen-year-old militiaman (and future president of Princeton). On the morning after the battle, he looked around him at the corpses and the fire-gutted houses and wondered: "Is the contest worth all this?" A moment later, down the road came George Washington on his horse. Something about the way the big Virginian held the reins, the determination emanating from that large physique, restored hope in the amateur soldier's battered soul.[21]

New Jerseymen not only sustained the Revolution on land, they played an active role in the war at sea. At least thirty privateers, equipped with letters of marque, sailed from Little Egg Harbor, just north of modern Atlantic City. The damage they did to British ships sailing in and out of New York sparked a ferocious retaliation. On October 4, 1778, a British naval force and 300 regulars and loyalists under Captain Patrick Ferguson burned ten large ships and many smaller ones. They rampaged up the Mullica River, torching shipyards and saltworks and homes for twenty miles. But the seafaring New Jerseyans of Little Egg Harbor were by no means out of the war. In May 1779, a German officer glumly informed his diary: "The rebels have sixteen strong new privateers and a frigate there, and four weeks ago unfortunately captured six three- and two-masted ships among them a royal provision ship."[22]

Another aspect of the war that seldom appears in formal histories is the role New Jersey's women played in the conflict. They were as committed to the struggle as the men, on both sides. Cortlandt Skinner's wife, Elizabeth, maintained a secret correspondence with her loyalist husband, supplying him, one witness later testified, "with the most material intelligence of the designs & conduct of the enemy that was received."[23]

On the American side, we have the story of Susan Livingston, the governor's daughter. In 1780, when the British raided her family's home, Liberty Hall, in Elizabethtown, Susan threw herself in front of a chest containing vital documents about the state's rebel government and cried that if the raiders left the contents untouched, she would give them her father's papers. Assuming she was protecting love letters, the British officer in charge went into a perfect gentleman act and agreed. Susan led the raiders to a bookshelf and handed them dozens of her father's old law briefs, which the gleeful British stuffed in their forage bags. Not until they got back to Staten Island did they discover they had been gulled.

New Jersey's women were as exposed as the men to the terror of midnight guerillas. They were also frequently forced to confront in their homes and barns British regulars, who did not always conduct themselves as gentlemen. On March 22, 1777, a justice of the peace took testimony from a thirteen-year-old girl in Hunterdon County who told how she had been raped repeatedly by British troops over the course of three days. Five other women told similar stories. A committee of the Continental Congress proposed to publish this testimony, along with similar statements. But other Americans objected to ruining the women's reputation. In the eighteenth century, a raped woman was no longer respectable. Some historians suspect the number of rapes in New Jersey were far larger than those reported. Many women chose silence.[24]

African Americans also played an important role in the struggle. About 12 percent of East Jersey's population was black, most of them slaves. In some communities, blacks numbered 20 percent. By the end of the war, about 2 percent of the soldiers in the state's Continental brigade were black. Some were slaves, sent by masters to avoid conscription into the ranks. Others were volunteers, attracted by the bounty offered to enlist. Oliver Cromwell, a free black from Burlington County, served as a private from 1777 to 1781 and fought bravely at Monmouth and half a dozen other battles. He received a pension from the government after the war. Many other blacks served in the militia. Others played important roles as teamsters transporting supplies for the Continental army when it was in winter camp.[25]

When the war began, New Jerseyans did not have a newspaper. They were forced to rely on papers from Philadelphia and New York. Governor Livingston attempted to remedy this problem by persuading a printer named Isaac Collins to launch the *New Jersey Gazette* in Burlington. But the paper did not circulate in East Jersey, where New York papers, crammed with misinformation and British propaganda, held sway. Washington decided to remedy this information vacuum by creating his own newspaper. He permitted Shepherd Kollock, a printer turned artilleryman, to resign from the army and begin publishing the *New-Jersey Journal* in Chatham. Kollock quickly became a fiery spokesman for the American cause.

The guerilla war in New Jersey was fought mostly by militia. But whenever Washington had a chance to use his Continentals to strike a retaliatory blow at the British, he seized it. One ripe target was the British fort on Paulus Hook, in present-day Jersey City. Before dawn on August 19, 1779, Major Henry Lee led 300 men through waist-deep marshes to launch a bayonet assault that caught most of the garrison by surprise. A remnant held out in an inner redoubt, and Lee retreated with 159 prisoners.[26]

Less successful was an American attack on another British fort at Bulls Ferry (modern Hoboken) the following year. The fort was headquarters for midnight raiders who burned and robbed in Bergen County. Major General Anthony Wayne assaulted it with 1,000 men, backed by artillery. But the 84 loyalists in the fort defended themselves with cannon and musketry. The only approach had towering cliffs on both sides and a stockade with a ditch and an abatis of sharpened stakes. After losing 59 men, Wayne retreated.[27]

The British worsened the savagery of the guerilla struggle by creating the Board of Associated Loyalists, with ex-governor William Franklin, exchanged for a captured American general, at its head. The loyalists were given a charter that permitted them to profit from anything they plundered. The British army made little or no attempt to control their depredations or monitor their tactics.

In the ebb and flow of what Washington called this "desultory war," the important thing was not victory in every battle but a determination to show the enemy that New Jersey's commitment to the struggle remained unquenched. Washington's policy of keeping the British on the defensive whenever possible and striking back at midnight raiders and foragers was vindicated in September 1781.

The American army and the French expeditionary force began their march to Yorktown, Virginia, where they hoped to trap a British army under Lord Cornwallis. Strung out in a long, exposed line of march, the Franco-American force was as vulnerable as the British army that had retreated through New Jersey in 1778. Benedict Arnold, by this time a British brigadier general, rushed to Sir Henry Clinton and begged him for 6,000 men, guaranteeing that he would destroy Washington and his army. Clinton refused him. The British commander said he feared to arouse the "bold persevering militia of that populous state." Washington and his French allies marched to the victory that won the war.[28]

Although the "desultory war" continued for another year in New Jersey, it gradually subsided as the loyalists in New York realized the struggle was lost. William Franklin signaled their surrender when he boarded a ship to England to escape the possibility of being prosecuted for some of the outrages committed by the Board of Associated Loyalists. With peace came a statistic that certified New Jersey as the "Crossroads of the American Revolution": soldiers fought no less than 238 battles on its soil—more than in any other state in the confederation.[29]

Perhaps the most appealing thing about New Jersey's Revolutionary story is its link to freedom. The reliance on a combination of a regular army and militia rested on faith in the courage of free people. It was a realistic faith. It did not expect men and women to commit suicide in defense of freedom. But George Washington—and New Jersey's leaders—believed free people would take grave risks if they thought they had a reasonable chance of succeeding.

This was a faith New Jersey's men and women amply fulfilled in the long struggle. In this book, we are commemorating more than the 225th anniversary of a victorious war. We are also celebrating the emergence of the Americans on the world scene—the creation of a new people who combined freedom and courage, realism and idealism, in a way that has established a different kind of country.

New Jerseyans should be proud of their state's crucial role in this epochal turning point in world history. They can be equally proud of their effort to keep the memory alive in the minds and hearts of twenty-first-century Americans in books such as this one.

"THESE WERE
TROUBLESOME TIMES INDEED":

Social and Economic Conditions in
Revolutionary New Jersey

* * *

DAVID J. FOWLER

I N 1775, THE ANONYMOUS AUTHOR of *American Husbandry* described New
Jersey thus:

> The inhabitants of this province consist almost entirely of planters; and though
> there are many considerable estates . . . among them, yet in general they are little
> freeholds, cultivated by the owners; they have no town of any note, New York
> and Philadelphia being their places of export and import . . . : they live in a very
> plentiful manner . . . ; for no where . . . are the necessaries of life in greater plenty.
> . . . [T]he lower classes . . . are all very well cloathed and fed; better than the same
> people in Britain.[1]

Although the writer's portrayal of idyllic rustic simplicity is in many respects percep-
tive, it tends to oversimplify a more complex social and economic structure. How the
people of this small, agrarian colony on the periphery of a far-flung empire accommodated the disruptions of the first American civil war will be the focus of this essay.

Three years earlier, William Franklin (see fig. 2), the colony's last royal governor, had calculated the population of the thirteen counties "commonly called the
Jersies" at 120,000, a figure remarkably close to the modern estimate of 122,000.[2] The
well-traveled "great road" from New York to Philadelphia crossed a corridor along
which not only people and goods but also ideas, information, and rumors moved.[3]

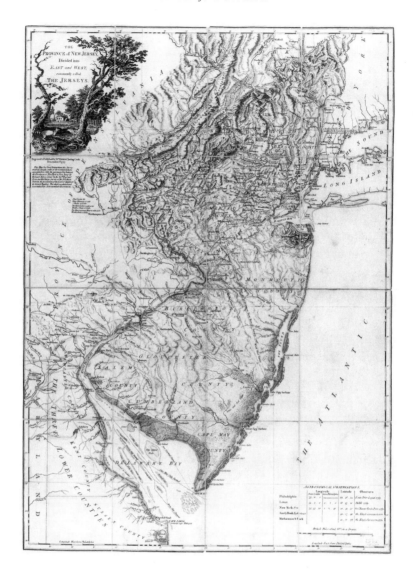

FIG. 6 *William Faden,* The Province of New Jersey, Divided into East and West, commonly called The Jerseys, *1777. Courtesy of Richard B. Arkway, Inc., New York.*

The dichotomy between the two divisions—East Jersey and West Jersey —was not merely an "idle distinction," as Governor Franklin thought, but instead belied their different settlement histories, landholding systems, ethnic composition, legacies of civil disorder, and orientation to the neighboring colonies of New York and Pennsylvania (fig. 6).[4] An accident of geography had many repercussions, for good or ill, throughout the colony's (and later the state's) history.

Diversity—ethnic, cultural, religious, economic—was this society's "defining characteristic."[5] More than a century of immigration had resulted in a cultural mosaic in the province. Settlers of English descent comprised slightly more than half of the population; the remainder was divided among Dutch, Scots, Scots-Irish, German, French, and Swedish.[6] Within this plural society were "ethnic communities" that maintained distinctive cultural, economic, religious, and even political spheres. Bergen and Somerset counties, for instance, were predominately Dutch, while remote Cape May was preponderantly English. A Scottish "ethnic network" spread throughout central New Jersey. Counties such as Monmouth and Middlesex were more mixed. The colony overall exhibited "marked homogeneity within a larger heterogeneous milieu."[7] Frequently overlooked by commentators, however, was the presence of "ethnic others." By 1774, the surviving Lenape on the Brotherton reservation reportedly numbered a mere sixty people; perhaps a couple hundred more lived scattered in other small villages. Much more numerous were enslaved and free African Americans, who comprised 7 to 8 percent of the general population; their numbers were more concentrated, however, in certain East Jersey counties than in Quaker-dominated West Jersey.[8]

An "extraordinary, almost unimaginable diversity of religion" characteristic of the Middle colonies matched New Jersey's ethnic variety.[9] The major sects and denominations were Quakers, Baptists, Dutch Reformed, Anglican, and Presbyterians (including Congregationalists). This "spiritual pluralism," along with rural conditions and a shortage of clergy, fostered many "ubiquitarians" who were "indifferent," that is, they were not particular about which services they attended.[10] Although religion sometimes surfaced in voting alignments in the assembly, it did not, as in neighboring Pennsylvania, result in the formation of cohesive blocs. For pragmatic reasons, the cultural and religious diversity of New Jersey tended to promote compromise, accommodation, and tolerance.[11] But as events in the period 1775–1783 demonstrated, serious fractures in society lay just below the surface.

There were "Gentlemen in the first rank of Dignity & Quality" in the province, such as the councilor, proprietor, surveyor-general, and would-be earl of Stirling, William Alexander (see fig. 4).[12] Many well-to-do merchants and professionals had personal, kinship, and business contacts in Philadelphia or New York; conversely, several prominent individuals from these cities eventually retired to estates across the Delaware or the Hudson. Perhaps the most famous was William Livingston (color plate 4), the New York attorney and politician who in 1772 retired to Elizabethtown—he was shortly to play a decisive role in his adopted home. The bastions of elitism and conservatism (and ultimately, Toryism) were the western capital of Burlington and especially the eastern capital of Perth Amboy, which were dominated by the largely Anglican and anglicized proprietors and royal officials.[13]

Despite notable examples of "high-born, long recorded families," contemporaries often recognized the overall equality of colonial New Jersey society. In 1771, a Swedish minister in Gloucester County noted that "here almost everyone is of the same stamp."[14] Such statements were exaggerations, of course, but they did emphasize that New Jersey was representative of colonial America in that it was a "truncated society," the majority of which—perhaps half—consisted of white male farmers of "middling" status.[15] The goal of colonial Americans was to achieve a "competency," that is, "the power to govern their own working lives."[16] The means of attaining this colonial American dream was the basic unit of farm production, the patriarchal family (husband, wife, children), sometimes assisted by servants, slaves, and hired laborers.[17]

As an older colony with no extensive western domain, inexpensive fertile land in New Jersey close to transportation networks was becoming more difficult to obtain. A growing number of people occupied hardscrabble soils with little hope of economic betterment or chose tenancy, became artisans, or removed from the province. In truth, many immigrants were ultimately sojourners, and geographic mobility was often a sine qua non to upward mobility.[18] By the late colonial period, nearly half of the householders of Bedminster Township were landless, and in nearby Bernardstown, more than a third were tenants or cottagers. Some tenants were prosperous, however, and for many, tenancy was merely a strategy whereby young farm families strove to achieve freehold status.[19]

At the bottom of this hierarchy of dependency were the most exploited: the poor, apprentices, indentured servants, and slaves. The poor were often recently arrived immigrants or, more often, young laborers entering the workforce on their own. If a farmer could afford it, during busy seasons of planting and harvesting this transient rural proletariat augmented the labor of the farm family; because wages were high in colonial America, after a few years these laborers might obtain enough to rent or purchase their own land, as might newly freed servants (fig. 7). The bondage of African Americans was usually permanent and definitely the most brutal and degrading. Whether slave or free, African Americans typically worked as agricultural laborers, sometimes as domestics, occasionally as skilled or unskilled workers at manufactories.[20] Black or white, free or bound, the labor of all the various kinds of workers was integral to the successful operation of many family farms as well as nascent industries.

New Jersey early earned the reputation as "the garden of North America," a testament to the variety of crops that could be grown there.[21] Typical of the regional economy that characterized the breadbasket Middle colonies, farm families engaged in mixed grain-livestock husbandry. Winter wheat was the major cash crop, along with rye and corn; myriad other vegetables and fruits were also grown. Animals were kept for draft as well as for meat and other by-products. On more marginal soils along the coast, people subsisted by "raising cattle in the bog," hunting, fishing, gathering shellfish, harvesting (often poaching) timber, and part-time farm-

FIG. 7 *Unknown artist*, Colonial Family Working Together. *Courtesy of the New Jersey Museum of Agriculture's Dow Brown Collection, New Brunswick.*

ing.[22] During winter months, the farm family was kept busy processing crops and produce, harvesting wood, working at part-time crafts, and engaging in numerous other tasks. Along with these employments, the household economy, guided by women—spinning wool and flax, raising barnyard fowl, dairying, making cheese, tending a garden—was crucial to the annual success of the farm family.[23]

A persistent myth that has been laid to rest is that of the self-sufficient yeoman farmer. Everyone to a greater or lesser extent participated in the market economy either by local bartering or by exchanging produce or cash on the intracolonial or intercolonial level for goods—tea, coffee, chocolate, sugar, molasses, rum, salt, gunpowder, and especially textiles—that they considered "necessaries" or "luxuries" and were either unable or unwilling to produce for themselves.[24] The degree of participation was, of course, affected by one's wealth and proximity to markets, but virtually no one in New Jersey was very far from a peddler or rural retailer, who in turn was connected to a merchant in a larger country town, who in turn was linked to a provisions or dry goods wholesaler in New York or Philadelphia, who in turn bought merchandise on generous credit from a large mercantile house in England or Scotland. An important phenomenon of the post-1740 period was the burgeoning consumer society, in which colonial Americans were eager participants.[25]

The downside of all this consumption was indebtedness. With the infusion of heavy military expenditures during the Seven Years' War, the American standard of living rose, and consumption increased correspondingly. With the advent of peace, credit contracted down the line, and economic hardship—foreclosures, bankruptcy, lawsuits for debt—multiplied. Colonial Americans, who were acutely sensitive regarding anything that smacked of dependency, resented what they perceived as economic servitude. Ironically though, on the eve of the Revolution, His Majesty's subjects in America, including the Jerseys, enjoyed the highest standard of living in the world, higher even than in Britain itself.[26]

As a small, relatively prosperous agrarian colony on the fringe of empire that was largely dependent on its neighbors for external commerce, New Jersey was a "reluctant rebel" that in reality had "no substantive quarrel" with Great Britain. People's concerns were sometimes provincial—as with agitation for paper money, which dominated the decade before the Revolution—but more often local.[27] There is scant evidence of serious threats to political or social stability. Some smuggling of goods (rum, molasses) to Philadelphia in contravention of the revenue laws was carried on, apparently with the complicity of customs officials, via the Salem customs district. In 1769–1770, riots convulsed Essex and Monmouth counties; in the former, the issue was antiproprietary sentiment and in the latter debtor relief.[28] Again, the source of the problems was local and provincial, not imperial.

The colony's reaction to the sequence of revenue legislation—the Stamp Act, the Townshend duties, the Tea Act—that so inflamed the more commercially oriented colonies tended to be comparatively moderate and restrained; the influence of the Quakers in several counties no doubt played a role. Neither the enactment nor the repeal of most of the obnoxious laws evoked much of a public outcry.[29] The colony in general tended to watch its more influential neighbors. Richard Stockton (see fig. 14) feared that if the colony did not send delegates to the Stamp Act Congress, it would look "like a speckled bird among our sister colonies." As in other colonies, there were Sons of Liberty, mass meetings, inflammatory rhetoric, liberty poles.[30] The boycotts of British imports that attended the protests were "a tentative declaration of American economic independence." Although Governor William Franklin expressed skepticism, there was apparently some increase in the manufacture of homespun cloth.[31] By taxing tea in 1773, Parliament in effect politicized a ubiquitous consumer item, which thereby assumed a "radical, new, symbolic function" for Americans. In December 1774, one year after the more famous Boston Tea Party, patriots at Greenwich in Cumberland County demonstrated empathy with their Massachusetts brethren by burning a shipment of tea.[32]

New Jerseyans were influenced by the ideology of the protest movement, but it is difficult to assess its impact.[33] One strain was the dissenting tradition of the Great Awakening at midcentury, which in general challenged traditional authority; but religion probably "followed politics rather than leading it."[34] More pervasive was the secular awakening occasioned by the republicanization of Anglo-American society. The classical republican tradition was akin to the dissenting religious tradition in that it emphasized virtue versus vice; in addition, good republicans feared arbitrary power and tended to view imperial problems as a conspiracy of corrupt, venal bureaucrats intent on enslaving the colonies.[35] And Americans displayed an "extraordinary touchiness" regarding any perceived threat (such as taxation without representation) to their liberty and property.[36] Evidently local conditions, tensions and anxieties that pervaded society, and the rhetoric of religious rationalists and republicans intersected at a momentous point when pragmatic imperial administrators launched a "rational, logical, and equitable" program to tighten fiscal control of a vast empire.[37]

The role of local committees in the protest movement demonstrates that "a behind-the-scenes aura invariably shrouds rebellions."[38] Committees of correspondence first emerged during the Stamp Act crisis of 1765–1766 when they served the vital function of coordinating opposition colonywide as well as communicating with committees in other colonies. Revived during the Townshend duties crisis of 1768, the committees enforced the boycott with the threat of social ostracism or ritual degradations such as tar-and-feathering. When on October 20, 1774, the Continental Congress passed a nonimportation, nonexportation, nonconsumption agreement known as the Association, the infrastructure was already in place for its enforcement. The Association quickly evolved into an instrument for flushing out dissenters and enforcing conformity.[39] A committeeman in Cape May County boasted that he personally "handed an Association Paper to most of the Inhabitants . . . and that only one Man . . . refused signing it."[40]

Concomitant with the activities of the committees was the takeover of the local militia. It was a crucial process that unfortunately has left little evidence; by 1775, however, membership in the militia had become "a political act." Gilbert Giberson of Monmouth County, who ultimately joined the British, later claimed that he accepted a militia captaincy "to prevent a troublesome man from being elected."[41] Although the mechanics of the process are frustratingly elusive, with greater or lesser difficulty patriots did achieve control of the local instruments of indoctrination and enforcement. Even as late as 1776, most people in New Jersey still sought reform and reconciliation with Britain, not independence. As the popular movement became more radical, confrontational, and militant, conservatives and some moderate Whigs who had supported it recoiled from its more repressive aspects. Many Quakers, who had formerly exerted considerable political influence in the province, retreated from public life. Presbyterians such as Rev. John Witherspoon (see fig. 13) filled the vacuum and became the dominant religious element in politics.[42] The interrelated roles of committees and militia bear out the observation that the Revolution, especially in its early phases, was effected by "an organized and wilful minority."[43]

The New Jersey Provincial Congress was indeed prescient when in August 1775 it expressed the commonly held fear that the province was likely to be immersed in "all the horrors of a civil war."[44] Independence, more than any other issue, provoked a crisis of conscience for many individuals. Joseph Cogil of Gloucester County, for one, declared that "he was as Good a Whig as Ever Sat on a pot till Independicy Was Declared."[45] Emboldened by the arrival of British forces in early July 1776, covert loyalism now became active. Patriots suppressed royalist uprisings in several counties; in volatile Monmouth, at least six counterinsurrections broke out. In Shrewsbury and other locales, the specter of slave revolt reared its head, and many slaves also fled behind British lines.[46] Although patriot forces quelled the revolts, it proved to be only the first phase of civil violence. The reverberations were felt at all levels of society. In March 1777, Thomas Farr, deacon of the Upper Freehold Baptist Church (fig. 8), recorded the uneasy lull: "No meeting—these were troublesome times indeed."[47]

The interrelated issues of motivation and allegiance are two of the most vexing; in general, "efforts to define persons in a revolution run afoul of insuperable

FIG. 8 *Upper Freehold Baptist Church ("Yellow Church"), 1776. Imlaystown, N.J. Photo courtesy Upper Freehold Baptist Church.*

problems of definition." It might be prudent to adopt John Adams's estimate that patriots, loyalists, and neutrals and the apathetic each comprised one-third of the population.[48] But it is essential to keep in mind that the situation was a highly fluid one that could literally change daily based on factors such as proximity to American or British forces. The state itself was a patchwork of allegiances. Areas remote from enemy posts and the threat of invasion generally contained relatively few disaffected, while counties in the arc surrounding occupied New York contained many.

There were many shades of disaffection to the American cause. Some became "Refugees" who fled into New York and sat out the war there; others stayed at home and endured harassment, fines, and distraint of property. The reaction of others was more militant: they either joined Provincial regiments or became partisans who took the war home to the rebels. One of the latter was James Moody of Sussex County, who attempted to remain neutral until 1777 when his patriot neighbors shot at him.[49] Keeping in mind that there were always exceptions, the motives of New Jersey's loyalists were various. Anglicans, royal officials, and most of the proprietors (especially in the East) supported the crown. Others were content with the status quo or feared the consequences of loss of membership in the "empire of goods."[50] Family and kinship exerted a powerful force. Although examples of families rent by discord are dramatic, they actually were rare—most people went to war as part of family and associational networks. There is no evidence of class warfare: loyalists, like patriots, came from all ranks of society.[51]

While it may be true that "religion did not cause the Revolution," once the fighting began the disaffected, especially Anglicans and Quakers, viewed it as a religious confrontation. It was a commonplace among loyalists, as one Quaker insurgent claimed in 1776, that "the Presbyterians are the cause of all this bloodshed."[52] Conversely, because of their refusal to support the war effort, Whigs regarded Quakers as "Drones of Society."[53] A prewar schism between *Coetus* and *Conferentie* factions in the Dutch Reformed church evidently influenced wartime alignments in the Hackensack Valley.[54] Both contemporaries and later observers agree that private grudges and local conditions doubtless also played a part in determining allegiance. The decision to be Whig, Tory, neutral, or trimmer was essentially influenced by factors of temperament, experience, and locale.[55]

Whatever the initial sources of people's motivation, it is certain that as civil violence escalated, the *lex talionis* (law of retaliation) was frequently invoked. On their part, patriots could point to numerous acts of murder and robbery perpetrated by enemy raiders. Indeed, the general derangement of society gave rise to gangs of "banditti" who utilized the Pine Barrens of south Jersey or the Highlands of the New York–New Jersey border. While some of the latter engaged in bona fide partisan activity, others seem to have been more opportunistically inclined. One such band, in a nocturnal raid in 1779, murdered Thomas Farr and his wife.[56] The reaction of patriots in war-torn Monmouth that year was to create the Association for Retaliation, a vigilante organization that acted as a parallel government to the duly elected county authorities. Loyalists, enraged by property confiscation and "Acts of cruelty and Barbarity," countered in 1780 by establishing the Board of Associated Loyalists.[57] The culmination of the war of retaliation occurred in April 1782 when Joshua Huddy (a Retaliator) was taken from prison under questionable authorization by Richard Lippincott (an Associator) and summarily hanged opposite Sandy Hook. Clearly, an "ethic of . . . self-redress" was operative.[58]

When the British occupied New York in September 1776, northeastern New Jersey was destined for the next eight years to become a military frontier. The so-called neutral ground was actually "a grim twilight zone" of marauding expeditions that threw the civilian populace into a state of protracted siege.[59] Gangs of blacks and whites launched many of the raids from Refugee-Town, a makeshift settlement centered at the Sandy Hook lighthouse (fig. 9). Patriots feared being plundered or kidnapped or of suffering the fate of Joseph Murray of Monmouth County, who was killed "at his harrow in his corn field."[60] The southwestern part of the state experienced a similar situation during the British occupation of Philadelphia; an officer reported that the inhabitants were "afraid of every person they see."[61] Proximity to enemy garrisons, particularly New York City, is key to understanding the disequilibrium that recurrently afflicted large parts of the state.

The British seizure of the "gateway ports" of Philadelphia and especially New York also disrupted the elaborate network of internal and external trade between the two entrepôts and their respective hinterlands. Naval blockades interdicted coastwise trade to New England and the West Indies.[62] The re-

Vol. I.   New York Mag. Aug. 1790.   Nº VIII.

Anderson Del.   Tiebout Sculp.

VIEW of the LIGHT HOUSE at SANDY HOOK.

FIG. 9 View of the Lighthouse at Sandy Hook. *Reproduced in* New York Magazine, *August 1790.* *The Mariners' Museum, Newport News, Va.*

FIG. 10 Thirty Shillings, 1776. *The Collection of the Newark Museum. Gift of Ralph E. Lum Jr.*

percussions on the essentially agrarian economy of New Jersey were soon evident. The campaign season, as well as frequent alarms, conflicted with the planting and harvesting schedules of crops. During the summer of 1776, for instance, tenant farmers who mustered in Hunterdon County felt that "they may as Well knock their famalys in the head for . . . they will be Ruined." The prospect of windfall profits in privateeering or higher wages paid to teamsters also enticed farmers and laborers.[63] In the absence of men, women sometimes took over management of farms.[64] Between 1777 and 1780, the legislature also embargoed the export of enumerated commodities. Both armies expropriated or destroyed crops. The height of the grain crisis between 1778 and 1780 coincided with encampments of the Continental army in the state. Farmers were reluctant to accept devalued continentals or commissaries' and quartermasters' certificates, and the legal procedure of impressing supplies was both unpopular and cumbersome.[65] Despite myriad problems, the "erratic but timely" supply system did, after all, keep the army from disbanding at Morristown.[66]

The complicated problem of wartime currency finance exerted a pervasive influence on all aspects of Revolutionary society. The disruption of normal trade and pressing needs for goods, services, and soldiers' pay dictated that ever increasing amounts of money be printed. Congress, in response, "stuffed the maw of the Revolution with paper money."[67] In January 1778, for instance, $152 continental equaled $100 specie (silver); by March 1780, the ratio had skyrocketed to 3954:100. Sensitive to their tenuous hold on power, legislators were reluctant to levy heavy taxes, but by 1779 it became imperative to pay for congressional requisitions. Citizens also recognized that hyperinflation was itself a form of taxation. Although the lawmakers attempted to be fiscally responsible, the problem was that the state's money (fig. 10) was tied to the rapidly declining continental: a nadir occurred in May 1781 when $15,000 in state currency was equivalent to $100 specie. The British, in a novel subterfuge to undermine the rebel economy, further compounded the problem by circulating counterfeit money.[68] By late 1780, the state was "drained of supplies, drained of cash, over-run with certificates, and burdened with taxes." Inflation tended to stifle trade, lessen confidence in the new regime, pit creditors against debtors, and foster speculators, profiteers, and monopolizers.[69]

A concomitant of the deflation of currency was the inflation of prices. Depending on the season of the year, the weather, demands of the armies for provisions and troops, and British blockades and privateers, commodity prices could fluctuate wildly. In 1779, the state led in petitioning Congress to establish uniform price-fixing laws.[70] As numerous complaints about "forestalling, regrating, and engrossing" attest, however, such attempts met with mixed results. Farmers resented price regulation, and some either reduced their output, withheld crops from the market, or held out for the highest price. Attempts in the countryside to maintain customary prices indicate that a "moral economy" was operative.[71] New Jersey's experiment with price regulation was relatively short-lived, however, and its communities did not experience the class conflict over the issue that erupted in Philadelphia.

The necessity of accommodating wartime disruptions of the domestic economy by finding alternative employments and import-substituting industries presented opportunities for entrepreneurial innovation.[72] Although some industries were well established, others had been conducted sporadically or as cottage industries, or not at all. Because salt was essential for the preservation of provisions for both military and civilian consumption, numerous saltworks mushroomed along the coast. In December 1777, the assembly exempted a large number of laborers at saltworks and ironworks. One ironmaster complained, however, that local farmers sought employment "solely to be clear of the militia."[73] At the beginning of the war, lack of almost all war matériel hampered the mobilization. Both civil and military officers entered into contracts with blacksmiths and gunsmiths for the fabrication and repair of arms. Critically important was the need for gunpowder. In response, the Provincial Congress in 1776 offered bounties for the production of saltpeter, and in March 1778 the legislature exempted from militia duty workers at the powder mill in Morristown. Because of abuses and complaints from recruiting officers and civilians in nonexempt occupations, however, in 1779 the legislature repealed most exemptions.[74]

Of all New Jersey's wartime industries, the production of iron for munitions is the best documented. Although well established in the northern counties and in the Burlington County pinelands, the industry was nonetheless plagued by problems common to all manufactories during the war.[75] Despite a shortage of blasting powder, in 1776 Hibernia Furnace in Morris County produced nearly 100 tons of cannonballs. Many owners were loyalists who shut down operations, but furnaces such as Andover, with its high-grade ore, were deemed so essential that they were placed under rebel management. Other enterprises were solidly in patriot hands, such as the Batsto ironworks in Burlington County: beginning in 1779, Batsto was owned by a partnership consisting of Continental quartermaster general Nathanael Greene and his two assistants.[76] Although ironworks such as Hibernia, Andover, and Batsto made significant contributions to the patriot cause, in general the war was probably "more disruptive than stimulating to the iron industry."[77]

In 1778, "Camillus" boasted that "domestic industry has nearly supplied the want of trade," but lack of evidence prevents an accurate assessment.[78] Sporadically if not continuously, scores of gristmills and sawmills continued their vital functions, approximately 300 tanneries produced leather for various civilian and military uses, and the production of homespun linen and woolens in unknown amounts was carried on as a cottage industry.[79] By the latter part of the war, however, imported textiles from both legal and illegal sources again became available (and more desirable). At one time or another, all the domestic industries—iron, salt, milling, cloth—suffered to greater or lesser extent from enemy troop movements and depredations, labor shortages, and lack of raw materials. Although the war may well have provided the "moment of opportunity for every domestic industry," there is scant evidence to support the claim.[80]

The greatest frenzy of venture capitalism resulted in March 1776 when the Continental Congress authorized commerce raiding by private men-of-war. Privateering had a long history in the Anglo-American world, and although its tactics were akin to piracy, in practice it was circumscribed by numerous rules and instructions.[81] Purchasing and outfitting even a small vessel was a risky and expensive business, and consequently the majority of privateers were owned by partnerships and syndicates based in Philadelphia. One of these was Thomas Leaming, Jr. and Company. A native of Cape May County, Leaming later boasted that he was "very lucky in . . . Privateering (which I considered the most beneficial Way, in which I could serve Myself and the Public)." Among the fifty prizes he claimed was the storm-damaged *Triton* transporting 224 Hessians, which was captured in September 1779 by the schooner *Mars* and the sloop *Comet* (fig. 11).[82]

The lowly as well as the highborn were attracted to the allurements—patriotism, profit, and adventure—of privateering. Shareholding in privateer cruises democratized investment in the nascent economy. For most people, however, inflation probably ate away their prize money. With the flurry of activity revolving around frequent auctions where prize vessels and cargoes were sold, minor ports such as The Forks of Little Egg Harbor became boomtowns. The numerous gadfly attacks of privateers using New Jersey bases stung British and loyalist merchants in their pocketbooks, provided alternative employment for both seamen and "land-men," and furnished an as yet unassessed source of income for the new government.[83]

During the waning years of the war, a full-blown subterranean economy developed in New Jersey that revolved around trade in contraband. From the start, patriot civil and military officials tried to prevent supplies in the prosperous "neutral ground" opposite New York from falling into enemy hands. A similar situation

FIG. 11 Comet, the Sloop, *eighteenth-century sailing vessel reproduced in the Captain Wiederholdt Diary. J. G. Rosengarten Collection. Rare Book and Manuscript Library, University of Pennsylvania.*

developed in West Jersey in 1777–1778 during the British occupation of Philadelphia. By the early 1780s, however, the "London trade" emanating from the eastern counties proved to be an intractable problem. The dynamics of the trade involved the British supplying luxury and manufactured items and in turn paying in specie for much needed provisions and lumber. Laws prohibiting the trade were passed throughout the war, but patriot officials simply could not command the resources to enforce them.[84]

Scores of indictments "for going into enemy lines" indicate that traders of all allegiances, occupations, ages, genders, and colors were drawn into the vortex.[85] In November 1780, for instance, the sheriff of Monmouth was ordered to apprehend thirty-five county residents "concerned with corresponding with the enemy and supplying them with provisions." Among those named was "Negroe Joe the servant of the widow Stevens."[86] In 1781, the Monmouth County grand jury accused Elizabeth Newell of Freehold of sending "one calf" to Staten Island; Newell's case notwithstanding, indictments naming women were rare.[87] As evidenced by their anonymity in the records, because of the relative ease with which women could travel between the lines, they were particularly effective in fencing goods. Late in 1780 a scandal occurred when several prominent New Jersey Whigs were implicated in the illicit trade.[88] In 1782, "A Plain Farmer" attempted to invoke the spirit of '76 against "these moon-light pedlars" who were subverting the cause "with British gew-gaws."[89] But goods that formerly served to politicize a segment of society now served to de-politicize a segment. What ended the trade in contraband was the end of the war.

On April 3, 1783, militia hunted down and killed the Tory partisan John Bacon. His death marked the literal and symbolic end of the conflict: he was the last reported casualty. Eleven days later, Governor Livingston proclaimed a cessation of hostilities. For residents of New Jersey, the war had truly been "a protracted, strenuous public event": the state suffered the largest number of military engagements (238), but doubtless some raids and skirmishes went unrecorded.[90] In 1784, a British officer observed that the state "suffered extremely by the war, much more in proportion than any other." But some parts of the state—the Hackensack and Raritan valleys, central Jersey, northern Monmouth County—disproportionately bore the brunt of invasion, supply, and debt. The sordid chronicle of brutality, retribution, venality, and profiteering negatively affected the moral tone of society. While the violence seemed to politicize some people, others became alienated and isolated.[91] Within the context of a home front convulsed by internecine strife, "imperatives of survival" help to explain much of the behavior on all sides.[92] Sometimes overlooked is the fact that the patriots prevailed largely because of the unsung citizens who, albeit grudgingly, tilled the soil, paid their taxes, and bore arms.

Even before the end of hostilities, goods that had been stockpiled in New York began to flood the market. Import-starved Americans went on a consuming frenzy. Consequently, many of the domestic industries established during the war could not withstand the competition. The loss of former markets, heavy taxes occasioned by the enormous war debt, and the general readjustment of the economy soon led to postwar depression, a malaise that was to last for most of the 1780s. As in the colonial period, credit contracted, and indebtedness and foreclosures increased; politics was defined, as in the prewar period, by the paper money issue. By the late 1780s, in order to bring money back into the state, even the detested loyalists were allowed to return. Depending on locale and people's wartime experience, the reaction to them could be violent; loyalists who had existing family networks in the state were more successful at reintegrating into society.[93]

If the causes of the rebellion seem elusive, its social and economic consequences seem ambiguous. For a few who were aggressive, calculating, and strategically situated, the war provided lucrative opportunities: "Patriotism and personal profit were often inseparable." An emerging liberalism characterized by acquisitiveness, self-interest, and individualism—always present to some degree in society—ultimately crowded out the old republican values of virtue, frugality, and "disinterestedness."[94] Many others—farmers, laborers, tradespeople, veterans, blacks—did not fare as well. Sales of confiscated loyalist estates, which were tainted by fraud, did not result in a "democratization of landholdings," nor did they generate much revenue for the new government. During the war and well into the postwar period, there was a general decline in the standard of living.[95] In six townships in East Jersey, for instance, there existed a "low ceiling on opportunity": population expanded while farm sizes declined, and marginality, landlessness, tenancy, tax delinquency, and mobility increased. Fully two-thirds of taxpayers in each township were either landless or farming on a near-subsistence level. It became more difficult than before, in short, to achieve "yeoman independency." Not until the end of the decade, with prosperity stimulated by war in Europe, were Americans able to retrieve their former standard of living, the highest in the world.[96] As throughout early American history, the option of migration facilitated the possibility of economic betterment.

NEW JERSEY:

Radical or Conservative in the Crisis Summer of 1776?

★ ★ ★

Maxine N. Lurie

HISTORIANS HAVE LONG debated the question of whether the American Revolution was, in fact, revolutionary. They have argued over what changed, how much it changed, and whether the changes were slight or significant. In examining this issue, historians have looked at government and politics, landholding, thought and culture, religion, and what happened to loyalists, women, blacks, and Native Americans.[1] Despite all that has been written on the issue, including a number of recent efforts at synthesis that have tried to bridge different interpretations, this debate has not been resolved. The old divisions between early-twentieth-century Progressive historians, such as Carl Becker, and nineteenth-century Whig scholars, for example, George Bancroft, have been replaced by controversies between "Neo-Progressives" and "Neo-Whigs." The Progressives saw social and economic differences between groups as central to an understanding of all history. They argued that the Revolution was a dual one; in Carl Becker's famous statement, it was both "the question of home rule" and "over who should rule at home."[2] They further maintained that the Revolution created a radical break with the past, later undone by a counterrevolution embodied in the U.S. Constitution. The Neo-Whigs, also known as the Consensus School of historians, saw intellectual and political ideas as central. Bernard Bailyn, for example, examined over 300 pamphlets produced in the 1760s and 1770s and summed up the ideas they contained in *The Ideological Origins of the American Revolution*. These historians argued that change was evolutionary, beginning in the colonial period and spreading through the Revolution and its aftermath; that from 1765 to 1776 the colonists were conservatives trying to preserve what they had; and finally, that the Constitution represented the culmination of what the Revolutionary generation learned through experience. Thus in 1956 Edmund Morgan referred to the Constitution as the "final fulfillment" of the war.[3]

Beginning in the 1960s, some historians of the American Revolution began to look at history "from the bottom up," to investigate ordinary people—including women, blacks, and Native Americans—to see whether they participated in the Revolution and how it changed their lives. While Jesse Lemish looked at "Jack Tarr" sailors and Alfred Young at a little shoemaker with the long name of George Robert Twelves Hewes, both as representatives of those on the bottom rungs of society, other historians turned to a discussion of "republicanism" and what it meant for the Revolutionary generation.[4] More recently, the focus has been on use of public spaces (including taverns) and participation in popular events (such as parades).[5] Nevertheless, the basic issue was and remains the nature and consequence of the American Revolution.

Several historians have tried to bridge the divide by offering a synthesis of interpretations. In *The Creation of the American Republic* (1969), Gordon Wood emphasized the importance of ideas and essentially argued that a conservative Revolution produced radical results. However, twenty-three years later, in *The Radicalism of the American Revolution* (1992), his thinking had shifted to an assertion that the American Revolution "was as radical and as revolutionary as any in history."[6] In reaching this conclusion, as a number of critics have pointed out, he omitted women, blacks, and Native Americans and extended his discussion of the results of the Revolution through the 1830s.

If one looks at historians of New Jersey who have written about the American Revolution in the state within the context of the broader interpretations noted above, it is clear that most of those who have studied New Jersey during this period have emphasized the conservative nature of the state. Larry Gerlach referred to New Jersey as a "reluctant rebel," while John T. Cunningham saw the state as a cautious one.[7] The proof often given for this evaluation is that the state hesitated to join the "common cause" supported by the other states, dragged its heels on independence, and wrote a constitution that not only continued to refer to New Jersey as a "colony" but also concluded with the statement: "Provided always, and it is the true Intent and Meaning of this Congress, that if a Reconcilation [*sic*] between Great Britain and these Colonies should take place, and the latter be again taken under the Protection and Government of the Crown of Great Britain, this Charter Shall be null and void, otherwise to remain firm and inviolable."[8] Finally, historians writing about the state have concluded that when the war was over, not much had changed; this had been a conservative revolution from beginning to end.[9]

With this ongoing debate in mind, it is logical to take a fresh look at New Jersey at the beginning of 1776, the events of July and August, and changes that had occurred by December of that year. By examining the political documents and

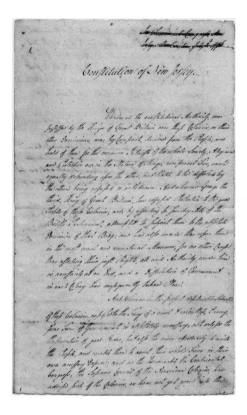

FIG. 12 *New Jersey Constitution, 1776. First and last pages.*
New Jersey State Archives, Department of State.

government adopted in the period surrounding the passage of the Declaration of Independence in July, and in particular the New Jersey Constitution of 1776 (fig. 12), we are provided with insight into what New Jersey patriot politicians meant by "revolution" and "republic" and the changes they meant to ensure by providing for both. This closer look at what happened in New Jersey in 1776, sometimes called the "year of crisis," reveals a significant shift that produced radical changes in the structure of its government. From this perspective, New Jersey no longer appears to be the conservative place many have described; instead, its revolution more closely resembles Wood's radical model.

The Crisis Summer of 1776

In January 1776, New Jersey was a small place, both in area and population when compared, for example, to Massachusetts or Virginia. It was also mainly rural (the largest city, Elizabethtown, containing only an estimated 350 houses), with an economy primarily based on a mixed agricultural production of grains, cattle, and other products.[10] In early 1776, the state's royal governor, William Franklin (see fig. 2), still held office, as did members of the royal assembly and council; they would survive longer than their counterparts in any other colony. Elections had been held for two extralegal Provincial congresses, but neither had as yet replaced the government sanctioned by the crown; instead, the two governments shadowed each other. New Jersey's representatives to the Second Continental Congress, including William Livingston (see color plate 1), were seen as conservative Whigs. On the other hand, John Witherspoon (fig. 13), Presbyterian minister and president of the College of New Jersey (now Princeton University), was an early advocate of independence, but his was as yet a lonely voice.[11]

On July 1, 1776, it was reported in the *New York Gazette and Weekly Mercury* that General William Howe and 113 ships (a gross underestimation of the British fleet) were massed at Sandy Hook, off the coasts of New York and New Jersey, and ready to attack (see fig. 17). At the same time, the Second Continental Congress was meeting in Philadelphia to consider the question of independence. Its members included five delegates from New Jersey—John Witherspoon, John Hart, Richard Stockton (fig. 14), Abraham Clark (fig. 15), and Francis Hopkinson (fig. 16)—all recent replacements for previous representatives and now ready to vote in favor.[12] Governor William Franklin recently had been arrested and sent off to Connecticut to be confined under the watchful eyes of patriot governor Jonathan Trumbull. And the Third New Jersey Provincial Congress was meeting in Burlington to discuss and complete a new constitution. New Jersey, therefore, already had moved quite far in a short time toward radical change and was about to go much farther.

The shift in sentiment in New Jersey, as elsewhere in early 1776, can be attributed to several factors: the continuing de facto war to the north, King George III's refusal to repeal the "Intolerable Acts" and his declaration that the colonies were in rebellion, his hiring of German mercenaries (Hessians) to fight for Britain, and the rabble-rousing sentiments of Tom Paine's *Common Sense* (see fig. 47), with its attack on monarchy and an appeal to Americans to save "freedom" for the world. In New Jersey can be added Governor William Franklin's ongoing correspondence with English authorities; his deliberate efforts to differentiate the colony from the other twelve, especially those leaning toward independence; and his call for the old assembly and council to meet. It is ironic that Benjamin Franklin's loyalist son helped precipitate the shift to American independence by trying so hard to maintain New Jersey's position within the British Empire.[13]

Most residents of New Jersey, as elsewhere in the American colonies, objected to British taxation, from the Stamp Act of 1765 to the Tea Act of 1773, as a violation of their rights. The 1765 resolutions of the New Jersey Assembly are explicit on this position. They stated that New Jersey's citizens would meet "constitutional requisitions," that is, legitimate ones, but: "Resolved . . . that it is . . . essential to the freedom of a people, and the undoubted right of Englishmen, that no taxes be imposed on them but with their own consent." The people of New Jersey, they continued, were not represented in the British Parliament. Therefore, they believed that taxes could only be imposed "by their own legislature." Toward the end of the statement, the assembly went beyond dependence on their rights as Englishmen by referring to "those privileges and immunities which God and nature seem to have intended [for] us." Finally, they concluded with a declaration of loyalty and a pledge of allegiance to the king worth noting, because in it they promised to "faithfully adhere to his royal person, and just government."[14] That final qualification of a "just government" is significant, for it demonstrates their belief that only "just" laws were legitimate ones.

Despite the firm resolve to prevent "taxation without representation," in the ten years that followed the 1765 resolutions New Jersey residents appeared to be more interested in local affairs, primarily concerning themselves with issues including land conflicts, lawyers' fees, and the resolution of a dispute over the selection of the colony's two treasurers.[15] However, when in May 1776, more than a year after the Battles of Lexington and Concord in Massachusetts, the Second Continental Congress resolved that those colonies without established governments should create them, New Jersey acted quickly. As noted, it arrested Governor Franklin, replaced its delegates to the Continental Congress,

FIG. 13 (TOP) *Charles Willson Peale,* John Witherspoon, *n.d. Oil on canvas. Princeton University. Presented by friends of the University. Photo: Bruce M. White PP19.*

FIG. 14 (BOTTOM) *John Wollaston,* Richard Stockton ("The Signer") Class of 1748, *n.d. Oil on canvas. Princeton University. Bequest of Mrs. Alexander T. McGill. Photo: Bruce M. White.*

FIG. 15 *James Read Lambdin,*
after John Trumbull, Abraham Clark,
ca. 1872. Oil on canvas. Independence
National Historic Park.

and elected the Third Provincial Congress, a body that voted fifty-four to three to form a government and then appointed a committee of ten to write a state constitution—a document that was discussed, completed, and adopted all in the space of about a week.[16]

On July 2, the delegates voted in favor of adopting the new state constitution—twenty-six to nine. They voted again on July 3, but few historians have noticed that the second vote specifically dealt with the deletion of the final paragraph concerning reconciliation: "Whether the draught of the constitution be now printed, or the printing thereof be deferred for a few days, in order to reconsider, in a full house, the propriety of the last clause in the constitution, containing the proviso respecting reconciliation?" A no vote was a vote to defer. In the end, it was seventeen to eight not to defer but to print the original version, which retained the last clause.[17]

William Paterson, who may have become a "conservative" Federalist politician in the 1790s, was a patriot in 1776 and served as the state's attorney general throughout the war.[18] Because he was the secretary of the Provincial Congress, the earliest copy of the New Jersey Constitution that has come down to us is in his hand—but he voted no on both days. Also, five of those delegates present on the first day changed their vote on the second—from yes to no. John Dickinson Sergeant, who had excitedly written Massachusetts patriot Samuel Adams shortly before the Provincial Congress met that New Jersey would "have a Republik established by the end of the week," changed his vote and on July 3 voted no.[19] It appears that they, and several other delegates, who voted no were New Jersey radicals who wanted a constitution that clearly included a permanent break with England. They voted no because they assumed that when the document was reconsidered, with all the delegates present (the "full house" of the resolution compared to only half of the delegates who attended on July 2 and 3), they would win their point and delete the objectionable clause.[20]

A number of historians have noted the absent delegates, using the fact as further proof the state was conservative. However, the same was true at the same time in New York. Clearly a number of New Jersey patriots in July 1776 thought it wiser to be home rallying the local militia, or moving their own families away from the coast to safety, than to be sitting in a tavern in Burlington writing a constitution. Considering that the British would later capture General Charles Lee, Declaration of Independence signer Richard Stockton, two of Abraham Clark's sons, and a number of other patriot leaders, as well as lay waste to their property, such action made sense. In the end, not enough delegates returned and not enough were willing to risk voting no; they preferred accepting the document with that final clause.[21]

There is yet another factor to consider, which puts the reconciliation clause in context and makes it appear less conservative. On July 2, virtually no one in New Jersey knew what had that day transpired in Philadelphia—that the vote in the Second Continental Congress had, in fact, been for independence. Only four colonies wrote constitutions before the Declaration of Independence—and three of them, New Jersey included, contained some reservations in case the war ended with reconciliation.[22] Thus, by writing a constitution, New Jersey delegates moved to the forefront of the Revolution, taking an enormous risk at a critical point in time. If the American colonies ultimately failed to win independence, the leaders of the four colonies that had produced constitutions would surely have been executed.

Also of great interest and providing a perspective on the events that occurred later that summer is the next move of the Provincial Congress after the passage of the

FIG. 16 *Robert Edge Pine*, Francis Hopkinson, *1785. Oil on canvas. Courtesy of the Historical Society of Pennsylvania Collection, Atwater Kent Museum of Philadelphia.*

Declaration of Independence. On July 17, it officially noted that the "United Colonies" had been declared "Free and Independent States"; the next day, just sixteen days after the state Constitution was adopted, it "Resolved, That New Jersey . . . adopt and assume the style and title of . . . [a] State."[23] Still, the New Jersey Constitution continued to refer to New Jersey as a colony, to the increasing embarrassment of its citizens, until a new one was adopted in 1844, but all other documents written after July 18, 1776, referred to New Jersey as a state.[24]

With the passage of the Declaration of Independence, thoughts of reconciliation seem to have been abandoned during the course of that summer. In July, the Provincial Congress considered the wording of an oath of allegiance for those serving under the new constitution—an oath required by the constitution itself. Section 23 said that "every Person" elected to the Legislative Council or House of Assembly had to take an "Oath of Affirmation," the word "Affirmation" provided to accommodate Quakers. But this was an oath to uphold the constitution, which included a pledge not to alter several of its sections (those pertaining to rights to be discussed later), with the wording for that purpose specified in the document. What the Provincial Congress preferred to do in mid-July, however, was to combine an oath of allegiance to the state with the constitutionally required pledge to protect rights. By August, a combined oath of this nature was prepared and presented when members of the first council and assembly elected under the new constitution met, and they all signed it.[25] The oath begins: "I [blank] do swear that I do not hold myself bound to bear Allegiance to George the third King of Great-Britain . . . and [it continues] that I do and will bear true Allegiance to the Government established in this State under the Authority of the People."

Nowhere is there any mention of possible reconciliation, and New Jersey is referred to as a state. It appears that those who lost the vote on July 3 won what they had wanted all along—a permanent revolution. If the constitution and oath are viewed together, it is clear that what New Jersey accomplished in the summer of 1776 was the creation of John Dickinson Sergeant's "republic." Gordon Wood has noted the radicalism of the Revolution, which replaced the monarchy with a republic. New Jersey did just that. Furthermore, those who wrote New Jersey's constitution told us what a republic meant to them, as the following discussion illustrates.

The constitution of 1776 opens with a statement of fundamental principles dealing with where government comes from and why it exists. It begins with the compact theory of government: "Whereas all the constitutional Authority, ever possessed by the Kings of Great Britain . . . was, by Compact, derived from the People, and held of them for the common Interest of the whole Society." Popular sovereignty is the creation of a government by the people; the government then exists to serve them. Its purpose is to provide for the "Happiness," "Safety," and "Well-Being" of the people.

The constitution then notes that this compact had been violated, because the king broke its "reciprocal ties." He failed to protect those in New Jersey and had in fact "assent[ed] to Sundry Acts of the British Parliament" and "made War on them in the most cruel and unnatural Manner, for no other Cause than asserting their just Rights." Their rights were just, but George III no longer represented justice (which absolved them of their promise of loyalty given, for example, in the Stamp Act Resolutions).

The right of revolution was included in the preamble, which is, in fact, New Jersey's own Declaration of Independence: "all civil Authority under him [the king] is necessarily at an End, and a Dissolution of Government in each Colony has consequently taken Place." As a result, no government existed, but it was clearly recognized that "some Form of Government is absolutely necessary, not only for the Preservation of good Order, but also . . . to unite the People" and for them to defend themselves. Therefore, the need followed to create a new government—and the remainder of the constitution specifies its provisions. Though the words are less eloquent than those of Thomas Jefferson, author of the contemporary Declaration of Independence, the basic arguments are the same.[26] The 1776 New Jersey Constitution also defined what its framers meant by a republic—a government in which representatives of the people dominated and where certain specific and crucial rights were forever protected.

The 1776 New Jersey Constitution provided for a form of state government containing a strong legislature and a weak governor. The legislature consisted of a council and assembly, as had the colonial government that preceded it. While the royal governor had been appointed by the king, it specified that the governor of New Jersey would be selected annually by both houses of the legislature meeting "jointly" to "elect some fit Person within the Colony." The result was that in addition to being totally dependent on the legislature for his position, the governor also had to accept its laws, because he was given no veto power. At the same time, with this strong legislature in place, no longer could a distant king, Privy Council, any person, or any other body overturn New Jersey's laws (although this would change after 1789 under the federal Constitution). In the seventeenth century, proprietors and their governors had vetoed laws, and until this point in the eighteenth century both the royal governor and English authorities could do so and regularly did, sometimes immediately and sometimes years after a law had been passed. Under the provisions of the 1776 New Jersey Constitution, this could no longer happen. Moreover, where royal governors had called the colonial legislature into session and had been the only ones authorized to ask for special sessions, the new and weaker governor could do neither. Instead, the constitution provided for the automatic yearly meeting of the legislature, and, at the same time, the Speaker of the assembly was given the power to call a special session.

While the creation of a weak governor seems strange to us today, at the time of the Revolution New Jersey was not unusual in its desire to rest the major portion of power in the legislature. Other states did the same, for with imperial power gone and only a provisional Continental Congress acting as a central government, the delegates of the people were intent on taking as much control as possible.

Rights

The New Jersey Constitution also defined the essential rights of the people in a republic. These included annual elections, trial by jury, and religious toleration. Although there is no separate "Bill of Rights" in this constitution (as there would be in those of 1844 and 1947), these specific rights are mentioned within the text of the document. In fact, they were considered so important that the oath required of legislators to take office prohibited them from ever changing the relevant portions of the constitution. Thus these crucial rights were to be permanent—or as the document repeatedly states, they were to be "forever."

A logical question arises as to the reasons for their selection and the accompanying language contained in the constitution. Long before 1776, parliamentary elections were required every seven years. While American colonists generally preferred frequent elections and annual legislative sessions, without written constitutional provisions the only way they could obtain them was to pass limited duration revenue bills. When New Jersey became a royal colony in 1702, the nature of its government was determined by instructions from Queen Anne, which simply ordered that legislative meetings were to alternate between Perth Amboy in East Jersey and Burlington in West Jersey; there was no stated requirement for periodic elections. As a result, between 1754 and 1776 assembly elections occurred only four times, and legislative sessions, while more frequent, were held on an irregular basis.[27]

Protests beginning with those related to the Stamp Act made clear that "no taxation without representation" meant that proper taxes should be enacted by local and frequently elected representatives meeting regularly. This issue was clearly of concern to the New Jersey Assembly, which noted in 1767 that the assembly should be elected "at proper Periods" in order to "secure the Liberty of the People."[28] Beginning in 1775, under provisions for electing a Provincial Congress and required by the language contained in the constitution, this meant requiring annual elections. The constitution stated that these were to begin in October 1777 and be held in October every year "forever."

A second concern was trial by jury. The lack of such trials (in, for instance, the Admiralty courts) was an issue for colonists from at least 1696 through the 1765 passage of the Stamp Act and the subsequent "Intolerable Acts." Early New Jersey documents provided for trial by jury, with the judgment passed "by twelve good and Lawfull men" of the "neighborhood."[29] The New Jersey Constitution mandated that "the inestimable Right of Trial by Jury" be "confirmed . . . for ever." Such trials served two purposes: they prevented government tyranny while protecting the rights of individuals.

The third concern, religious toleration, resonated in the state for reasons related to both tradition and necessity. Provisions for religious freedom had existed in New Jersey since the Concessions of 1665. Even if contrary to English law, that document provided that there would be freedom of conscience for all in the colony as long as they kept the peace. Subsequent documents, including the Instructions from the Queen in 1702, repeated the guarantee, and therefore most New Jersey residents were free to worship as they wished (except for "Papists," i.e., Catholics, specifically excluded in the Royal Instructions).[30] New Jersey residents also were free of the requirement that they pay tithes to a state (i.e., established) church. Although the Concessions of 1665 stated that the assembly could by law establish churches as long as liberty was given to all "to . . . maintain what Preachers or Ministers they please," and the later Instructions from the Queen mention the "maintenance" of the Orthodox, that is, Anglican Church, no state church was ever established. These freedoms attracted to the colony a religiously diverse population. Thus even by 1700 there were Quakers, Dutch Reformed, Swedish Lutherans, French Huguenots, New England Puritans, Scottish Presbyterians, Anglicans, and Baptists, among others. None was strong enough to dominate; hence the failure to establish one church and the need for toleration.[31]

By the 1770s, however, some feared a move to establish the Anglican Church in all of the British colonies and that this would be followed by the appointment of a bishop. It was the state church in the Carolinas, Virginia, Maryland, Georgia, and several New York counties, while the Congregational Church was the established church in New England (except Rhode Island). New Jersey's own Rev. James Odell, an Anglican minister and strong loyalist (who would resettle in Canada after the Revolution), apparently hoped to become the first Anglican bishop in America, an ambition supported by Governor William Franklin.[32] If this had occurred, a state church, maintained by mandatory taxes, would have resulted.

The authors of the New Jersey Constitution moved to protect that to which they were accustomed. They provided for both liberty of conscience and the prohibition of an established church. Section 18 of the constitution stated that everyone would have "the estimable Privilege of worshiping Almighty God" according to the "Dictates" of their "own Conscience." No one would be forced to attend a church "contrary" to their "own Faith or Judgment." Significantly, Catholics were no longer excluded; the provision overrode the Royal Instructions of 1702 and extended toleration to Catholics as well.

In addition to insisting on the freedom to worship as they wished, New Jersey residents refused to support the establishment of a state church. Indeed, the constitution clearly stated that no one would "ever be obliged to pay Tithes, Taxes, or any other Rates" to build or maintain a church or support a minister, except voluntarily. This was immediately followed by Section 19, stating: "That there shall be no Establishment of any one religious Sect in this Province in Preference to another."

Nevertheless, the constitution went on to restrict voting and office holding to Protestants (a provision common elsewhere at the time, including Pennsylvania). Despite this contradictory limitation, the guarantees of religious freedom in the constitution were both clear and broad and more comprehensive than what had existed previously. The Provincial Congress that wrote and approved this constitution reflected the religious diversity of New Jersey. It was signed by delegates who were Quakers, Dutch Reformed, Presbyterians, and members of other religious groups. Sections 18 and 19, therefore, resulted from the delegates' diversity, colonial practice, and desire to maintain their religious freedoms.

At a time when concepts of a constitution were still to be worked out and when the legislature was dominant and might presume to change it, New Jersey's 1776 constitution required those elected to take an oath never to touch the provisions for annual elections, jury trials, and religious freedom. The second half of the oath comes directly from the constitution. It states, "I [blank] A.B. do solemnly declare that, I will not assent to any Law, Vote or Proceeding which shall . . . annul or repeal," and then it goes on to list the relevant sections protecting those rights.[33]

There were limits to what was changed by New Jersey's constitution of 1776; it did not totally alter all aspects of government that had existed under royal rule. The religious qualification for voting and office holding has already been discussed; in addition, there were property requirements. The 1776 version of republicanism included the notion that to participate in government, one needed a stake in society, commonly defined as property ownership. Thus women, blacks, and Native Americans were usually disqualified.[34] The New Jersey Constitution required £1,000 for membership in the council, £500 for the assembly, and £50 to qualify to vote. The last requirement repeated a recent change made by the Provincial Congress—from a freehold (land-owning requirement) to any property.[35] Calculated in proclamation money (local paper currency rather than pounds sterling), this actually made it easier to vote, although office holding was still largely restricted to the more well-to-do.

The constitution also specified "That all Inhabitants of this Colony of full Age" worth £50 could vote, which meant that until 1807 widowed or single women and blacks with property could vote in New Jersey.[36] It is clear that in the 1790s some of them did in fact vote. Strange as it was for the times, this development has been explained in two ways: either the haste with which the document was written and adopted or the influence of Quakers, who were so prominent in New Jersey and believed in equality. Most probably an accident, whatever the cause, the practice caused laughter, consternation, and finally a backlash. In 1807, the legislature passed a law restricting voting to "white adult males," and the constitution of 1844 included that phrase.

What Was Revolutionary in the Revolution

Between July and the end of December of 1776, a number of significant events took place in New Jersey. The war arrived with a vengeance and would continue until 1783. Once invaded, and fearing a disastrous conclusion to the Revolution, many New Jersey residents flocked to take up British general William Howe's offer of a pardon, and the number of loyalists was high. But by the end of the year, General George Washington and his ragged forces had won a stunning victory at Trenton, and the new "state" had changed in five truly significant ways:

First, there was no king, no rule by any form of monarchy, and no "nobles." William Alexander, Lord Stirling, would be the last New Jersey resident to ever claim a title of nobility.

Second, the government was now a republic based on the "authority of the people." The royal council was gone—replaced by an elected upper house. The appointed royal governor, formerly the agent of the king, was no more. In his place was a chief executive elected annually by both houses of the legislature and hence dependent on them. In August, the legislature met for the first time and selected William Livingston as the first state governor. Although the British reacted by putting a price on his head and chasing him from place to place, Livingston remained strongly committed to the cause of independence. The legislature also had the power to pass whatever laws it chose, including provisions for paper money, without fear of a veto from above (governor) or abroad (the king). Previously a violation of British regulations, the desire for such a law in the past had soured relations between William Franklin and the colonial legislature. The issue would continue to embitter politics in the 1780s, but it was now the state's choice, since it was in control of its own affairs.[37] There was no higher authority other than the people themselves.[38]

Third, provisions for annual elections (or the present regularly scheduled elections and set terms of office) had been made.

Fourth, there was an assurance that jury trials would continue.

Fifth, the colonial legacy of religious toleration and diversity would be maintained.

Added to the foregoing were concerns for rights and, based on the Declaration of Independence, a thankfully bothersome mention of equality for all. The phrase "all men created equal" soon would be used by New Jersey residents to argue for the abolition of slavery, an institution some believed contradicted this premise.[39] Not everything changed, but enough had to consider the New Jersey Constitution of 1776 to be the culmination of a "radical" revolution.

THE "COCKPIT" RECONSIDERED:

Revolutionary New Jersey as a Military Theater

✷ ✷ ✷

MARK EDWARD LENDER

IN WAR, AS IN REAL ESTATE, location can be everything; during the War for Independence, location virtually decreed that New Jersey would be one of the chief military theaters. Situated between the de facto rebel capital in Philadelphia and the chief British garrison in New York City, the state was the contested middle ground. Armies maneuvering in either direction had to plan operations in the province. Generations of historians have referred to New Jersey as the "Cockpit of the Revolution," and from a purely quantitative perspective, the term is apt.[1] More fighting took place in New Jersey than in any other state: between October 16, 1775, with the seizure and destruction of the British transport *Rebecca & Francis* on Brigantine Beach, and a final incident on April 3, 1783, with a fugitive loyalist near Tuckerton, the state and its rivers and coastal waters were the scene of at least some 296 battles, skirmishes, and naval engagements—and one authoritative compilation has counted over 600.[2] Revolutionary New Jersey was a dangerous place.

If the fighting was frequent, it was also varied and complex. There were major battles between Continental and British regulars; there were smaller-scale actions involving mixed Continental and militia forces; and there were patrolling skirmishes where both sides got off no more than a few shots. Some fights involved only irregular forces operating under local authority or completely on their own initiative, occasionally with little interest in the wider war. Maritime privateers used New Jersey's rivers and coasts to wage war as a matter of free enterprise. In some instances, one side or the other tried to force a decisive action—to inflict a campaign-winning or even war-winning defeat; other actions aimed only at harassing enemy outposts or foraging operations, disrupting communications, or simply terrorizing neighborhoods. Bitter local actions reflected the civil war "within the war" between Whigs and loyalists. New Jersey was host to war in virtually all of its guises.

Location helped determine not only the frequency of combat but also the activities of the armies when not actually on campaign, for war also included recruiting, planning, training, civil and political relations, supply and intelligence operations, communications, and all the rest of the minutia of maintaining armed forces in the field. It was simply waiting for the enemy to make a move. Washington spent about half of the War for Independence in the state, devoting most of his time and attention to these noncombat tasks. In addition, New Jersey commanded the lines of communication between New York and Philadelphia, and its roads and rivers were important to each side. Rebels and redcoats both tried to exploit the state's physical geography: the British tried to force major actions on the plains of central New Jersey, terrain suited to traditional European tactics, while Washington used the defensive landscapes of northern New Jersey to establish relatively secure base and headquarters areas.

The frequency and duration of military operations meant that military concerns intruded prominently into daily affairs. For almost eight years, war, or the prospect of war, was a fact of life, and residents learned to live with it and interacted routinely with the military. Local farms fed both armies, often involuntarily, and pillaging troops from both sides did enormous property damage. Civilians also supplied combatants with intelligence, helped with recruiting, and, among patriots, rotated in and out of the militia. Thus distinctions between soldiers and civilians often blurred, and civilians would be very much a part of the war effort.

Indeed, the military experience of New Jersey became a microcosm of the wider war. The conflict assumed such scope and complexity that it touched on virtually every military question raised in other theaters. Granted, New Jersey's location made it a battleground, but how did such factors as terrain, supply, and communications shape actual operations? How, for example, did the British cope with the tactical problems inherent in operations in the interior of the state? How did patriots counter British superiority in numbers, naval support, matériel, and experience? To what extent did civilians play a role in active operations? And how, of course, did these matters help explain the ultimate victory of patriot arms? A focus on New Jersey offers a broader understanding of the conflict, and this essay argues that to understand events in the "Cockpit of the Revolution" is to understand the military history of the Revolution generally.

Early Operations: Retreat and Revival

The war came to New Jersey through the happenstance of geography: it engulfed the state because of New Jersey's proximity to operations in and around New York City.[3] There were several early incidents in New Jersey, mostly militia brushes with

FIG. 17 *Thomas Davies (attrib.),* An original sketch by an English officer on board of one of Adml. Howe's Fleet while at anchor in New York Harbor, just after the Battle of Long Island, *1776.* *Watercolor. I. N. Phelps Stokes Collection, Miriam and Ira D. Wallach Division of Art, Prints and Photographs, The New York Public Library, Astor, Lenox and Tilden Foundations.*

British vessels or crews coming ashore to forage, all minor affairs. The real force of the war struck only in the summer of 1776. In August, the British landed on nearby Staten Island, and beginning in September, General William Howe, the British commander in chief, launched assaults that successively drove Washington from New York City and its environs (fig. 17)—and then across New Jersey. On December 8, the remnants of Washington's army crossed the Delaware River into the relative safety of Pennsylvania.

The rebel cause appeared on the verge of collapse. Washington was battered, and most local militia had scattered. Thousands of New Jersey residents had declared allegiance to the king, and some had taken up arms against the patriots. Even the state legislature had dispersed. In fact, the seeming lack of nerve and disaffection of patriots bothered Washington even more than General Howe. "I think our affairs," Washington wrote his brother,

> are in a very bad situation; not so much from the apprehension of Genl. Howe's army, as from the defection of New York, Jerseys and Pennsylvania. In short, the conduct of the Jerseys has been most infamous. Instead of turning out to defend

their country and affording aid to our Army, they are making their submissions as fast as they can. If they the Jerseys had given us any support, we might have made a stand at Hackensack and after that at Brunswick, but the few Militia that were in arms, disbanded themselves . . . and left the poor remains of our Army to make the best we could of it.[4]

New Jersey, with its stores of produce, strategic location, and ambivalent revolutionaries, seemed secure for the crown.[5]

Yet the British had not finished off Washington's battered corps. Howe believed—with some reason—that the rebel army would largely disintegrate by spring. In his view, it was better to allow winter to run its destructive course with the rebels; he could clean up any pathetic remnants later. Thus on December 13 the British general ordered his command into winter quarters. Detachments would hold key towns across central New Jersey—including New Brunswick, Princeton, Trenton, and Burlington—thus maintaining security and communication. Howe admitted that these commands were too far apart to support one another; but he considered trouble very unlikely, and if there was any, he expected the garrisons to hold out until the arrival of reinforcements.[6] His decision constituted one of the greatest blunders of the war.

Howe had badly misread the situation. As the initial trauma of invasion faded, New Jersey patriots began to rebound. By mid-December, militia had engaged the British in some two dozen actions. Small enemy units venturing into the countryside did so at their peril, and even large bodies could run into trouble. On December 17, for example, at Hobarts Gap, militia stopped 800 redcoats short of Morristown.[7] (Royal success at the gap would have been disastrous for the Americans; at the very least, it would have denied the safe haven of the village to Washington's men after Trenton and Princeton.) Patriot naval harassment prevented the British from establishing winter headquarters at Burlington, and when they moved inland to Bordentown, militia patrols kept them on alert. By late December, things were so bad around Trenton that the garrison commander, Colonel Johann Rall, needed an escort of 100 men with artillery support to get a dispatch through to Princeton. Comfortable in New York, Howe missed the import of this, but many of his field commanders in New Jersey were getting nervous.[8] The state was not pacified, the interior was dangerous, and the New Jersey militia, so scorned by Washington only a week before, had revived.

Patriot political authorities also recovered from the initial shock of invasion. Most New Jersey officials were able to maintain civil order, work with militia units in dealing with Tory activity, and retain contact with senior patriot military leaders. Patriot command and control remained functional, and resistance in New Jersey was increasingly well organized.[9] Popular support for continued resistance grew as well, spurred in part from reactions to the Royal Army. Troop conduct was egregious and alienated even many residents originally well-disposed toward the crown. Soldiers pillaged freely; farms and homes were looted, public buildings were damaged or destroyed, and there were incidents of personal violence and rape. Tabulated damage claims reached the modern equivalent of millions of dollars.[10] By late 1776, Howe had lost whatever chance he had to win New Jersey's hearts and minds.

The British commander also underestimated Washington. During the retreat, Washington had lost heavily to desertion, expired enlistments, and matériel shortages; but his army remained operational. Reinforcement and logistics efforts faltered but never collapsed. Even before crossing into Pennsylvania, the rebel general had been looking for a chance to strike back; once across the Delaware, he focused on plans for a counterattack.[11] Frantic efforts to rally reinforcements succeeded. Washington was no match for the British main body, but he scraped together enough of a force to target the isolated British detachment at Trenton. He planned the operation for Christmas night.

The plan almost misfired. Washington had wanted an attack in three columns, but weather and river conditions prevented this, and only the commander in chief's column of some 2,500 men got across the Delaware in force (see color plate 4). He and his own column attacked by themselves and, aided by the fortunes of war, achieved complete tactical surprise. The Battle of Trenton was more a raid than a major engagement. The serious fighting lasted only some forty-five minutes, but the Hessian defeat was complete: Rall was mortally wounded, over 100 were killed or wounded, and another 918 fell prisoners (see color plate 5). Washington's lost only three wounded and two frozen to death during the initial advance.[12] Knowing the British would have to react, Washington quickly withdrew to Pennsylvania—but he had struck a startling blow.

He also had regained Howe's attention. Trenton was more an embarrassment than a major defeat, but Howe understood its impact on patriot morale—which was euphoric—and that it reflected a deteriorating military situation. Circumstances demanded a decisive response, and on January 2, three days after Washington had again occupied Trenton along Assunpink Creek, Howe dispatched Lord Cornwallis toward the village with some 6,000 men. Washington was in trouble; a British rush across the Assunpink bridge could have pushed him into the Delaware River. But confronted with a rebel delaying action, Cornwallis reached Trenton only at dusk. When a half-hearted attempt at the bridge failed, he decided against a night action. He would "bag the fox" in the morning.[13] Thus for the second time in the campaign, a British general elected not to make a final thrust against a vulnerable rebel army.

The mistake was fully the equal of Howe's earlier decision to end the campaign. Daybreak found the Americans gone. In a classic *ruse de guerre*, Washington had left a few militia to keep campfires burning and make the noise of an army and then slipped away along an unguarded road. Early on January 3, just outside Princeton, his forces collided with some 700 redcoats and, after an initial check, overwhelmed them in a brief but violent action (see color plates 6 and 7). Once again, Washington quickly left the field—and wisely, inasmuch as a furious Cornwallis had counter-marched and was closing rapidly.[14] The patriot general also decided not to attempt a descent on New Brunswick and seize a lightly guarded British pay chest. His men were tired, and he headed out of harm's way; by January 7, his army was safely at Morristown. The so-called ten crucial days were over and, with them, perhaps Britain's best chance to win the war on the battlefield.

The Lessons of '76

The main British army, of course, remained undefeated—but it hardly mattered. The reverses at Trenton and Princeton left British commanders off balance, and unsure of Washington's next move, Howe gave up most of New Jersey. For the rest of the winter, the Royal Army held only a strip of territory between Perth Amboy and New Brunswick.

With Howe's withdrawal, patriot authorities quickly reasserted political control. The significance of this for the rest of the war was stark: the British army would command only the territory on which it stood. As the British moved on, the rebels, almost always hovering on their flanks, moved in and reestablished themselves. The courts, law enforcement, local markets, public records—including the land titles so vital to an agricultural economy—all remained in patriot hands. Without control of these critical social and political assets, the British stood little chance of rekindling any broad New Jersey allegiance to George III. They never did root out the rebel civil structure in New Jersey, a defeat as telling as any they suffered on the battlefield.

This failure sealed the loyalists' fate. With the British retreat, hundreds, and eventually thousands, of Tories who had come out for the king during the early days of the invasion were left to look to themselves. They stood no chance. The re-surgence of patriot military and civil authority included a settling of accounts with the loyalists, who were crushed as a political force. In early 1777, for example, at Morristown, the Council of Safety condemned thirty-five loyalists taken in arms. Two Tory officers were duly hanged, at which point the committee put an offer to the remaining men: join their officers on the gallows or enlist in the Continental army. They enlisted.[15] In June of the same year, the state legislature passed the first of a series of acts allowing the condemnation and sales of Tory estates. The seizures struck at the economic base of loyalism, and hundreds of families lost everything, forcing many to seek protection behind British lines in New York.[16] Measures like these had the desired effect: they broke the back of loyalism as an effective threat to the Revolution. There was no pretense at allowing what might be termed "fair play" (or civil liberties, for that matter) for the Tories. This was a civil war, and loyalists were the internal enemy. Just as Whig families fled to avoid the British onslaught in late 1776, early 1777 found Tories trying to escape their patriot neighbors. It was a grim reversal of fortunes and demonstrated to loyalists everywhere that they were safe nowhere beyond the immediate presence of British troops.[17]

There was no effective counterrevolution in New Jersey. The loyalists fought on but never established an effective regional base to support a revival of royal political authority. Tories waged a persistent guerilla war, and some 2,450 served as regulars for the king, but they could not dislodge the Whig grip on the political apparatus of the state.[18] In the spring of 1777, the long-term importance of all of this may not have been fully apparent, but it was clear enough that New Jersey loyalists were as embittered and demoralized as their patriot neighbors were reanimated.

A New War: The Morristown Encampment and Its Consequences

As patriots and the British pondered the impact of the 1776 campaign, Washington took up quarters in the Arnold Tavern at Morristown (see fig. 27). His choice of destinations was limited after Trenton and Princeton, and he settled on the town because it was relatively secure. The terrain favored the defensive. The town was on high ground, protected south and east by the Great Swamp and the Watchung Mountains. As an added precaution, troops built a hilltop redoubt close to the center of town. As there never was an attack, the post became known as Fort Nonsense, but it made good sense in early 1777.[19]

As a base area, Morristown was almost ideally located. Before the war, it was a hamlet of only some 250 people; but the population was friendly, and a rebel political structure was firmly in place, a boon to army administration as it dealt with civilian authorities and state militia. Local farms were productive, a key factor in sustaining growing numbers of troops and animals. The town's location also facilitated communications. Morristown was situated to control new inland transport routes that ran from New England through New York State and northern New Jersey and hence to points south. It was also ideal for intelligence gathering. Units posted in the Watchung Mountains kept an eye on the British in the New Brunswick area, and those on the Hudson Palisades watched the enemy garrison in New York—and these outposts reported regularly to Morristown. In addition, the village screened approaches to New Jersey's nascent iron and gunpowder industries, resources increasingly helpful to patriot munitions supply.[20] Such a base was vital for a successful insurgency, and Morristown remained in service until 1782, earning informal status as military capital of the Revolution.

Washington made good use of his time at Morristown. Between January and April, he created a new Continental army able to fight a protracted war. The one-year enlistments of 1775 were gone, replaced by troops enrolled for three years or "for the war." All recruits received cash bounties of $20, and the "for-the-war" men were promised 100 acres of land.[21] In an agricultural world, 100 acres offered an entree to yeoman status, a real inducement to the young or poor with little previous stake in society. The result was an army of rank and file largely from the lower socioeconomic strata, with a middle-class or wealthy officer corps.[22] The arrangement afforded Washington the promise of stable regiments, and over time he intended to train "a respectable army" capable of meeting the redcoats on equal terms.

Again, location helped. Suited to the defensive, Morristown also provided a staging point for offensive operations, and Washington was looking for small fights. Between January and April, patriots fought some eighty actions, mostly across from New York and around the strip of British-occupied territory between New Brunswick and Perth Amboy.[23] A primary goal was to keep the British out of the countryside and away from New Jersey's ample stores of food and forage. No one would refer to New Jersey as the "Garden State" until the nineteenth century, but the state was renowned for its agriculture, and Howe had intended to feed his army from local farms. But foraging parties frequently met opposition, and the British had no choice but to cover foragers with armed escorts, which drained resources and nerves.

Two examples illustrate the point. On February 8, no less than Lord Cornwallis marched from New Brunswick at the head of over 2,000 redcoats and Hessians. His target was the store of food and forage at Quibbletown (now in Piscataway Township). But a patriot attack killed and wounded over sixty men at the cost of six rebel dead and another twenty wounded. This was a high price for hay. Two weeks later, 1,500 troops on a foraging operation at Spanktown (modern Rahway) were attacked by 1,000 rebels who not only disrupted the foraging but punished the column all the way back to Perth Amboy. It was Napoleon who famously noted that armies "traveled on their stomachs," but Washington was equally aware of the fact, and he made the British fight just to eat.[24] Without a battle-tested army, Washington had found a winning formula: "By keeping four or five hundred men well advanced," he wrote another officer, "we not only oblige them to forage with parties of 1,500 and 2,000 to cover, but every now and then, we give them a Smart Brush."[25] Hessian captain Johann Ewald, who served in many of the foraging actions, thought much the same thing. The British army, he noted in his diary, "would have been gradually destroyed through this foraging."[26]

In the end, patriots won the "forage war."[27] Washington simply made the New Jersey countryside too dangerous, and for the British, the loss of the state as a granary was a major disaster, ultimately forcing British commissaries to import the bulk of their foodstuffs from Ireland, a hugely expensive and time-consuming operation. Transatlantic supply operations compelled one of the largest maritime efforts in British history, and the supply ships required naval escorts to ward off swarms of American privateers. Consequently, the Royal Navy, one of the real advantages the British enjoyed over the rebels, had to divert considerable strength from other operations.[28] Thus the cumulative effect of small battles such as Spanktown and Quibbletown—and scores of others—had far-reaching implications.

The forage war also served another important purpose. The practice of sending small units into harm's way provided invaluable field experience; troops learned the practical skills of soldiering even as Washington reorganized the army. By late spring, when he was ready to consider more ambitions operations, a significant proportion of the men had seen at least some action. When the general moved south in April and May, his army was not entirely green.

1777: Middlebrook and After

Success at Morristown allowed Washington to confront the British more directly in the spring. Again, he enjoyed the advantage of location, shifting his base of operations to the Watchung Mountains at Middlebrook. Washington was on excellent defensive terrain and virtually dared Howe to come after him.[29] Perhaps recalling the horror of Bunker Hill, the royal commander never did.

Instead, Howe tried to lure Washington down—but the patriot chief refused to be lured. Once more, location told against the British. Howe's plans for 1777 called for a strike on Philadelphia, and the shortest route was across New Jersey. But such a march would force him to cross the Delaware, perhaps in the face of Washington's army. He could not risk this. Thus in mid-June, in a final effort to bring the rebels to battle, he feigned an evacuation of New Jersey, hoping Washington would come down from the hills. Washington reacted cautiously, noting that whatever the British were doing, they had retained their artillery. Thus when Howe turned to fight on June 26, he met only advanced American detachments. The day saw a series of sharp engagements between Oak Tree, Scotch Plains, and Westfield. But when Washington declined a general action and pulled back to the Watchungs, Howe quit the state.[30]

Major consequences followed. Refusing to march across New Jersey, Howe went to Pennsylvania by sea. Landing at the head of Chesapeake Bay in late August, he took until mid-September to break through Washington's troops (who had plenty of time to march from New Jersey) and into Philadelphia.[31] Yet holding the city depended on the ability to feed and supply the army, and after his experience in New Jersey, Howe understood the problems inherent in local foraging. Thus the British needed control of the Delaware River, allowing navy transports to supply the city. Until river navigation was secure, Philadelphia was not.[32]

This meant more fighting, as two rebel forts commanded the river. Fort Mifflin sat on Mud Island, just off of the Pennsylvania mainland; across from Fort Mifflin was Fort Mercer, in Red Bank, New Jersey. On October 19, British artillery opened on Fort Mifflin, and on October 22 some 2,000 Hessians assaulted Fort Mercer (fig. 18). It was a slaughter: firing from concealed positions, the Continentals killed or wounded 400.[33] Fort Mercer held out until November, abandoned only after the evacuation of Fort Mifflin made the New Jersey post untenable. The British had won the Delaware and seemingly the campaign. But it was a costly victory: the fighting had consumed over a quarter of Howe's effective strength.[34]

The delays in taking Philadelphia helped doom another British army. Even as Howe was dealing with Forts Mifflin and Mercer, the troops of General John Burgoyne were coming to grief at Saratoga, New York. Howe's orders from London never specifically required him to assist Burgoyne, but his operations in Pennsylvania concluded at so late a date as to preclude a supporting deployment. Burgoyne was lost, and soon afterward the French recognized American independence and declared war on Britain. What had begun as a colonial rebellion had become an international war—a godsend to the Americans.

Thus the period from January to June 1777 marked an extraordinary passage in arms. Washington rebuilt the Continental army as a credible force and worked effectively with militia and civilian authorities to maintain control of the countryside. He used location at Morristown and Middlebrook to offset superior British numbers and experience, and without risking a major battle, he compelled the British to commit vast and unanticipated resources to feed themselves and their animals. He made it too dangerous for the British to leave their garrisons in anything but major force, and he kept them off balance tactically as well as strategically. Finally, he cost the British invaluable time during the spring, a delay with disastrous consequences for the royal cause. True, he lost Philadelphia, a blow to rebel pride—but in the end it hardly mattered. Later in the war, notably in the Yorktown campaign, Washington certainly equaled his performance in the first half of 1777—but he never surpassed it.

The Monmouth Campaign and American Military Maturity

The French declaration of war altered the military equation. Confronted with a widening war, the British realized that they could not fight everywhere. Bitterly, they elected to forgo pursuit of a military decision in the North, redeploy troops to protect vital Caribbean colonies, and invade the southern states. The crown hoped that southern Tories would rally in numbers sufficient to restore royal authority. The new strategy meant abandoning Philadelphia. But the Royal Navy lacked the transports to evacuate the entire army and terrified loyalists, who were well aware of what had happened to New Jersey Tories the previous year. Thus on June 18, 1778, the new British commander in chief, General Henry Clinton, began to march some 12,000 troops and camp followers overland to New York—directly across New Jersey.[35]

FIG. 18 *Irwin Bevan,* Attack on Mud Island, *ca. 1918. Watercolor.*
The Mariners' Museum, Newport News, Va.

The march brought on the longest single day of fighting of the entire war. Clinton reached Freehold, in Monmouth County, only on June 26; poor roads, hot and rainy weather, and patriot harassment had slowed his movement, and the army needed a rest. Washington, breaking camp directly from his winter quarters at Valley Forge, had followed the British into New Jersey. Clinton had resumed his trek early on the 28th, when the Continental vanguard, under Charles Lee, struck his rear. A strong counterattack pressed Lee, but Washington brought up the main army by midday, and the lines stabilized after bitter fighting (see color plates 8 and 9). The afternoon was spent in a spectacular cannonade and localized American attacks, all in brutal heat. The battle was a tactical draw, although Clinton had the worst of it. That night, Clinton broke off and eventually got his army safely back to New York.

The Battle of Monmouth was an important benchmark in the war, a measure of rebel progress in arms. Changes effected the previous winter at Valley Forge had vastly improved the Continental army. French arms and equipment reached the army in quantity, and training improved under the tutelage of General Frederick von Steuben. Recruiting operations began to replenish depleted ranks, and some states, including New Jersey, even sent draftees to the Continental regiments. The artillery arm reorganized, and quartermaster operations, placed in the capable hands of General Nathanael Greene, got supplies moving to camp. When it became clear that a

New Jersey campaign was a possibility, Greene stockpiled supplies along probable lines of march. The army that broke camp in June 1778 was a rejuvenated force.

Monmouth was the first test of the new Continentals, and they did well against the best regiments in the British army. There were still serious problems. Field communications and resupply were not on a par with the British, there were too few mounted troops, and Washington's staff still lacked experience in conducting large-scale operations.[36] But on the whole, the Continentals were a force to reckon with at Monmouth, and even the British conceded as much. The battle marked the "coming of age" of the Continental army—a maturing of the force Washington had begun to build at Morristown in early 1777.

Monmouth also reflected the civilian commitment to the war. In 1776, the effects of the first British invasion were devastating: much of the militia dispersed, residents fled in alarm, many loyalists came out to declare for the king, and state government scattered. The story was different in 1778. Militia rallied and operated effectively with the Continentals, few Tories came out, and state government followed events carefully. Most civilians were hostile to the invaders. They hid valuables and drove livestock into the woods and swamps, passed information on British movements to militia and Continental troops, and assisted enemy deserters. Some picked up weapons and joined the fight. By 1778, the British faced a civilian population willing to support rebel troops while denying vital intelligence, supplies, and moral support to the crown. Even with an enemy army in their midst, state patriots remained firmly in political and civil control. In military terms, the Monmouth campaign was an important passage of arms, but in addition, it was a telling measure of the extent to which New Jersey was lost to the Empire.

The Long War: Skirmishes, Raids, and Exhaustion to 1783

In the aftermath of Monmouth, the focus of active operations shifted to the South, although this did not diminish the significance of New Jersey's military role. After a mild winter at Middlebrook in 1778–1779, the army endured the appalling 1779–1780 winter—the coldest ever recorded—at Morristown. This experience shook the army profoundly. Snows were four to six feet deep; pay was five months late; firewood, food, and forage were scant. Deteriorating rebel finances exacerbated problems—the army had no money to purchase local produce—and some troops pillaged just to survive. By January 1780, Washington had to impress supplies and take stern measures to protect civilian property from desperate soldiers. By spring, troop protests verged on mutiny.[37] Open revolt flared the following winter. On New Year's Day 1781, the Pennsylvania line mutinied at Morristown, and the troops marched for Philadelphia to demand satisfaction from Congress. Emissaries met them at Trenton, however, and most men returned to duty with promises of better conditions and, in some cases, discharges. Shortly thereafter, Washington put down rebellious New Jersey Continentals at Pompton, shooting two ringleaders.[38] It was as close as the army had come to dissolving since the darkest days of 1776.

Yet these episodes, however bitter, served to underscore the value of New Jersey's secure location. Even in the bleak winter of 1780, there was plenty of food in the state, and when Washington impressed it, he was able to work through established civil authorities. This expedited the process and limited the political damage inherent in a blunt military seizure of private property.[39] Nor were the British able to take advantage of the mutinies. In 1780 and 1781, Morristown's protected location kept them from learning the full scope of patriot difficulties until it was too late to act. In late August and early September of 1781, the British also missed the import of a rapid and skillfully disguised march across the state. Continental and French troops moved south from positions around New York and Rhode Island to arrive in Virginia in October—to trap Cornwallis at Yorktown.[40] Washington and French general the Comte de Rochambeau made good use of New Jersey's interior communications routes. Even when not a battlefield, New Jersey remained vital ground.

Until the end, however, the war of skirmishes and raids continued in New Jersey. After Monmouth—that is, after the end of major combat—the state saw some 266 small-scale incidents.[41] Some were well-planned raids against specific targets—blockhouses, prominent individuals, forage operations, and the like—while others were the result of rival groups stumbling across one another. Casualties were usually minimal. In January 1779, for example, the *New Jersey Gazette* reported the death of three "Pine-Banditti" at the hands of Monmouth County militia; in May 1781, militia and Tories skirmished in Shrewsbury with no known casualties.[42] In aggregate, however, hundreds were killed, wounded, or captured—hardly "small" losses in a state with fewer than 130,000 residents.

Some of these operations were larger. In 1779, 400 Continentals stormed the British outpost on Paulus Hook (modern Jersey City), taking 158 prisoners and killing or wounding another 50. The following year, 400 Hessians struck rebel positions at Hoppertown in Bergen County, killing or capturing some 49 men.[43] But these were raids, never intended to capture and hold territory or settle a decisive point. As such, they were of a piece with rest of the local hit-and-run actions. The northern war had devolved into a grinding series of small-unit and guerrilla operations; such wars usually ended through attrition and exhaustion rather than a knockout blow, and neither side was capable of throwing such a punch.

The only exception to the "desultory war," as Washington termed it, came in 1780. In June, British commanders in New York learned of the Continental near-mutiny at Morristown. Unsure of what was really happening, they launched a reconnaissance in force into New Jersey. On June 7, about 5,000 British and Hessians drove inland toward Springfield. Continental and militia resistance stopped them at Connecticut

Farms (now Union), which the British burned before pulling back to Elizabethtown. On June 23, General Clinton, just returned from the invasion of the Carolinas, reinforced the troops and sent them in again. With luck, they could force Hobarts Gap, as they had failed to do in 1776, and get to Morristown. Tough opposition stopped them at Springfield, which they also burned before pulling out for good—harassed virtually every step of the way by infuriated local militia.[44] It was the last major British incursion into the state.

The Battle of Springfield was instructive. By 1780, property damage, a shattered economy, and the near constant threat of enemy raids had left New Jersey residents profoundly war-weary. Yet this did the British little good. The burning of Connecticut Farms and Springfield reflected their understanding that civilian New Jersey was against them and that raids, no matter how severe, would not dislodge patriot authority. They also knew that these same civilians were the source of the militia that sniped at their flanks. Enough militia came out to cooperate with the Continental regulars to make a penetration of the state interior prohibitively expensive. The British could still handle the patriot regulars, but they could not wage war successfully against a war-wise populace.

The naval war also lost none of its intensity. Between late June 1778 and 1783, there were 108 engagements on New Jersey's rivers or off of its immediate coasts.[45] Many of these actions were privateer assaults on British shipping bound in and out of nearby New York, and predations were a galling and expensive drain on the British merchant fleet. In 1777 alone, privateer operations drove up marine insurance rates 20 percent, and captured goods became important to the patriot war effort and to the civilian economy. British attempts to strike at the privateers also motivated several shore engagements, including a large attack in 1778 on General Casimir Pulaski's cavalry at Osborne (or Minnock) Island.[46] To the end of the war, however, New Jersey's privateers were a thorn in the British side.

The partisan warfare, ashore or afloat, was intertwined with New Jersey's civil war. Unable to reestablish themselves in their home state, refugee Tories raided actively from New York. Many of their operations came under the aegis of the Board of Associated Loyalists, headed by New Jersey's deposed royal governor, William Franklin. They fought like what they were: men with nothing left to lose. Black troops, often escaped New Jersey slaves, were active participants, sometimes in ventures against the neighborhoods of former masters.[47] The civil aspect of the war was the most likely to target specific civilians, and it engendered some of the deepest bitterness of the era.

"The Banks of the Delaware": Retrospection on a War

In the end, failure to hold and pacify New Jersey, or any substantial part of it, weighed heavily against the British war effort. With the British unable to maintain a significant presence in the state, their hopes of a rebel political collapse never materialized. Indeed, the patriot civil structure proved resilient even during the darkest periods of the war, and Whig political authority only consolidated as the war lengthened. This proved of critical importance to the military effort. Firmly in place, local Whig committees and courts dealt with suspected Tories and offered a constant source of vigilance against counterrevolution. Loyalists had no chance to reassert the authority of the crown in New Jersey. Civilian officials also worked with Continental military authorities in matters of civil-military relations, including Continental recruiting and commissary operations. The assistance rendered in impressing supplies for the army in 1780 was a case in point. None of this worked perfectly everywhere or all of the time—but civil authority, even when embattled, kept the state in the war.[48]

Significantly, the political infrastructure lay in back of the militia—the armed embodiment of the civil structure. Militia participation was never complete or equitable: perhaps 30 percent of the state's eligible manpower was lost to loyalism or Quaker pacifism, and militia laws allowed the well-to-do to hire substitutes to serve for them.[49] There also were shirkers who did their best to avoid their tours of duty, and there were frequent complaints about dilatory militia responses in times of crises. Thus Governor William Livingston complained that military burdens fell disproportionately on the shoulders of the "willing."[50] But war is seldom fair, and enough men did serve to make the militia effective. Never intended to fight major battles—that was obvious in November 1776—the militia learned to handle local tasks admirably. It bore the brunt of the "desultory war" of skirmishes and raids, security patrolling and intelligence gathering, and intimidation of loyalists. Militiamen eventually learned to work well with the patriot regulars, and they did good service at Monmouth, Springfield, and smaller operations with the Continentals. To a considerable degree, then, New Jersey became a society in arms and, with Washington's regular army, a full military partner in holding the state for the Revolution. It was this partnership that won the war.

Skillful patriot use of New Jersey's location and terrain contributed as well. Protected positions at Morristown and Middlebrook provided the secure bases necessary to support organizational as well as operational missions. Washington used them to counter British numbers and assume the posture of a "force in being"—perhaps not strong enough to challenge the redcoats directly but too strong to ignore. Certainly Howe considered Washington too strong to attack on good defensive ground or to leave in his rear; he could never entice Washington into the open for a decisive battle in New Jersey, even as the rebel general used terrain and position to support persistent and damaging "brushes" with the enemy without risking a major defeat. Location helped level the playing field, which advantaged only the rebels.

The same was true of New Jersey's strategic interior. In patriot hands, the interior was an invaluable sanctuary, of which Morristown was the paramount example. This region also offered relatively secure communications, including the best links between the northern and southern colonies, which was amply demonstrated in the march of Washington and Rochambeau to Yorktown. In addition, it protected many of New Jersey's contested farms, which contributed far more to patriot than to British commissaries—again, a fact with serious and adverse consequences for the crown.

No British commander found the key to operations in the New Jersey interior. This was the lesson of scores of small battles and of some larger ones such as Hobarts Gap and Springfield. British forces could pass through the state—Clinton proved that in 1778—but not without moving in major force, not without a fight, and not with any intention of lingering. This lesson was confirmed repeatedly elsewhere during the rest of the war. Small enemy forces were always at risk, and far from bases of supply, reinforcement, or naval support, even sizeable British formations would come to grief on battlefields across the colonies. In varying degrees, Bennington, King's Mountain, and, in perhaps the best examples, Saratoga and Yorktown were the New Jersey experience writ large. The American interior was dangerous, and the British never learned to tame it.

The last Continental troops filed out of the Morristown encampment on August 29, 1782 (fittingly, they were from the New Jersey Brigade).[51] It was the last of many marches through the state, so many that New Jersey has earned informal recognition as the "Crossroads of the American Revolution." In their various marches, the British never subdued New Jersey, but they always understood its military importance. No one was clearer on this than Lord Cornwallis. At a social moment after his surrender at Yorktown, he was gracious and candid enough to offer a toast to Washington: "And when the illustrious part your Excellency has borne in this long and laborious contest becomes matter of history, fame will gather your brightest laurels rather from the banks of the Delaware than from those of the Chesapeake."[52]

PICTURING
REVOLUTIONARY NEW JERSEY:
The Arts

✶ ✶ ✶

BARBARA J. MITNICK

I resumed my studies with Mr. West, and at the academy, with ardor; and now began to
meditate seriously the subjects of national history, of events of the Revolution, which have
since been the great objects of my professional life.

– JOHN TRUMBULL, *AUTOBIOGRAPHY,*
REMINISCENCES & LETTERS, 1841

THE "GREAT OBJECTS" THAT WERE to arise from the extraordinary ability
and palette of John Trumbull (1756–1843) and other important history painters
ultimately became the major components of America's national visual archive. In a
new country, the American Revolution provided the initial subject matter to establish
new traditions and to catapult the nation's early heroes into lasting fame. Because of
the significance of New Jersey's pivotal location, it became the center of the fighting—the "Crossroads of the American Revolution"—where more battles took place
than in any other state. America's early history painters began to travel to New Jersey
in the 1770s—some to take part in the action but all in quest of subject matter and
sources for their work. Within the course of the war and for many years thereafter,
they documented the memorable scenes of the colonists' quest for independence.

Prior to the Revolution, the colony and (after July 1776) the state of New Jersey
was generally considered to be little more than a corridor between the major cities of
Philadelphia and New York—"a barrel tapped at both ends," as allegedly asserted in

1783 by none other than Benjamin Franklin (1706–1790; see fig. 46).[1] There is no doubt that Philadelphia (America's largest eighteenth-century city and capital of the colonies during most of the Revolution) and New York were two major centers of culture. New Jersey's location fell in between and was overshadowed; thus its fine and decorative artists and artisans found it difficult to be recognized for their skills, to secure appropriate training, and even to begin to rival the output of the more sophisticated and well-trained painters, printmakers, and craftspersons at work nearby. Moreover, New Jersey, as was generally the case in the rest of the country, was a rural enclave—mainly populated with farmers trying to carve out a basic living. It seems that with only a few exceptions, its residents had neither the time nor the inclination to be involved in cultural activities; nor were many able to acquire the financial resources to participate in the fine or decorative art marketplace. Thus, following Franklin's early lead, many scholars have continued to maintain that New Jersey was and has remained an "artistic desert."[2] Happily, however, by the middle of the twentieth century, this generally accepted notion began to be dismissed, as new research uncovered documentation for a more thriving cultural climate. Although by no means overlooking the emphasis on practicality in everyday New Jersey life, historians such as Richard P. McCormick have come to understand that "artistic expression was not entirely neglected."[3] It also is now abundantly clear that as a result of the American Revolution, beginning with the successes of the Battles of Trenton and Princeton, the former "barrel tapped at both ends" became important in its own right, and the "Crossroads of the American Revolution" began its ascent to truly become a major "crossroads" of art and culture. As the Battles of Trenton and Princeton became the first turning points of the Revolution, so did those events signal the transformation of New Jersey from an "artistic desert" to a major source of subject matter for America's finest history painters. However, it appears that the same Revolutionary War activities that spurred the fine arts resulted in an upheaval that produced the opposite effect with regard to several of the decorative arts, as the concurrent devaluation of currency generally caused producers of marketable crafts to locate fewer outlets for their wares.

The Fine Arts

THE PRE-REVOLUTIONARY PERIOD Despite the economic circumstances of most New Jerseyans during the eighteenth century, artists did manage to find employment—mainly as itinerant portrait painters or creators of "landskips," which were usually intended for overmantel decoration. As for sculptors, the production of stone grave markers kept several of them employed, and New Jersey also was the home of the production of early wax portrait images. The success of these practical forms of art is not surprising, even though it is understood that most Americans of the period eschewed art for decoration, art "for art's sake," or indeed art for anything but utilitarian purposes. At the same time, in that prephotography world, most citizens deemed it important to record their appearances for their descendants; thus it was typical to find people even of modest means commissioning painted or wax likenesses. And grave markers were certainly necessary for remembrance and identification of the burial locations of the dead. Even rural New Jerseyans seemed to find the means to pay the fees of itinerant portrait painters roaming the countryside, typically carrying partially finished canvases of men and women that required only individualized heads to fill in the empty spaces. Wealthier New Jerseyans were able to "sit to" more proficient artists for longer periods in order to obtain professional results.[4]

Although most of the portrait painters who plied their craft in New Jersey during the period before the Revolution are unknown today, a few did achieve a modicum of recognition. John Watson (1685–1768), who emigrated to America possibly as early as 1714 from Scotland, chose to establish himself in New Jersey's then-capital, Perth Amboy, where he achieved success in several activities, of which painting was one.[5] In 1730, after a trip back to Scotland, he reportedly returned to New Jersey with a group of paintings and set up an art gallery—possibly the first in America. Yet the early-nineteenth-century art critic William Dunlap, writing in his 1834 *History of the Rise and Progress of the Arts and Design in the United States*, stated that by the date of the publication of this two-volume study, no surviving pictures by Watson could be located.[6] Today, some have been attributed to his hand, but his lasting importance appears to be his pivotal position in fostering art in the state's early capital rather than in his paintings, which tend to be somewhat flat and lifeless imitations of contemporary English portraits.

At the same time, as we look back at artistic production in New Jersey in the late eighteenth century, we can proudly point to Patience Lovell Wright (1725–1786), who not only pioneered the production of wax portrait images but also became a self-appointed spy and informant to Benjamin Franklin and later George Washington and Thomas Jefferson after settling in England before the Revolution. Her son, Joseph Wright (1756–1793), is known to have created a life mask of Washington at the general's headquarters at Rocky Hill in 1783; he then went on to portray him in both painting and sculpture. Even the famous Gilbert Stuart (1755–1828) worked for a time in Bordentown.[7]

THE REVOLUTIONARY PERIOD The tradition of conventional itinerant portraiture and practical forms of art might have continued unabated in New Jersey were it not for the onset of the Revolution. Suddenly, whether winning or losing, the battles and events of the war were understood to contain important material for history painters—and it was sources for this form of narrative (storytelling) and didactic (instructive) art that the more talented and ambitious painters of the late eighteenth century sought for their life's work.

For centuries, beginning in Renaissance Italy, it was clearly understood that the finest artists aspired to be history painters, that is, the primary recorders of scenes from history, literature, religion, or mythology.[8] To writers and critics, including Leon Battista Alberti (1404–1472) in fifteenth-century Italy, André Félibien (1619–1695) in seventeenth-century France, and Sir Joshua Reynolds (1723–1792) in late-eighteenth-century England, history painting was at the top of a hierarchy of subject matter. Alberti, for example, called it the *istoria*, the "chief business of a serious painter," which will move the soul of both the learned and the unlearned as it reveals a rebirth of the styles and emphasis on civic virtue that had originated in the ancient world.[9]

The first major American painter to follow this path was Benjamin West (1738–1820), who left his Pennsylvania home for Europe in 1760 and three years later established a studio in London; he ultimately became known and is still identified as the father of American history painting. With West's departure from America and art training still severely limited in the colonies (basically to apprenticeships), it did not take long for promising history painters to come to the conclusion that they must find the means to travel to London to study in West's atelier.[10]

With the coming of the Revolution to New Jersey, some local artists tried their hand at documenting its major events; few are widely remembered. But two major practitioners who worked in New Jersey, Charles Willson Peale (1741–1827) and John Trumbull, have firmly secured places in the pantheon of American history painters. Peale was a saddler and watchmaker from Maryland who also had learned the basic techniques of portraiture from the mid-eighteenth-century Maryland painter John Hesselius (1728–1778) and subsequently, on a visit to Boston from America's undisputed preeminent pre–Revolutionary War portraitist, John Singleton Copley (1738–1815). After arriving in West's London studio in 1767, Peale soon found himself copying some of the master's recent historical works as well as painting drapery and other subordinate portions of West's large commissions—many intended for the collection of King George III.[11] However, only two years later, after enduring great homesickness for his wife and family, Peale returned to Annapolis until the onset of the Revolution. He spent the next few years traveling through the colonies to paint portraits of George Washington and other early American leaders.[12]

By returning to the colonies, however, Peale missed the excitement generated by West's "revolution in art," for in 1770, just one year after his departure from London, West caused an upheaval in British art circles as his newest painting, *The Death of Wolfe* (1771, National Gallery of Canada, Ottawa; color plate 11), was nearing completion. Intended to commemorate the death of British general James Wolfe on September 13, 1759, on the Plains of Abraham in Canada during the Seven Years' War (French and Indian War), the work reveals the fallen soldier wearing contemporary military dress, rather than the traditionally accepted costume of antiquity.

To visiting potential patrons questioning the propriety of this change, Dr. Robert Hay Drummond (1711–1776) (archbishop of York) and Sir Joshua Reynolds (then president of England's Royal Academy), West insisted that the event in question took place in an area of the world "unknown to Greeks and Romans." And in the following statement, he revealed his reason for including what he regarded as truthful contemporary details: "I consider myself as undertaking to tell this great event to the eye of the world; but if, instead of the facts of the transaction, I represent classical fictions, how shall I be understood by posterity!"[13]

Nevertheless, despite this logical declaration, the work was severely criticized by Drummond and Reynolds for compromising the dignity of the general's death, and it was therefore rejected for inclusion in the royal collection of King George III. West, however, remained undeterred and responded to Reynolds's and Drummond's complaints by declaring that if on completion of the work they still disapproved, he would "consign it to the closet." But that did not prove necessary, for on his return to West's studio, Reynolds was so thoroughly impressed with the final product that he was moved to declare that it would "not only become one of the most popular, but occasion a revolution in art."[14] In fact, that is just what happened, and soon a replica was ordered for the king. News of the "revolution" traveled everywhere, and despite Peale's absence from London, there is no doubt that he learned of the story and its ramifications and began to realize that his own history paintings could be favorably influenced by this new (for the period) and radical departure from traditional practice. Moreover, he had been provided with the tools to do so, for his early training with West and knowledge of the master's daring technique had undoubtedly been an inspiration. Thus Peale clearly saw an opportunity to extol the major events of the American Revolution by painting the participants wearing accurate military uniforms within a grand-style format, which could potentially evoke feelings of nationalism and patriotism along with adoration for the new nation's heroes. The battles and events surrounding the Revolutionary War were eventually to provide the subject matter for the creation of America's most important and lasting representations of that crucial period in our history, and Peale was there when it all began.

In 1776, Peale enlisted in the city militia of Philadelphia as a private, and by December of that year he was elevated to the rank of first lieutenant.[15] By the end of the month and during the first week of January 1777, he participated in the crucial Battles of Trenton and Princeton, although there is no evidence to suggest that he was either a trained soldier or a military strategist. Nevertheless, he was interested in the battles, and particularly in the role of General Washington, whom he managed to lionize in paint long before Washington ever succeeded in becoming the supreme hero of the war. Four years earlier, the general had begun to "sit to" the artist, a session that resulted in the creation of the first known life portrait of Washington. During the remainder of Washington's life, he actually went "to the painter's chair," as he characterized it, on some twenty-three occasions for Peale, more than for any other artist, despite his known aversion to the practice.[16]

On January 8, 1779, the Supreme Executive Council of Pennsylvania commissioned Peale to paint *Washington at the Battle of Princeton* (color plate 6). The council hoped that along with preserving Washington's appearance at the time of the monumental battle, "the contemplation of it may excite others to tread in the same glorious and disinterested steps which led to public happiness and private honor."[17] It was a work that firmly although somewhat prematurely established Washington as America's grand-style hero, a larger-than-life-size, full-length image of the general dressed in his blue and buff uniform, blue ribbon revealing his rank as commander in chief, and the sword that he used throughout most of the war. He stands majestically before a rendition of the distant Princeton battle; the cannon and the captured Hessian battle flags at his feet symbolically refer to his recent success at the Battle of Trenton. Begun fully two years before the final American victory at Yorktown, Virginia, in 1781, its purpose was to provide a monumental and inspirational remembrance of the event and historical portrait in the tradition of grand-style history painting; it was never intended to be an accurate account of the battle.[18]

Major events inspire artists, and therefore during the Revolution and in the years to follow, John Trumbull also set about recording America's fight against Great Britain. He was the son of Jonathan Trumbull (1710–1785), a strong supporter of independence who became the governor of Connecticut in 1769, and Faith Robinson, also a member of a distinguished family; she was a descendant of John Robinson, a Pilgrim leader who had arrived at Plymouth, Massachusetts, in 1620. John Trumbull's early childhood was beset by illness, and at the age of six he lost his left eye in an accident. However, it seems that he was not unduly hampered by this affliction, since he was soon reading Greek, and in 1773 he graduated from Harvard, the first American artist to receive a college education.[19]

After the first shots of the Revolution were fired at Lexington, Massachusetts, on April 19, 1775, a regiment of Connecticut troops, commanded by General Joseph Spencer, with Trumbull serving as his aide-de-camp, marched to Boston. In June 1776, Trumbull's rank was elevated to colonel, a promotion he believed resulted in large part from Washington's recognition of his artistic skill in his drawing of a view and plan of the enemy's works in Boston, which the general used to advantage during the ensuing campaign.[20]

By late February 1777, however, Trumbull resigned from the military, primarily as a result of his cantankerous reaction to a discrepancy in the date of his original commission. He returned to the family home in Lebanon, Connecticut, and "resumed my pencil," as he described his art work.[21] But he soon came to understand that his access to copies of old masters brought to Boston by the eighteenth-century Scottish-born portrait painter John Smibert (1688–1751) and some black-and-white engravings would not substitute for formal training. Beyond that discouraging situation, his father opposed his interest in making art a career, believing that it was not a suitable profession for a man of Trumbull's social or intellectual status; instead, his father wanted him to enter the ministry or become a lawyer. But Trumbull managed to persevere; he determined that he would become a history painter and resolved to travel to London to study with Benjamin West.

Despite the fact that America was at war with Great Britain, in 1780 Trumbull entered West's London atelier. However, as the son of Connecticut's governor who was also a prominent patriot, it is not surprising that his presence in England's capital city raised the suspicions of the British government; soon he was accused of spying and summarily dispatched to Bridewell prison. Fortunately, he survived his incarceration, and when hostilities ended in Yorktown a year later, Trumbull was released and returned to America. By this time, he had firmly resolved not only to become a history painter but specifically to paint a "Hall of the Revolution," a distinctive visual archive for the new nation.[22] Finally, by 1784, long after hostilities had ended, Trumbull was able to safely return to London to resume his studies with West and during the next few years to complete his first major Revolutionary War paintings, *The Death of General Warren at the Battle of Bunker's Hill, 17 June 1775* and *The Death of General Montgomery in the Attack on Quebec, 31 December 1775*.[23] During the mid-1780s, he also began to widen his artistic horizons by traveling to Paris, where he met Jacques-Louis David (1748–1825), Elisabeth Vigee Lebrun (1755–1842), and Jean-Antoine Houdon (1741–1828), three of the finest French artists of the day. Newly inspired by his recent travels, Trumbull began adding to his series of works depicting Revolutionary War battles and events, including his famous *Declaration of Independence* and compositions related to the battles of Yorktown, Trenton, Princeton, and Saratoga.[24]

In *The Capture of the Hessians at Trenton, 26 December 1776* (color plate 5), which Trumbull began in 1786 and completed about 1828 (after the installation of his four Capitol Rotunda paintings), he created a scene that could not have taken place, for although the pictured Hessian commander, Colonel Johann Rall, had been a participant in the Trenton battle, he had in fact been mortally wounded and therefore could not have been standing, as he is in the painting, beside the victorious Washington on horseback. It is reported that on realizing the gravity of Rall's situation, Washington had directed Major William Stevens to care for the mortally wounded Hessian, and thus Trumbull resolved to "compose the picture, for the express purpose of giving a lesson to all living and future soldiers in the service of [their] country, to show mercy and kindness to a fallen enemy—their enemy no longer when wounded and in their power." Trumbull's invented composition therefore presents a formal (albeit mythological) scene of mercy shown after the American victory—one meant to inspire viewers with Washington's leadership as well as encourage gratitude for his military prowess.[25]

In the second of Trumbull's major New Jersey Revolutionary War scenes, *The Death of General Mercer at the Battle of Princeton, 3 January 1777*, of 1787–ca. 1831 (color plate 7), he chose to emphasize the heroism of a fallen general during an action-filled battle, rather than something akin to the more ceremonious Princeton battle scene that Charles Willson Peale had completed in 1782. Following the lead of depicting heroic death as had West in *The Death of Wolfe*, Trumbull achieved glorious immortality for the American general Hugh Mercer, as he shows him dying for the cause of independence. In the work, General Mercer's horse is killed from under him; before he could get away, two grenadiers attacked, and he fell mortally wounded.[26]

THE NINETEENTH CENTURY Although other eighteenth-century artists painted scenes related to the Revolution in New Jersey, the history paintings of Peale and Trumbull clearly set the stage for later practitioners. In the nineteenth century, the most significant artists to picture Revolutionary War battles and events in New Jersey were Dennis Malone Carter (1827–1881) and Emanuel Leutze (1816–1868).

Born in Ireland, Carter came to America in 1839 with his family and settled in New York.[27] A painter whose work included still life, religious images, as well as depictions of important historical figures (including Abraham Lincoln), he is best known in New Jersey for two major paintings recalling Molly Pitcher's role in the Battle of Monmouth, *Molly Pitcher at the Battle of Monmouth* of 1854 (color plate 9) and *Molly Pitcher Being Presented to George Washington* of 1856 (color plate 10). Although serious questions remain concerning the true identity of the so-called heroine of Monmouth and the nature and extent of her actual accomplishments during that battle, it seems that the mythological image of Molly Pitcher lives on as the quintessential female supporter of the Continental army.[28] In *Molly Pitcher at the Battle of Monmouth*, the feisty heroine succeeds in taking over the cannon duties of her husband after he falls beside it; in *Molly Pitcher Being Presented to George Washington*, a meek and subdued Molly is presented the next day to General Washington, who, according to legend, reportedly commended her for her bravery and possibly even commissioned her a sergeant in the American army, a unique accolade for an eighteenth-century woman.

The honor of creating the finest American grand-style history paintings in the nineteenth century, particularly with respect to New Jersey's role in the Revolution in Trenton and Monmouth, must be awarded to Emanuel Leutze. Born in Germany in 1816, by 1825 he and his family immigrated to the United States. In 1840, at the age of twenty-four, he decided to return to his native land to study, since by that time American artists had begun to travel to the Düsseldorf Art Academy for its excellent formal training in drawing from both the antique and life. Leutze also learned the principles of the grand style of his American predecessors, West, Peale,

PLATE I *John Wollaston*, William Livingston, *late eighteenth century. Oil on canvas. Fraunces Tavern Museum, New York.*

PLATE 2 *Wistar Glassworks, sugar bowl, eighteenth century.*
Courtesy Winterthur Museum.

PLATE 3 *Jean Leon Gerome Ferris*, Washington's March Through the Jerseys, *ca. 1906. Oil on canvas. Private Collection.*

PLATE 4 *Emanuel Leutze*, Washington Crossing the Delaware, *1851. Oil on canvas. The Metropolitan Museum of Art, Gift of John Stewart Kennedy, 1897 (97.34). Photograph © 1992 The Metropolitan Museum of Art.*

PLATE 5 *(above) John Trumbull,*
The Capture of the Hessians at Trenton,
26 December 1776, *1786–ca. 1828. Oil on*
canvas. Yale University Art Gallery,
Trumbull Collection.

PLATE 6 *Charles Willson Peale,*
George Washington at the Battle of
Princeton, Jan. 3, 1777, *1779–1782.*
Oil on canvas. Princeton University.
Commissioned by the Trustees.
Photo: Bruce M. White PP222.

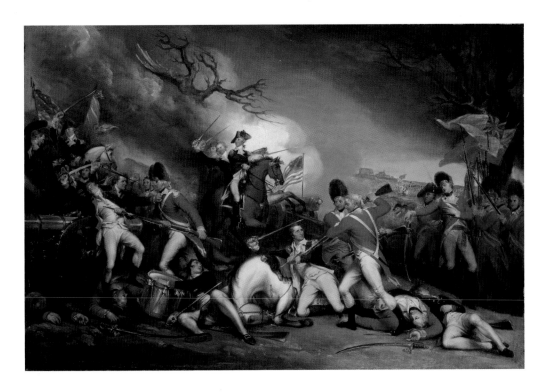

PLATE 7 *John Trumbull,* The Death of General Mercer at the Battle of Princeton, 3 January 1777, *1787–ca. 1831. Oil on canvas. Yale University Art Gallery.*

PLATE 8 *Emanuel Leutze,* George Washington at the Battle of Monmouth, *1857. Oil on canvas. Monmouth County Historical Association, Freehold, New Jersey; Gift of the descendants of David Leavitt, 1937.*

PLATE II *Benjamin West,* The Death of General Wolfe, *1770. Oil on canvas.*
National Gallery of Canada, Transfer from the Canadian War Memorials, 1921.
Gift of the 2nd Duke of Westminster, Eaton Hall, Cheshire, 1918.

PLATE 9 *(opposite, top) Dennis Malone Carter,* Molly Pitcher at the Battle of Monmouth, *1854. Oil on canvas. Fraunces Tavern Museum, New York.*

PLATE 10 *(opposite, bottom) Dennis Malone Carter,* Molly Pitcher Being Presented to George Washington, *1856. Oil on canvas. Monmouth County Historical Association, Freehold, New Jersey.*

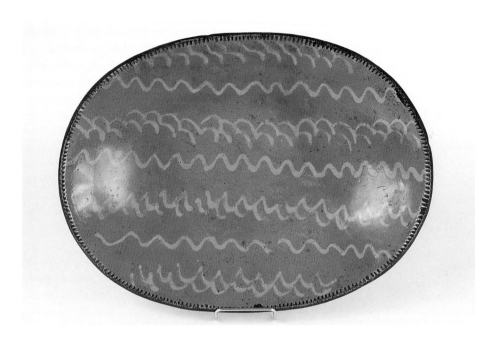

PLATE 12 *J. McCully, Trenton, N.J., oval platter, late eighteenth–early nineteenth century. Redware. New Jersey State Museum Collection, Museum Purchase, CH264.*

PLATE 13 *Unknown*, Annis Boudinot Stockton, *late-nineteenth-century copy of an eighteenth-century original. Photo courtesy Historic Morven, Inc.*

and Trumbull, along with the most up-to-date advancements in European art. In Düsseldorf, after his training was complete, Leutze established his own atelier at the academy and managed to attract students from several countries.[29]

By the late 1840s in Germany and elsewhere in Europe, as discontent reigned and revolutions began, Leutze conceived of his most important Revolutionary War painting, which comes down to us as the tour de force of his career, *Washington Crossing the Delaware* (color plate 4). It depicts the general and his ragtag army approaching the New Jersey shore on Christmas night, 1776, as they make their way to surprise the Hessian garrison at Trenton.

Leutze had several reasons to choose the subject. He knew of the paintings of Trumbull, Peale, and others, but he undoubtedly also was interested in creating an inspirational piece that would play a role in encouraging the salvation of the American Union, an issue on the minds of many Americans by the late 1840s. It is also important to understand that the work was conceived and painted in Germany, where many citizens were fighting their own revolution against tyranny. Therefore, in 1849, when he began the painting (also the year the Frankfurt Parliament disbanded), it seems that Leutze was equating German struggles with the American fight for independence; indeed, Germany's contemporary revolutionary hero Heinrich von Gagern (1799–1880) was compared favorably with Washington by many of his compatriots. Thus Leutze's principal biographer, Barbara Groseclose, has appropriately concluded that the artist's subject matter can be considered "both a historical symbol and a brilliant metaphor for psychological encouragement."[30]

In 1851, Leutze brought the painting to the United States to display it first at the Stuyvesant Institute in New York and subsequently in the Capitol Rotunda, where he hoped it would be approved for inclusion as one of the scenes related to the establishment of the nation that remain on view to this day. Although it was not selected, critics lauded the work throughout its tour. A writer for the *New York Evening Mirror*, for example, praised it as "the grandest, the most majestic, and most effective painting ever exhibited in America . . . the best commentary upon the times that 'tried men's souls' that we have ever seen, and we hope it will be exhibited in every city of the Union, until it has been visited and revisited by every man, woman and child in the Republic of Washington."[31]

Although technically inaccurate, the intention of the artist both to glorify and mythologize the image of the Continental army as troops struggled to cross the icy Delaware River was admirably fulfilled. Washington could not be expected to remain standing in the moving boat as he appears in the painting; the flag on display was not put into use until some six months later; and the ice floes in the river may have been incorrectly drawn. However, when one considers the inspirational importance of the composition, these issues are inconsequential. To this day, for both New Jersey and the nation, the work has monumental significance, for George

Washington's finest moments and the subsequent first turning points of the Revolution are recalled when viewing this great painting.

Beginning in 1852, on his return to Germany, Leutze resolved to create a companion piece for *Washington Crossing the Delaware* titled *Washington Rallying the Troops at Monmouth* (color plate 8). Why Leutze chose a composition dealing with the only occasion in Washington's career when he showed anger is an open question. Regardless, the work documents another major New Jersey subject: the occasion during the Battle of Monmouth on June 28, 1778, when Washington saved the day, after General Charles Lee's unauthorized retreat, by rallying disorganized troops and repelling the British. He had the help of the Marquis de Lafayette and Alexander Hamilton, who are pictured in the work leading the troops, just behind the figure of Washington on his rearing horse.[32]

While contemporary critics overwhelmingly had applauded *Washington Crossing the Delaware*, little evidence of admiration was forthcoming for the Monmouth composition. The main problem appeared to be Leutze's selection of an incident thought at the time to be lacking in heroism; thus Washington's character and deeds were not considered to be elevated in the work. On the other hand, it can be argued that Leutze was portraying the true virtue of Washington—one of his finest hours, not his weakest. He was angry and admonished Lee, but he saved the day in an act of valor.[33]

Leutze died in 1868, and for many Americans his demise also signaled the death of grand-style history painting. But only three years earlier, the Civil War had ended with almost no American family left unaffected by the tragic loss of life and limb. Understandably, Americans did not want to view battle scenes filled with blood and carnage, and since most people narrowly equated history painting with battle painting, the grand style went out of favor. It was a crucial moment in the history of American art, for until recently, it was believed by many scholars that history painting never revived. However, in 1876, only eleven years after the conclusion of the Civil War, when the nation embarked on the celebration of its hundredth birthday (the famous 1876 United States International Exhibition, commonly referred to as the "Centennial"), a new wave of patriotism and nostalgia for America's early history was encouraged, which, in fact, did bring about an altered form of history painting.[34]

This new approach to the painting of historical events began as the United States entered a period known today as the "American Renaissance." Although some Americans began to study the art and architecture of the fifteenth-century Italian Renaissance, others focused their attention on another kind of "rebirth"—a uniquely national art inspired by their own past. Known today as the "Colonial Revival," Americans began to collect eighteenth-century relics; manufacturers produced decorative arts and furniture from eighteenth-century designs; composers wrote patriotic music; and architects created plans for Colonial and Federal-style homes.[35]

One of the foremost practitioners of what has come to be known as Colonial Revival history painting was the lifelong Philadelphian Jean Leon Gerome Ferris (1863–1930), who also maintained a summer home at Cape May Point, New Jersey.[36] Just after the turn of the century, Ferris painted his largest Revolutionary War scene, *Washington's March through the Jerseys* (color plate 3), which is based on a familiar story that took place after the defeat of the Continental army at Long Island, Harlem Heights, and Fort Washington. From Fort Lee, New Jersey, in December 1776, Washington was compelled to lead his troops in a retreat from what is now known as Historic New Bridge Landing at the Hackensack River and then across New Jersey to the Delaware River, where they crossed into Pennsylvania. Known to be deeply discouraged by this state of events, in a letter of December 18, 1776, Washington made the following famous plea to Congress to increase his manpower: "[I]f every nerve is not straind [*sic*] to recruit the new army with all possible expedition I think the game is pretty near up."[37] Despite that obvious state of depression, in the true spirit of the postcentennial painting favored during the Colonial Revival, when the nostalgia, sentimentality, and bright side of any incident were encouraged, Washington appears as a hero waving to his men, rather than the leader of a retreating army.

The Decorative Arts

As pre–Revolutionary War eighteenth-century artists in New Jersey generally concentrated on filling the practical needs of their clients, creators of glass, pottery, silver, furniture, textiles, and the like also tended to focus on utilitarian requirements. However, unlike paintings related to the Revolutionary War, which came into favor as a result of a need to develop traditions and laud America's new heroes, industries related to the decorative arts were thwarted by the concurrent devaluation of currency. It was not until after the end of the hostilities and the establishment of a free and independent nation, which intended to prosper by developing homegrown industries and discouraging imports, that the decorative arts really began to flourish. As in other colonies, the farming families and communities of New Jersey created a need for artisans to produce not only implements related to rural occupations but also objects necessary for the conduct of their everyday lives. Consequently, local craftspersons could be found in every town, although some played dual roles—plying their crafts from September to June, while reserving the summer months for farming. There was often overlap in professions that today would be quite distinct. For example, a furniture maker typically would supply coffins to the local undertaker.[38]

Shortages of glass in eighteenth-century England, which caused the export of window glass and other household glasswares to be virtually impossible, made the development of that industry a priority in the colonies. As early as 1608, settlers in Jamestown, Virginia, attempted to establish a glass-making operation, and later in the century other short-lived businesses were begun at Salem, Massachusetts; New Amsterdam; and Philadelphia. But it is to New Jersey's credit that the first glass furnace to survive and prosper was established here. Realizing the need and therefore the opportunity, Caspar Wistar (1695/96–1752), the German-born owner of a Philadelphia brass button factory, negotiated an agreement to pay four glass experts from Holland (John William Wentzell, Caspar Halter, John Martin Halton, and Simon Kreismeier) to "teach the art of glass making to him and his son Richard, and no one else."[39]

Wistar's business began in 1739 on a large tract in Allowaystown, Salem County, about six miles from the town of Salem. After he built homes for his workers along with a "mansion house" for himself near the glass furnace, the area became known as Wistarberg. Glasswares in various colors—ranging from clear and opaque white to aquamarine and other variations of light to olive green, along with tones of amber, blue, and brown—emerged from the factory in designs usually emanating from the individual ideas of the Wistar artisans (color plate 2). Thus surviving objects tend to be unique, rather than examples from multiples of a single pattern; window glass also was produced in several sizes.

The South Jersey sand combined with the abundant local forests created the perfect location for the production of glass, and before long Wistar's plant became known as the "cradle of American glass making."[40] It contained certain distinctive characteristics, which Newark Museum decorative arts curator Margaret E. White, in her groundbreaking 1964 volume, *The Decorative Arts of Early New Jersey*, described as follows:

1. Pieces free-blown from bottle or window glass and shaped by manipulation;

2. Applied decoration, such as threading around the neck of a pitcher; superimposed swirls or swagging, known as "lily pad"; and

3. Crimping, that is, dents or flutes made with a tool to serve as ornament on the foot of a vessel or the end of a handle.[41]

In 1759, Wistar died, leaving the glassworks to his son, Richard, who continued the business until 1780, when he put it on the market. It was a difficult operation to sell, undoubtedly in large part due to the devaluation of currency during the Revolution, which had severely cut into profits. Richard died in 1781 before the business was sold.

Long before its ultimate demise, workers continually fanned out from the glassworks at Wistarburg with their newfound knowledge. Some began their own glass enterprises. Most notably, Jacob Stanger (or Stenger) reportedly set up his own business, the Olive Glass Works, with five of his brothers (Solomon, Daniel, Francis, Peter, and Philip); two other brothers (Adam and Christian) became blowers in the factory in the New Jersey town now known as Glassboro.[42] But in 1780, with the

Revolution continuing and currency severely devalued to about two or three cents on a dollar in gold, the Stangers found themselves in debt and compelled to sell off portions of their 200-acre property to pay their creditors. It was not until the business was taken over by Colonels Thomas Heston and Thomas Carpenter that it was put on a sound footing and made profitable.[43]

Since the establishment of the first glass industry in South Jersey, some 200 glassworks have been established in the state. Most were in South Jersey, but others began in the north, such as the Columbia Glass Works and the P. C. Dummer Glass Company.[44]

Eighteenth-century New Jersey is also remembered for the beginnings of the New Jersey pottery industry. Margaret White reminds us that in seventeenth-century America, "earth and wood were the only materials available from which to make the ordinary utensils required in a home," so it is no surprise that potters were needed in every town and village.[45] Major figures in the early pottery industry, which centered around Burlington, were William Crews, who is recorded as having worked in New Jersey as early as 1685, and the Londoners Dr. Daniel Coxe, Stephen Soames, and Benjamin Bartlett, who ran a business through their agent, John Tatham. Between 1687 and 1692, Coxe and Bartlett were also proprietors of West Jersey.

It appears that the Coxe firm's purpose was to produce "white and painted earthenware and pottery vessells" utilizing a tin-glazed technique, which attempted to imitate Dutch and English delftware. However, in New Jersey, this "white and painted earthenware" had to be made from the red earthenware found locally rather than its light-colored counterpart available in England; thus the clay had to be coated with an opaque white glaze to achieve the desired effect. Believing that objects made in this manner "are in great request," Coxe made sure that an appropriate production method was developed.[46]

Until the end of the eighteenth century, New Jersey was known first for redware pottery, made from red earthenware, and subsequently stoneware, made from blue clay found near South Amboy. Redware pieces were typically glazed only on the inside of such kitchen objects as plates, jugs, platters, and bowls, so that grease and liquids would not penetrate. Some examples contained incised decoration or ornamental designs usually painted in a yellow, white, or green liquid called slip. Examples of redware businesses established in the late eighteenth century are those of J. McCully Sr. in Trenton, beginning in 1780 (color plate 12), and Phillip Durell of about 1781 in Elizabethtown. As for stoneware, records indicate a pottery begun by James Morgan between 1775 and 1785 in Cheesequake, near South Amboy, which continued to offer stoneware pots, jugs, and mugs for sale until 1828. Early on, it appears that it survived the era of currency devaluation during the Revolution to go on to become one of the major sources for these wares after the war, when free Americans were no longer reliant on imports from Great Britain and the Continent.

In the nineteenth century, New Jersey became a leading center for pottery production, and with the purchase by David Henderson of the Jersey Porcelain and Earthenware Company of Jersey City, such innovative techniques as casting of objects in molds, rather than creating pieces one by one on potters' wheels, revolutionized the industry. The great New Jersey pottery tradition continued well into the twentieth century, particularly in the area around Trenton.[47]

Strong practical notions regarding the arts in colonial New Jersey took an interesting turn in the development of the production of household silver. Since crime in colonial America often involved theft, and proving ownership of any recovered coins was difficult, it became a common custom for silver currency to be converted into household objects. Not surprising, however, was the plainness of the designs, due in part to the mixture of provided coin, limitations on available tools, and simply taste.

Perth Amboy, then capital of New Jersey, attracted the first goldsmith in the state, David Lyell (fl. 1699–1725). In addition, two French Huguenot silversmiths, Abraham DuBois and Elias Boudinot, arrived in New Jersey in the late seventeenth century; in 1753, Boudinot moved to Princeton. In addition to his skill as a silversmith, Elias Boudinot also was the ancestor of Elias Boudinot IV, a signer of the Declaration of Independence and president of the Continental Congress, and Annis Boudinot (color plate 13), who married Richard Stockton, another signer of the Declaration from New Jersey.[48]

As for New Jersey furniture making, its history through the era of the Revolution was largely unstudied until 1958, when the Newark Museum mounted the exhibition *Early Furniture Made in New Jersey*. This groundbreaking display and its catalog created an opportunity to research and document the existence of New Jersey furniture makers from the seventeenth to the mid-nineteenth century; incredibly, a list of over 1,000 names was compiled at the time.[49] From Fenwick Lyell (1766–1822) in the late seventeenth century to John Jelliff (1813–1893), the best-known nineteenth-century parlor and cabinetmaker in the state, the list indicates a surprising level of activity, given the state's former reputation as an "artistic desert." However, only about a dozen are known to have been working in the eighteenth century: they include the chair and cabinetmakers Oliver Parsell (1757–1818); three generations of Egertons: Matthew (1739–1802), his son, Matthew Jr. (fl. 1785–1837), and his grandsons, John Bergan (1791–1838) and Evert (1795–1838); Maskell Ware (1766–1846); and Isaac Alling (1749–1819) and his son, David (1773–1855).

As one might suspect, the early furniture of New Jersey consisted of basically plain, straight-lined items such as joint stools and gateleg tables, which were often constructed by carpenter-joiners or craftspersons trained in their native countries before emigrating to the colonies. Generally, designs followed European sources. By the eighteenth century, more and more furniture makers were arriving from both England and the Continent—bringing with them their knowledge of the newest

FIG. 19 *Chest of drawers, Queen Anne style, Lawrenceville, N.J., ca. 1740.*
Walnut, pine, and holly; original engraved brasses. The Collection of the Newark Museum.
Purchase 1962: The Members' Fund.

styles (fig. 19). Thus greater refinement of both form and design was introduced, for example, the curved lines of the cabriole leg as well as claw and ball designs. However, after the discovery of the classical ruins of Herculaneum and Pompeii in the 1730s and 1740s, the designs of the Englishman Robert Adam became popular. From 1760, George Hepplewhite's English furniture, which essentially followed Adam's classical approach, and Thomas Sheraton's inlay work also set a standard for the colonies, although the full flowering of this so-called Hepplewhite-Sheraton period did not occur in the United States until the early nineteenth century.

It has long been thought that immigrants who were well trained gravitated to Philadelphia or New York on arrival in the colonies, but it is also now known that competent craftspersons did settle in New Jersey and that several surviving fine pieces can be attributed to them. Margaret White points to Benjamin Randolph, who was born and died in New Jersey and made fashionable furniture for residents of the state.[50] The fact that by 1958 the names of over 1,000 furniture makers were compiled by the Newark Museum provides evidence that much of the surviving fine furniture of the eighteenth century could very well have been produced in New Jersey.

The Arts in New Jersey

The battles and events related to the American Revolution in New Jersey established the sources for some of the finest productions of American history painters. Beginning in the late eighteenth century and continuing into the twenty-first, the state's strategic location as the "Crossroads of the American Revolution" has literally put it on the nation's artistic map. The war itself was the main stimulus for the production of paintings intended to tell the story of history's first revolution of its kind to succeed. Peale's glorification of the success of George Washington at Princeton along with Trumbull's creation of major Trenton and Princeton battle scenes originally intended for his "Hall of the Revolution" were greatly admired in their own time; after the Revolution, as the nation grew stronger and wealthier, patronage for such works of art increased.

At the same time, the development that had taken place in the decorative arts before the Revolution was negatively affected by circumstances arising from a nation at war; as a result, the decorative arts did not reach their potential until well after the establishment of independence. Taken together, however, the art and artifacts that survive today provide us with extensive insights into life in New Jersey in the era of the American Revolution.

NEW JERSEY ARCHITECTURE
IN THE REVOLUTIONARY ERA

✴ ✴ ✴

HARRIETTE C. HAWKINS

The farmhouses you meet with on the road, the beautiful cultivated fields and enclosures,
remind you of old England. I have not seen any part of America that resembles that country
more than the State of Jersey.

— ROBERT HUNTER JR., A SCOTTISH
TRAVELER TO NEW JERSEY, 1785

AT THE TIME of the Revolution, New Jersey was one of the smallest colonies in both area and population. Its most striking feature was the mixture of its peoples; in fact, New Jersey was the most ethnically and culturally diverse of the North American colonies.[1] Its people included the descendants of settlers from Connecticut, Rhode Island, Massachusetts, Long Island, and New Hampshire; Swedes, Finns, English, and Scots; native tribes; enslaved and free Africans; Scottish emigrants from British settlements in Ulster, Northern Ireland; and the "Jersey Dutch"—an amalgam of Dutch, Flemish, French Huguenots, Walloons, Scandinavians, Germans, Poles, Hungarians, and Italians who came to New Jersey either directly from Holland or were once part of the New Netherlands colony. English settlers or their descendants made up slightly less than half of the white population in New Jersey at the beginning of the Revolution.[2] Most of the colony (approximately 60 percent of the people) was concentrated in the northern counties, with Hunterdon the most populous.

This diverse mix of New Jersey's colonists is manifested in the buildings and structures of the late eighteenth century. They echo the cultural roots of those who built them, but they also reflect the distribution of wealth and something of the countervailing forces of assimilation and differentiation that were at work during this period of political and cultural turbulence. By the 1770s, there was evidence of assimilation into what could be roughly construed as a culture shaped largely by British settlers, although it is worth remembering that Great Britain itself was a relatively new amalgam of several countries with many distinct traditions.[3]

The fertile lands of the inner coastal plain and the Piedmont regions of central and western New Jersey saw their first European settlers during the last quarter of the seventeenth century, and in the beginning of the eighteenth century the arable lands in the upper Piedmont and Highlands began to attract a second wave of settlers. By the third quarter of the eighteenth century, New Jersey's economy was overwhelmingly reliant on agricultural production, and its social system was dominated by middle-class farmers.[4] Communities along the lower Delaware, Raritan, and Hackensack river watersheds and near the major stagecoach routes impressed visitors by the beauty and abundance of the cultivated landscape; New Jersey's reputation as a fertile, well-tended "garden state" appears to have been established by the 1760s. Many were struck by the similarity of the natural landscape to that of England.[5]

When visiting New Jersey in the 1740s, the widely traveled Swedish scientist Peter Kalm described Woodbridge, which was chartered as a town in 1669, as a "small village consisting of a few houses" and Elizabethtown (present-day Elizabeth), as a small town with "a few stone buildings" and for the most part scattered "well built" houses "generally of boards, with a roof of shingles and walls of shingles."[6] To the well-traveled eyes of one English diplomat, Thomas Pownall, Elizabethtown in the 1750s looked "more like a collection of country places of a rich and thriving Germany than a Town."[7] In the 1790s, Irish traveler Isaac Weld described Trenton as having 200 houses and four churches; Princeton's highlights included a college in a "wretched" state and some eighty dwellings. Weld estimated New Brunswick to have some 200 houses, and Newark, "built in a straggling manner," had the "appearance of a large English village."[8]

The older communities of East and West Jersey had been settled for a century by the outbreak of the Revolution, and it is no surprise that travelers were struck by their resemblance to England and the European continent. The impression taken away by visitors to these older settlements was one of neat, prosperous, well-tended farms and orchards; small towns and villages interspersed with small hamlets; and a few larger, older "cities" such as Perth Amboy, Burlington, Trenton, and Elizabethtown, the colony's largest community with an estimated population of 12,000.[9]

Most commercial and domestic buildings in the major settlements were timber-framed structures covered with boards or planks. The three-bay, two-story circa 1766 clapboard house owned by Continental army quartermaster Alexander Douglas, which was briefly utilized by George Washington in early 1777 for a council of war, is considered "an excellent example of a small eighteenth century dwelling of the type common in Trenton during the Revolutionary war years."[10]

Most settlers in the colony began life in modest one- or two-room buildings of fieldstone, timber, or log construction. New Jersey was well forested and for many decades had ample and cheap supplies of wood, with easily quarried brownstone and ironstone also available in many parts of the state. Although West Jersey had abundant clay, settlers in Burlington began colonial life in what were described in 1679 as "block houses being nothing else than entire trees, split through the middle, or squared out of the rough, and placed in the form of a square, upon each other, as high as they wished to have the house."[11] The same account notes that English settlers and "many others" in the area settled by West Jersey Quaker proprietors were living in drafty timber-framed houses covered with lapped boards 5 to 6 feet long.[12] Throughout the state, log construction continued to be used for temporary buildings, for secondary outbuildings on farmsteads, and for interim shelter in frontier settlements. During the ferocious winter of 1779–1780, the Continental army found enough timber around Morristown to erect log huts for soldiers and officers. Designed for up to twelve enlisted men, the huts were 14 feet wide and 15–16 feet long, 6½ feet from the ground to the roofline, with a fireplace and chimney. George Washington ordered that a log kitchen and an office be constructed during his tenancy at the Jacob Ford Mansion in Morristown in 1779–1780 (see fig. 23).[13]

In East Jersey, wood seems to have been the most common building material, with brick or stone reserved for the more important homes and public buildings. In West Jersey, however, the soils soon provided ample raw material for the young colony's brickyards. Although the settlers who arrived in Burlington in 1677 built log houses, they quickly shifted to more durable materials—perhaps as a result of reports of the devastation wreaked by London's great fire of 1666—and the dimensions and quality of brick made in West Jersey were soon regulated by the West Jersey Assembly. By 1698, a Burlington account mentions the "many stately brick houses built . . . and many Fair and great Brick houses on the outside of the Town, which the Gentry have built for their Country Houses."[14] By the mid-1740s, Burlington, the chief port and capital of West Jersey, was described as a town of 250 families living in well-built brick houses, in contrast to the towns to the north and east.[15]

Building Types in Revolutionary New Jersey

At the time of the Revolution, the homes of New Jersey's colonists tended to follow inherited regional or ethnic traditions with respect to design, use of space, and construction techniques. However, selective borrowing and adaptation were evident as once-distinct cultural groups began to assimilate with other settlers.

In general, the built landscape of New Jersey's lower Delaware region is strongly identified with Quaker traditions and culture, even though Quakers did not comprise a majority of the population by the time of the Revolution (by 1745, Quakers represented only 16 percent of Salem County's largely English population). But as was the case in many other parts of colonial New Jersey, building styles in Salem County tended to change slowly. In the late seventeenth century, most of the county's first settlers came from more populated areas in England and had attained middle-class (or higher) socioeconomic status. For much of the eighteenth century, they continued to use building styles and organize domestic space in traditional ways. Late-medieval building traditions imprinted on the early settlers proved to be remarkably durable, and brick homes with distinctive decorative patterns in vitrified (lead glazed) brick have remained West Jersey's most celebrated architectural form. Nevertheless, frame houses were probably more common than the collection of surviving eighteenth-century buildings suggest.

Although the population was more diverse and more affluent by the second half of the eighteenth century, the domestic buildings of West Jersey largely followed traditional hall/parlor plans and tended to be modest in size. As additional space was needed, rooms were added laterally. A study of Salem County probate records for the period 1700–1774 noted "neither wealth nor time made a significant difference in the basic types of houses built by the inhabitants of Fenwick's Colony, the first permanent English speaking settlement in the Delaware Valley. . . . Nearly four-fifths of the inventories for this period showed two to three room houses; only a minority owned houses that were larger or smaller."[16] At the "high end" of the homes built by the original settlers of Fenwick's Colony and their descendants is the remarkably well preserved two-and-a-half-story, three-bay house constructed by Abel and Mary Nicholson in 1722 (fig. 20).[17] Abel Nicholson and his father were part of the original group of settlers led to Salem County by John Fenwick in 1675. Forty-nine years later, the Nicholsons built a handsome brick dwelling house that possibly replaced an earlier frame structure. This new dwelling has been described as "one of the finest and most complete examples of patterned brick work from the earliest years" of the style's development in Salem County and reflects a decorative building tradition popular in sixteenth-century France and seventeenth-century England.[18] Although the Nicholsons' house is slightly larger and has more surface decoration, it is stylistically similar to the house built a generation later (in 1752) by their son, Samuel, as well as the John and Mary Dickinson house (1754) and others in the area that can be dated to the 1760s.[19]

According to cultural geographer Peter Wacker, the most common type of eighteenth-century New Jersey house was the "I" house, which is thought to have an English pedigree.[20] This type is generally a rectangular, two-and-a-half-story, one-room-deep house, 22 or 23 feet wide, with a gable roof, interior gable end chimneys, and a simple exterior without a porch; additions take the form of an ell or are built laterally to the main block. Although the "I" house is the most common form, other housing types appeared and reflected the many immigrant populations in the colony.[21]

FIG. 20 *The Abel and Mary Nicholson House, 1722. Salem County Historical Society, Salem, N.J.*

An example of another style of house, the Flemish cottage type, was found in "Jersey Dutch" settlements in Bergen County and the Raritan watershed. These long, low cottages were usually built of coarse or dressed stone with recessed windows, a sharply pitched roof with a pronounced overhang, and a rear lean-to. Identified by historian Thomas Wertenbacker and further described by Peter Wacker, the design of these houses was probably derived from those found in the Flemish-speaking areas of Southern Zeeland, western Belgium, and the northern tip of France.[22] Still another dwelling type once common in colonial New Jersey has been dubbed the East Jersey cottage; it is associated with English settlements, particularly those areas colonized by New Englanders. According to Wertenbacker, the East Jersey cottage was typically a 45-by-18-foot, one-and-a-half-story structure with small windows, an interior chimney or chimneys, and a sloping roof with a narrow rear annex. The similarity between the Flemish and East Jersey cottages suggests that cross-pollination between two cultural groups was under way by the early years of the eighteenth century.[23]

It is important to bear in mind that the few large houses and grand buildings that have influenced popular perceptions of eighteenth-century life were relatively rare in a colony of farmers, merchants, and tradespeople. In 1748, the cosmopolitan Swede Peter Kalm, traveling in the colony, seemed surprised at the modest house in Burlington provided for the royal governor, and a British officer in 1765 expressed a disdainful opinion of the quarters provided for the colonial governor and other officers.[24] Thus it is no wonder that the generous spaces and relative comforts afforded by the colony's few larger houses are the main reasons they were pressed into service as headquarters for the commanders and other leaders of the Continental and British armies.

By the time of the Revolution, the "new fashion" for elegantly balanced houses with wide central halls, symmetrically arranged rooms, generous double-hung sash windows, as well as articulated doorways, cornices, window surrounds, and other hallmarks of the Georgian style, were being built by New Jersey's well-to-do farmers and merchants. In New Jersey, as in other colonies, the floor plans, along with the classical ornamentation that characterized the architectural fashions of Georgian England, were adopted selectively from sources in circulation at the time, including treatises on classical architecture, pattern books, and builders' manuals. As a result, the Georgian style became associated with upward mobility and served as a physi-

FIG. 21 *William Trent House. Photo courtesy City of Trenton, Department of Recreation, Natural Resources and Culture.*

cal symbol of the rationality and order that marked the last stages of the English Renaissance and the flourishing of Enlightenment thought.[25]

One of New Jersey's earliest and most important Georgian manors was completed in the 1720s by William Trent, the Scottish émigré, Philadelphia merchant, real-estate speculator, and first chief justice of the colony. Trent was a Philadelphia merchant who developed an agricultural and industrial plantation on an 800-acre tract at the falls of the Delaware River, a settlement subsequently known at Trent's town.

Trent's brick manor house (fig. 21) was one of the colony's earliest examples of a style developed in the sixteenth century by the Italian Renaissance architect Andrea Palladio (1508–1580) for the merchants and landed gentry of northern Italy and then reinterpreted by English architects and builders beginning in the seventeenth century. Many of the Palladian manors were the centers of country estates located on rivers and canals of the Veneto region of northern Italy, so the style readily transferred to the landed gentry of Europe and America, who used rivers as highways. Trent was invested in transatlantic import and export, was married to the daughter of a royal governor, and would have been aware of the latest fashions for household design and furnishings.[26] Trent's "pretty box of a house" on the Delaware was still drawing the admiration of visitors decades after it was built and was home to some of New Jersey's most prominent citizens throughout the eighteenth century. A 1759 advertisement describes a courtyard on each side of the house, with an allée of English cherry trees leading down to the Delaware ferry and a large, handsome garden. Outbuildings included a 30-by-20-foot, two-story brick kitchen (erected in the 1740s) with four apartments above for servants; it was connected to the main house with a paved "gangway." The property's 40-by-38-foot barn, with stables for ten horses, was only slightly smaller than the manor house. The estate also featured a "chaise house," a "poultry-house," other unspecified farm buildings, and an orchard with 350 trees.[27]

By the 1740s, the new Georgian style had gained favor among wealthier New Jerseyans: "gentlemen's houses," as distinct from "rich farmers' places," were being built throughout the colony.[28] A main feature of the Georgian style is the center hall, which generally but not always runs the full width of the house and served as the formal reception area as well as a multipurpose room. Approximately twenty years after William Trent built his home on the Delaware, the "Dutch" merchant, surveyor, and attorney Cornelius Low (who settled in New Jersey in 1730) used the Georgian idiom to make a similar statement of his wealth and status with a new manor on the northeast bank of the Raritan River. The manor overlooked his bustling commercial enclave at Raritan Landing (fig. 22). Built with 300 tons of sandstone, the house is five bays wide, measures 40 by 30 feet, and features fine interior woodwork and double interior chimneys. A long central hall bisects four rooms arranged symmetrically on either side. A high basement story and 9-foot chimneystacks emphasize the prominence of the house.

FIG. 22 *Cornelius Low House, 1741. Courtesy of the Middlesex County Cultural and Heritage Commission, New Brunswick, N.J.*

Around the time that Cornelius Low constructed his river mansion above Raritan Landing, Anthony White, a wealthy young resident of New Brunswick (and son-in-law of the colony's former governor), built a slightly larger (50 by 41 feet) manor in the Georgian style on a slight rise on the southwest bank of the Raritan River. Low's heritage was Dutch, while White came from English colonial stock, but both used the same five-bay double-pile Georgian plan for their grand river mansions.[29]

One of the attractions of the Georgian style was a standardized design vocabulary, which could accommodate individual taste, budgets, or building materials. In New Jersey, self-conscious (and perhaps cost-conscious) builders sometimes reserved the more expensive materials for the all-important main facade. Peter Kalm observed that houses in New Brunswick reserved the use of brick for the street facade, "all the other sides being merely of planks."[30] Likewise, three sides of Anthony White's mansion are constructed of beaded clapboard, but the house's main (river) facade was built of brick and was stuccoed and scored to resemble dressed stone. Similarly, the Low manor and the Henry Guest house in New Brunswick, also in the Georgian mode, have dressed stone facades but employ random fieldstone on the side and rear elevations.[31]

In 1761, the proprietors of East Jersey commissioned a New York builder to design and construct a Georgian-style house in Perth Amboy for the royal governor (currently known as Proprietary House). One of the largest and most ambitious of

FIG. 23 *The Jacob Ford, Jr. Mansion ("Washington's Headquarters"), 1772.*
Courtesy of Morristown National Historical Park.

New Jersey's Georgian residences built during the third quarter of eighteenth century, the house reflected the proprietors' desire to attract an official who could bring
greater prestige and commerce to the struggling capital of East Jersey (see fig. 42).
The final cost of the three-story brick building, including land, was estimated to be
more than £6,600—considerably above the amount budgeted; more than £500 was
spent for materials imported from England. The formal rooms were handsomely finished and appointed. That the building was to entertain and house the best people of
the colony and their important visitors is apparent in the generous spaces allocated
for support functions, such as the full third-floor garret and "lower offices" of the
cellar story, which included rooms for a butler and housekeeper and a servants' hall,
in addition to kitchens and a wine vault. The facade's projecting centered gable is a
design feature of high-style buildings of the American colonies.[32]

Several of the larger homes, now Revolutionary War landmarks, were chosen by
George Washington for his personal use during his lengthy stays in New Jersey. The
simple but commodious frame and clapboard house built in 1778 by William Wallace
in Somerville was barely finished when General Washington made it headquarters
for his family and key officer corps during the winter of 1778–1779 and the following
spring. The next year Washington, his family, key officers, and servants, as well as
the builder's widow and son, crowded into another new manor in the small village of

Morristown (fig. 23). Completed in 1774 by Colonel Jacob Ford Jr., a member of one of Morris County's most prominent families, the manor was once part of a 200-acre parcel and was prominently sited on a hill with commanding views above the area's main roads.[33] The central block of the two-and-a-half-story frame mansion features a long central hallway with two rooms on either side and a large, two-story kitchen wing. The size and ornamentation of this new home were visible reminders of Ford's social and economic status. Built of timber, the manor had unusually fine and stylish details, such as the Palladian windows, a hipped roof with heavy cornice, a belt course between the first and second floors, and an elaborate pedimented doorway with a fanlight, sidelights, and Ionic order half columns. The use of ship lap cladding helped to create the illusion of dressed stone.[34]

In 1873, after the death of Ford's grandson, the mansion was purchased by four prominent citizens of Morristown, who then formed the Washington Association of New Jersey to oversee the care and interpretation of the headquarters. It was among the first Revolutionary War sites preserved in New Jersey, and after it was given to the National Park Service in 1933, it became the centerpiece of America's first National Historical Park.

Houses of Worship

> There are in America a number of such places called towns, where one must look for the houses, either not built or scattered a good distance apart . . . the residents of which live apart on their farms, a particular spot being called the town where the church and tavern stand and the smiths have their shops—because in one or the other of these community buildings the neighbors are accustomed to meet. And when later professional men, shop-keepers and other people who are not farmers come to settle, their dwellings group themselves around the church and the shops.[35]

From its earliest days, New Jersey's built landscape reflected religious diversity within the largely middle-class, agrarian population. Lords Carteret and Berkeley (lord proprietors of New Jersey in the seventeenth century) and successive owners were real-estate speculators, and toleration of religious differences was an important and needed incentive to attract settlers. By the time of the Revolution, there were six major Protestant sects in the state: Quaker, Anglican, Dutch Reformed, Presbyterian, Baptist, and Methodist; the most numerous were the Presbyterians.[36] Thus religious life in New Jersey during the last half of the eighteenth century could be characterized as both diverse and dynamic. A missionary for the Church of England reported in 1756 that he found the population lively and democratic, with many religious sects, "the choice being determined by the wives."[37] Disputes over organizational structure, governance, and/or theology, such as the *Conferentie* versus *Coetus* split in the Dutch Reformed church, the "new light" and "old light" sects among Presbyterians, and the Hicksite and Orthodox schism among Quakers only added to the complexity of the colony's religious life.

There was no established or state-supported religion in New Jersey, and it was up to individual congregations to find the financial means to support a minister and raise a building. A shortage of religious structures sometimes produced creative arrangements among colonists. Just before the Revolution, an Anglican missionary noted that he had to hold services in a borrowed Presbyterian church, a barn, and a field. In addition, he also reported encountering at least a dozen different denominations.[38] Sharing of houses of worship by different sects was also noted by the Quaker missionary Samuel Bownas in the late 1750s, when he reported that Middletown Baptists had loaned their meetinghouse to the Quakers; he observed that the Baptists arrived early and "joined the Quaker meeting without dissention or caviling."[39] This apparent ease with which different sects could share facilities is explained in part by the similarities in basic liturgical requirements among the various Protestant sects, which sprang from the Reformation.

Reformation theology required active participation by the congregation in worship and that the congregation see and hear worship leaders. Ornamentation of the worship space was anathema, and the divine word in the form of preaching and scriptural lessons was given pride of place in the worship space. Thus, despite the popularity of the "new" classically influenced Georgian style for important Protestant houses of worship in colonial America, New Jersey's Protestants tended to be more conservative when designing their religious buildings. As was true with the colony's houses, the Georgian style was used selectively and on a modest scale. The simple "meetinghouse" plan appears to have been an especially durable embodiment of contemporary ecclesiastical ideals, and the term "meetinghouse" seemed to be applied universally to houses of worship in eighteenth-century New Jersey. The first buildings for religious worship were probably simple log or timber-framed spaces for relatively small congregations. But by the first decades of the eighteenth century, more substantial houses of worship could be found in the larger settlements, such as the brick church built by Anglicans in Burlington.[40]

The most consistent design for meetinghouses is the form employed by the colony's Quakers, whose worship spaces generally followed the dictates of Reformation theology but without the theological or social hierarchy implied by a pulpit, altar, or assigned or owned pews. By the early 1720s, the Quakers of West Jersey had erected substantial one-room rectangular buildings with double-hung windows, well-illuminated interiors containing simple wooden pews, interior balconies or lofts, and sliding partitions for use during business meetings. Most were built of brick or stone, with separate entrances for men and women. In addition, most meetinghouses tended to have wagon or horse sheds on the grounds.

New Jersey has an unusually fine collection of Quaker meetinghouses from the eighteenth century; they are an especially prominent part of the historic landscape of the lower Delaware region. One of the earliest surviving examples is in Woodbury, sections of which date from 1715 to 1722. Most are brick, often laid in Flemish bond, but a few smaller examples, such as the meetinghouse at Arney's Mount (ca. 1775) in Burlington County and the one at Stoney Brook outside Princeton (ca. 1724, rebuilt 1760), are constructed of local fieldstone. Some Quaker meetinghouses from the eighteenth century are frame, such as the small one (24 by 20 feet) near Seaville in Cape May County; the 1758 structure (25 by 26 feet) in Dover, Morris County; and the larger (34 by 48 feet) 1788 Plainfield Meetinghouse. All adhere to the same basic design formula.[41]

New Jersey Quakers, for the most part, tried to honor their beliefs and remain aloof from the secular conflict that swept through the state during the Revolution. Their buildings, however, did not always fare as well. Larger buildings with an open plan were quickly put into service by armies (or legislative bodies) desperate for temporary shelter. Examples include the Evesham Friends Meetinghouse (1760), which was used as a British barracks in General Henry Clinton's 1778 march from Philadelphia toward New York; the meetinghouse at Stoney Brook that served as a hospital during the Battle of Princeton; and the meetinghouse in Woodbury that was used as a hospital for colonial troops during the 1777 Battle of Red Bank and subsequently by General Cornwallis to house British officers (fig. 24).

The staying power of the simple meetinghouse form is evident in the buildings erected by other Protestant sects. The pre-Revolutionary Old Yellow Meeting House in western Monmouth County is a simple two-story frame and clapboard example built by one of the colony's oldest Baptist congregations to replace an earlier (1720) building (see fig. 8). One of the earliest Baptist meetinghouses remaining in the state, it may indicate the influence of the Quakers who also settled in the area.[42]

By the middle years of the 1770s, the religious buildings found in older settlements were often the second or third house of worship for a congregation. Reports from Anglican missionaries in the first half of the eighteenth century mention simple log or frame buildings for worship, with more elaborate structures built a generation or two later, once there was a critical mass of congregants and enough income to support a minister and more ambitious construction. Although Anglican churches in the larger communities tended to be more elaborate and made of brick or stone, in smaller communities Anglicans worshipped in simple frame buildings, such as the parish churches at Mount Holly and Coles town in Burlington County.[43]

On the eastern side of Monmouth County, the fine church built by the Anglican congregation at Shrewsbury is an example of this evolution. Anglicans were holding services in Middletown by 1692, and a congregation was meeting in

FIG. 24 *Woodbury Friends Meetinghouse and wagon shed, ca. 1715. Gloucester County Historical Society, Woodbury, N.J.*

Shrewsbury by 1702.[44] The first church, reportedly of brick, was not erected until 1732, and by the late 1760s a larger building was needed to accommodate a bigger congregation.[45] The handsome frame church is a good example of how Georgian fashion was interpreted on the local level, and it is also indicative of the aspirations of Anglicanism transplanted to a colony with many competing religions.

Progress on the new church was not rapid; the 68-by-32-foot timber-framed building took four years to complete. It was built by local carpenters (including church member and local tavernkeeper Josiah Halstead) after the designs of Scottish-born master carpenter Robert Smith, designer of the College of New Jersey's Nassau Hall as well as a number of important institutional buildings and churches in Philadelphia. When Shrewsbury's Christ Church was dedicated in 1774, the handsome building presided over the main intersection of one of the important coast roads and routes to the interior. It must have seemed a very modern architectural statement with its large Palladian window at the east end, Doric order doorway surrounds, octagonal cupola, and elegant canopied pews in the chancel. A configuration of roof trusses (probably borrowed from builders' manuals of the period) allowed a more expansive, open interior.[46] The building is clad in the durable cedar shingle favored for framed buildings in eastern New Jersey and represents the mingling of consciously high-style design and local building traditions. The choice of material may also reflect economic constraints, since an important church building in an urban setting would more likely have been built of stone or brick.

A few years earlier, New Brunswick's Anglican congregation built a second church that was a vernacular version of the "new" classically inspired style popularized by British architect and mathematician Christopher Wren (1632–1732) in his designs for parish churches in London following the fire of 1666. Also known as Christ Church, the building was constructed of sandstone and employed a fashionable longitudinal plan rather than the meetinghouse plan of the other Protestant denominations in the town. It had a gambrel roof and a large Palladian window in the rear wall; a large square tower, reminiscent of Wren's London churches of half a century earlier, was added in 1773 and dominated the skyline of New Brunswick.[47]

Presbyterian churches were among the most substantial buildings in older settlements of East Jersey, such as Newark and Elizabethtown, and followed the meetinghouse form used by New England Puritans. On the eve of the Revolution, the Middlesex County courthouse proved too small to accommodate all the citizens who assembled to discuss relations with England, and the assembled throng moved to the more commodious Presbyterian meetinghouse.[48] Presbyterians were an important group in colonial East Jersey and figured prominently among Revolutionary leaders. Of the eleven New Jersey delegates to the 1775–1776 Continental Congress, eight were Presbyterian. Elizabethtown's Presbyterians included two generals and one captain in the Continental army, one New Jersey signatory of the Declaration of Independence, the president of the Continental Congress in 1782–1783, as well as the colony's governor, a former Anglican.[49]

In Elizabethtown, prominent Presbyterians and Anglicans made their presence known by constructing large, handsome buildings, "either one of which made a much better appearance than any one in Philadelphia," according to Peter Kalm. He admired the "meetinghouse" of the Presbyterians, which was described as built of wood and covered with shingles "but has both a steeple and bells."[50] As a result, the strong link between the cause for independence and the Presbyterians meant that Presbyterian houses of worship were sometimes singled out for destruction or desecration. The Presbyterian meetinghouses in Mount Holly, Elizabethtown, and Springfield were burned by the British; Princeton's Presbyterian Meetinghouse served as a barracks. Princeton's College of New Jersey had a high-profile Presbyterian divine as its head, and the college's Nassau Hall (fig. 25), one of the largest buildings in the colonies, changed hands three times during the Battle of Princeton. The building and its furnishings suffered much ruin from Continental and British troops who were quartered there.

One of the finest surviving examples of a rural Presbyterian meetinghouse from the mid-eighteenth century is the Old Tennent Meeting House in western Monmouth County. The church was built by the Scots and "Scots-Irish" Presbyterian farmers whose families had settled in western Monmouth County several generations earlier. In 1751, the congregation followed traditional ideas for worship space—albeit on a larger scale—when they collected subscriptions from 192 congregants and began construction of a large, two-story frame building midway between Monmouth Courthouse (Freehold) and Englishtown to replace an older church.[51] Old Tennent Meeting House (also known as Old Scots) is a capacious (60 by 40 feet) two-story frame building clad in cedar shingles and finished with high-backed pews and pine paneling. Sited on a slight hill, its importance to the surrounding community was announced by a cupola with weathervane. The primacy of preaching is apparent in the handsome elevated pulpit, which is surmounted with a tester or sounding board. Below the pulpit is the lower desk where precentors, or leaders of congregational singing, stood, and beyond are the prominent seats reserved for the senior church leaders, the "elder's square."[52] The U-shaped interior features galleries around three sides. The long arched windows along the first floor and the cornice modillions are nods to the classically inspired fashions of the day.

The "Jersey Dutch" were nearly 17 percent of New Jersey's free white population at the time of the Revolution and were one of the most culturally distinct groups in the colony. The Dutch Reformed Church, in spite of protracted internal struggles over its independence from the founding church in Holland, clung to its languages and rituals; as a result, it was less successful in attracting other Protestant members. Dutch ministers, however, tended to support the Revolutionary cause, and Dutch Reformed

FIG. 25 *Rev. Jonathan Fisher,* Nassau Hall, A North West Prospect, *n.d. Oil on canvas. Princeton University Art Museum. Presented by alumni headed by A. E. Vondermuhll, Class of 1901.*

churches were singled out for reprisals by the British in New York City, Staten Island, and the Raritan Valley.

Some of the early Dutch churches were small hexagonal or octagonal build-ings and had very plain interiors in keeping with dictates of reformed worship.[53] Although the Dutch church wrestled with issues of cultural integration, the Dutch Reformed church built in New Brunswick in 1767 employed such fashionable Georgian elements as stone quoins, long round-headed windows, and rusticated doorways. The small square building was dominated by a steeply pitched hipped roof with steeple.[54] Thus even the Dutch, who chose to preserve their cultural tradi-tions as long as possible, were building churches on the eve of the American Revo-lution in the same style as the Presbyterian churches at Newark, Elizabethtown, and Paramus.[55]

No Ordinary Town:
Taverns in Revolutionary New Jersey

One of the most ubiquitous establishments in eighteenth-century New Jersey was the tavern, a public house that supplied food and drink, or an "ordinary," where public meals were provided at fixed times and prices.[56] By the middle of the 1780s, legislative records indicate there were 400–500 licensed places for public dining, drinking, and lodging, evenly split between the eastern and western parts of the colony.[57] Trenton had at least a dozen taverns to serve those involved in shipping and transportation from the city during and after the war. Although it did not see much stagecoach traffic until after the Revolution, the small market town of Shrewsbury supported an average of twelve taverns between 1763 and 1784.[58]

Almost as soon as settlers began to trickle into the colony, the Assembly of East Jersey acted to ensure that settlements accommodated travelers and provided a public establishment where food, drink, and lodging could be obtained at regulated prices; by law, tavern owners were also required to provide a minimum of two beds, stabling, and pasture. In West Jersey, there were rules at the county and town level for the provision of food, drink, and lodging.[59] The quality of food, drink, and lodg-ing varied enormously, however, and inn-keeping did not seem to be a particularly lucrative enterprise.

New Jersey's public houses also served as information centers, post offices, and community centers, in addition to their sometimes more colorful role as havens for drinking and gambling. The legislature recognized their important place in com-munity life in a 1739 act, which described the purpose of "taverns, inns and ordinar-ies" as accommodating "Strangers, Travellers and Other Persons, for the Benefit of Men's Meeting together for the dispatch of Business, and for the entertaining and refreshing of Mankind in a reasonable manner."[60]

FIG. 26 *Unknown artist,* Potter's Tavern, *ca. 1759. Pen-and-ink sketch. Bridgeton, N.J. Photo courtesy Cumberland County Historical Society.*

The simplest ordinaries were likely one- or two-story frame structures, such as the Shrewsbury tavern operated by Josiah Halstead, Potters' Tavern (1773) in Bridgeton (fig. 26), and the Village Inn (ca. 1732) in Englishtown. Some of West Jersey's taverns were built of brick, such as the two-story, three-bay, brick Gabreil Daveis Tavern (1756) in Blackwood, Camden County, and Seven Star Tavern (1762) in Salem County; both were laid in Flemish bond. Some of the more rudimentary establishments were made of logs. To replace a dilapidated tavern in a small settlement in Hunterdon County in 1767, the lessee was instructed to build a good log house (at least 28 by 22 feet), with a full cellar walled with stones and a "good barn and stables."[61]

During the years leading up to and including the Revolution, "business" at a public house sometimes included debating and organizing for the revolutionary cause. In Hunterdon County, citizens met at John Ringos Tavern in Amwell in the summer of 1774 to form their first revolutionary body, the committee of correspondence; the Council of Safety, a key decision-making body of New Jersey's rebel government, met there in December 1777. Haddonfield's Indian King Tavern was a meeting place for the colonial legislature in 1777. These community gathering places also hosted meetings of local civic and religious groups and occasionally served as courtrooms.[62]

Most of New Jersey's eighteenth-century taverns have vanished. The surviving examples are simple buildings of one to three stories; almost none retain the ensemble of the auxiliary buildings needed for storage and housing of coaches and animals. At a minimum, a tavern would have had at least one room for serving beverages and food, and sometimes there was an anteroom to accommodate meetings. Some of the larger establishments provided separate rooms for lodging, but privacy and cleanliness in sleeping arrangements were rare. Fancier taverns, such as the three-story Arnold Tavern in Morristown, had parlors, a dining room, and a second-floor ballroom, as well as the usual barroom and kitchen (fig. 27).[63] A few even catered to the tourist trade, such as the new tavern advertised by Abraham Godwin near the falls in Passaic. The owner assured prospective visitors that they "may depend on the best and genteelest treatment" and offered as additional inducement "a convenient room for dancing, and a fiddler, will always be ready. . . . Also a guide to attend any strangers who shall shew them all the natural curiosities at the falls."[64] Communities on the major coach roads or near courthouses tended to offer better accommodations. In 1765, one of Princeton's taverns, the Sign of the Hudibras, was offered for sale. The establishment was described as having "12 rooms and 2 good kitchens, 1 with a loft overhead with 2 rooms." A separate sale of the furnishings in-

THE ORIGINAL ARNOLD TAVERN.
FROM PEN AND INK SKETCH BY MISS S. HOWELL.

FIG. 27 *Miss S. Howell,* The Arnold Tavern, *1891. Pen-and-ink sketch. Courtesy of the Local History Department, the Morristown and Morris Township Library.*

cluded "thirteen Good Feather Beds, plentifully furnished with sheets, Pillow Cases and other Bedcloths, 13 Bedsteads 7 of them with Sacking bottom."[65]

Harnessing the Bounty of Nature:
The Utilitarian Buildings of the American Revolutionary Era

Although taverns were the most ubiquitous commercial buildings in New Jersey at the time of the Revolution, there were other structures that supported the livelihoods of the colonists. Since most of the population at the time of the Revolution made their living from farming, the utilitarian buildings of a New Jersey farmstead would have been a common sight, although few have survived. An eighteenth-century New Jersey farmstead consisted of many buildings, ranging from the largest secondary structure, the barn, to others, which could include a smokehouse, springhouse, granary, wagon shed, privies, washing house, and baking oven. New Jersey's barns must have been impressive. Thomas Anburey, a British officer, thought that farmers lavished more care in the construction of their barns than they did their houses.[66] Since the barn housed the tools and livestock, which formed the core of a farmer's equity, a well-constructed barn was essential. During his tours of the colony, Peter Kalm described a barn type typical of the north of Germany, Holland, Prussia, and southern France. These large buildings had long, sloping roofs covered with shingles; there was a threshing floor in the middle, a hayloft above, and stables for cows and horses on either side of the threshing floor. Kalm thought the size of these buildings was "almost to equal a small church."[67]

Another type of barn found on New Jersey farmsteads, known as the English barn, was a rectangular frame building of three bays, with a gable roof and doors on the longer side. Period advertisements refer to English and Dutch barns (fig. 28), so the cultural associations of each type were clearly identified in the period.[68] As was characteristic of much of New Jersey's architecture during the eighteenth century, assimilation and adaptation among different cultural groups occurred within a generation or two. There are barns found today that appear to be hybrids of Dutch, English, and other northern European building traditions, particularly in the pre-Revolutionary "frontier" of northwestern New Jersey.

Mills

As an agricultural colony, most exports consisted of agricultural products shipped to New England, southern Europe, and the West Indies.[69] Manufacturing of any product that competed with English manufactured goods was discouraged by the protective English trade laws and duties, a situation that eventually bred great resentment among the burgeoning capitalists in the American colonies. But some

FIG. 28 *Wortendyke Barn ("New World Dutch Barn"), Park Ridge, N.J.*
Photo: Rich Veit and Michael Gall.

manufacturing activities were too important to basic survival to be discouraged. Along with brickyards and tanneries, grain and lumber milling were critical industries. Gristmills and sawmills were among the first commercial buildings, in addition to the ordinary or tavern, to be established in settlements with streams large enough to power waterwheels. The abundance of mills and the busy regional market for goods can be seen in a 1751 census of industries. For example, in Burlington County (which then included a milling enclave at Trenton), there were twenty gristmills, twenty-two sawmills, three fulling mills, one furnace, two forges, two brew houses, and nine ferries.[70] By the 1930s, when the first Historic American Buildings survey teams were sent to record early buildings in New Jersey, only a handful of mills from the mid-eighteenth century remained; it is not surprising since mills were adapted for new technology and shifting market demand. Milling was often the route to success for the colony's entrepreneurs. Trenton's first industrial enterprise was a log gristmill established in 1679 by Mahlon Stacy, who had emigrated a year earlier from England. Stacy also became a trader in grain. His business acumen served him well; by 1692 he became a proprietor of West Jersey.[71]

Although data on the appearance of early mills is incomplete, most mills were simple frame, log, or log and frame buildings. Except for the grinding stone, these mills could be made entirely of wood and did not require a large volume of water to operate. A survey of the Musconetcong watershed in northwestern New Jersey suggests that such simple mills were once very common in the frontier communities of this area. Larger and more productive mills would have been located along waterways with a higher volume of water.[72] Proximity to waterways and ample supplies of wood were also inducements to the construction of sawmills, which were sometimes built in conjunction with gristmills. A sawmill was a less capital-intensive investment than a gristmill and helped increase the supply of building material dramatically; otherwise, lumber had to be produced by a labor-intensive process of pit sawing, which could yield only about 100 board feet of wood a day.[73]

Ironworks

New Jersey's abundant woodlands, many streams and rivers, ore-rich soils in the coastal plain, and accessible iron deposits in the Highlands of northwestern New Jersey provided the basis for the colony's only significant nonagricultural export, iron. The most productive deposits of magnetite and hematite ore in the Highlands had been surveyed before the Revolution; the Dickerson mine at Succasunna was in operation by 1700. Plentiful bog iron deposits in the Pine Barrens in the south had supported extractive and production facilities for iron early in the eighteenth century. With the elimination of British duties on colonial iron in the mid-eighteenth century, production increased in the colonies, reaching a peak of 5,000 tons in 1751.[74] There were three different types of iron production facilities: furnaces, which produced pig iron from ore; forges, which transformed pig iron into iron bars; and bloomeries, which transformed bar iron into wrought iron.[75] Furnaces, forges, and bloomeries of varying sizes were developed by entrepreneurs to supply iron products for settlers and for export. A 1784 report listed eight furnaces for smelting and seventy-nine forges, with the largest numbers in Morris and Sussex counties.[76]

As revolution threatened and Britain choked off supplies of manufactured iron and other materials needed for munitions, the importance of New Jersey's iron operations escalated, and ironworkers were exempted from military service. Among several important furnaces in New Jersey was the one built in 1741 in Oxford, the oldest remaining hot blast furnace in the state (fig. 29). The principal structure of the furnace complex was the stack, a square structure at least 20 feet high made of stone or brick and built into the sides of a hill. Forges contained a hearth and water-activated hammer and transformed brittle pig iron into more valuable bar iron.

The importance of these ironworks can be seen in the size of the houses built for their managers. Examples include Shippen Manor (1754) in Oxford and the large residence built in 1768 by Jacob Ford for the ironmaster of his Mount Hope furnace and forge.

One of the largest and most important of the colony's iron mining and manufacturing operations was Ringwood Ironworks, which proved to be of critical strategic importance to the Revolutionary army and was visited by General Washington five times. Managed by Robert Erskine, the Continental army's mapmaker and first surveyor general, Ringwood was developed in the 1740s to take advantage of the plentiful natural resources of the Ramapo Mountains. At the time of its purchase in the 1760s by the German immigrant and investor Peter Hasenclever, Ringwood contained a new furnace, iron mines, two forges, coal houses, a sawmill, and dwelling houses. Hasenclever's iron empire included three ironworks and more than 150,000 acres in New York, New Jersey, and Nova Scotia. He expanded the Ringwood operation to include an ironworks at nearby Long Pond, an elaborate system of waterpower (including a dam 22 feet high and over 850 feet long), and a manor house. More than 500 skilled and unskilled workers were brought from Germany and England.[77]

Iron forges had been established in the first half of the century in Bordentown, in Mount Holly and New Lisbon, and in the Musconetcong watershed of northwestern New Jersey. Other important iron-making operations were located in the sparsely populated Pine Barrens. At Batsto Furnace, bog ore was converted into pig iron, bar iron, and assorted iron products. The importance of iron as a commercial venture can

FIG. 29 *Oxford Furnace, ca. 1741 (mid-nineteenth-century photograph). Warren County Cultural and Heritage Commission, Oxford, N.J.*

be seen in the ambitions of Batsto's developer, Charles Read, who assembled more than 12,000 acres of pinelands and in less than a decade had established iron forges or furnaces at Taunton, Aetna, Atsion, and Batsto.

Saltworks

Another necessity of life was salt, and wartime disruptions underscored its importance. Wartime scarcity raised the price of salt seventy times over its prewar price, and by 1777 the New Jersey legislature felt compelled to enact price controls. Even with a regulated price, salt production on almost any scale could be very profitable. Saltworks ranged from small-scale boiling and drying operations using simple equipment to larger ventures involving reservoirs, sluice gates, windmill-driven seawater pumps, and boiling and storage buildings.[78]

Speculators rushed to build saltworks, and several of these operations were targeted for destruction by the British army or loyalist forces. One of the largest and most ambitious of the Revolutionary-era saltworks was financed by the Pennsylvania Council of Safety and located near Tom's River. The complex included a large, brick boiling house; a drying house; two storehouses; a windmill; and a smith's shop. The works were destroyed in a Tory raid in 1782.[79]

A Built Legacy of People and Cultures

On the eve of the American Revolution, New Jersey had the most diverse population of any American colony—a demographic distinction that has continued throughout the state's history. By the last quarter of the eighteenth century, a diverse mixture of peoples from New England, the British Isles, northern Europe, and Africa had created a built landscape that varied in forms, materials, and styles. In one sense, New Jersey was a colony of separate cultural regions, but the process of assimilation and acculturation among different groups seemed to be well under way by the last quarter of the century. New Jersey's moderate climate, its natural abundance, and the relative ease of cultivation won it the moniker the "Garden State" early in its history; despite two "capital cities," it was a colony of towns and villages interspersed with small-to-moderate-sized farms and areas of wilderness to the south and northwest. Nassau Hall, home of the College of New Jersey, was the largest structure in the colony, while governmental buildings such as courthouses and jails were modest in size and material.

The most ubiquitous commercial buildings were taverns or ordinaries, sawmills, and gristmills. Although nearly forgotten, the colony's salt extraction and drying industries were an important and strategic component of the economy during this period, as were its iron extraction and production industries.

Religious toleration for all Protestant sects was one of the most important ingre-
dients in attracting settlers, and the resulting mix of religious sects was a rich one. The
forces of cultural assimilation were at work from an early date in the colony; this is
evident from the sharing of worship spaces among various Protestant sects throughout
the eighteenth century. For all but New Jersey Quakers, houses of worship and support of a minister hinged on the economic surplus of many or the benefaction of a few,
and the relative modesty of most colonial religious structures reflects the economic
realities and wealth distribution of the time. As the economic base improved and the
population grew, churches and meetinghouses moved from simple log or frame buildings to larger and more finely appointed structures. By the mid-1770s, some congregations were worshipping in the third building on a particular site. The liveliness and
diversity of the colony's religious life are evident in the number of religious structures.
The dominant form for houses of worship was the meetinghouse, which reflected the
tenets of Reformation theology and the attraction of less hierarchal, more self-directed
religions, as well as the largely agrarian middle-class nature of the population.

The new, classically inspired Georgian fashion in architecture provided a common
stylistic language for an upwardly mobile, entrepreneurial population with a worldlier
frame of reference. The Georgian idiom, which was available from pattern books and
builders' manuals, was used selectively and conservatively, and it generally incorporated local traditions in materials and construction. When the Georgian style does
appear, it is usually in larger settlements or in the homes of the wealthier merchants,
tradespeople, or landowners.

Beginning with the industrialization of the nineteenth century, New Jersey has
endured wave after wave of development, which has erased or obscured much of its
eighteenth-century built landscape. It is hard to visualize the thriving farms, small
towns, and hamlets of the young "Garden State" described by soldiers and travelers:
the many farmsteads with their signature barns, the distinctive profiles of English
and Dutch framed buildings, the handsome meetinghouses, the sawmills and gristmills that provided materials needed for daily life, and the fashionable Georgian-
style institutional buildings and homes of the prosperous. Thanks to the work of
history-minded New Jerseyans who began saving Revolutionary-era sites more than
a century ago and continuing work by succeeding generations of preservationists, an
important collection of sites do survive from this critical stage of the colony's history. They offer a fascinating glimpse into the blending of many different building
styles and traditions and deserve to be better known.

CAUGHT IN THE MIDDLE:

New Jersey's Indians and the American Revolution

✳ ✳ ✳

LORRAINE E. WILLIAMS

O N MAY 12, 1779, General George Washington received a delegation of
Delaware Indians at his headquarters at Middlebrook, New Jersey.[1] "Delaware" was the name the English had given to the native peoples sixteenth- and seventeenth-century explorers found occupying the area that is today all of New Jersey,
northern Delaware, eastern Pennsylvania, southeastern New York, and southwestern
Connecticut. The native peoples called themselves "Lenape," but by the 1740s they
had come to refer to themselves as "Delawares" when they dealt with the English.

The delegation was escorted by George Morgan, a resident of the farm "Prospect" in Princeton, New Jersey, adjoining the land of the College of New Jersey
(today Princeton University). Morgan was also the agent for Indian Affairs for the
central states. In his care on the visit were three Delaware boys—eight-year-old
George Morgan White Eyes, the son of Chief White Eyes, Morgan's good friend;
sixteen-year-old John Killbuck, the son of Chief Killbuck; and eighteen-year-old
Thomas Killbuck, Chief Killbuck's half brother. The boys were to be schooled in
Princeton under Morgan's supervision. Young White Eyes would go on to graduate
from the college in 1789.[2]

Washington greeted the Delawares with a military parade and made a speech
emphasizing the importance of the recent treaty alliance between the two parties to
the future of each. The Delawares had become the first American Indian nation to
conclude a treaty with the new United States in September 1778.[3] They had pledged
that they would

give a free passage through their country to the troops aforesaid [the American forces], and the same to conduct by the nearest and best ways to the posts, forts or towns of the enemies of the United States, affording to said troops such supplies of corn, meat, horses, or whatever may be in their power for the accommodations of such troops . . . [and] engage to join the troops . . . with such a number of their best and most expert warriors . . . and act in concert with them.[4]

In exchange for the Delawares' support of the Americans' effort against the British, the United States had promised to provide a fort for the Indians' safety against retaliation from the British or their Indian allies and to provide the trade goods—metal tools, guns, and cloth—upon which the Indians had become dependent.

This first treaty of the young rebellious nation followed the format of older treaties made by the British with North American Indians for more than a hundred years. It was also the format the United States would follow in other treaties it would make with Indian allies. But this treaty of 1778 concluded with a clause that had never before appeared in a North American treaty and would never appear again: "[S]hould it for the future be found conducive for the mutual interest of both parties to invite any other tribes who have been friends to the interest of the United States, to join the present confederation, and to form a state whereof the Delaware nation shall be the head, and have a representation in Congress."[5] Chief White Eyes is credited with the idea that the nation's fourteenth state should be an Indian state. He signed the treaty along with Chiefs Killbuck and Captain Pipe. Perhaps the urgent desire to make this first treaty with the Indians made the United States offer a status of equality to the Delawares that it would never offer again.

The Delawares who visited Washington at Middlebrook were not, however, from New Jersey. These Delawares had come to the state from villages in the Ohio country (the colonial name for the drainages of the Allegheny and Ohio rivers). They were offering to guide the American forces along the western frontier between the American stronghold at Fort Pitt (present-day Pittsburgh) and Fort Detroit, the British stronghold to the north in Canada. Washington was welcoming the Delawares back to their old homeland for only a brief visit. Then they were to journey to Philadelphia, where Congress was in session. These Delawares' home in 1779 was no longer in New Jersey or any of their ancestral lands on the East Coast. It was out on the western frontier. There they had been caught solidly in the middle of the American Revolution between the British and the Americans. Both combatants at first argued that all Indians should remain neutral; later, each demanded military aid from them. The Delawares had to choose a side. They picked the United States and hoped they had made the right choice.

At the beginning of the American Revolution there were Delawares still living in New Jersey. They had English names, and if they owned land, it was by English

law as members of the colonial population. Perhaps as many as 200 Delawares occupied a colonial reservation, Brotherton, in Burlington County. There is no record
of George Washington or the Congress meeting with these New Jersey Delawares.
They were not a numerous and separate society to be courted as potential allies.
When New Jersey declared itself a state in 1776, the Delawares within its borders
became citizens of a state in rebellion and at war, and the reservation population at
Brotherton became wards of the state (formerly, they had been wards of the colonial
government). These Delawares were caught between the combatants' armies, which
were to crisscross New Jersey repeatedly. Indeed, the constant warfare in the state
earned New Jersey the name "Cockpit of the Revolution."

By 1776, the Delawares were dispersed widely across North America, below
Canada and east of the Mississippi River. They lived in radically different circumstances in and out of New Jersey. How had this come to be? How well did these two
populations—the Delawares on the Ohio and those in New Jersey—survive while
being caught in the middle of the American Revolution?

A Complex Colonial History for New Jersey's Indians

The Europeans who first explored and then attempted to establish colonies in what
is today New Jersey encountered the Lenape living in small, unfortified settlements,
moving seasonally to hunt, fish, collect shellfish and wild plant foods, and grow corn,
beans, and squash. During the seventeenth century, the Dutch, Swedes, and English
competed for colonial sovereignty over the area and also competed with one another
for the Indians' furs and wampum or sewant (strings or belts of small shell beads for
which Indians were eager to trade). The furs brought high prices in European markets, and the wampum was much prized by Indians farther from the coast, particularly the Iroquoian groups such as the Five (later the Six) Nations of New York and
the Susquehannocks of Pennsylvania. Until the English won total control of what
became New Jersey and New York in 1664 by the conquest of the Dutch colony of
New Netherland (which had conquered New Sweden in 1655), colonists were few in
number. Aside from the Dutch-Indian warfare around New Amsterdam (New York
City after 1664) in the 1640s, relations between the Indians and the various European
colonists in New Jersey were largely peaceful. The small numbers of colonists did not
keep the Indians from using their territory in traditional ways, and the Europeans
were welcomed as a source of the metal tools, guns, and cloth the Indians avidly
sought in exchange for wampum, furs, and sometimes corn and deer meat.

This peaceful situation did not long outlive the English conquest of 1664. Not
only did more and more settlers arrive from Great Britain, but New Jersey also attracted settlers from New England. By the 1720s, the numbers of colonists were

FIG. 30 *Work basket, Delaware Indians, Hunterdon County, before 1735. Wood-splint. New Jersey State Museum Collection. AE 66.286.*

interfering with the Indians' access to resources. With fur-bearing mammals trapped out, the Indians had only their lands to exchange for the tools and cloth they desired—and needed. The Indians were learning the hard lesson that the English idea of land ownership denied them access to continuing to hunt, fish, or cut down trees even on large expanses the colonists owned but did not yet occupy. Since the colonists most coveted the best farmland, the Indians were quickly dispossessed of any but marginal agricultural land.

At this point, some Delawares decided they could no longer live with the Europeans and took advantage of an invitation from the Miami Indians to move west to the Ohio country, recently depopulated by the fur wars of the Iroquois. The Miamis welcomed the Delawares, as did the Iroquois, who claimed the Ohio territory by conquest but had sent few of their own people to settle there.[6] There was plenty of room for the Delawares to farm, hunt, and fish and even to revive the fur trade as a way to secure European goods. In the Ohio country, the British and the French competed for influence among the Indian bands and for access to their furs. This competition provided the Indians with many material and political advantages.

In the 1730s and 1740s, Delawares who became disaffected with New Jersey life continued to migrate to the Ohio country. By the late 1740s, there were at least three Delaware villages on the Allegheny River near Fort Pitt. These villages were surrounded by those of other refugee Indians from the eastern colonies, including Shawnees, Senecas, and Mohawks.[7] Sometimes different Indian peoples shared towns. In 1748, Conrad Weiser, a colonial emissary, found that Shingass Old Town (named for the Delaware chief who lived there) was occupied by both Delawares and Mohawks.[8]

Indians who remained in New Jersey from the 1720s through the 1750s tried to adapt to a life enclosed within a Euro-American population. No longer able to follow traditional subsistence patterns, these Delawares became wage laborers to supplement the meager farming and hunting still available to them. They worked at such jobs as harvesting crops, building houses, and coastal whaling.

They also learned to make the European-style wood-splint baskets that the colonists needed for domestic and agricultural use (fig. 30). Delaware Valley Indians became extremely successful basket makers and are credited with starting an adaptation to colonial life that spread to other Indian groups from the Carolinas to southeastern Canada. Teedyescunk (also commonly spelled "Teedyuscung"), the leading Indian signer of the 1758 agreement to relinquish to the colony of New Jersey all Indian land claims south of the Raritan River, had supported himself for decades before as a basket and broom maker.

By 1758, Teedyescunk and many other Delawares had moved either to Easton, Pennsylvania, or to the Susquehanna River valley farther west, seeking pockets of land not yet overrun by colonists. With the onset of the Seven Years' War in 1756 (popularly called the French and Indian War in British America), the Delawares in the Susquehanna Valley and the Ohio country supported the French (fig. 31). They had old scores to settle with the English colonists and hoped to gain a better supply of trade goods from the French. Governor Francis Bernard initiated negotiations to extinguish Indian land claims in New Jersey as part of an effort to end the Delawares' raids from Pennsylvania into the northwestern part of New Jersey.[9]

Many New Jerseyans who lived nowhere near the frontier feared attacks by the Indians still living among them within the colony. In an effort to calm the public, the colonial government required resident Indians to register with a magistrate, take a loyalty oath, and wear a red ribbon to show they were friends rather than foes.

When this did not produce calm, in 1758 Governor Bernard created the Brotherton reservation in Burlington County. It was to be a haven for all Indians south of the Raritan River who cared to move there. Near the present town of Indian Mills, the reservation's location offered several advantages. A house and at least one sawmill were already on the property. The land adjoined the pinelands, where the Indians could continue to hunt and forage free of the colonists who disdained the pinewoods as "the barrens."

Governor Bernard described the new reservation in 1759 with evident satisfaction.

> It is a tract of Land Very suitable for this purpose, having soil good enough, a large hunting country and a passage by water to the Sea for fishing . . . & has a saw mill upon it which serves to provide them with timber for their own use & to raise a little money for other purposes. [W]e laid out the plan of a town to which I gave the Name of Brotherton & saw an house erected being one of ten that were ready prepared.[10]

The location of Brotherton had another advantage—it was in an area heavily populated by English Quakers, who had long promoted an attitude of friend-

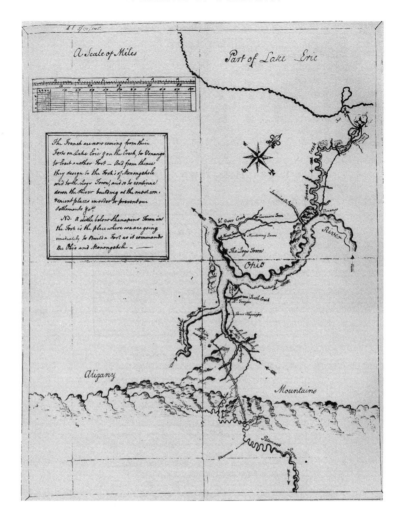

FIG. 31 *George Washington's Map, Accompanying His Journal to the Ohio, 1754. Facsimile.*
Reprinted in the Proceedings of the Massachusetts Historical Society *61 (1927–1928).*
Boston: Massachusetts Historical Society, 1928. Courtesy of the Massachusetts Historical Society.

ship and solicitude toward the Indians. The development of the nearby Atsion Iron Works after 1766 also offered the Indians employment and a company store from which to buy provisions.[11]

At Brotherton, Presbyterian missionary John Brainerd could continue the ministry to the Delawares his brother, David, had begun in the 1740s. A log meeting-house was built, and Brotherton became both a reservation and a mission community when John Brainerd was appointed guardian of the Indians there in 1762.[12]

Not all Indians still living in New Jersey moved to Brotherton, which seems never to have had a population of more than 300. The 1758 treaty made specific reference to

Indians continuing their fee simple rights to lands they already held as individuals. In the 1760s, John Brainerd ministered to Indians living in areas near Brotherton and referred to Indians still living in Monmouth County.[13]

By the 1760s, the Indians in New Jersey had adopted English names. They had been missionized by different Christian denominations. The Quakers and the Presbyterians had been most active. The latter were supported by the Presbyterian Society for Propagating Christian Knowledge, based in Scotland. The Scottish society collected and sent funds for the Indians' benefit, which were dispensed by the College of New Jersey at Princeton. With this support, John Brainerd was able to establish a school at Brotherton, at least one graduate of which attended the college at Princeton. The funds were important to the quality of life at Brotherton because the colonial government expected the reservation to be self-supporting after its initial investment in construction and moving costs.

The disaffected New Jersey Indians who crossed the Delaware and filtered westward were drawn to the Moravian Brethren at Bethlehem, Pennsylvania. The Moravians baptized numbers of Delawares and settled some of their converts in nearby mission towns (fig. 32). The mission towns proved to be unpopular with both the local colonists in Pennsylvania and with non-Christianized Indians. After the French and Indian War, the disaffected Delawares still living in eastern Pennsylvania (along the west bank of the Delaware and in the Susquehanna River valley) moved west to join the Delaware settlements in the Ohio country, and the Moravians moved with them. Missionaries John Heckewelder and David Zeisberger ministered to the Indians in the Ohio settlements and began new "praying towns" there. An English trader named Cresap visited one of them in 1775 and described it this way: "Christianized under the Moravian Sect, it is a pretty town consisting of about sixty houses, and is built of logs and covered with Clapboards. It is regularly laid out in three spacious streets which meet in the centre, where there is a large meeting house built of logs sixty foot square covered with Shingles, Glass in the windows and a Bell."[14]

After the French and Indian War, the Delawares moved their villages away from Fort Pitt into the valley of the Muskingum River (a tributary of the Ohio). By 1775, therefore, there were two distinct populations of Delaware Indians. One still lived in New Jersey, extremely anglicized and adapted to life within the colony. The other lived in the Ohio territory. The latter maintained in their villages on the Muskingum freedom from colonial oversight but had become dependent upon commerce with the colonists for tools and clothing. In fact, during Cresap's 1775 trading visit, a veteran trader told him that to be accepted by the Indians he met, he should wear a calico shirt like they did, not the buckskins the Indians associated with the land-hungry colonial frontiersmen.[15]

In both New Jersey and the Ohio country there were professedly Christian communities of Delawares—Moravian towns in the Ohio country and the Presbyterian

Brotherton reservation in New Jersey. The American Revolution would bring drastic changes to the Delawares in both locations.

On the Frontier

In 1775, the Ohio country Delawares were divided about how to deal with the Americans. Chiefs White Eyes and Killbuck believed it was possible to coexist with the settlers, even as the colonists expanded their settlements westward. White Eyes, in particular, supported the influence of the Moravian missionaries among the Delawares. Captain Pipe believed any accommodation to the settlers moving into the Ohio country would only cost the Delawares land and autonomy. At the beginning of the Revolutionary War, these leaders vied for control of their people as they tried to decide which side to support.

Although both the British and the Americans at first urged the Indians on the western frontier to remain neutral, the Indians were immediately affected by the

FIG. 32 Baptism of American Indians, Moravian Mission, Bethlehem, Pennsylvania, 1758.
Courtesy of Rare Books Division, The New York Public Library, Astor, Lenox, and Tilden Foundations.

disruption of trade the hostilities caused. The Americans had difficulty supplying trade goods while mobilizing resources for the war effort to the east. But the British could continue supplying "their" Indians through Canada. It was not long, as the Indians had expected, before entreaties for neutrality became entreaties to join one side or the other. George Washington was particularly concerned that an eruption of warfare by the frontier Indians against the western settlers should force him to draw off forces he needed to use against the British in the middle states, specifically in New Jersey. He had gained firsthand experience of the frontier Delawares when, as a young colonel of the Virginia militia, he had been sent during the French and Indian War to their territory in an unsuccessful attempt to attach them to the English cause.[16] In the 1770s, the Moravian missionaries pressured the Delawares strongly to join the American cause. Like most dissenting Protestants, the Moravians thought their future religious freedom lay with the Americans.

At the same time, the Delawares were subjected to pressures from the Iroquois, nominal overlords of the Ohio country, who continued their long-standing support of the British. The Delaware leaders wanted to choose the right side. They had backed the losing French in the previous war; this time, they wanted to back the winner. But it was difficult to foretell who that would be.

After much debate, the Delawares agreed to support the Americans and concluded the treaty of 1778. Unfortunately, by the time their delegation visited Washington at Middlebrook in 1779, the relationship was already under stress. Chief White Eyes, the leading supporter of the treaty, had been killed earlier that year by some Americans he was guiding in conformity with treaty provisions.[17] The Americans feared Indian reaction to his murder. They reported falsely that the chief died of smallpox. They brought his son and Killbuck's son and half brother from the frontier, nominally for their protection but perhaps also to serve as hostages should the Delawares break the treaty.

As the Delaware delegation traveled toward New Jersey in 1779, Colonel Daniel Brodhead, the commander at Fort Pitt, wrote to Washington about a plot to kill the visiting Indians and thereby plunge the frontier into an Indian war. Washington did not receive the message until after the Indians had left Middlebrook. He sent George Morgan a warning to take particular care during the Indians' visit to Philadelphia and added that he had ordered Brodhead to meet them with a military escort on their return to ensure safe passage back to their villages.[18]

Once back in the Ohio country and lacking White Eyes's strong support for the Americans, the Delawares found that they also lacked the fort Congress had promised them to protect their villages and the trade goods they needed to survive (fig. 33). It was not long before Captain Pipe took his group to join the British at Detroit. The Delawares who continued to back the Americans were helpless in the face of attacks by other Indians who were supplied by the British.

In 1782, the last blow to the Delaware-American alliance was the murder by Pennsylvania militia of ninety-six Delaware men, women, and children at the Moravian mission settlement of Gnadenhutten.[19] Killbuck was forced to retreat for protection to the Americans at Fort Pitt as a wave of anti-American feeling swept through the Delaware settlements on the frontier. The enmity engendered outlasted the end of the Revolution. The western Delawares continued to war with the United States until they were finally defeated in 1794. The disheartened Moravians moved their converts to Canada, where their descendants remain today. The remaining frontier Delawares again moved westward, away from the incoming settlers, and eventually they settled in Oklahoma, where there are today two reservations populated by Delawares who well remember their roots in New Jersey.

There turned out to be no winning side for any of the Indians on the western frontier. By the Treaty of Paris, which concluded the Revolutionary War in 1783, the British ceded to the United States all frontier lands westward to the Mississippi River, including the lands of their own Indian allies. In consolation, the British offered their Indian allies the option to move to reservations in Canada.

In New Jersey

From its creation in 1776, the state of New Jersey seems to have ignored the Indians still living within its boundaries. Unlike decades earlier, there seems to have been no fear that these Indians would connect with the Delawares on the frontier. We know that

FIG. 33 *Seventeenth-century trade goods, New Jersey State Museum Collection.*
Top (left to right): axe head, hoe blade, knife, padlock. Bottom (left to right): axe head, axe head.

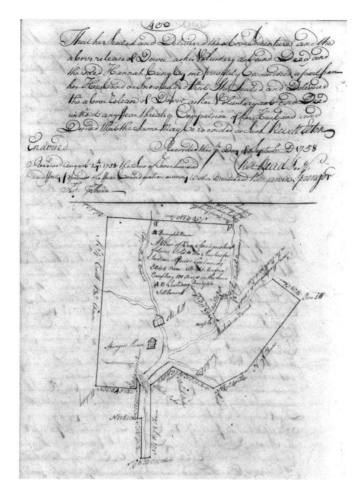

FIG. 34 Original Survey of Brotherton Indian Reservation, Burlington County, N.J., ca. 1758. *New Jersey State Archives, Department of State.*

some Indians in the state served in the American military forces during the Revolutionary War. They were following a long-standing tradition of volunteering for military service that John Brainerd reported.[20] The Indians at Brotherton (fig. 34) participated in the war effort through their work at the nearby Atsion Iron Works. Atsion was active throughout the Revolution and supplied the Continental army and navy with shot and other military products.[21] The Indians must have been particularly dependent on the ironworks and its company store, as there is no record of the state supporting the reservation during the war. With the severing of ties between Great Britain and New Jersey, funds were also no longer available to the Indians from the Scottish Society for Propagating Christian Knowledge.

In 1777, worried about his family's safety and lacking financial support for his ministry to the Indians, John Brainerd moved to Deerfield in Cumberland County, where he died in 1781. No missionary to the Indians was appointed to succeed him. The Indians at Brotherton and in the surrounding area lost not only pastoral care but a spokesman of consequence to protect their rights. Southern New Jersey Quakers had also spoken for the Indians' rights, but the Quakers lost status in the eyes of other New Jerseyans because of their pacifism. The Indians, even on the reservation, were very much left to their own devices in war-torn New Jersey.

The records provide no evidence of New Jersey Indians' struggles during the Revolution, but we do know that the population at Brotherton declined. In 1801, the state bought the reservation lands from the remaining Indians. The fewer than a hundred Indians still resident there wished to join the Stockbridge Indians in New York State. After this move, Bartholomew Calvin, the Brotherton Indian who had attended the College of New Jersey, petitioned the New Jersey government for an award of $2,000 in return for the Indians' relinquishing their hunting and fishing rights south of the Raritan River. The state legislature granted the funds and assisted the Indians to meet their expenses in relocating to Wisconsin, where their descendents can be found today.[22]

During the Revolutionary War and the years afterward, most of New Jersey's Indians who remained in the state blended ever more into the general population. There was no category of "Indian" in the state census of 1790. Indians who remained were henceforth citizens of the state and the nation, a status that reservation Indians of the West would not gain until 1924. New Jersey's resident Indians survived the Revolutionary War and its aftermath, and a few communities, such as Monmouth County's Sand Hill Delawares, were able to maintain a clear group identity into the 1950s. Many residents in New Jersey today still proudly claim Indian ancestors among the Delawares who remained in the state in the seventeenth and eighteenth centuries.

MOVING TOWARD
BREAKING THE CHAINS:

Black New Jerseyans and
the American Revolution

✳ ✳ ✳

GILES R. WRIGHT

IN 1855, WILLIAM COOPER NELL, abolitionist, lecturer, journalist, and a pioneering black historian, wrote *The Colored Patriots of the American Revolution*, perhaps the first full-length study to narrate the historical experience of black Americans.[1] This work also provided a nexus between persons of African descent and the American Revolutionary War.

In examining the intersection of the American Revolution and blacks in New Jersey, this present essay is part of a rather extensive historiography; it continues in the tradition of Nell and other black historians, including William Wells Brown in the 1860s, George Washington Williams and Joseph T. Wilson in the 1880s, Benjamin Brawley in the 1920s, Luther P. Jackson in the 1940s, and Benjamin Quarles in the 1960s.[2] In doing so, it suggests that the War of Independence can be viewed as instructive in at least two significant ways; both go beyond a chronicling of blacks as participants in the war, the focus of the aforementioned studies.

First, the Revolutionary War marked a watershed—a juncture in history by which time several key developments had occurred in New Jersey black life: a large increase in the slave population since its introduction to New Jersey; the emergence of the slave family; the existence of a small free black population; and the cultural metamorphosis of Africans into African Americans. Second, the American Revolution can be considered in terms of its impact on black New Jerseyans. The nature of the war's meaning for this segment of the population in New Jersey is of course part of the conflict's effect on the lives of all northern blacks. Given that it was the North, led by Vermont in 1777, that ushered in the "First Emancipation" (the initial full-scale effort to eliminate slavery in America), the central question remains whether the Revolution, through its cascading torrents of historical change, was the major reason for this occurrence—the disappearance of chattel bondage in the North. One school of thought has suggested that it was; its historians have argued that it was the Revolution's ideology of freedom, equality, and moral rectitude that dealt a crippling blow to the North's system of bondage. In 1961, for example, Leon Litwack noted:

> The liquidation of slavery in the North should not be considered simply on the grounds of profits and losses, climate and geography. Abolition sentiment generally ignored these factors and chose instead to emphasize one particular theme: that the same principles used to justify the American Revolution, particularly John Locke's natural rights philosophy, also condemned and doomed Negro slavery. Such an institution could not be reconciled with colonial efforts to resist English tyranny; indeed its existence embarrassed the American cause.[3]

Echoing these sentiments in 1967, Arthur Zilversmit ended his chapter on abolition during the American Revolution by writing:

> The years of the Revolutionary War had brought great gains for northern Negroes. . . . Undoubtedly the Revolutionary elan was a moving force behind the policy of abolition. . . . In the preamble to their abolition acts, both Pennsylvania and Rhode Island appealed to the ideology of the American Revolution to justify their actions.[4]

In 1973, another historian, Edgar J. McManus, took a similar position:

> The greatest thrust for Negro freedom came during the Revolutionary era. Public opinion veered sharply against slavery almost in direct proportion to the deterioration of relations with England. White militants demanding political freedom for themselves found it difficult to justify chattel bondage for Americans of darker pigmentation. . . . Everywhere the natural rights doctrine espoused by the patriot party forced change in attitudes about the Negro and his place in American life.[5]

Other historians have questioned whether the spirit of liberty and equality generated by the American Revolution convinced appreciable numbers of Northerners that bondage was morally wrong, contending that the Northerners' effort to abandon slavery was rooted in economic factors. For example, some have argued that slavery disappeared in the North because the region's economy was not dependent on slave labor and that the relatively small number of slaves in that part of the country, where free white workers basically prevailed, made northern employers far less resistant to abolitionist efforts than southern slaveholders.[6] In explaining the institution's demise in New Jersey around the time of the Revolution in terms of fundamental economic determinants and considerations, Frances Pingeon has noted:

> During at least half of the eighteenth century the desperate need for labor of all kinds obscured the problem inherent in Northern slavery. With the approach of the Revolution, these tensions began to develop. It is my contention that conflicts arose more from economic need and social problems created by slavery in New Jersey than from Revolutionary ideology. The message of New Jersey Quakers and enlightened liberals of the Revolutionary epoch evoked a response in New Jersey because the strain of the slavery system in this particular society outweighed its advantages. The Revolution gave a moral strength to questions that were already being asked.[7]

Pingeon concluded that by the time of the Revolution, slavery in New Jersey had become uneconomical and was a dying institution. "The long New Jersey winters, which forced idleness on many Blacks employed in farming; the increased competition with white labor; and the ingrained prejudice against Blacks, a legacy of the colonial era, raised questions about the profitability of slavery," she observed.[8] Pingeon further indicated that the response of New Jersey slaveholders to this lack of economic benefit varied. Now viewing bondage as a matter of short-term speculation rather than a more permanent investment as in the South, some hired out their bondpersons and collected their wages. Others sold their slaves in the nation's booming southern markets. Still others relocated to the South with their slaves.[9]

It appears that the Revolution itself succeeded in undermining slavery in New Jersey and served as a liberating instrument for New Jersey blacks. Perhaps it was the lofty egalitarian and libertarian rhetoric of the Revolution that helped weaken New Jersey bondage. At the same time, another factor of equal significance was at play: the chaos and turbulence spawned by the Revolution. The Revolution's severe dislocations invested black New Jerseyans with an unprecedented opportunity to realize their yearnings for freedom, and thus caught up in the vortex of the Revolution, they used their increased bargaining power to their own advantage. The Revolution thereby had a profound impact on black New Jerseyans, affecting their well-being and reshaping their lives in an unprecedented manner. The forces unleashed during the Revolutionary War in fact produced cataclysmic changes in the lives of black New Jerseyans that were still reverberating by 1810, a year that some have identified as the end of the Revolutionary War era.[10] Indeed, by marking 1810 as the end of an era that began in 1776, a period of considerable social upheaval, two key pieces of evidence of slavery's decline in New Jersey are accommodated: An Act for the

Gradual Abolition of Slavery (fig. 35) that was passed in 1804 and the unprecedented size of the free black New Jersey population in 1810.

Before the Revolution: 1630s–1776

Although by the time of the American Revolution New Jersey had not become what historian Philip D. Morgan has defined as a "slave society," one in which slavery is the determinative institution, it had become a "slave owning society."[11] It had come to possess an economy that featured a considerable reliance on enslaved labor, making the forced labor of blacks an important thread in New Jersey's social fabric. Indicative of this development was the immense growth in the slave population over the nearly 150 years slavery had been on New Jersey soil. Identified as numbering 200 in 1680, seemingly the earliest year for which New Jersey slaves were counted, by 1770 the total had reached 8,220, a roughly forty-fold increase.[12] This enabled New Jersey, on the eve of the American Revolution, to rank second only to New York among northern colonies in terms of actual numbers of blacks and their percentage of the total population. In addition, this expansion of New Jersey's blacks mirrored their overall growth in the American colonies. By the onset of the Revolution, the number of blacks in America had reached at an all-time high: approximately 500,000, roughly 20 percent of the total American population. It was the highest percentage of blacks ever to be found in this country.[13]

The growth of the New Jersey black population before the onset of the Revolution was understandable given the increase in demand for slave labor and the availability of Africans. This growth coincided with the rapid expansion of the transatlantic slave trade during the eighteenth century, a period that witnessed the arrival of 60 percent of all slaves brought into the New World. The trade's volume peaked in the 1780s, when nearly 80,000 slaves per annum crossed the Atlantic from Africa. Initially coming into New Jersey from the West Indies (e.g., Barbados) and the southern mainland colonies (e.g., Virginia, Georgia, the Carolinas) as incidental residue of the overall transportation of Africans across the Atlantic, by 1750 slaves were brought into New Jersey directly from the African continent, increasingly to be used to replace white indentured servants in the labor force. Between 1761 and 1765, regular advertisements of public auctions held in Coopers Ferry (present-day Camden) of slaves from West Africa appeared in Philadelphia newspapers, indicating the substantial influx of bondpersons into New Jersey during that period. The Seven Years' War (French and Indian War), which took place between 1756 and 1763, accentuated the demand for African slaves, since the participation of white males in the war limited their availability for indentured servitude. Moreover, expanded opportunities for economic advancement for workers in Europe also affected the demand for African slave labor in New Jersey.[14]

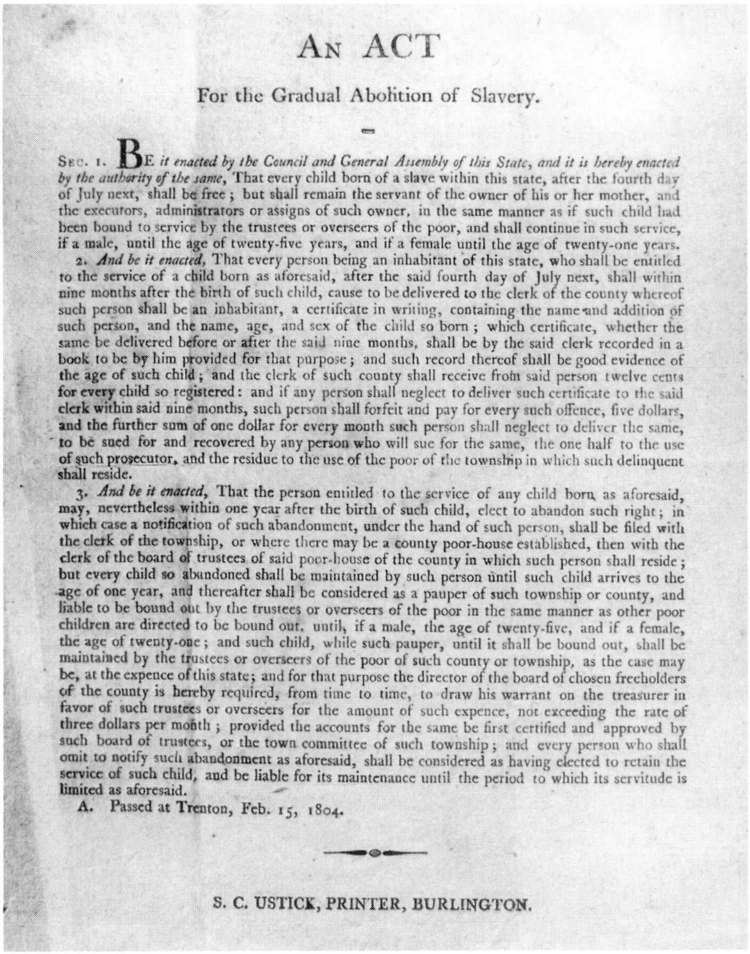

An ACT

For the Gradual Abolition of Slavery.

SEC. 1. BE it enacted by the Council and General Assembly of this State, and it is hereby enacted by the authority of the same, That every child born of a slave within this state, after the fourth day of July next, shall be free; but shall remain the servant of the owner of his or her mother, and the executors, administrators or assigns of such owner, in the same manner as if such child had been bound to service by the trustees or overseers of the poor, and shall continue in such service, if a male, until the age of twenty-five years, and if a female until the age of twenty-one years.

2. And be it enacted, That every person being an inhabitant of this state, who shall be entitled to the service of a child born as aforesaid, after the said fourth day of July next, shall within nine months after the birth of such child, cause to be delivered to the clerk of the county whereof such person shall be an inhabitant, a certificate in writing, containing the name and addition of such person, and the name, age, and sex of the child so born; which certificate, whether the same be delivered before or after the said nine months, shall be by the said clerk recorded in a book to be by him provided for that purpose; and such record thereof shall be good evidence of the age of such child; and the clerk of such county shall receive from said person twelve cents for every child so registered: and if any person shall neglect to deliver such certificate to the said clerk within said nine months, such person shall forfeit and pay for every such offence, five dollars, and the further sum of one dollar for every month such person shall neglect to deliver the same, to be sued for and recovered by any person who will sue for the same, the one half to the use of such prosecutor, and the residue to the use of the poor of the township in which such delinquent shall reside.

3. And be it enacted, That the person entitled to the service of any child born, as aforesaid, may, nevertheless within one year after the birth of such child, elect to abandon such right; in which case a notification of such abandonment, under the hand of such person, shall be filed with the clerk of the township, or where there may be a county poor-house established, then with the clerk of the board of trustees of said poor-house of the county in which such person shall reside; but every child so abandoned shall be maintained by such person until such child arrives to the age of one year, and thereafter shall be considered as a pauper of such township or county, and liable to be bound out by the trustees or overseers of the poor in the same manner as other poor children are directed to be bound out, until, if a male, the age of twenty-five, and if a female, the age of twenty-one; and such child, while such pauper, until it shall be bound out, shall be maintained by the trustees or overseers of the poor of such county or township, as the case may be, at the expence of this state; and for that purpose the director of the board of chosen freeholders of the county is hereby required, from time to time, to draw his warrant on the treasurer in favor of such trustees or overseers for the amount of such expence, not exceeding the rate of three dollars per month; provided the accounts for the same be first certified and approved by such board of trustees, or the town committee of such township; and every person who shall omit to notify such abandonment as aforesaid, shall be considered as having elected to retain the service of such child, and be liable for its maintenance until the period to which its servitude is limited as aforesaid.

A.   Passed at Trenton, Feb. 15, 1804.

S. C. USTICK, PRINTER, BURLINGTON.

FIG. 35 *Act for the Gradual Abolition of Slavery, 1804. From the Collections of the New Jersey Historical Society.*

The increased dependency on slaves in New Jersey was particularly noticeable in its northern region, where the Dutch, who were the first to bring bondpersons into New Jersey and among the world's main traffickers in slaves during the seventeenth century, settled in large numbers. Northern New Jersey was thus, along with southern New England and the New York City area, part of the region in the North that featured the highest concentration of slaves. For example, by the mid-eighteenth century, enslaved men outnumbered propertyless single white men 262 to 194 in Monmouth County. Neighboring Middlesex County had 281 enslaved men and only 81 free wage workers, white and black. The numbers for Bergen County for the same categories were 306 to 8. Conversely, slaves in the southern part of New Jersey were relatively few in number on the eve of the American Revolution—only about 5 percent of the total population in 1772.[15] They were part of an economy that was less diversified than that found in northern New Jersey, and they lived in a region that traditionally featured a greater availability of white workers.

With the rising need for Africans in New Jersey during the years leading up to the Revolution came an increase in their value, a point that runs counter to the notion of slavery's unprofitability. Prices seemingly reached a nadir around the mid-1730s, when the average cost of a male slave was about £20.[16] An examination of New Jersey estate inventories for the 1750–1760 decade, however, reveals an average price of roughly £47 for thirty-two males. After the Revolution, however, prices were substantially higher. Seventy-two men included in New Jersey estate inventories between 1794 and 1801 had an average value of roughly £76; twenty-seven of them were worth at least £100. Thus the average price had increased more than 50 percent beyond the 1750–1760 level.[17]

The growth of the New Jersey slave population by the time of the Revolution was also influenced by the ability of enslaved people to reproduce themselves. This process of natural increase among slaves in America was a key way in which American bondage could be distinguished from slave systems in other parts of the New World. Commenting on this prevailing pattern, as it was revealed in British slave colonies in the Caribbean, Morgan has written:

> In 1780 the number of blacks in British America was less than half of the total number of African emigrants received in the previous century and a half, whereas the white population exceeded its emigrant group almost three times over. The key to the black disaster lay in their experiences in the Caribbean, where about one in four Africans died within the first three years of residence and where sugar production proved a veritable destroyer of life. In this region as a whole, African slaves and their descendants never produced enough children to offset the staggering number of adult deaths.[18]

The increase in New Jersey's slave population was not without worry on the part of white New Jerseyans. Their preference was for laborers like themselves, considered more assimilable than Africans who were perceived as uncivilized, primitive, savage, vicious, dangerous, and capable of the greatly dreaded acts of rebellion. Given the fact that whippings, brandings, and mutilations were common punishments even for free persons in colonial New Jersey, it is not surprising that harsh, severe, even barbaric punishment was regarded as essential to addressing the danger that subversive slaves posed. For example, the 1704 slave code provided that a slave guilty of stealing an item worth five shillings receive forty lashes on his or her bare back and be branded with the letter "T" on the left cheek near the nose.[19] Under this same code, burning served as a punishment for slaves committing arson or murder and castration for "any carnal knowledge of a white woman." The 1713 slave code that replaced that of 1704, while removing castration and any allusion to burning, continued to prescribe severe penalties against slaves, allowing for immediate execution for such crimes as arson, rape, or murder.[20] Even minor infractions brought severe punishment. Examples include a 1751 law that subjected slaves to twenty lashes by the constable for meeting in groups of more than five or for being out of doors after 9:00 P.M. without their owner's permission. A 1760 law imposed a punishment of thirty lashes upon a slave for setting an illegal trap.[21]

The concern about acts of servile insurrection, one of several common forms of both overt and covert slave dissent (e.g., running away, theft, arson, sabotage, murder of slave owners, and feigning illness), was well founded, for such acts are well documented in pre-Revolutionary New Jersey. In 1734, for example, two slave conspiracies were unearthed, perhaps New Jersey's first significant examples. Occurring miles apart, they nevertheless were remarkably similar. The first was discovered near Somerville, where it was alleged that hundreds of slaves plotted to gain their freedom by a massacre of whites. A belief by the slaves that their bondage was contrary to the orders of King George seemingly helped fuel their subversion. According to the plot, as soon as the weather became mild enough to permit them to survive in the woods, at some midnight agreed upon, all of the slaves were to rise and slay their owners. Buildings were to be set afire and the draft horses killed. Finally, having secured the best saddle horses, the conspirators intended to flee to the Indians and join them in support of the French. However, the impudent remarks of a drunken slave aroused suspicion of the plot and led to the arrest of several hundred bondmen, two of whom were hanged and many others flogged.[22]

In the second example, also in 1734, a group of slaves in Burlington County somehow became convinced that England had outlawed slavery and therefore they were being held in bondage illegally. Thus enraged against their owners, a large number formed a plot to gain their freedom by armed rebellion. A Philadelphia newspaper reported that it had been decreed by the leaders of the uprising that every male and female slave in every family was to rise at midnight and cut the throats of their masters and sons. They were not to meddle with the women, whom they intended to plunder and ravish the following day. As in the Somerville example, when the massacre was over, the rebels intended to seek refuge among the French and Indians. The plot failed after it was uncovered following an investigation prompted by a remark one of the plotters made while arguing with a white. He asserted that he was as good as any of the slave owners and they would soon know it. Although most of the county's slaves were suspected of complicity, only thirty of the ringleaders were brought to trial. One slave was hanged, several had their ears cut off, and the rest were severely flogged.[23]

A subsequent slave plot surfaced in 1741 in Hackensack, where three bondmen were burned alive after being convicted of setting fire to seven local barns. In 1772, in Perth Amboy, another slave plot was discovered when a slaveholder, alarmed by reports of a conspiracy, urged that all blacks, including seven of his own, be sent to Africa at their owners' expense.[24] Obsessive fear of a slave rebellion led the committee of correspondence in Shrewsbury and Freehold in 1775 to order that "all arms in the hands of or at the command of negroes, slave or free, shall be taken and secured by the militia officers of the several districts." This action was taken in response to "numerous and riotous meetings of negroes at unlicensed houses," which the committee perceived as threatening and fraught with dangerous implications.[25]

While the need for black labor overrode concerns about slave insurrections, it is likely that the growth in the population of black New Jerseyans by the time of the American Revolution would have been greater if not for the high mortality rates and decline in fertility that accompanied the arrival of slaves directly from Africa during the middle of the eighteenth century. These slaves lacked immunity to common diseases such as measles, whooping cough, and smallpox. Fertility also fell, it has been argued, because as slave owners replaced indentured servants, they preferred the replacements, like those they replaced, be single men without families.[26]

The slave family, the enslaved population's most important instrument for its survival, had also surfaced in New Jersey by the time of the American Revolution; a familial life—the African family—which had initially been destroyed through enslavement, had been rebuilt. The manner in which colonial slaves in New Jersey and elsewhere came to acquire a sense of being connected by blood—a feeling of affinity based on an awareness of common descent—is still not that well understood. However, it probably did involve the existence in New Jersey of several generations of native-born blacks, a more favorable balance of the sexes (still, males outnumbered females throughout the colonial period, reflecting the emphasis placed on importing black males for the labor force), and the defining among New Jersey slaves of new, non-African marital roles and familial structures (e.g., the extended family) that addressed the most obvious problem of physical separation.

The importance of early New Jersey slave families cannot be minimized, for they performed at least two vital functions. Slave families aided the process of natural reproduction which, as previously noted, contributed to the size of the population of black New Jerseyans by the time of the American Revolution. Black families also served as socializing agents, helping younger generations acquire adaptive mechanisms that would facilitate their survival in the face of the stresses and strains of bondage.

Further, the early black family was connected to a common form of slave resistance. Bondpersons in New Jersey, as elsewhere in colonial America, frequently absconded from their owners in order to be reunited with family members. Extant runaway slave notices thus often provide some clues about the early formation of New

Jersey slave families. The following few lines from a 1772 example revealing a man's interest in seeking out either his mother or wife offer insight into the level of familial consciousness among black New Jerseyans on the eve of the American Revolution.

> RUN-AWAY from the Subscriber, on Sunday Evening the 27th Day of December last, a Negro Man named Jack, about 33 Years old, a short spare Fellow. . . . He was purchased from Hendrick Emons, of Rockey-Hill in New Jersey, about 9 years ago, and it is supposed he is either gone that Way, where he has a Mother, or else to Anthony Ten Eyck's at Albany, where he has a Wife.[27]

Of course, not all New Jersey black families were enslaved and subject to being torn apart; the oldest consisted of free persons. Such families on the eve of the American Revolution were part of a small group of free blacks in New Jersey that numbered roughly 400 in all—about 5 percent of the total black population.[28]

Free blacks could be found in New Jersey as early as the 1680s. Some of the earliest had migrated from Manhattan to Bergen County, where they became owners of original Tappan land grants. They were Afro-Dutch, bearing such surnames as Van Donck, De Vries, and Manuel.[29] The pathway to joining free blacks was somewhat blocked in the aftermath of the rebellion of 1712 in neighboring New York, in which a group of slaves killed nine whites and wounded five or six more.[30] Alarmed over the prospects of similar insurrection on New Jersey soil, the legislature passed a law in 1713 that provided for greater strictures on the enslaved population; it required that a manumission (a formal act of freedom from slavery) be accompanied by a security or bond of £200 and a guarantee of £20 a year for the upkeep of any freed slave.[31] This financially prohibitive arrangement for most New Jersey slave owners would prove to be the greatest impediment to manumission efforts in pre-Revolutionary New Jersey. By 1776, most of those who comprised the small number of free blacks in New Jersey were either the descendants of seventeenth-century free blacks or manumittees who fell into one of two categories: those who through age or circumstance had become liabilities to their owners or those who were the descendants of mixed racial unions—mulattoes.

Perhaps the most notable native-born mulatto New Jerseyan who had been manumitted by the time of the American Revolution was Cyrus Bustill, an individual whose life actually intersected with the conflict. A native of Burlington, Bustill was born in 1732, the son of his owner, Samuel Bustill—an English-born Quaker and prominent lawyer—and his female slave, Parthenia. At his death in 1742, Samuel Bustill left a will that gave Cyrus to his wife, Grace, who later sold him to a local baker—a Quaker—with the understanding that Cyrus undertake an apprenticeship that would enable him to purchase his freedom. By 1774, Cyrus had secured his freedom, opened a bakery in Burlington, and married. During the

American Revolution, he worked at his trade in Burlington and, in all probability, baked bread for Washington's troops during the 1777–1778 winter ordeal at Valley Forge. While there is an oral tradition in the Bustill family that he even received a silver coin from Washington for such service, there is actual documentary evidence, also possessed by Bustill's descendants, that in fact he was given official commendation for his baking services for the Continental army. After the war, he moved his family to Philadelphia, where he became one of the city's early black leaders; he was a founding member of the historic Free African Society in 1787 and later opened a school for black youth in his home. Bustill also would gain recognition as the great-great-grandfather of Paul Robeson, the celebrated twentieth-century singer, actor, and civil rights activist, arguably New Jersey's most illustrious native.[32]

The life of Bustill suggests the pioneering role that free blacks, given their greater personal autonomy, understandably played in the early life of black communities in America. In pre-Revolution New Jersey, however, they were victimized because of their color in ways similar to those in bondage. Although it failed enactment, a bill that came before the 1773–1774 session of the legislature illuminates the subordinate status sought for free blacks; it required manumitted slaves to pay taxes and fulfill all other duties of citizens, but it denied them the right to vote, serve as a witness except against each other, and marry whites. In addition, free blacks who ran into debt or who were sentenced to prison could be bound out as indentured servants.[33]

Free blacks were also in the forefront of the cultural transformation black New Jerseyans had experienced by the time of the American Revolution—from African to African American. On the eve of the Revolution, the great majority of New Jersey blacks were no longer complete aliens in a strange land. As uprooted Africans, they had indeed become hybrids or hyphenated Americans—new products of a two-pronged process of acculteration.[34]

Scholars are still debating the extent to which Africans maintained and transmitted their culture in the New World. One acknowledged process involved the melding of different traditional African customs into a Pan-African culture and the retention of some aspects of this heritage—what have been termed Africanisms or African survivals. Affecting the preservation of African cultural traditions (the rekindling of African ways of thinking and behaving) was, of course, the arrival in New Jersey of slaves directly from Africa. Their importation enhanced the possible infusion of New Jersey's native black population with firsthand knowledge of the continent and its cultural heritage.

One of the ways in which New Jersey slaves revealed a Pan-African associational life was through the African burial ground. Suggesting a sense of unity and social cohesion, as well as solidarity and common purpose, these burial sites were probably the first public places where black New Jerseyans congregated. While the actual locations of such eighteenth-century places have yet to be unearthed in New Jersey, they have been discovered elsewhere; a neighboring example is the African Burial Ground in New York City. We can surmise, therefore, that they existed in New Jersey as well and could provide further evidence of the continuation of such African burial practices as the placing of favorite objects of the deceased on top of the grave. In fact, the Gethsemane Cemetery in Little Ferry, a burial place established in 1860 for Hackensack's African Americans, has yielded broken white pottery and clay pipes, also suggestive of death rituals derived from African peoples—in particular, the Bakongo of present-day Congo.[35]

Slave owners, aware of African cultural continuities present among their slaves, sometimes used them to their advantage. One example, drawing on supranatural beliefs associated with the practice of trial by ordeal in some African societies, was a 1767 case in which a slave was suspected of murdering a white man, but no evidence could be found against him. As a last resort, the suspected slave was ordered to touch the face of his victim; when blood then ran out of the dead man's nose, the slave was induced to confess, convicted of murder, and duly burned alive. New Jersey historian David Steven Cohen has pointed out that this incident also revealed the "bloody corpse" motif found throughout the Western world, perhaps an example of cultural syncretism.[36]

Through their cultural borrowing and reinterpretation, the acculturative process experienced by New Jersey Africans also involved the adoption of the beliefs and behavior patterns of their land of enslavement—the absorption of the culture of the larger society. African slaves revised their languages, for example, learning to speak such European languages as English, Dutch, and German. Their fluency naturally varied considerably; runaway notices often referred to fugitives who spoke "low Dutch," "Negro Dutch," or "bad English," as well as to those who exhibited a bilingual proficiency ("speaks good Dutch and English") and to those who could "read and write, and 'tis supposed will forge a pass."[37]

Clothing was another area that reflected the acculturative process. Again, advertisements for escaped slaves are instructive. In some instances, they document slaves having a taste for fine clothing, perhaps in imitation of wealthy slave owners. A 1773 notice that referred to three runaways from Hopewell, for example, showed that they wore or carried with them items that belied their lowly status. "A suit of black clothes, a brown silk camblet coat, three linen shirts, good shoes and stockings" described the first; "a yellowish brown close bodied coat, a vest, the foreparts calf-skin, with the hair on, new buckskin breeches, a new felt hat, good shoes and stockings" identified the second; and the last was in possession of "a green sagathy coat, a light coloured cut velvet vest, two striped Holland jackets, a brown coat, a red great coat, a pair of leather breeches, three shirts, the one ruffled, a pair of tow trousers, a new castor hat, good shoes and stockings."[38]

Another example of the degree of Americanization present among black New Jerseyans before the Revolution is one captured on occasion in runaway slave notices.

Witness a 1772 notice that identified a thirty-year-old runaway from "Boontown" (Boonton) as being "much addicted to strong drink."[39] Virtually all African societies from which slaves were taken had very strong strictures against intoxication for everyone except the elderly—those who, as a reward of old age, had earned the right to use intoxicants to excess. It would thus be virtually unthinkable in traditional African society for those as young as thirty to consume large quantities of intoxicating beverages.

Religion serves as an area where black New Jerseyans exhibited both African cultural continuities and the internalizing of Euro-American culture, drawing on the African past as well as the American present. By the time of the Revolution, many black New Jerseyans had been affected by the desire of white colonists to bring Africans to a belief in Christ and had become Quakers, Anglicans, Lutherans, Presbyterians, Moravians, or members of the Dutch Reformed Church. Through the example of William Boen, a conversion to Quakerism can be seen as informing nonviolent protest against slavery. Born into bondage in Mount Holly in 1735 and manumitted at age twenty-eight, Boen's antislavery convictions led him to refuse to use or wear any article manufactured or transported by enslaved labor.[40] By attaining a position of influence among early Lutherans, Arie Van Guinee also personified the religious acculturation that occurred among some early black New Jerseyans. In 1714, several years after moving to the Raritan Valley from New York City, where he was a member of a Lutheran congregation, he held the very first local Lutheran service in his home. Van Guinee later assisted in the baptisms of his niece and nephew and became a man of considerable means, purchasing sizeable plots of land over the years.[41]

In contrast to Boen and Van Guinee were those black New Jerseyans whose conversion to Christianity still allowed for the expression of their African religious heritage—the fusion of Christian and African religious beliefs and rituals. Often their conversion could be attributed to the Great Awakening that began in 1740, an evangelistic movement anchored in the notion of equality before God that featured camp meetings and revivals and an emphasis on immediate conversion rather than spiritual growth through study and discipline. It attracted New Jersey blacks, along with those in other colonies, because the emotional fervor and convulsive behavior it sanctioned permitted several African cultural survivals. One of those was the drum-like rhythmic hand clapping that accompanied their responsive singing; another was "spirit possession," the supreme religious experience so fundamental to traditional African religious beliefs and practices in which a deity momentarily takes over the mind and body of a devotee, allowing for a trance or altered state of consciousness. Behaving like a possessed person has persisted to the present-day in some African American churches. Terms for the conduct include "shouting," "getting happy," and "getting the Holy Ghost."[42]

Naming practices among black New Jerseyans also offered proof of the coexistence of a long memory of Africa and newly acquired American ways. Such West African names as Sambo (of Hausa origin), Kuff (a derivative of the Akan "Kofi"), and Sukey (probably the Wolof female name "Suki") could be found among New Jersey slaves before the Revolution, as well as such African-sounding names as Bonturah, Cudjo, Mingo, Quameny, Quamino, Quaco, Quashee, and Jemima.[43] In answering to European names by the eve of the Revolution, however, black New Jerseyans also signaled a change in their identity. A perusal of pre-Revolution runaway slave notices, wills, and inventory lists reveals a common use of names clearly non-African, such as Tim, Peter, Jack, Joe, Sybil, Betty, Elizabeth, Sylvia, and Sarah. Among these names are some that suggested a kind of comic jest that played off of the slaves' lowly status; for example, fanciful names like Free, Hero, and Prince were used, as were classical names such as Plato, Caesar, Phoebe, Cato, Pompei, Medea, and Chloe. That slave owners never carried these names themselves indeed suggests the degree to which they often sought to mock, ridicule, and demean their human property.

The use of aliases—multiple names—by runaway slaves, as a way of avoiding detection and capture, indicates still another manner in which the naming process revealed a degree of Americanization among New Jersey bondpersons. A 1771 notice, for example, indicated that Jem, a slave of Isaac Wilkins of Newark, "calls himself by the several names of James, Gaul, Mingo, Mink, and Jim." A 1764 notice, stating that Jacob, of Freehold, New Jersey, "has several times changed his name, calling himself James Stuart, and James Pratt, &ct . . . he passes himself as an Indian," reveals a fugitive not only using several names but one artful enough in adapting to his environment to change his ethnic identity as well.[44]

Finally, New Jersey slaves in their daily work revealed skills associated with occupations in Africa, as well as those learned through their experiences in bondage. In the first category would be the work that New Jersey slaves did as farm laborers, cultivating grains for domestic use and export to the West Indies and raising hogs, cattle, and horses on small farms or small slave holdings. Women who toiled as house servants or were engaged in cooking, laundering, and spinning also fell into this category, as did male slaves serving as seafarers and dockworkers who drew upon work habits found among African groups situated close to bodies of water. Other occupations found among black New Jerseyans that were akin to African work traditions included blacksmithing, weaving, and one often mentioned in fugitive slave notices: fiddling, a talent related to that of professional musicians found among the West African coast who played stringed instruments such as the kora of the Mandingo people.[45]

Mining, at which blacks from Angola and the Congo were especially skilled, also engaged the services of New Jersey slaves. In fact, one of the largest mines in colonial America, employing over 200 slaves, was the Schuyler mine in lower Bergen County. It was discovered by an elderly black, whose reward was a "fancy dressing gown like his master and some pipe tobacco." In the mines, blacks worked with skilled and journeymen whites and indentured servants, as well as in skilled positions at forges and blast furnaces.[46]

By the onset of the Revolution, black New Jerseyans had become chimney sweeps, bakers, masons, farriers, coopers, wheelwrights, shoemakers, carpenters, and barbers—all radical departures from African work traditions. In one notable case, Peter Hill became one of the nation's earliest black clockmakers. Born a slave in 1767 in Burlington, Hill was able to serve an apprenticeship while in bondage to the clockmaker Joseph Hollingshed Jr. After gaining his freedom in 1795, Hill established his own workshop and purchased land in Burlington; he later moved his shop to Mount Holly. Hill's work revealed a cultural transformation that involved the traditional African perception of time, a critical function of the African cosmology or worldview that for some New Jersey slaves had been discarded by the time of the Revolution. In turn, they embraced a new concept of time, which became both linear as well as an abstraction measurable in such finite units as hours, minutes, and seconds. Essentially, they moved away from a sense of time derived from the repetitive rhythms of nature and the regularities of social life.[47]

The Revolution and After: 1776–1810

Considering the breakdown of traditional measures for the social control of bondpersons that accompanied the often near-anarchic conditions of the American Revolution, it is not surprising that two slave conspiracies were plotted in New Jersey during the Revolution. One occurred in Somerset County in 1776 and involved a group of slaves who armed themselves and attempted to unite against their owners. Three years later, in Elizabethtown, slaves, allegedly incited by the Tories, conspired to rise and murder their owners.[48] The liberation of the insurrectionists that would have resulted from the success of their insurgency helps to underscore the central place of the word "freedom" in any assessment of the Revolution's enormous impact on black New Jerseyans. In short, there occurred during the Revolutionary War era, the years between 1776 and 1810, impressive gains in the struggle to break the chains binding New Jersey's enslaved population. By 1810, slave imports had ceased; the number of free blacks had increased dramatically; and the slave population had been lowered appreciably.

The American Revolution radically altered black New Jerseyans' lives by greatly widening opportunities for slaves to escape the yoke of bondage. The most common escape route to liberty was through simply running away. Although it is difficult to quantify such slave flight during the Revolution, it is clear that the numbers of such men and women "exceeded those in any previous era."[49] They were certainly among the thousands of bondpersons in America who, as active agents in their own liberation, used the war's turmoil and tumult to flee from their owners (fig. 36). In the process, they helped shrink the number of American slaves by roughly 100,000 by the war's end, "the largest black escape in the history of North American slavery."[50] Second- and third-generation New Jersey–born slaves who had gained familiarity with the neighboring countryside therefore were especially prone to take flight, often passing themselves off as free blacks. As can be seen in the following slave notice, which appeared in the *Pennsylvania Packet*, January 4, 1780, even among slaves only briefly in New Jersey there was an inclination to use the war as a cover for flight:

> Was taken up, and is now confined to Trenton gaol, by the subscriber, living in New-Germantown, Hunterdon County, State of New Jersey, a young Negro Man, who says his name is Peter; he is nearly six feet high, of slender make, speaks and understands very little English, and appears to have been but a short time in America, had scarce any clothing. The owner is desired to apply, pay charges and take him away.[51]

Runaways were among the New Jersey slaves who gained their freedom through military service. As one scholar has noted, "Fugitives often fled to the opposing armies to seek freedom in return for military service. A New Jersey master reported in 1778 that his runaway had 'gone to join the enemy,' and another advertised that his Negro would probably 'endeavor to get . . . to the American camp, as he is fond of soldiery.'"[52]

The British were the first to encourage slave defections by offering freedom to fugitives who took refuge with their military forces. On November 7, 1775, John Murray, Lord Dunmore, the last royal governor of Virginia, declared martial law and promised freedom to any slave who was willing and able to take up arms in His Majesty's service (fig. 37). Other British commanders followed Dunmore's lead and recruited slaves; ultimately, approximately 1,300 blacks served with the British.[53] When the British left America at the end of the war, they carried an estimated 20,000 free blacks to Great Britain, the West Indies, and Canada (Nova Scotia); some of these eventually relocated to Sierra Leone. This number includes

FIG. 36 *"Three Pounds Reward," Runaway Slave Notice, Nov. 8, 1775. Facsimile, Monmouth County Historical Association, Freehold, N.J.*

THREE POUNDS Reward.

RUN away from the fubfcriber, living in Shrewfbury, in the county of Monmouth, New-Jerfey, a **NEGROE** man, named TITUS, but may probably change his name; he is about 21 years of age, not very black, near 6 feet high; had on a grey homefpun coat, brown breeches, blue and white ftockings, and took with him a wallet, drawn up at one end with a ftring, in which was a quantity of clothes. Whoever takes up faid Negroe, and fecures him in any goal, or brings him to me, fhall be entitled to the above reward of *Three Pounds* proc. and all reafonable charges, paid by

Nov. 8 1775.　　JOHN CORLIS.

black New Jerseyans who were among the 3,000 who evacuated with the British from New York City in 1783, further reducing New Jersey's slave population.[54]

The most celebrated black who saw service with the British was a native New Jerseyan: Cornelius Titus, who later became known as Colonel Tye. A runaway slave from Monmouth County (see fig. 36), he distinguished himself at the 1778 Battle of Monmouth, then went on to become the scourge of American patriots. Tye looted and raided farms, carrying off silver, clothing, and badly needed cattle for British troops in Staten Island and New York City. For these accomplishments, he and his men were paid handsomely, sometimes receiving five gold guineas. In September 1780, while attempting his greatest feat—the capture of Captain Josiah Huddy, who was famed for his leadership in raids against British positions in Staten Island and Sandy Hook, Tye was shot in the wrist. Originally thought to be a minor wound, within days lockjaw set in and, lacking proper medical treatment, Tye died. Pertinent to any assessment of Tye's importance to the British is the observation by Graham Hodges that "Tye's title is noteworthy." Hodges has noted that while the British army did not formally commission black officers, it often granted blacks officers' titles out of respect.[55]

Dunmore's proclamation helped move patriot commanders and decision-makers to rethink their policy of excluding blacks, both slave and free, from the war—a policy that seemed to ignore the fact that blacks occasionally had served in colonial militias and had participated in the Revolution's first battles. Coupled with the fact that as the struggle for independence lengthened and the number of soldiers grew critically short, the proclamation prompted col-

> **By his EXCELLENCY, &c.**
> **A PROCLAMATION.**
>
> AS I have ever entertained hopes that an accommodation might have taken place between *Great Britain* and this colony, without being compelled, *by my duty*, to this most disagreeable, but now absolutely necessary step, rendered so by a body of armed men, unlawfully assembled, firing on his majesty's tenders, and the formation of an army, and that army now on their march to attack his majesty's troops, and destroy the well-disposed subjects of this colony: To defeat such treasonable purposes, and that all such traitors, and their abetters, may be brought to justice, and that the peace and good order of this colony may be again restored, which the ordinary course of the civil law is unable to effect, I have thought fit to issue this my proclamation, hereby declaring, that until the aforesaid good purposes can be obtained, I do, in virtue of the power and authority to me given, *by his majesty*, determine to execute martial law, and cause the same to be executed throughout this colony; and to the end that *peace* and *good order* may the sooner be restored, I do require every person capable of bearing arms to resort to his majesty's STANDARD, or be looked upon as traitors to his majesty's crown and government, and thereby become liable to the penalty the law inflicts upon such offences, such as *forfeiture of life, confiscation of lands*, &c. &c. And I do hereby farther declare all *indented servants, negroes*, or others (appertaining to rebels) *free*, that are able and willing to bear arms, they *joining his majesty's troops*, as soon as may be, for the more speedily reducing this colony to a *proper sense* of their duty, to his majesty's crown and dignity. I do farther order, and require, all his majesty's liege subjects to retain their quitrents, or any other taxes due, or that may become due, in their own custody, till such time as peace may be again restored to this at present most unhappy country, or demanded of them for their former salutary purposes, by officers properly authorised to receive the same.
> *Given on board the ship* William, *off* Norfolk, *the 7th day of* November.

FIG. 37 *"Lord Dunmore's Proclamation,"* Virginia Gazette, *Purdie Edition, November 24, 1775. Colonial Williamsburg Foundation.*

onists to overcome their fears that a slave revolt or mass defections would result from the arming of slaves. By the end of the war, out of a total force of 300,000, roughly 5,000 blacks, had served the patriot cause.[56]

While we have no estimate of the number of black New Jerseyans who fought on the side of the patriots, we know that most of those who did came from southern New Jersey.[57] This area had the larger free black population and the greater physical presence of Quakers, who, as America's first organized abolitionists and despite their pacifism during the Revolution, were probably more willing to promise freedom to their slaves for wartime duty. Oliver Cromwell was among those black South Jerseyans who served with the patriots. Born free in 1752 in Columbus, Burlington County, Cromwell's distinction lies in part in his having lived to be 100 years old and his ability, at that age, to provide oral testimony regarding his participation in the war. Among the reminiscences recounted by Cromwell, who enlisted in a company attached to the Second New Jersey Regiment, was his having accompanied George Washington when he crossed the Delaware in 1776 (color plate 4) and his participation in the Battles of Princeton, Brandywine, Monmouth, and Yorktown. Adding luster to Cromwell's Revolutionary War service was Washington's signing on June 5, 1783, of Cromwell's honorable discharge (fig. 38) as a private and Cromwell's receipt of a yearly federal pension of $96.[58]

With the change in the military policy of excluding blacks, New Jerseyans were among the American slave owners who now offered freedom to their slaves for war service, sometimes promising freedom if they served in their place. Benjamin Coe

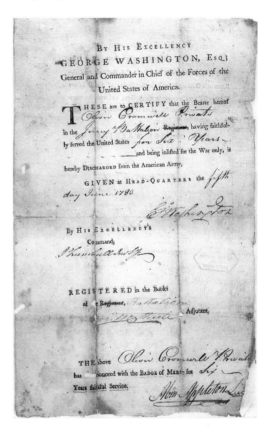

FIG. 38 *Honorable Discharge of Oliver Cromwell, June 5, 1783. Military and Civil Records, National Archives.*

of Newark, owner of a slave named Cudjo, was among these. For serving as a member of the Continental army as a substitute for Coe, Cudjo not only received his freedom but nearly an acre of ground on High Street in Newark.[59] At the other end of the spectrum was the tragic case of Samuel Sutphen of Readington, Somerset County; it involved reneging on a promise of freedom for military service.

Born in 1747 into bondage in Somerset County, by the onset of the American Revolution Sutphen had become the principal farmhand on his owner's plantation. With the outbreak of hostilities, his owner, Barnardus LaGrange, sided with the loyalists and ultimately fled to British-occupied New York. His property was confiscated, and the ownership of Sutphen passed through two individuals before he was bought by Casper Berger, a tavern owner and member of the New Jersey militia. Berger promised to free Sutphen at the end of the war if he would serve in his stead. Sutphen accepted Berger's commitment and participated in numerous military engagements, but Berger failed to keep his promise. At the war's conclusion, Sutphen then experienced a succession of two owners. The widow of the second owner permitted him to earn money with which to purchase his freedom. Sutphen's story of injustice finally ended around 1805 with that purchase; he had endured a life of bondage until his midfifties.[60]

New Jersey also provided several examples of slaves whose participation in the war led to their freedom through action by the legislature. At the heart of their rather unique cases was the question: What was to be the disposition of slaves who were part of the confiscated estates of loyalists?

The first of three slaves to be freed by legislative decree in New Jersey as a reward for American military service was Peter Williams, who belonged to a Tory from Woodbridge. Taken behind British lines by his owner, he escaped in 1780 and then served first with the state militia and then the Continental army until the end of hostilities. His manumission occurred in 1784 and established a precedent for the well-documented case of Prime, who belonged to a Princeton loyalist, Absalom Bainbridge, and whose case ended in November 1786 when the legislature passed an act manumitting him. Three years later a slave named Cato received his freedom in the same manner. Like Peter Williams, he belonged to a Woodbridge loyalist and served in both the state and Continental armies.[61]

The impact of the American Revolution also extended to the number of manumissions in New Jersey; there were considerably more after the Revolution.[62] Among those granting manumission to their slaves was William Livingston, New Jersey's first governor (color plate 1), who set his slaves free during the war, stating that bondage for "Americans who have almost idolized liberty" was "peculiarly odious and disgraceful."[63] Another New Jersey slaveholder who seemingly took to heart the Revolution's egalitarian and libertarian principles was Moses Bloomfield. Father of Joseph Bloomfield, the state's governor (1801–1802 and 1803–1812), Moses Bloomfield freed his slaves in a public ceremony on July 4, 1783, that celebrated the end of the war. Mounting a platform in Woodbridge, he stated: "As a nation, we are free and independent—all men are created equal, and why should these, my fellow citizens— my equals, be held in bondage? From this day forth they are emancipated and I here declare them free and absolved from all servitude to me and my posterity."[64]

The Revolution even emboldened slaves to seek freedom through the courts by attacking defects in title deeds and in some cases by challenging the very legality of bondage itself. The February 2, 9, and 16, 1780, editions of the *New Jersey Gazette*, for example, ran notices of one New Jersey bondman suing for his liberty in which he warned prospective buyers that he expected "freedom, justice and protection . . . by the laws of the state."[65]

Aside from reducing the number of those in bondage in New Jersey, the American Revolution gave impetus to New Jersey's burgeoning abolitionist movement. In providing the perfect context for those opposed to slavery to voice their opposition, it helped foster an antislavery sentiment that led to the further weakening of New Jersey bondage. While earlier a denunciation of slavery had been couched largely in terms of its immorality, an antislavery position could now be based on slavery's existence running counter to the very pronouncements of liberty and equality used to justify rebellion against Great Britain. An excellent example of this is seen in the writing of David Cooper, a New Jersey Quaker who in 1785 joined with other Quakers to present a bill to the legislature seeking to abolish both slavery and the slave trade.[66] His attack on slavery, written in 1783 and titled *A Serious Address to the Rulers of America, On the Inconsistency of Their Conduct Respecting Slavery*, noted the incompatibility of slave ownership and the ideals of the Revolution. Urging his compatriots not to appear hypocritical to subsequent generations, Cooper eloquently penned the following:

> Ye rulers of America beware: Let it appear to future ages, from the records of this day, that you are not only professed to be advocates for freedom, but really were inspired by the love of mankind, and wish to secure the invaluable blessing to all; that, as you disdained to submit to the unlimited control of others, you equally abhorred the crying crime of holding your fellow men, as much entitled to freedom as yourselves.[67]

Although New Jersey generally lagged behind its northern neighbors in terms of antislavery efforts, such efforts were very much in evidence well before the American Revolution, enabling Cooper to draw on well-established antecedents. As early as 1696, the Quakers of West Jersey and southeastern Pennsylvania voted in their yearly meeting to recommend to their coreligionists that they cease the further importation of slaves.[68] Considerably later, the Quaker John Woolman, a native of Rancocas, Burlington County, became one of America's foremost early advocates of abolition. Believing that slaves should be freed by the personal action of their owners rather than by political measures, he traveled extensively throughout the colonies, from New England to the Carolinas, on horseback and by foot championing the cause of emancipation. His *Considerations on Keeping Negroes* (fig. 39), first printed in 1754, is considered a benchmark among antislavery statements written in America.

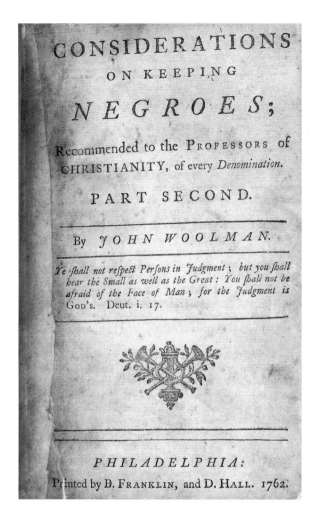

FIG. 39 *John Woolman,* Considerations on Keeping Negroes. *Philadelphia, 1762.*
Rare Books Division, The New York Public Library, Astor, Lenox and Tilden Foundations.

Woolman's humanitarian message no doubt contributed to the 1769 tariff on the importation of slaves into New Jersey, which can be interpreted as an attempt to limit the expansion of slavery in the colony. It most certainly facilitated the action taken in 1776 by Pennsylvania and West Jersey Quakers who, in their respective yearly meetings, agreed to excommunicate those coreligionists who refused to divest themselves of bondpersons. It also probably influenced the numerous petitions that the colonial assembly received from Quaker counties in 1773 and 1774 that asked for duties that would end the importation of slaves into the colony, as well as for a law to ease the requirements for manumitting slaves. In 1775, a strong petition asking for an act "to set free all of the slaves now in the Colony" was presented to the assembly by fifty-two Quakers from Chesterfield in Burlington County.[69] These petitions are significant in that they mark a movement by Quakers to go beyond seeking to persuade those of their own faith of the immorality of bondage and to alter public policy instead; they sought to have their antislavery views sanctioned by law.

In 1786, in the aftermath of the American Revolution, Governor William Livingston gave impetus to the approach of employing legislation in the antislavery struggle by securing the passage of An Act to Prevent the Importation of Slaves into the State of New Jersey, and to Authorize the Manumission of Them Under Certain Restrictions, and to Prevent the Abuse of Slaves. As its title suggests, this landmark law banned slave imports by levying a fine of £50 for each slave imported from Africa after 1776 and £20 for each slave imported before 1776; encouraged manumission by allowing a slave owner to free a slave between twenty-one and thirty-five years of age and of sound mind and body without posting a bond of £200; and allowed owners to be indicted for the inhumane treatment of slaves.[70] Continuing this trend two years later, the state enacted legislation that forbade the removal of slaves from New Jersey without their consent; provided that slaves convicted of a criminal offense receive the same punishment as white lawbreakers; required slave owners to teach slave children to read; and permitted the state to seize and sell slave ships.[71]

A decade later, in 1798, New Jersey passed the Act Respecting Slaves, a more detailed slave code that repealed virtually all preexisting slave legislation. While a gradual abolition clause was removed from this bill, under its provisions slaves were now allowed to own real estate; the terminal age at which slaves could be manumitted was raised to forty from thirty-five; manumitted blacks could reside in any county; and the penalties for abusing slaves or failing to educate them were raised.[72]

It is likely that the more progressive attitude toward the treatment of slaves found in the aforementioned laws of 1786, 1788, and 1798 can be attributed to the Revolution, revealing another way in which the war helped to improve the plight of New Jersey bondpersons. Although the Revolution did not convince a majority of New Jersey inhabitants of the need for the outright support of manumission, the Revolution's emphasis on natural rights seemingly made these inhabitants more favorably disposed to ameliorating the conditions of bondage. Efforts to make New Jersey bondage less onerous seem to undercut the argument that New Jersey slavery declined because of its unprofitability; there appears to be little evidence that those inclined to rid themselves of slaves for economic reasons were in the forefront of any efforts to improve the well-being of New Jersey bondpersons.

The Revolution also seemingly produced a judicial climate in New Jersey more favorable to bondpersons, as the courts gave increasingly liberal interpretations to the laws governing manumission. In 1795, the state supreme court ruled that a mere promise of manumission, although unsubstantiated by legal consideration, created a valid claim to freedom. "It is far better to adopt this rule," the court declared, "than to suffer promises thus made . . . to be violated or retracted at pleasure."[73]

Another important step in the antislavery struggle in New Jersey was taken in 1793, when, at the instigation of the Pennsylvania Abolition Society, the state's first abolition society was formed. Representatives of the Pennsylvania society traveled to Burlington on January 26, 1793, and supervised the birth of the New Jersey Society for Promoting the Abolition of Slavery.[74] Focusing initially on "defending the rights of free blacks and winning some important cases for slaves wrongfully kept from freedom," it did not press for immediate and unconditional manumission, supporting instead the pattern of gradual emancipation already established in Pennsylvania in 1780 and to be established in New York in 1799.[75]

The year 1800 witnessed the kind of paradox that has often characterized the black historical experience in general and that in New Jersey in particular. On the one hand, in that year black bondage reached its peak in New Jersey; the state had a total of 12,422 slaves. Of this number, the overwhelming majority—11,915, were found in the northern counties, reflecting a similar regional imbalance that had characterized New Jersey slavery from its earliest days. On the other hand, the free black population, which stood at 2,762 in 1790, had increased to 4,402 ten years later, its highest to date. The southern counties, as they had in 1790 when they had 1,466 free blacks, accounted for most of these free blacks—2,374, almost 85 percent of the total black population of the southern counties.[76] These counties were part of the Delaware Valley, encompassing southeastern Pennsylvania and southern New Jersey, an area that has been termed the "Cradle of Emancipation," where black people were first emancipated in the United States on a massive scale. The dominant presence in this area of Quakers, the nation's first organized abolitionists, again helps to explain why the area led in the emergence of a free black population.

By 1804, the stage had been set for the final development in erasing the moral blot of bondage in post-Revolutionary New Jersey: the passage of New Jersey's first abolition law, An Act for the Gradual Abolition of Slavery. Success in the neighboring states helped New Jersey abolitionists to achieve this milestone. The Gradual Manumission Act passed in New York in 1799, like the Pennsylvania act of 1780, indeed exerted pressure on New Jersey. Could New Jersey remain a bastion of slavery, immune from the liberty offered in neighboring states? If it attempted to do so, would New Jersey slaves flee to join free black communities in the neighboring states?

In addition to the gradual abolition laws of Pennsylvania and New York, the position on manumission taken by the state's abolition society helped New Jersey's emancipation process to be a gradual one. In fact, realizing fully that the idea of total and immediate emancipation stood little chance of success, in February 1804 the society presented a impassioned plea for gradual abolition. While pointing out that slavery was indefensible "in a land of freedom, and by a people distinguished for reason and humanity," the plea stated that to emancipate those who were enslaved at present would violate the property rights of slaveholders. This argument, the plea continued, should not apply to the proposed emancipation of unborn blacks, "that to enslave Children to the latest posterity for the cost of the parent . . . is a satisfaction vastly disproportionate."[77]

Crucial to the nearly unanimous acceptance of the 1804 abolition law was the scheme to compensate owners for the ultimate loss of the children of their slaves, a plan first enacted in New York. Under the provisions of this act, all children born of slaves after July 4, 1804, were to be emancipated after serving apprenticeships to their mother's owner, females after twenty-one years of age and males after twenty-five.[78] In this concession to slave owners, which amounted to "the nearest approach to financial compensation to expropriated slaveholders in any northern emancipation law," the law provided that slave children over the age of one could be abandoned to the poorhouse, where they would be bound out to individuals who would receive compensation from the state for their maintenance.[79] Since the children were often bound to their former owners, the law benefited the latter because they now had an "apprentice" paid for by the state. The maintenance fees led to considerable abuse and fraud. Amid efforts to repeal the entire bill because it allegedly deprived individuals unconstitutionally of their property without their consent, the fees were discontinued by the legislature in 1811, the abandonment clause having been repealed in 1805.[80] Evidence that these children became a tremendous financial burden to the state is reflected in the fact that, in one year, the support of the bound children amounted to over 40 percent of the state budget. In terminating the payments, it was observed that in some instances, the state had paid the guardian, usually the former slave owner, more than the lifetime price of the slave.[81]

Passage of the 1804 abolition law made New Jersey the final state to join the effort to eradicate slavery in the North. What has been termed the "First Emancipation," the illegality of slavery in the North, was now a reality. Six years later, roughly a generation removed from the firing of the last shot at Yorktown (the Revolution's final battle), 75 percent of blacks in the North were free. Massachusetts, New Hampshire, and Vermont had no slaves; Pennsylvania and Rhode Island had black populations that were 97 percent free, Connecticut's 95 percent free, and New York's 63 percent free.[82] With 42 percent of its black population free, New Jersey ranked last in this regard, a fact not surprising given that its gradual abolition act had only been in existence since 1804. Sixteen years later, in 1820, the state's free black population was 62 percent, a percentage that compares somewhat favorably with the 63 percent reached in New York in 1810, some eleven years after its gradual abolition act went into effect.[83]

The free black population in New Jersey in 1810 stood at an all-time high: 7,843.[84] Of this number, the majority, for the first time, were found in the state's northern counties. Here free blacks numbered 4,316, compared to 3,527 in the southern counties, although in the latter they constituted 91 percent of the total black population as opposed to roughly 29 percent in the former—a drastic difference.[85] Still, New Jersey slavery, confined principally to the northern counties, especially Bergen, Somerset, Monmouth, and Middlesex, had started down the road to extinction; the growth of the free black population had become irreversible.

Although having escaped the bonds of involuntary servitude, by 1810 free New Jersey blacks were still the objects of hostility and discriminatory legislation from Revolutionary War–era white New Jerseyans; they faced hardship, persecution, and physical insecurity. In fact, the prolongation of slavery in New Jersey after the Revolution encouraged the notion that free blacks were actually slaves without masters; it helped to reinforce the willingness of the larger society to impose many social injustices and disabilities upon free black persons. They were denied the right to sit on juries or testify in court, subjected to curfews, restricted in their travels, confined to certain occupations, and not allowed to stand in the militia. While the 1798 slave code, for example, required that free blacks, both from other states as well as New Jersey, traveling outside their home county carry with them certificates of freedom signed by two justices of peace, perhaps the most egregious social disability they suffered was the loss of the franchise.[86] This occurred in 1807 when both single white women and blacks lost the right to vote that was given under the 1776 constitution to all persons worth £50. This would become the grievance that black New Jerseyans would campaign against most vigorously during the antebellum period. Yet despite the indignities and degradations experienced by free New Jersey blacks and regardless of hardship, persecution, and physical insecurity, their life was far preferable to bondage.

The significance of a relatively large free black population in New Jersey in 1810 as a consequence of the American Revolution cannot be exaggerated. Such freedom found expression in a more fully developed black associational life in New Jersey. Around 1800, for example, the black community's most precious and enduring social institution—the black church—began to emerge, committed from the outset to meeting both the spiritual and temporal needs of its members. Owing to their early appearance, black New Jersey churches are among the oldest to be found in the North. The Mount Pisgah African Methodist Episcopal (AME) Church in Salem is regarded as the earliest of these congregations; it was present at the first and organizing conference of the AME Church in Philadelphia in 1816. The formation of black churches—in particular, AME congregations—was facilitated by the presence of Richard Allen in southern New Jersey in the early 1780s. Founder of the AME Church and its first bishop, Allen had served as a wagon driver during the Revolution and at the end of the war traveled as an itinerant preacher in this area, as well as in southeastern Pennsylvania and Delaware.[87]

With the enlargement of the number of free blacks in the wake of the Revolution came another development worthy of mention: the darkening of the free black New Jersey population. This shift away from a population disproportionately mulatto increased the chances of success of darker-hued runaways. The greater chance of success in turn encouraged others to flee. The following statement by Ira Berlin regarding this process indeed applies to New Jersey: "The larger, darker-skinned free Negro population camouflaged fugitives, increased their chances of success, and encouraged still other blacks to make their way from slavery to freedom. The increase in runaways begun during the tumult of the Revolution continued into the postwar years."[88]

The American Revolution, more than any other single event, sounded the death knell for New Jersey slavery. While New Jersey slaves may have been hard pressed to debate the ideological underpinnings of the war, they quickly fathomed how the war could be made to serve their interests and concerns, and they responded accordingly. To those who were escape-minded, it served as an unprecedented blessing. For others, it was the opportunity to parlay military service into freedom, an opportunity that was seized upon and applied to both of the opposing combatants. The war also aided the work of those who were opposed to slavery, their efforts to abolish black forced labor gaining momentum in the war's aftermath. The theory of natural rights and the slogans of liberty and independence that were promulgated to denounce the tyranny and despotism of the British now became the perfect justification for any number of antislavery activities, ranging from manumissions, to laws that sought to ease the treatment of the enslaved, to the creation of an abolitionist society. In short, as a recent study suggests in a reference that includes New Jersey, "the war itself proved the greatest solvent to the master-slave relation."[89]

The positive effects of the American Revolution on the lives of black New Jerseyans would also foreshadow the gains African Americans would derive from the nation's subsequent major wars—creating the ironic situation of blacks benefiting from armed conflicts that gave rise to considerable misery and suffering. Indeed, the Civil War led to the freeing of all of America's bondpersons, creating the "Second Emancipation," while World Wars I and II brought about the foremost development in twentieth-century African American life: the Great Migration, the unprecedented movement of black people out of the South in search of the Promised Land. Since New Jersey was the destination of many who trekked northward as part of the Great Migration seeking to escape the inequities, injustices, and cruelties of Jim Crowism in the South—considered by some to be a newer form of bondage—the story of the two world wars prompting black settlement in New Jersey can be viewed as connected to that of the American Revolution and black New Jerseyans. Both stories involve African Americans using war-related developments to improve their circumstances, to break the chains of bondage in seeking their right to life, liberty, and the pursuit of happiness—an ideal first given prominence by the American Revolution roughly 225 years ago.

"TROUBLESOME TIMES A-COMING":

The American Revolution and New Jersey Women

✦ ✦ ✦

DELIGHT W. DODYK

I was told the inhabitants of our little town were going in haste into the country, and that my nearest neighbours were already removed. When I heard this, I felt myself quite sick; I was ready to faint. . . . I thought of my own lonely situation, no husband to cheer with the voice of love my sinking spirits. My little flock, too, without a father to direct them how to steer. All these things crowded into my mind at once, and I felt like one forsaken; a flood of friendly tears came to my relief.[1]

MARGARET HILL MORRIS (1737–1816; fig. 40) had good reason to be fearful. In December 1776, as English and Hessian troops advanced up the Delaware River toward her Burlington, New Jersey, home, Morris, a widow and a Quaker, had a decision to make. Morris chose to remain in her house with her children as Burlington was occupied by Hessian troops and bombarded from the river by patriot forces. "Oh, that the cruel contest was over and the present distinctions amongst us at an end; that friendship might extend her kindly influence to either part alike and all be friends again," she wrote to her brother in October 1777 (fig. 41).[2] Too often in history written about the Revolutionary War, the violent reality of warfare is submerged in the hyperbole of patriotism. A few heroes are celebrated, while ordinary acts of bravery and humanity go unremarked. During the war, women were thrown into hostilities; some served as medics, cooks, messengers, even combatants. In a war that involved their homes and children, survival itself was political as well as personal, and the domestic became heroic.

FIG. 40 Portrait of Margaret Hill Morris, *n.d. Haverford College Library, Haverford, Pa., Quaker Collection.*

In colonial New Jersey, women's lives were circumscribed by tradition and English common law, under which women were "subordinate in private life and marginal in public life."[3] At the same time, the subordinate status of women under British rule was tempered by colonial conditions; the scarcity of labor and particularly of women gave women a "functional independence and importance" not found in the British Isles. According to historian Joan Hoff-Wilson, "Woman's role as a household manager was a basic and integral part of the early political economy of the colonies. Hence she occupied a position of unprecedented importance and equality within the socioeconomic unit of the family."[4] At the "Crossroads of the American Revolution," a conflict that often seemed more like civil war, New Jersey women played a significant part.

The years before the outbreak of hostilities were fraught with uncertainties for women in New Jersey. The interruption of trade brought shortages of domestic products that drew women into the politics of the day, whether such a role was sanctioned or not. In a rare firsthand reflection by a New Jersey farm woman, nineteen-year-old

Jemima Condict wrote in October 1774, "It seems we have troublesome times a coming for there is great disturbance abroad in the earth and they say it is tea that caused it. So then if they will quarrel about such a trifling thing as that, what must we expect but war and I think or at least fear it will be so."[5]

The elite women who lived at the edge of male political leadership were aware of the complexities of opposition to the crown. The wives of many prominent New Jersey men, shielded at first by wealth and status, uprooted their families to seek safe haven in less contested areas. Others remained at home. The experiences of Elizabeth Downes Franklin (1728–1777), the wife of the last royal colonial governor, and Susannah French Livingston (1723–1789), the wife of the first governor of the state of New Jersey, illustrate the experiences of elite women. On opposite sides of the conflict, both suffered from the political and military turmoil.

In May 1775, the colonial New Jersey Assembly was displaced by the independent Provincial Congress of New Jersey. Governor William Franklin (see fig. 2) struggled unsuccessfully for several months against the changes and was imprisoned in 1776, while Elizabeth, his aristocratic wife, was destroyed by her husband's downfall. The daughter of wealthy sugar planters in Barbados, Elizabeth was educated in England, where she met William Franklin, the illegitimate son of Benjamin Franklin who had gone to London in 1757 with his father, staying on to dabble in the law and enjoy English society. Elizabeth and William were married on September 4, 1762, and, shortly thereafter, William was appointed royal governor of New Jersey. In 1763, the couple came to New Jersey and joined elite Tory circles. Elizabeth gave ample expression of her taste for luxury as they moved to the elegant Proprietary House (fig. 42) in Perth Amboy, close to the Tory stronghold of New York.[6]

Elizabeth was completely unprepared for the maelstrom. While many New Jersey women found their families torn by political disagreement during this period, William and Benjamin Franklin were totally at odds by the end of 1775. When patriot militiamen broke into Elizabeth and William's home in Perth Amboy in January 1776 to keep the governor from fleeing, Elizabeth was

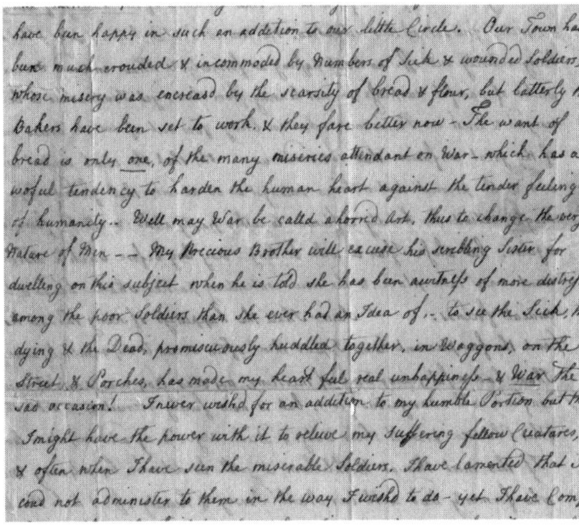
have been happy in such an addition to our little Circle. Our Town has
been much crouded & incommoded by Numbers of Sick & wounded Soldiers,
whose misery was encreasd by the scarsity of bread & flour, but latterly the
Bakers have been set to work. & they fare better now - The want of
bread is only one, of the many miseries attendant on War - which has a
woful tendency to harden the human heart against the tender feelings
of humanity.- Well may War be called a horrid Art, thus to change the very
Nature of Men -- My Precious Brother will excuse his scribbling Sister for
dwelling on this subject when he is told she has been a witness of more distress
among the poor Soldiers than she ever had an Idea of.- to see the Sick, the
dying & the Dead, promiscuously huddled together, in Waggons, on the
Street, & Porches, has made my heart feel real unhappiness - & War the
sad occasion! I never wishd for an addition to my humble Portion but that
I might have the power with it to relieve my suffering fellow Creatures,
& often when I have seen the miserable Soldiers, I have lamented that I
coud not administer to them in the way I wishd to do - yet I have Comfor

FIG. 41 *Excerpt of Letter from Margaret Hill Morris to her brother, Henry Hill, October 12, 1777. Haverford College Library, Haverford, Pa., Quaker Collection, Gulielma Howland Collection no. 1000, Box 7.*

FIG. 42 *Proprietary House, 1762–1764 (later photograph depicting the building as it appeared in 1809 during its hotel period). Proprietary House Association, Perth Amboy, N.J.*

deeply traumatized. Although William urged her to leave for Barbados or London, she remained in Perth Amboy. Her health deteriorated when William, loyal to the crown, was put under house arrest in June 1776. The Provincial Congress arrested him in Burlington on June 21, 1776, and Elizabeth never saw him again.[7] Perth Amboy was occupied by American troops in the summer of 1776 and then by the British military during the winter of 1776. The local inhabitants fled the town as British troops commandeered every house, and Elizabeth, terrified, lived in a few upper rooms as British officers took over Proprietary House. Continental forces effectively cut off supplies to the town and shot any British soldiers foraging at local farms. Meanwhile, William was sent to prison in Connecticut. Elizabeth's pleas for help went unheeded by Benjamin Franklin, so she fled to New York with retreating British troops in June 1777. Weakened by her hardships, she died in New York City on July 28, 1777. Her family possessions, stored in New York, were later destroyed by fire.[8]

Susannah Livingston, the wife of William Livingston (color plate 1), took over Elizabeth Franklin's role as First Lady of New Jersey. She was a fifty-three-year-old grandmother when her husband was appointed governor by the state legislature on August 31, 1776.[9] When the British invaded New Jersey in November 1776, Susannah and her adult daughters, Judith and Susannah, fled the Livingston's country estate, Liberty Hall, in Elizabethtown (fig. 43) for Basking Ridge, where they found refuge on the estate of her brother-in-law, William Alexander, Lord Stirling (see fig. 4).[10] On May 30, 1777, her daughter wrote to William Livingston from Parsippany that "Mama received your Letter of the 17th., last evening, & is very busy preparing to go to Elizth Town again. . . . We are pretty near settled here, very contrary to our own Inclinations, tho' as it was the Advice of the Gentlemen of the Army, we thought it best for if any thing should have befallen us, our Conduct would have been condemned."[11] The women moved back to Liberty Hall where, fortunately for the Livingstons, the officer of the Hessian troops who occupied the house was "not inclined to turn robber, and everything was left undisturbed save for a few provisions."[12]

Women in trouble sometimes sought out the First Lady's assistance. In November 1777, the frantic wife of John Mee, who had been sentenced to death as a traitor in Morris County, came with a petition for reprieve to Susannah. Married women such as Mee had no civil identity apart from their husbands. Considered *feme covert* under English common law, married women were assumed to have the political views and loyalties of their husbands.[13] Though moved by the woman's plight, Susannah told her that she had no influence in the case. "[T]he poor Creature like [a] drowning Man is willing to catch at a straw, she says her Husband will comply with any terms & religiously abide by them, if he can obtain a pardon, if that cannot [be?] granted begs he may be imprisoned during the War." John Mee was hanged for treason in 1778.[14]

The British invasion of New Jersey under General William Howe in November 1776 forced many New Jerseyans to be decisive about their loyalties. Some women, such as the widow Margaret Morris, could make that decision for themselves. She was the head of her household and made decisions for her children. Once the invasion began, however, wives and daughters were in peril whether their sympathies, personal or assumed, were loyalist or patriot. The fortunes of a family could change drastically overnight. This was the

FIG. 43 *Liberty Hall, ca. 1772. Photograph courtesy Liberty Hall Museum, Union, N.J.*

situation in which Jannetje Vrelandt Drummond (?–1790; fig. 44) found herself on the evening of November 20, 1776. Drummond's husband, Robert, was a prosperous local merchant, an officer in the local militia, and a member of the New Jersey Assembly and the Provincial Congress. In the assembly, Robert sought to correct the crown's injustices, but he was no advocate of independence.[15] Returning from a trip to New York, he sported the uniform of a major in the British army of General Howe. With Washington's army in flight, it appeared to many people, including Robert, that the British army would prevail. Robert successfully recruited some 200 local men into the Third Battalion of the notorious General Cortlandt Skinner's brigade. Early in 1777, local patriot mobs plundered Drummond's store and carried off some 1,000 pounds worth of goods. Later, in April, Drummond's Tory forces attacked in Bergen County, no doubt with retribution in mind.[16]

As declared loyalists, the Drummonds bore the weight of punitive legislation passed by the New Jersey Provincial Congress. The Provincial Congress had begun taking some Tories into custody even before the New Jersey Constitution was adopted on July 2, 1776, but it was later that generally applicable measures against loyalists were enacted. In October 1776, New Jersey passed an act declaring that New Jerseyans—like Robert Drummond—who went to war against the state were guilty of high treason.[17]

The wives and families of loyalist men were suspect for several reasons. They sometimes were outspoken of their own convictions, and they moved into and out of British-held areas, raising suspicions that they were giving aid to the enemy. On June 4, 1777, an act was passed making travel within the state without official permission from the Council of Safety a capital offense. Many loyalist wives were found to be interfering with the confiscation of their husbands' estates by hiding family possessions. To deal with this resistance, Governor Livingston, as head of the Council of Safety, was given the power (on June 24, 1777) to send the wives and children of loyalists into British-held territory, a power he exercised early in July. Jannetje Drummond was charged as one of those wives who "secrete the goods, and conceal everything they can" in a list sent from Newark to Governor Livingston in July 1777.[18] In 1779, Drummond was indicted and convicted of treasonable acts. Land she had inherited from her father in what is present-day Passaic was confiscated and later sold. Such confiscated properties were snapped up by well-to-do patriots.[19] Public records in the United States and Great Britain reveal the fates of many New Jersey loyalist women and their families, particularly the wives of Anglican clergymen, lawyers, merchants, and colonial officials, but many are unaccounted for. Some fled to England or Nova Scotia. Some were compensated by the British government, some not, their hardships obscured by time.

A fortunate group of loyalist wives were able to preserve their way of life. Theodosia Bartow Prevost (1746–1794), also of Bergen County, negotiated the system much more successfully than Jannetje Drummond. The wife of James Marcus Prevost, an officer in the Royal American Regiment who served in the Seven Years' War (French and Indian War), Theodosia came from an old American family. She and her husband settled on a farm estate, known as the Hermitage, in remote Hoppertown (now Ho-Ho-Kus) near Paramus in 1767. During the Revolution, Theodosia Prevost was in a precarious position. In 1776, James Prevost was called back to full-time military service, leaving Theodosia and her mother to manage the estate with a few servants, the five Prevost children, and Theodosia's half sister. They survived the threat of foraging by Tory militia and Continental soldiers, and Theodosia was extremely careful in her neighborly relationships.[20]

Despite her husband's career, Theodosia Prevost preserved appearances of neutrality. In the fall of 1777, she made the acquaintance of Aaron Burr Jr., a young lieutenant colonel in the Continental army commanding Malcolm's regiment guarding the army supply station near Suffern, whom she later married. Thanks to her friendship with Burr, other patriot leaders, and family connections with prominent New Jerseyans, Prevost had allies in the effort to preserve her estate.[21] Her position deteriorated when the legislature passed an act on December 10, 1777, ordering the confiscation of the personal property and permitting the compulsory use of real property owned by loyalists. In July 1778, Prevost seized upon a significant opportunity to improve her position. After the Battle of Monmouth, when Washington's forces marched north through New Brunswick toward Paramus, Prevost sent a message to Washington offering her home as his headquarters. Her invitation was accepted by the general for himself and a group of his officers, including Alexander Hamilton, the Marquis de Lafayette, and James Monroe. Four days of rest and relaxation at the Hermitage from July 11 to 14 proved valuable when the Prevost estate was threatened with confiscation in December 1778. Future president James Monroe, Aaron Burr, and Burr's friend William Paterson, attorney general of New Jersey, all interceded on her behalf.[22]

FIG. 44 *Unknown artist,* Portrait of Mrs. Robert Drummond (Jannetje Vrelandt), *ca. 1776. Pastel on paper. From the Collections of the New Jersey Historical Society, Newark. 1898.2 Bequest from the Estate of Allen Claus.*

Unlike Theodosia Prevost, most women depended upon their husbands or fathers for their safety and economic well-being. Wartime life without a husband was precarious. According to Harriet Stryker-Rhoda, "No woman who had actively aided the patriot cause could risk falling into enemy hands. . . . Many New Jersey women were forced to join their men because they could not manage and were left destitute when their husbands were in service."[23] Women whose homes were destroyed sometimes had to take their children and follow their menfolk in the army, sewing and laundering for the troops, foraging for supplies, and nursing the wounded in return for food and protection. If they were lucky, wives of Continental soldiers were assigned rations for performing services for the army. Others, mostly from the poorer ranks of society with nowhere to go, simply attached themselves to the moving army, picking up work and food where they could. Washington bemoaned the encumbrance of families traveling with the army, disrupting discipline, and making movement cumbersome. Had he evicted the women, however, he would have faced higher levels of desertion, since there were no provisions for the support of a soldier's wife and children. "Sometimes welcomed, oftentimes denigrated, they [women] were a visible, vocal, and patriotic part of the Continental Community."[24]

Life as an army follower was wretched. A Continental officer who witnessed the Continental army passing from New Jersey into New York State in 1780 commented that the women "were the ugliest in the world to be collected . . . their visage dress etc every way concordant to each other—some with two others with three & four children & few with none—I could not help pitying the poor innocent Creatures—their way of living and treatment with the many low & Scandalous examples ev'ry day shown them."[25] This dismal image is not the one publicized by the legend of Molly Pitcher at the Battle of Monmouth (see color plate 9). Pitcher's true identity is contested; some assert she was Mary Hays McCauley, the wife of a Pennsylvania foot soldier.[26] Others claim she is a composite of women with the army who gained recognition by taking up arms when the army was under fire. Whether bringing water to soldiers during the heat of the battle or fighting, the many "Molly Pitchers" of the Revolution were an army of intrepid women performing many tasks that the modern military does itself. In Monmouth County, women were listed along with men as people capable of bearing arms. A list dated April 30, 1780, "A Classed Returne [sic] of Captain James Green's Company," included the names of nineteen women intermixed with those of ninety-five men raised to help defend the frontier of the county.[27] In November 1778, a runaway teen-age girl, disguised as a boy, tried to enlist in the New Jersey Regiment in Newark. After suspicious officers searched her and found her to be a female, they marched her through town to the drumbeat of the "Whore's March."[28] It was a humiliating spectacle.

Nursing was an important but uncelebrated aspect of women's contributions to army life. While some nurses were hired by the Continental army, many camp followers routinely cared for the sick. Hospital nurses were relatively well paid. However, as more women sought such employment, wages declined to the point where nurses were paid less than stable hands.[29] Hospitals were unsanitary and understaffed. Many women nursed sick and wounded soldiers right in their own homes. Margaret Morris of Burlington, a lay medical practitioner, wrote, "A number of Sick & wounded brought into Town, calls upon us to extend a hand of Charity towards them . . . several of the Soldiers who were brought into Town Sick, have died, & it is feard the disorder by which they were affected, is infectious—."[30] Her Quaker ideals led her to serve wherever there was need and to bemoan the loss of life on both sides. Similarly, Ann Cooper Whitall (1716–1797), also a Quaker, cared for Hessian soldiers wounded during the Battle of Red Bank. She refused to leave her home during the battle, nursed and fed the soldiers in her home, and came to be known at the "Heroine of Red Bank."[31]

Households near army encampments were continually disrupted. The most comfortable homes were requisitioned for officers' housing; any home could become billets or a hospital. Hungry, unruly soldiers stole from local residents. After the Battle of Princeton, dysentery and smallpox attacked soldiers and civilians. During the Continental army's winter encampment in the Morristown area in 1777, smallpox attacked civilians and troops alike, and despite pleas from the local population regarding the risk of the procedure, Washington insisted that all be inoculated.[32] During the 1777 encampment, Theodosia Johnes Ford's large home was used by Captain Thomas Rodney's light infantry; then again, during the bitter winter of 1779 and 1780 it was taken over by Washington for his headquarters. Squeezed into two rooms with her four children, Ford carefully stored away valuables to protect them from the soldiers passing through.[33]

Families who lived along the main roads bore a special burden during the war. Advancing and retreating armies, whether patriot or loyalist, passed their houses, often desperately hungry.[34] Women and girls watched helplessly as food, livestock, firewood, clothing, and equipment disappeared. Impoverished soldiers accosted farm women on the road for handouts of food and drink, and farmwives stood by as soldiers wrung the necks of their precious fowl to fill a soldier's kettle or roasted the chickens over their kitchen fires.[35] The Continental army was so poorly supplied that women of wealth helped to support it. In 1780, women across the state raised $15,488 for George Washington to use as he thought proper.[36]

British and Hessian soldiers were particularly vicious in their acts of plunder and destruction.[37] Along the march, farms were systematically sacked by British troops, and homes were plundered for anything of value by officers and soldiers alike. In Piscataway, one observer reported hearing "their [the women's] lamentations as the soldiers carried off their furniture, scattered the feathers of beds to the winds, and piled up looking-glasses, with frying-pans in the same heap, by the roadside. The soldier

FIG. 45 Caldwell's Monument.
Reproduced in Benson J. Lossing,
Pictorial Field Book of the Revolution
(New York: Harper Brothers, 1850), 1:326.

would place a female camp follower as a guard upon the spoil, while he returned to add to the treasure."[38]

The British military strategy of looting and wholesale destruction of patriot property struck directly at women. Home, the stage for women's role in society, became their battlefield. In what Leonard Lundin describes as "the last heavy blow of the war" in New Jersey, the village of Connecticut Farms near Springfield was attacked on June 7, 1780, by troops commanded by General Wilhelm von Knyphousen. The troops burned "ten dwelling houses, the meeting house, the parsonage, the school house, and numerous barns, shops, sheds, bee houses, milk houses, and cow houses." The depredations included "the destruction of the Widow Clark's four hundred apple trees; extensive looting; the wanton murder of Mrs. Caldwell, wife of the Presbyterian minister, as she sat quietly with her children indoors" (fig. 45).[39]

Hannah Caldwell's husband was away during the attack, serving as a chaplain to Washington's army at Jockey Hollow. While he was absent, she managed their family of nine children, relocating when loyalist forces came near. On the day of her death, she had decided to remain in the parsonage with her two youngest children, another young girl, and her housekeeper. According to her housekeeper, a soldier shot at her through a window. Her home was then pillaged and burned. The British later claimed she was accidentally caught in the line of fire.

On occasion, women challenged enemy troops, earning a place in local legend. Annetje Van Wagenen Plume, for example, a wealthy Newark wife and mother, was alone on her farm while her husband was serving in the Continental army during the winter of 1777. The story goes that when British and Hessian troops occupied Newark that winter and Hessian soldiers invaded looking for supplies, she reportedly chastised them as they chopped firewood on her parlor floor. Watching a Hessian soldier sneak into her dairy room, she shut and bolted the door after him. Plume subsequently turned him over to patriot authority. As a souvenir, she was given his metal helmet, which she used as a door-knocker.[40]

Plume was fortunate in her encounter with the Hessian soldiers. Rape was a real danger to women, especially by British and Hessian troops. A diarist recounting the horrific Battle of Princeton noted that the plundering and vandalizing of local homes paled beside the sexual abuse of women: "another horrid outrage, . . . (which by a Great Defect in Human Nature that is against Justice and Reason) We Despise those poor Innocent Sufferers in this Brutal Crime Even as long as they live." He noted that, in peacetime, "many virtuous women have suffered in this Manner and kept it Secret for fear of making their lives miserable." In wartime the "unnatural Miscreants are sure of getting of [sic] with Impunity."[41] Loyalist troops developed a reputation for sexual brutality, and tales of young women fleeing to the woods to escape their predictable fate were widely circulated. Though most victims of rape were not inclined to testify, a committee of the Continental Congress was able to obtain some testimony.[42] Abigail Palmer from Hunterdon (age thirteen) reported that during the winter of 1777, she was with her grandfather at home. "A great number of soldiers Belonging to the British Army came there, when one of them said to the Deponent, I want to speak with you in the next Room & she told him she woud not go with him when he seizd hold of her & dragd her into a back Room and she screamd & begd of him to let her alone . . . her Grandfather also & Aunt intreated . . . telling them how Cruel & what a shame it was to Use a Girl of that Age after that manner, but finally three of Said Soldiers Ravished her." Apparently Abigail and another child were then taken to camp by the soldiers and gang-raped before an officer returned them home. Three other Hunterdon County girls testified to their similar abuse.[43]

Women of means fared better than the wives of farmers and laborers. When poet Annis Boudinot Stockton (color plate 13) had to flee from Morven, her estate in Princeton (see fig. 5), in November 1776, she was forced to abandon her library. Instead of securing her own papers, she went to the college to conceal the papers of the Whig Society, revealing what she most valued. Returning later, after Cornwallis had abandoned the ransacked Morven, she found only a few fragments of her poetry "culled from among soldiers straw."[44] Annis Stockton and her husband, Richard Stockton (see fig. 14), were part of the New Jersey elite. After Richard's death in 1781, Annis emerged as a public figure. She valorized the patriot cause in her published poetry, entertained major military and political figures at Morven, and forged a friendship with George and Martha Washington. In several of her poems, she extolled George Washington's leadership and virtues.[45]

Stockton's was a public voice of patriotic womanhood. A Federalist by conviction, she celebrated the military elite and American independence. Although she believed in the intellectual abilities of women and a role for women passing on republican virtues to their children, she did not advocate new rights for women, as did Massachusetts Federalist women, such as Abigail Adams and Judith Sargent Murray.[46] Perhaps, having experienced the chaos and tragedy of revolution firsthand, she wished only for peace and a return to normalcy. Advocating women's continued submission to men, she did not press for further social change. "[W]ith rev'rence treat in ev'ry place, The chosen patron of your future days; For when you shew him but the least neglect, Yourself you rifle of your due respect.—" she wrote to her niece in 1786.[47]

The 1776 New Jersey Constitution (see fig. 12) reflected Stockton's patriarchal perspective. New Jersey women gained none of the self-determination for which the Revolutionary War had been fought. The new state's laws affecting women aped the English common law principles of coverture—investing married women's property and civil rights in their husbands. New Jersey women of property, a fraction of the state's women, obtained the right to vote under the constitution, not as an early recognition of women's rights but by virtue of economic privilege. Some historians claim that this franchise resulted from oversight and sloppy constitutional drafting. Others suggest that this provision was later upheld by Quaker men seeking to expand their voting strength.[48] It is doubtful that most women even knew of their rights, although some exercised their short-lived franchise in local elections at the turn of the nineteenth century. In 1807, the legislature revoked this franchise. It took the next 113 years for women to regain the right to vote in New Jersey and considerably longer to untangle the bonds of coverture.

THE SURPRISING
NEW JERSEY LITERATURE OF
REVOLUTIONARY TIMES, 1750–1800

✱ ✱ ✱

MERRILL MAGUIRE SKAGGS

ALMOST ANYONE ASKING about New Jersey literature in Revolutionary times would begin first by looking for American patriots' writing: so
many crucial battles and retreats occurred in New Jersey that it has been called the
"Cockpit of the Revolution."[1] That nickname helpfully locates us in a place from
which one sees action closest. After finding the fighters, however, one is startled
to discover that more than one kind of revolution fomented in the state between
1750 and 1800. Of course, when it comes to rebelling patriots, military challenges,
governmental experiments (the Continental Congress met for a while at Princeton
to avoid confronting veterans marching to Philadelphia to demand back pay), and
voluble representatives of diverse population groups, New Jersey is at the center.
From its beginnings, New Jersey illustrated American pluralism, not homogeneity.
Even when prepared for diversity, however, one finds unexpected writers recording
New Jersey events. For example, in an age concerned predominantly about male
literacy, New Jersey boasted exceptional women writers.

As an example of literary good fortune, New Jersey could claim by the middle
of the eighteenth century writings by three remarkable women who represent that
half of the population often left out of historical accounts. Moreover, these three
women writers eloquently illustrate on paper three alternate attitudes toward the
written word at a time when most colonial women could not write.[2] Esther Edwards Burr (1732–1758) was a public wife par excellence, whose famous father (Jonathan Edwards) and husband (Aaron Burr), and eventually infamous son (Aaron Jr.),
made her an object of neighborhood scrutiny even beyond her death. She seems to

have been born without anonymity. In the public eye as she was, she kept a daily journal to gather her thoughts and wrench a little private time. Then she sent that journal, in the form of bundles of letters, to her friend Sarah Prince in Boston. She received Sarah's now-lost epistolary journal in return. But because the Prince family felt Esther was special, they saved her papers and eventually deposited them into the Harvard University library. These papers allow us day-by-day glimpses into the life of a woman required to serve as community role model at least from 1754 to 1757. In contrast, Esther's eventual friend and Princeton neighbor Annis Boudinot (1736–1801; color plate 13) chose a public role for herself. She was not only a woman poet (a category the age considered oxymoronic); she deliberately published her poetry while articulating political opinions in public conversations. Further, she was a committed patriot who eventually chose to save Whig papers from menacing British troops instead of rescuing her own poems. An even more unusual woman was Elizabeth Ashbridge (1713–1755). Her account of the "uncommon occurrences" of her life traces her story from runaway adolescent, to indentured servant, to Quaker preacher eventually honored on both sides of the Atlantic.[3]

Esther Edwards caught the eye of a family visitor named Aaron Burr when she was fourteen—the same age at which adolescent Elizabeth Ashbridge eloped. Yet Esther had not even been introduced to him when he returned as a widower, six years later, to ask for her hand in marriage. Since her family was then in difficult financial straits, barely making do between her father's pastorates, and since the match seemed fitting and the man seemed pleasant, she accepted Burr, who was sixteen years her senior, after five days of courtship. She followed him back to Newark, chaperoned by her mother. Following a Jersey wedding in his Presbyterian church, Esther served simultaneously as Burr's wife; mother of their two children, Sally and Aaron Jr.; hostess who fed and sometimes housed his ever-present visitors traveling on church business; and his adoring audience.

Although the household included servants and slaves (as did Morven, the Stockton estate where Annis Boudinot became mistress), Esther had, in fact, little time to write. While she complained that she never had any time to write at all, she at least enjoyed the education that prepared her to satisfy that writing impulse. Yet under the pressures in which she lived, she needed all the fortitude she could muster: Aaron Burr was first the leader of the New York evangelical synod, newly formed after its members had been ejected by Philadelphia conservatives; then he became the elected president of the College of New Jersey (later Princeton), which was established to serve evangelical youth. The college was to be located halfway on the post road from Philadelphia to New York, its position planned so it would miss no news from either direction. Esther's primary job was to maintain a cheerful home while Aaron did his work. However, because she came from an elite class—her grandfather founded Yale University and her father was an internationally recognized theologian—her letters were cherished until they were eventually published.[4] In 1757, her husband developed malaria while preaching the governor's funeral sermon in Elizabethtown and died three weeks later. Esther's father, Jonathan Edwards, was then elected Burr's presidential successor. But when he arrived to assume office, he and Esther were both fatally inoculated against the much-feared smallpox, and both died. Esther was only twenty-six years of age.

Esther's eighteenth-century spelling makes reading her journal feel like a transgressive act. Its value and charm, however, derive from the glimpses it gives of her daily routines: "I write just when I can get time. My dear you must needs think I can't get much, for I hav my Sally to tend, and domesteck affairs to see to, and company to wait of besides my sewing, [so] that I am realy hurried." This familiar voice of all overstressed women still resonates today: "you know I hant much time for reading now I have a young Child."[5]

When her husband leaves on business, she admits, "O my dear it seems as if Mr. Burr had been gon a little *Age*! and it is yet *but one Fortnight*!" When he returns, "to my unspeakable surprize my best self came home, all unexpected as much as the Man from the Moon." As soon as he arrives, however, "*All the World and his Wife comes here* but the worst of it is they hinder me from better company, I mean company at Boston, and that vexes me to death." And while the world soon includes the governor and his wife, who stop for tea, they remind Esther that "all the time I do get to write I steal." Yet in the cold winter months Esther observes, "Pray what do you think every body marrys in, or about Winter for? 'Tis quite merry, isn't it? I realy belive this for fear of laying cold, and for the want of a bedfellow. Well, my advice to such is the same with the Apostles, LET THEM MARRY."

When the family finally moved to the new site for the college at Princeton, Esther contended with ever-increasing hostess duties and annoyingly patronizing college tutors besides. One flare-up concerned her new friend Annis Boudinot, "a pleasant, sociable, Friendly Creture as ever you saw." A college instructor with "mean thoughts of Women" criticized Boudinot for writing about things she knew nothing of, such as friendship, for which women, he believed, "were hardly capable of anything so cool and rational." Esther indignantly "retorted several severe things upon him before he had time to speak again." But he got the last word: "One of the last things that he said was that he never in all his life knew or hear[d] of a woman that had a little more lerning then [common?] but it made her proud to such a degree that she was disgusfull [to] all her acquaintance."[6]

In contrast to Esther, Annis Boudinot could soon afford to be proud if she pleased, for she married Richard Stockton (see fig. 14), signer of the Declaration of Independence and builder of Morven, a major New Jersey mansion in Princeton, which is now a state government showplace (see fig. 5). Annis returned the favor of Esther Burr's friendship with a poem (punning on Samuel Richardson's *Clarissa*) entitled "To My Burrissa."[7] Annis Boudinot Stockton was once most important as the hostess who entertained any European "royalty" passing through East Jersey, who housed and entertained George and Martha Washington while the Continental Congress met in Princeton in 1783, and who, once widowed, earned the sobriquet the "Duchess of Morven." At present, she is much more interesting as the partisan poet whose verse concerning current political and business affairs was published in the newspapers and magazines of her time. The following is her defense of Alexander Hamilton, a key player in national politics and New Jersey history, the planner of industrial Paterson (and hence the archvillain who later haunted William Carlos Williams's imagination), and the founder of the national monetary system. From these poetic lines it is clear that the wealthy Stocktons looked favorably on Hamilton, considered the great stabilizer of American finances. Annis Boudinot Stockton writes,

For the GAZETTE OF THE UNITED STATES

Mr. Fenno,

The enclosed little *impromptu* on reading the several motions made against Mr. Hamilton. . . .

New-Jersey, March 12, 1793.

Have you not seen in saffron drest, *the Sun*
Burst thro' the crystal portals of the day;
While fogs, and blights, fast from his presence run—
And millions breathe but in his genial ray: . . .
So have I seen in our new hemisphere,
A star refulgent rise—whose potent ray
Pierc'd thro' the dread opaque that hover'd near,
And gave existance to our infant day.
So have I seen a man of honor shine,
And with nice rectitude begin his race;
Stringing each nerve with energy divine,
To save his country from the foul disgrace
Of blasted credit, and the *shades* of wealth—
Of broken faith, and infamy supreme;
Restoring strength, and confidence, and health,
To bankrupt funds, that were an empty name.
When vile intrigue, with all her little art,
And her dire nest of hornets, soon prepar'd
To vex the honest *veteran* to the heart—
And by surprize to throw him off his guard,

But fair Integrity repuls'd the foe,
And soon disolv'd the spells they had begun;
While well-earn'd fame with truths celestial glow,
Reflects new luster on *our* HAMILTON.[8]

By the standards of their time, the Stocktons were immensely wealthy and operated their estate with slave labor. Governors and statesmen consulted them for advice, and their gardens, which were modeled after Alexander Pope's Twickenham in
England, also made them famous. Many a misogynist editor might shrewdly choose
to publish Annis's verse and keep his "mean thoughts about women" to himself, unlike Esther Burr's uncivil college instructor.

But our last representative New Jersey woman writer enjoyed no such privilege.
In fact, the eventual prominence of Quaker Elizabeth Ashbridge, whose labor was
once sold and bought, helpfully highlights the radical divisions in New Jersey geography and demography. West Jersey was established as a Quaker refuge in 1676, before William Penn received his Pennsylvania charter in 1681. East Jersey, conversely,
effectively belonged to evangelical Presbyterians. For a short period when William
Franklin (see fig. 2) was royal governor, there were even two rival capitals: Burlington in the West and Perth Amboy in the East.

Literarily, Elizabeth Ashbridge commanded transatlantic attention when her
narrative was first privately circulated and then published in 1774. But her current
strong reputation can be traced to the inclusion of her journal, "Some Account of
the Fore-Part of the Life of Elizabeth Ashbridge," in recent American literature anthologies.[9] The subject of its own scholarly book after being recovered by Daniel B.
Shea (1990), the journal stands out among more formulaic Quaker spiritual narratives for its literary power.[10] That distinctiveness may or may not show the influence
of Samuel Richardson's novels, whose heroines Elizabeth Ashbridge resembles. Her
early life was dramatic. As an adolescent, she ran away with "the darling of my soul,"
only to be left a destitute widow and disowned by her father five months later.[11] She
lived with relatives in Ireland for five years, then decided she wished to emigrate
to America. Tricked into indentured servitude by a wicked woman kidnapper in
order to pay for her ship's passage, Elizabeth escaped the ship but then reboarded it
because she still wished to go to America. She overheard a mutiny scheme discussed
in the Gaelic she could now understand, in which sixty indentured Irish planned to
kill the English officers and seize the ship. Elizabeth warned the captain, who put
the ringleader ashore and saved his life and command. But the ungrateful captain
sold her as an indentured servant to a cruel master in New York, who assailed her
virtue and integrity. She barely escaped the disgrace of being stripped and publicly whipped by threatening to tell her master's wife of his unwelcome advances.
Then she experienced the temptations of the stage (for she was talented at singing

and dancing and had met theater people who admired her gifts). But she resisted and eventually purchased her last year's indenture contract with money earned at needlework. Soon Elizabeth married a second husband, whose name she omits, and discovered Quakerism while visiting relatives in Philadelphia. Her horrified husband fought her conversion by turning violent and hostile. Yet they both ended up in Mount Holly, a Quaker stronghold, each teaching a school. This personal account ends when her husband gets drunk, enlists in the army, sobers up and announces his scruple against fighting, is severely beaten, and soon dies. Elizabeth's course can then be followed through Quaker meeting minutes: she became a widely respected minister, married a wealthy Quaker named Aaron Ashbridge, and lived comfortably seven years before she felt moved to return and witness in Ireland, where she died.

What Elizabeth Ashbridge provides New Jersey literature is a kind of Horatio Alger heroine who makes her way from rags to riches. She commits bad mistakes and then finds her own solutions. She insists on her own kind of salvation and eventually enjoys power in her own right, which she has personally earned. She manages what few eighteenth-century women ever even imagined: travel, choices among a variety of lifestyles, close shaves and near-disasters averted, action, adventure. Thus these three women—the good wife Esther Edwards Burr, the politically savvy poet Annis Boudinot Stockton, and the activist preacher Elizabeth Ashbridge—supply in New Jersey literature a widely divergent and distinctive set of female prototypes.

Variety characterizes the New Jersey literature that reflects New Jersey life. Perhaps a poignant reminder of the state's political variety is the fact that the royal governor in office when the Revolution broke out was the son of the best-loved of all patriots, Benjamin Franklin. The letters between the two are part of the state's literature. When the fighting was over after the new nation had somewhat stabilized, William Franklin, released from prison, tried to reconnect with his now near-apotheosized father (fig. 46) serving in France. William wrote, "I uniformly acted from a Strong Sense of what I conceived my Duty to my King and Regard to my Country. . . . If I have been mistaken, I cannot help it. . . . It is an Error of Jedgment that the maturist reflection I am capable of cannot rectify, and I verily believe were the same Circumstances to occur Tommorrow, my Conduct would be exactly similar to what it was heretofore."[12]

Benjamin Franklin's response to his son reveals the unhealed hurt he still associated with this loyal Jersey Tory:

Passy, 16 August, 1784

DEAR SON: I received your letter of the 22d ultimo, and am glad to find that you desire to revive the affectionate intercourse that formerly existed between us.

FIG. 46 *Charles Willson Peale*, Benjamin Franklin, *n.d. Oil on canvas.*
Courtesy of the Historical Society of Pennsylvania Collection, Atwater Kent
Museum of Philadelphia.

It will be very agreeable to me; indeed, nothing has ever hurt me so much, and affected me with such keen sensations, as to find myself deserted in my old age by my only son; and not only deserted, but to find him taking up arms against me in a cause wherein my good fame, fortune and life, were all at stake. You conceived, you say, that your duty to your king and regard for your country required this. I ought not to blame you for differing in sentiment with me in public affairs. We are men, all subject to errors. Our opinions are not in our own power; they are formed and governed much by circumstances, that are often as inexplicable as they are irresistible. Your situation was such that few would have censured your remaining neuter, though there are natural duties which precede political ones, and cannot be extinguished by them.

This is a disagreeable subject. I drop it; and we will endeavor, as you propose, mutually to forget what has happened relating to it, as well as we can.

B. Franklin[13]

When Benjamin Franklin died in 1790, he disinherited William in his will. To the victors remained the spoils.

The ruptures produced by a revolution are no less painful because they seem inevitable. But where violent passions stir, passionate words and writings follow. As a major battleground in the fighting, New Jersey produced its commensurate share of revolutionary writing. Its best-known practitioner was the poet and journalist Philip Freneau, considered "the best of his time."[14] Like many an American writer who followed him (for example, Hawthorne, Thoreau, Twain, Cather, Faulkner), Freneau reconfigured his name and thus symbolically named himself. He was born to Pierre Fresneau and given an excellent education at Princeton, where he roomed with James Madison and socialized with Hugh Henry Brackenridge. The friends wrote "The Rising Glory of America" for their graduation exercises, and Bracken- ridge read it to hearty applause. Its style captures the characteristics of Freneau's future verse: portentous, public, prophetic. It begins:

> Now shall the adventurous muse attempt a strain
> More new, more noble, and more flush of fame
> Than all that went before—.

Thereafter, all the students' values are mentioned:

> Great is the praise of commerce, and the men
> Deserve our praise, who spread the undaunted sail,
> And traverse every sea . . . ;
> Yet all these bold designs to Science owe
> Their rise and glory—Hail, fair Science!

That popular exemplar of all virtues is acknowledged:

> Even now we boast
> Of *Franklin*, prince of all philosophy,
> A genius piercing as the electric fire.

All their lofty visions and recognitions bring the poem to its final claim:

> Haste, to your tents in fetters bring
> These slaves that serve their tyrant of a king,
> So just, so virtuous is your cause, I say
> Hell must prevail if Britain wins the day.[15]

Whether considering "The Prison Ship," such as the one on which he was incarcerated; "The Folly of Writing Poetry," such as he soon felt; or the inadequacies of his political enemies and Jefferson's, Freneau had a clear concept of hell and who belonged there, which he kept "at the white heat" for his poems.

New Jersey can claim to have generated at least some of the energy behind *The Federalist*, those eighty-five newspaper essays written to convince New Yorkers to ratify the Constitution; they have been called "the greatest American political discourse ever written."[16] New Jersey was where Alexander Hamilton, a key writer, wintered in Morristown's Ford Mansion (see fig. 23) in 1779 while he served as General Washington's private secretary. In that militarily slack season, he courted and eventually married Elizabeth Schuyler, who was visiting her aunt. The aunt, in turn, was married to Washington's surgeon and was quartered at the estate adjacent to Washington's headquarters in the Ford Mansion. James Madison, the second *Federalist* writer, was educated in Jersey at Princeton and there socialized with Philip Freneau, the state's patriotic versifier. Even John Jay, who wrote only five of the *Federalist* papers, married the daughter of William Livingston (color plate 1), commander of the New Jersey militia, who served until his death as first governor under the 1777 constitution. New Jersey helped link these three faces of "Publius," as they signed themselves, to each other. The document they produced together was regarded by Thomas Jefferson as "the best commentary on the principles of government . . . ever written."[17]

But finally, the most extraordinary literature either the state or the nation could display in the last half of the eighteenth century originated with two birthright Quakers.

John Woolman (see fig. 39) was a devout believer in the Inner Light. Thomas Paine (see fig. 3) exemplified what Melville called in *Moby-Dick* "fighting Quakers," or "Quakers with a vengeance."[18] Nevertheless, when the Revolution was in its worst predicament, Paine sat down in Newark, as legend has it, and wrote out his first *Crisis* paper on top of a drum. It begins with a paragraph so familiar and so brilliant that it can model the best persuasive rhetoric in English.

As a largely self-educated son of a Quaker corset-maker, Thomas Paine had known little but failure before he arrived in America in 1774 and settled in Philadelphia, where he wrote for magazines. He was the right man for the moment, however, and as indignation against Britain grew, he put all the frustrations of his own past into his pen as he wrote *Common Sense* (fig. 47), a call to arms and revolution published in January 1776. It quickly sold half a million copies. After fighting began, Paine served as personal secretary to General Nathanael Greene. When the patriots suffered a series of catastrophic losses and began to fall back across New Jersey in "the long retreat," Paine was present. As discouraged soldiers began to melt away home, Paine rallied the sore and disheveled ranks with a paper Washington ordered read to his troops. Its first paragraph became a classic:

> These are the times that try men's souls. The summer soldier and the sunshine patriot will, in this crisis, shrink from the service of his country; but he that stands it NOW, deserves the love and thanks of man and woman. Tyranny, like hell, is not easily conquered; yet we have this consolation with us, that the harder the conflict, the more glorious the triumph. What we obtain too cheap, we esteem too lightly:—'Tis dearness only that gives every thing its value.
>
> Heaven knows how to set a proper price upon its goods; and it would be strange indeed, if so celestial an article as FREEDOM should not be highly rated. Britain, with an army to enforce her tyranny, has declared, that she has a right (*not only* to TAX) but "*to BIND us in ALL CASES WHATSOEVER*," and if being *bound in that manner* is not slavery, then is there not such a thing as slavery upon earth. Even the expression is impious, for so unlimited a power can belong only to GOD.[19]

The first paragraph begins with one-syllable words that strike the ear like hammer blows. The last syllable of that sentence, strongest because it carries the weight of all that has preceded it, appeals to the spirit; by implication, it thus equates the adversary with the diabolic. The negative epithets "summer soldier" and "sunshine patriot" employ alliteration and assonance to catch the ear and point the derisive finger. Paine denigrates discouragement and extols virtue with a strong, active, oppositional verb—"stands" in contrast to "shrinks." He assures all that staunch patriots will be rewarded by receiving the love of men and women. He glamorizes resistance by equating tyranny with hell and struggle with glory. He reminds his audience of what they are fighting: British tyranny, false privilege and power, enslavement. Then he leaves it to God. And well he might, because nobody has written a better rallying cry. Its purpose is to overwhelm resistance, erase doubt, and embolden the fainthearted. It does the job. The rest of the pamphlet nurtures the emotional impulses that turn a man into a fighter. This emotional charge repeatedly sounds like iambic tetrameter blank verse:

"The heart that feels not now, is dead."
"I love the man that can smile in trouble."

"'Tis the business of little minds to shrink."
"Let them call me a rebel, and welcome."[20]

When one looks for the greatest poem of the Revolution, this declaration and the series it introduces are leading candidates.

Paine left Bordentown, New Jersey, in 1787 and returned to England and France to continue his fight. He was accused of treason in England, after which he was first honored, then imprisoned, by French radicals after assisting the French Revolution with *Rights of Man* (1792). Eventually, he was released from jail through the efforts of James Monroe. He returned to the United States to live in obscure poverty; was buried in New Rochelle, New York; and was eventually exhumed to be given a grander ceremonial burial back in England. There plans went awry, and his bones were lost. Philip Freneau wrote:

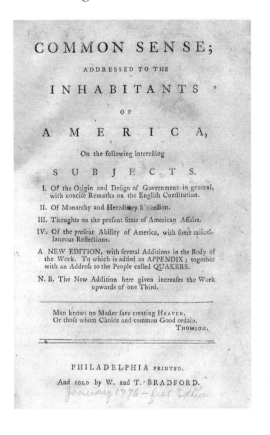

> Princes and kings decay and die
> And, instant, rise again;
> But this is not the case, trust me,
> With men like THOMAS PAINE.[21]

In a contrast as profound as the brain can comprehend, another Quaker son, John Woolman, produced a journal that still stands as a masterpiece of American colonial writing. But it is initially much harder for modern readers to appreciate because Woolman concentrated on making his words quiet, simple, plain, clear, and therefore unassailable. Over and over, as the best recent edition shows when it traces his revisions, he worked to make his prose blander,

FIG. 47 *Thomas Paine*, Common Sense, 1776. *From the Collections of the New Jersey Historical Society.*

devoid of distracting novelty and thus sounder, by deflating all possible emotion-charged vocabulary. His aim was not to stir but to instill conviction. While Paine was trying to energize the despondent spirits of discouraged troops through exhilarating rhetoric, Woolman was trying to facilitate the subtle workings of the spirit, the still, small voice of conscience. Paine strikes fire and rouses fury; Woolman's first sentence acknowledges "a motion of love."[22]

John Woolman's writing seems so antithetical to today's fashions that we need to start by reviewing the reasons he is considered so important. First, he is an obvious precursor to Henry David Thoreau and the doctrine of civil disobedience. Both Woolman and Thoreau respectfully declined to pay taxes levied to support a war of which they did not approve. But the parallels go a good deal further than that. Both men preferred to simplify their lifestyle and thus avoid the unnecessary work that could support a more elaborate or luxurious one. Both looked suspiciously on clothes that were too fashionable. Both believed no man had a right to make his way in the world while "sitting on another man's shoulders."[23] Both valued solitude and their own individual conscience. Both wanted "a life free of much entanglements," as Woolman said, in order to "get a living in a plain way, without the load of great business."[24] Both quit a prosperous trade once they had mastered it: Thoreau, pencilmaking; Woolman, shopkeeping.

The similarity between the two helps us easily to see the difference created by opposite and dominant verbal tones. Thoreau thunders, while Woolman approaches slaveholders so "tenderly" that he can say, "I expressed to him what rested on my mind, which he took kindly."[25] Thoreau is sharp-tongued, witty, cantankerous, curmudgeonly, full of verbal thrusts and parries, the master of satiric flourishes. Woolman works to make his words and manner unabrasive and undogmatic. It cost Thoreau nothing to say no, as Emerson pointed out in his funeral elegy. But contradicting or refusing another cost Woolman dearly. Thoreau laid down eternal truth, and Woolman "walked in uprightness before God" and inched his way forward slowly. Thoreau famously and contemptuously observed that "the mass of men live lives of quiet desperation," while Woolman admitted that "my heart was tender and often contrite, and a universal love to my fellow creatures increased in me."[26] Thoreau advised, "However mean your life is, meet it and live it; do not shun it and call it hard names. It is not so bad as you are."[27] Woolman acknowledged "man as the most noble amongst those [creatures] that are visible."[28]

Mostly, however, both Woolman and Thoreau are alike when they find no way to tolerate slavery and keep a sense of personal integrity. That issue is the key to Woolman's greatness, for his ability to empathize with the unfortunate is remarkable. In fact, however, his work is done not among the outcast and marginalized slaves but among comfortable, slaveholding Quakers who struggle with vital issues of their day: how to respond when under attack; how to regard the institution of slavery when one's estate depends on it; how to act responsibly toward the poor; how to be a good citizen when one does not approve of the acts of one's government; how to treat the culturally unfathomable—for example, the Native Americans who are scalping one's acquaintances.

Perhaps one answer lies in Woolman's life goals: "to be acquainted with operations of divine love" and to write down "the goodness of God." He believed that there was a "principle in the human mind which incites to exercise goodness toward every living creature," and that is what he tried to do.[29] Given the challenges of life in his time, the fascination of this journal has to do with how he managed to "live comfortably" and be quiet.

Woolman was born in Burlington County and moved from his father's house to Mount Holly when he was twenty-one. There he clerked for a shop owner and then ran his own store until it seemed to be generating unnecessary profits. At that point, he became a tailor and found he could earn enough by tailoring and writing legal documents, like wills, to support his family. Rather soon, however, he became an authorized Quaker minister and traveled throughout the colonies speaking and "reasoning together" with Friends, especially about slavery. His leadings eventually encouraged the Philadelphia Yearly Meeting to disapprove owning slaves altogether, although many prosperous Quakers held them. When asked to write a will in which a slave would be disposed of, he replied, "I cannot write thy will without breaking my own peace." Once he saw that "liberty was the natural right of all men equally," the question was settled. The value of the journal is that it traces the very long process through which Woolman worked out his conclusion and then persuaded others of it through "divine love and a true sympathizing tenderness of heart [that] prevailed at times in this service."[30] He is a primary reason that slavery was eventually abolished in these states.

Woolman was held in highest respect by most citizens of Philadelphia and West Jersey. He, in turn, knew the region's leaders, including Aaron Ashbridge, third husband of Elizabeth Ashbridge, whom he mentions as his friend. He did not impose on such friendships and announced a rule one wishes the nation understood better: "In three hundred minutes are five hours, and he that improperly detains three hundred people one minute, besides other evils that attend it, does an injury like that of imprisoning one man five hours without cause."[31] Such Quaker common sense could steady New Jersey culture today.

THE HISTORICAL GEOGRAPHY
AND ARCHAEOLOGY OF THE
REVOLUTIONARY WAR IN NEW JERSEY

★ ★ ★

RICHARD W. HUNTER AND IAN C. G. BURROW

Before we present you the matters of fact, it is fit to offer to your view the Stage whereon they were acted, for as Geography without History seemeth a carkasse without motion, so History without Geography, wandreth as a vagrant without a certaine habitation.

—CAPTAIN JOHN SMITH, *GENERALL HISTORIE OF VIRGINIA,
NEW-ENGLAND AND THE SUMMER ISLES,* 1624

NEW JERSEY'S ROLE IN the Revolutionary War is an abiding interest of many scholars, antiquarians and collectors, and countless reenactors and residents. This interest is kindled mostly through academic and popular writing, movies, school curricula, annual celebratory events, and interpretive programs at a handful of well-known, publicly owned historic sites.[1] In this most densely populated state in the nation, over the past century or more suburban development, urban redevelopment, and an expanding infrastructure have taken their toll on the land at an increasingly disruptive and ever-quickening pace, and sites associated with the events of the Revolutionary War have been among those affected.[2] With the earth so well turned and frequently obscured, it is difficult to appreciate that meaningful physical traces of the American Revolution still lie all around us in the landscape and that new and valuable information about the military conflicts, living conditions, and material culture of the period may yet reside in the ground. It is the purpose of this essay, through the two closely related disciplines of historical geography and archaeology, to elicit this "land visibility" of the Revolutionary War in New Jersey.[3]

The history of the Revolutionary War in New Jersey has been traditionally cast and recast through the study of the written record, chiefly through analysis of primary documents such as the orders and correspondence of American, British, Hessian, and French officers; the firsthand accounts of soldiers; political statements; and private letters. One class of documentary material in particular, historic maps and plans, provides a critical point of entry for both historical geographers and archaeologists interested in the Revolutionary War.[4] For the historical geographer, these informative and usually quite accurate documents can support a broad-based consideration of the cultural landscape and its constituent features (e.g., settlements, roads, river crossings, mills, industrial sites) and allow their relation to military strategy and maneuvers. For the archaeologist, historic maps and plans are of great value in locating and defining sites on the ground and a tool to be used in combination with other exploratory techniques, notably remote sensing and excavation.

An outcome of most archaeological endeavor in the field is the recovery of items of material culture—principally artifacts, skeletal remains, food waste, and environmental data.[5] While important in their own right as tangible evidence of the period, such materials may be systematically and scientifically analyzed, often providing insights not recoverable from a reading of the documentary record. Ultimately, it is the integration of these various lines of inquiry—archival study, historical geography, archaeology, material culture analysis—that will supply the most balanced and complete reconstruction of New Jersey's role as the "Crossroads of the American Revolution."

The Ebb and Flow of War in the Landscape

Making sense of the swirling events that occurred on the ground in the Middle colonies between the fall of 1776 and the summer of 1778, and then continuing on with lessening intensity, punctuated by occasional savage flare-ups, until the British abandonment of New York in November 1783, is no easy task. Lying at the heart of the conflict for much of this time and straddling several strategic land routes and navigable rivers between the key cities of Philadelphia and New York, New Jersey was the scene of a dizzying sequence of military advances and retreats, battles and raids, and occupations and evacuations.[6] All the while, the opposing forces also sought to develop and maintain sources of war matériel and lines of supply and to establish safe zones where troops could encamp and military strength could be built up. For seven long years, the Delaware and Hudson valleys, and the intervening territory that includes all of New Jersey, formed a zone of constantly and subtly shifting American and British control. As a New Jersey civilian during this turbulent period, to pursue a traditional family-based rural existence working on the land or to live and work in New Jersey's small towns and villages was a disconcerting experience indeed, fraught with uncertainty and distrust.

As it was for people at the time, be they military strategist or ordinary farmworker, for us today to mentally impose order on the whirling patterns of a multifaceted and fast-moving war, a grasp of New Jersey's geography is essential. Understanding the fundamental underlying physiography of the state, in particular its topography, helps bring the Revolutionary War into sharper focus, not only in a regional sense that can elucidate the relationship of military strategy and cultural landscape but also at the local level, where one may understand better, for example, why General George Washington and his officers might select a particular house for an overnight stay or why a particular mill might be selected as the subject of a British or American raid.

Just as the Philadelphia–New York corridor—that funnel of land transportation across the waist of New Jersey—continues to drive the regional economy to this day, so, too, was this seventy-five-mile-long strip of land connecting the two metropolises via the heads of navigation on the Delaware and Raritan rivers of paramount importance throughout the Revolutionary War. In the year between the fall of 1776 and the fall of 1777, with the British pushing south from Canada, the much longer Hudson River/Champlain Valley corridor may perhaps lay claim to an equal or greater strategic importance in military planning. However, in the broader and longer context of the entire war, the more compelling strategic interest for both American and British forces was unimpeded control of the main southwest-northeast-trending thoroughfares across central New Jersey and of the navigation of the Lower and Middle Delaware Valley, the Lower Raritan Valley and Raritan Bay, and New York's bays and shipping channels. It was only in the latter part of the war, when the British concentrated on the campaign in the southern colonies, that this area lost some of its centrality to the conduct of the war.

Indeed, even more than control of the major population centers at either end of the corridor (Philadelphia, New York) and the smaller towns and ports along its route (Burlington, Bordentown, Lamberton, Trenton, Princeton, Kingston, Raritan Landing, New Brunswick, Perth Amboy, Elizabethtown, Newark), whose loyalties and overlordship shifted back and forth, it was movement within the corridor itself that was at issue.[7] The key line of communication here was the King's Highway between Trenton and New Brunswick, with its northeasterly extensions to Perth Amboy, Elizabethtown, and Newark, which the British forces ostensibly controlled yet never felt secure enough in the cat-and-mouse period between December 1776 and September 1777 to use for a full-scale land assault on Philadelphia from New York.[8] Despite the existence of barracks at Trenton and New Brunswick, moving a large military force across central New Jersey was not logistically straightforward.[9] Crossing either the Raritan River at New Brunswick or the Delaware at Trenton was an awkward ferrying or fording prospect, as was ship-to-shore disembarkation at New Brunswick or shore-to-ship embarkation at Lamberton.[10] Along the highway itself between New Brunswick and Trenton, there were potentially difficult river crossings to negotiate at several locations, notably the Millstone River in Kingston, Stony Brook just outside Princeton, and Shabakunk Creek near Maidenhead (modern-day Lawrenceville).[11]

All the while, for five successive winters beginning in 1776–1777, Washington's forces lurked in the rolling hills of the Piedmont in New Jersey and Pennsylvania, adjacent to and immediately northwest of the corridor, well positioned to intervene in the event of large-scale British troop movements and with the capability of inflicting small-scale, debilitating, guerrilla-style raids on British patrols and sources of support. This was terrain that the American forces knew well and where they could count on support from the local citizenry. Only in northeastern New Jersey, directly across the Hudson from British-occupied New York City (in what was at the time eastern Bergen, Essex, and Middlesex counties), and in northern Monmouth County across Raritan Bay were there appreciable numbers of loyalists working against the patriot cause. From the relative security of the hills and valleys in Morris, Hunterdon, and Somerset counties, American forces could encamp and train safely and monitor British activity in the lowland of the corridor, making use most notably of vantage points along the First Watchung ridge. They also had access to milled goods (flour, meal, lumber, and fulled cloth) being produced along the North and South branches of the Raritan River and the headwaters of the Passaic River. Still more important, through its control of the iron-rich New Jersey Highlands and key water-powered industrial sites, the Continental army had the means to supply itself with munitions, wagons, and other items of military equipment.

Movement across the Piedmont and Highlands was considerably more difficult than along the main Trenton–to–New Brunswick corridor, but American forces made effective use of river corridors and the rudimentary road network, developing a familiarity with the terrain far beyond that which was attainable by the British. Riverbank routes along the North Branch and the Ramapo, for example, and cross-country alignments, such as that followed by the Old York Road, facilitated quite rapid American movement in the landscape, for the most part unobserved by the British. The importance of the road network to the American cause is clearly borne out in the extensive series of road maps surveyed for Washington by Robert Erskine and Simeon DeWitt between 1777 and 1781.[12] Mostly surveyed at a scale of one inch to a half mile and giving great attention to road-river relationships, mills, and taverns, these maps focus principally on Hunterdon, Somerset, and Morris counties and the western portions of Middlesex, Essex, and Bergen counties, that is, the area of American control and the northwestern side of the corridor where British control was most in dispute (fig. 48).

The Erskine and DeWitt maps of central New Jersey contrast noticeably with the less detailed maps of the same area by John Hills, cartographer to the British general Sir Henry Clinton, many of which were copied in New York from earlier

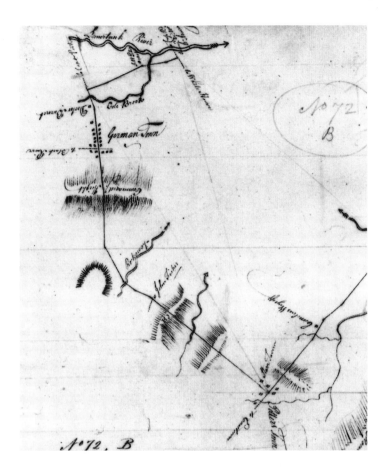

FIG. 48 *Robert Erskine*, Road from Garrison's Tavern to Somerset Ct.
H[ous]e and from Somerset to Van Nep's Mill & from Van Nep's Mill to
Boundbrook, *1779. Collection of the New-York Historical Society.*

surveys produced for the East Jersey proprietors in the 1760s (fig. 49).[13] The American knowledge of the central New Jersey landscape was likely a valuable asset in
planning the itinerary of General Rochambeau's French army in its march from
Newport, Rhode Island, to Yorktown, Virginia, in the late summer of 1781 and returning northward roughly a year later. This route traversed areas well mapped by
Erskine and DeWitt, following the Ramapo Valley; passing through Whippany,
Morristown, and Basking Ridge; and then heading up the Millstone Valley to join
the main Trenton–New Brunswick corridor at Princeton.

Figure 50 presents the military action of the Revolutionary War in New Jersey
in the context of the state's physiographic foundations and defines a generalized
"zone of conflict."[14] This zone is essentially the area in which the local population

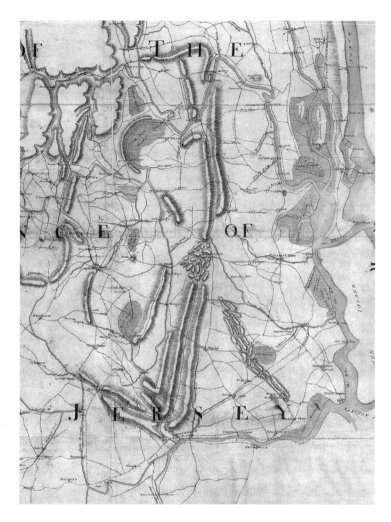

FIG. 49 *John Hills,* A Sketch of the Northern Parts of New Jersey, *1781.*
Reproduced in Peter J. Guthorn, comp., A Collection of Plans's Etc. Etc. In the
Province of New Jersey by John Hills, Asst. Engr. (Brielle, N.J.: Portolan, 1976).

either directly experienced military action in the form of hostile troop movements, looting, Tory and patriot conflicts, and battles and skirmishes or at least was seriously and frequently at risk of experiencing such events. Of course, there were degrees of severity of war experience within this zone. The so-called neutral ground of northeastern New Jersey, for example, was beset by almost constant insecurity, punctuated by major actions, from the fall of 1776 through to 1781. Much the same can be said of the northeastern coastal parts of Monmouth County on the south side of Raritan Bay. The Atlantic coast communities were also exposed to British

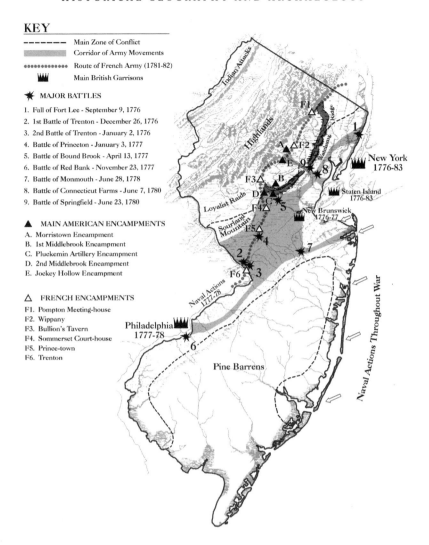

KEY

- ------- Main Zone of Conflict
- ▨ Corridor of Army Movements
- •••••••••• Route of French Army (1781-82)
- ♛ Main British Garrisons

✳ MAJOR BATTLES

1. Fall of Fort Lee - September 9, 1776
2. 1st Battle of Trenton - December 26, 1776
3. 2nd Battle of Trenton - January 2, 1776
4. Battle of Princeton - January 3, 1777
5. Battle of Bound Brook - April 13, 1777
6. Battle of Red Bank - November 23, 1777
7. Battle of Monmouth - June 28, 1778
8. Battle of Connecticut Farms - June 7, 1780
9. Battle of Springfield - June 23, 1780

▲ MAIN AMERICAN ENCAMPMENTS

A. Morristown Encampment
B. 1st Middlebrook Encampment
C. Pluckemin Artillery Encampment
D. 2nd Middlebrook Encampment
E. Jockey Hollow Encampment

△ FRENCH ENCAMPMENTS

F1. Pompton Meeting-house
F2. Wippany
F3. Bullion's Tavern
F4. Sommerset Court-house
F5. Prince-town
F6. Trenton

FIG. 50 Map Showing the Main Zone of Conflict, Major Battles and Principal Encampments in New Jersey during the Revolutionary War, 2004. *Hunter Research, Inc.*

and Tory raids and periodic naval engagements. The Delaware Valley and central New Jersey saw dramatic and destructive episodes over the winter of 1776–1777, on various occasions in the spring and summer of 1777, and again between the fall of 1777, when the British finally took Philadelphia, through the summer of 1778, when they evacuated the city, fought the Battle of Monmouth, and withdrew to New York City. With the exception of the British naval raid on the port of Chestnut Neck on the Mullica River in October 1778, southern and central New Jersey escaped further action for the remainder of the war following the Battle of Monmouth.

Despite the fact that large sections of northwestern and southeastern New Jersey were not directly affected by military events, it is clear that the majority of the population were nevertheless truly in the "line of fire." There was no significant population in the Pinelands, and substantial areas of northwestern New Jersey were either unsettled or only lightly so.[15] However, even these latter areas were vulnerable to attacks by loyalists and American Indians at various times.

In essence, the zone of conflict is defined by the same factors that had molded the settlement patterns of the colony for the preceding 150 years—namely, the productive agricultural soils and gentle topography of the Inner Coastal Plain and lowland Piedmont and the accessing of these areas through fall-line port settlements that sprang up along the Delaware, Raritan, and Lower Hudson. In the center of this zone is the Delaware-Raritan watershed that straddles, as noted above, the primary communication corridor between Philadelphia and New York. The main army movements shown in figure 50 naturally reflect the relative ease of travel and availability of provisions in this zone. The one exception here is the route of the French army in 1781 and 1782, which moved through highland country well to the west of New York to avoid detection and intervention by the New York garrison.

The northwestern boundary of the zone of conflict is the most strongly defined, both physiographically and militarily. The First Watchung Mountain marked the effective western limit of British military capability in the "neutral ground" throughout the war, and all efforts to breach this line—as at the Battle of Bound Brook in April 1777 and the Battles of Springfield and Connecticut Farms in June 1780—were stymied by American forces based in the Morristown area and along the Watchungs.

Military Encampments and Installations

Between the autumn of 1776, when the Continental army retreated southwest across New Jersey from Fort Lee into Pennsylvania, and the late summer of 1782, when the New Jersey Brigade finally vacated Jockey Hollow, numerous American encampments were established within New Jersey, mostly in the hills to the northwest of the Philadelphia–New York corridor (table 1). Some took the form of long-term permanent quarters occupied for many months and reoccupied over successive winters, as at Jockey Hollow and Middlebrook. Others were camps of shorter duration, a few days or weeks, housing troops that lay in wait, observing British movements along the Philadelphia–New York corridor, as was the case with General Anthony Wayne's brigade encampment set up in the early summer of 1777 on the First Watchung ridge overlooking Bound Brook. Still others were brief overnight stops made by American forces in advance or retreat, on their way to or from battle. In most instances, officers were separately quartered, usually in the homes of private citizens sympathetic to the patriot cause. The American forces threw up fortifications in conjunction with some of the longer-term encampments, as in the case of Fort Non-sense, outside Morristown. They also rapidly erected defenses at Billingsport at the mouth of Mantua Creek in July 1776, at Fort Lee on the Palisades toward the end of the same year, and at Fort Mercer on the Delaware River in 1777 (fig. 51), all to stem the tide of British advances.

While American troops fighting the Revolutionary War in New Jersey nec-essarily camped out, the British and their German (mostly Hessian) auxiliaries for the most part stayed in. For their long-term quarters, most British and Hes-sian troops were billeted in towns and fortifications that were under the control of the crown (e.g., Elizabethtown, Perth Amboy, Sandy Hook, New Brunswick, Princeton, Trenton, and Burlington)—in barracks, where these existed, or else in institutional buildings and private dwellings. Staten Island, throughout the war; New York City, from the time of its capture by the British in the late summer of 1776; and Philadelphia, during its nine months of British occupation in 1777–1778, all functioned as major military bases supporting British operations in New Jersey and elsewhere. Relatively few British encampments were made in the New Jersey countryside, and then most often as military forces gathered for or retreated from

TABLE I *Main Encampments of the Continental Army in New Jersey*

DATE OCCUPIED	NAME/LOCATION	ESTIMATED MAXIMUM TROOP STRENGTH	NOTES
January–May, 1777	Morristown	3,500	Various locations in Morristown vicinity
May–July, 1777	Middlebrook	7,500*	Summer encampment between First & Second Watchung ridges
December, 1778 – May, 1779	Middlebrook	10,000	Winter encampment in the Raritan Valley, north & west of Bound Brook
December, 1778 – June, 1779	Pluckemin	1,000	Artillery encampment
December 1779	Jockey Hollow	11,000	South of Morristown

No firm estimate available

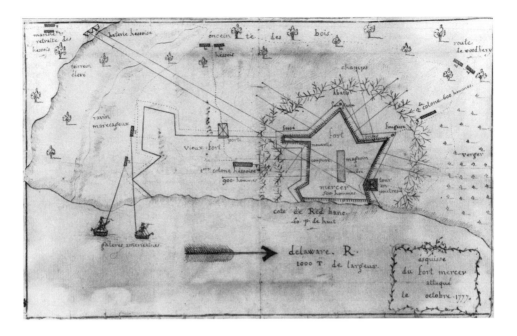

FIG. 51 *Chevalier Thomas Antoine Mauduit du Plessis (attrib.),* Esquisse du
fort mercier attaque, le octobre 1777. *Historical Society of Pennsylvania.*

battle. Again, officers typically stayed in the homes of sympathizers; the higher
their rank, the grander their lodgings. In the late summers of 1781 and 1782, a very
specific and select group of short-term encampment sites accompanied the French
army's marches through New Jersey.

With the exception of the Old Barracks in Trenton, a handful of institutional
buildings that briefly served as military quarters (such as Nassau Hall in Princeton;
see fig. 25), and a number of farmhouses and dwellings that provided accommodations for military officers or served as temporary outposts, there are very few surviving
buildings that can be directly associated with the military maneuvers and stationing of
troops during the Revolutionary War.[16] Reconstructed earthworks may be viewed at a
few fortifications (e.g., Fort Lee, Fort Nonsense, and Fort Mercer) and re-creations of
huts at Jockey Hollow, but most surviving physical evidence of military encampments
and installations in New Jersey lies below ground. Theoretically, in archaeological
terms, the longer the occupation, the more substantive the material culture remains
should be. Clearly, an overnight bivouac will not leave as powerful an archaeological
expression as months of soldierly occupation within a formally laid out encampment.
Indeed, the more permanent encampments were laid out according to well-established
plans, which allows for a measure of predictability in their archaeological exploration
(fig. 52). However, two-and-a-quarter centuries later, the survival situation is vastly

more complicated than this and has inevitably been affected by subsequent land use (chiefly, residential and commercial development and highway construction), by looters, and even by well-meaning but confusing interpretation and reconstruction.

The best-known American winter encampments of the Revolutionary War in New Jersey occurred in the Morristown area. In January 1777, fresh from dealing the British surprise defeats in Trenton and Princeton, a portion of the Continental army wintered in the Loantaka Brook valley between Madison and Morristown, with most officers and some rank and file lodging in nearby homes. Washington himself resided much of the winter at the Arnold Tavern in Morristown (see fig. 27). While extensive archaeological investigation has taken place at Valley Forge, Pennsylvania, where the bulk of the American forces spent the extraordinarily severe winter of 1777–1778, a systematic exploration of the Loantaka Brook valley for evidence of this encampment has yet to be conducted.[17] The one location connected to this first Morristown area encampment that has been the subject of archaeological study is Fort Nonsense, a redoubt built overlooking Morristown in the spring of 1777, which was excavated in the 1930s by the National Park Service with the help of Civilian Conservation Corps (CCC) labor. Some overly energetic trenching, with all too little documentation, preceded some elaborate reconstruction of the earthworks that has greatly complicated subsequent archaeological interpretation of the site.[18]

Beginning in December 1779 and stretching over three successive winters up until August 1782, a much more substantial American encampment was set up at Jockey Hollow, roughly three miles southwest of Morristown. In the first of these winters, again severe, more than 10,000 troops struggled to survive with inadequate provisions. Outlying camps were also established at Mount Kemble and near Mendham, while Washington established his headquarters in Morristown at the Ford Mansion (see fig. 23). Jockey Hollow and several related sites have been under National Park Service management since the early 1930s, and several programs of archaeological

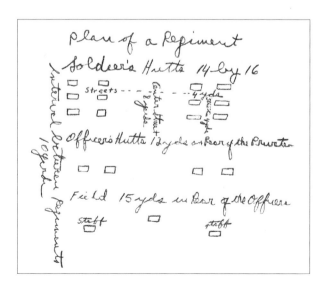

FIG. 52 *Joseph Harmar,* Hutting Plan for the 5th Pennsylvania Regiment at the Second Middlebrook Encampment, December 1778. *Redrawn from a sketch in the Harmar Manuscripts, William L. Clements Library, University of Michigan, Ann Arbor.*

excavation have been mounted since that time. Beginning with some CCC-assisted investigations, this work has evolved and become progressively more sophisticated, providing a proper basis for reconstruction and interpretation of important features of the site, such as the soldiers' huts, and allowing for an improved understanding of living conditions through analysis of food remains.[19]

No less important strategically were the Continental army encampments ten to twelve miles south of Jockey Hollow, where the First Watchung range noses southward almost to the Raritan River. Control of this upland position enabled the Americans to watch the lowland extending from Bound Brook toward Princeton, New Brunswick, and the King's Highway. In late May 1777, soon after the Battle of Bound Brook, the Americans deployed here to gauge the British resolve to advance on Philadelphia by land. Washington moved the bulk of the army from Morristown to the well-protected valley of the East and West Branches of Middle Brook between the First and Second Watchung ridges (today's Washington Valley), and two brigades took up forward positions on the brow of the first ridge. This occupation—the Middlebrook summer encampment—lasted only about six weeks. In mid-June 10,000 British and Hessian troops entered the Millstone Valley, but they neither continued toward Philadelphia nor lured the Americans down from the heights. A week later they retired to New Brunswick and Staten Island with the Continentals in intermittent pursuit. The Americans returned to Morristown in early July.

The main focus of the Middlebrook summer encampment has received little professional archaeological attention. However, one of the forward positions, General Wayne's encampment, has been investigated in some depth. About 1,400 men camped on the rim and back slope of the First Watchung ridge between Chimney Rock and present-day Vosseller Avenue. Although development and scavenging have depleted archaeological evidence over the years, recent exploration has helped to delimit and characterize the site.[20] The core of Wayne's brigade encampment site is now fortunately owned by Somerset County, its preservation assured.

In December 1778, with far fewer British troops in central New Jersey, a larger and longer-lived Continental army presence was established about a mile from Wayne's earlier position. This was the Middlebrook winter encampment.[21] Troops were quartered in huts on the slopes of the First Watchung Mountain on both sides of Middle Brook, just below Chimney Rock gorge. The Pennsylvania Line was across the Raritan, near today's Manville. Signal towers atop the First Watchung ridge alerted Middlebrook to incidents throughout the Raritan Valley and as distant as Bergen County and northern Monmouth County. The Wallace House in the nearby village of Raritan became Washington's headquarters; other officers lodged in several local farmhouses.[22]

Most of the site of the Middlebrook winter encampment now lies obscured and largely destroyed beneath the commercial and residential properties that line U.S.

Route 22 in Bridgewater Township, although it is not impossible that some patches of intact archaeological remains may yet come to light.[23] Farther north, quarrying and stone-crushing operations along the ridge, and continuing residential growth within Washington Valley, have also reduced the potential for archaeological survival. Sadly, while Somerset County's recent acquisition of the remainder of the site of Wayne's brigade encampment salvages some valuable Revolutionary War space in this strategic zone, the bulk of the Middlebrook encampments will never experience the type of preservation, field investigation, or interpretive treatment that has been accorded Jockey Hollow.

In the same winter that Washington installed the main body of the American army at Middlebrook, he also instructed General Henry Knox to develop an artillery training facility roughly seven miles to the northwest, on the west-facing lower slope of the First Watchung ridge overlooking the hamlet of Pluckemin (fig. 53). Knox's artillery camp was operational into the spring of 1779 and continued in use into the following year, first as a depot and then as a hospital. After fading into obscurity through the nineteenth century as successional vegetation reclaimed the hillside, this important site was partially rediscovered in 1916–1917 by the well-

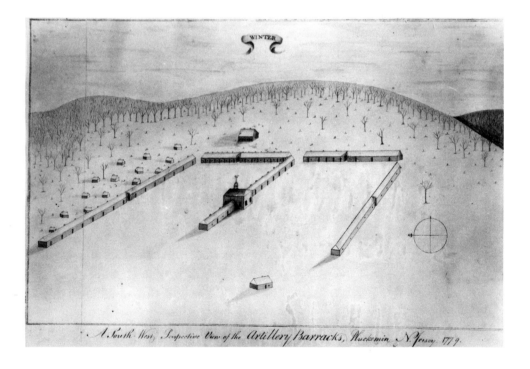

FIG. 53 *J. Lillie*, A South-West Perspective View of the Artillery Barracks, Pluckemin, N. Jersey. *1779. Pen sketch. Courtesy of Morristown National Historical Park.*

known avocational archaeologist Max Schrabisch, whose explorations were funded by wealthy local landowner Grant Schley. Unfortunately, Schrabisch did not fully report his finds, and it took another phase of rediscovery between 1979 and 1986, led by archaeologist John Seidel and historian Cliff Sekel, to establish the basic outline and critical features of the camp.[24]

While Schrabisch had approached the task of finding Knox's artillery camp through judgmentally placed trenches and test pits, which enabled him to find several soldiers' huts and a possible blacksmith shop, Seidel adopted a more revealing "open area" excavation strategy, along with carefully controlled remote sensing, elevated photography, and three-dimensional recording of artifacts. This latter program of study successfully related the field evidence to a drawing of the camp made in 1779 and identified a line of barracks, the main academy building, an armorer's shop, numerous waste disposal features, and many items of military equipment.[25] Support for this work came from a specially created nonprofit organization and a local developer. The developer, sensitive to the importance of the site, adjusted plans for residential development to preserve and avoid the core of the camp.

Undisputed archaeological traces of British and Hessian encampment and occupation activity in New Jersey during the Revolutionary War are hard to come by. In part, this may be attributed to the prevailing British and Hessian presence in the towns along the Philadelphia–New York corridor and their relative absence from the countryside in comparison with the American forces. In the towns, virtually all of which have continued to evolve and redevelop down to the present, much of the archaeological information base has been dispersed. It is also virtually impossible to isolate Revolutionary War–era archaeological deposits from occupation levels dating from the decades immediately preceding and following the conflict. Nevertheless, valuable, if somewhat fragmentary, data has been elicited from some key sites where the Revolutionary War years lie within a slice of a much longer sequence of occupation.

Archaeological work performed at the Old Barracks in Trenton in the 1980s and 1990s in connection with the restoration of both the barracks and the neighboring New Jersey statehouse has produced important information about the design of the building, parade ground, and surrounding terrain, as well as a wealth of artifacts, surprisingly few of which are of military derivation. The paucity of military artifacts from the surface of the parade ground has led excavators to suggest that this important space was swept clean on a regular basis. Excavations and observations in the basement of the building encountered several strata and pit deposits, some of which at least probably relate to the use of the building by the Continental army in the latter part of the war. A single sherd of a type of ceramic known as "colono ware" hints at the presence of African Americans from the southern colonies working at the barracks at this time. Another exceptional artifact recovered from the excavations is a ceramic inset from a sleeve link inscribed "Wilkes & Liberty No.

45," a telling testament to the Revolutionary spirit of the times immediately before and during the war.[26]

Excavations in and just outside the small port community of Raritan Landing, a few miles upstream from New Brunswick on the north bank of the Raritan River, have produced evidence of British military occupation in the area, which was at its peak in 1777 and early 1778. Controlled metal detection and ground penetrating radar survey, coupled with limited manual excavation and geographic information systems (GIS) mapping, defined a winter encampment location in the woods on the bluffs above the landing, while Revolutionary War artifacts from sites excavated along River Road support the hypothesis that the British occupied the port as a forward military post designed to block American advances from the Bound Brook area.[27] In the recently completed data recovery excavations conducted in connection with the improvement of the New Jersey Route 18/Metlars Lane intersection, one particular house site, on Lot 20, which produced numerous arms-related artifacts (including musket balls and brass and iron gun parts), was used and probably destroyed during the British occupation of Raritan Landing in 1777.[28] Archaeological explorations at Sandy Hook, which was fortified and occupied by the British and loyalists throughout the war, have yielded occasional military artifacts from the period, but the overwhelming preponderance of archaeological information from this topographically fluctuating setting relates to its later use as a proving ground and as the site of Fort Hancock.

Although some of the longer-term American encampments, notably Jockey Hollow and Pluckemin, and at least one key British military installation, the barracks at Trenton, have produced much useful archaeological data, campsites of shorter duration, many of which lasted only a night or two, have proved much harder to pin down in the field. Because of their relative invisibility in the landscape, many have probably been inadvertently built over, and it is difficult to assess their potential for yielding new information and consequently their historical significance. Nevertheless, some short-term encampment sites undoubtedly do still survive and may be expected to provide some archaeological manifestation, even if this may take the form of a widely dispersed scatter of artifacts spread across a patch of woodland or a series of residential backyards.

Tracking the main movements of American and British (and Hessian) troops across the New Jersey landscape with greater certainty and in greater detail will help in predicting where these more fleeting encampments may lie, as will careful oral history research among farmers and local residents into chance finds of artifacts. The American retreat and British pursuit across New Jersey in November and December 1776 and the American and British marches leading up to and following the Battle of Monmouth, for example, are strong candidates for study where evidence for short-term overnight camps may be found. In the case of the former movement,

CAMP # OUTGOING TRIP	CAMP # RETURN TRIP	MILES FROM PRECEDING CAMP	CAMP LOCATION	DATES OCCUPIED
20	34	15	Pompton Meeting-house [Pompton Plains]	Aug. 26–27, 1781; Sept. 12–13, 1782
21	33	15	Wippany [Whippany]	Aug. 27–29, 1781; Sept. 10–12, 1782
22	32	16	Bullion's Tavern [Liberty Corner]	Aug. 29–30, 1781; Sept. 12–13, 1782
23	31	15	Sommerset Court-house [Millstone]	Aug. 26–27, 1781; Sept. 9–10, 1782
24	30	14	Prince-Town [Princeton]	Aug. 30–31, 1781; Sept. 8–9, 1782
25	29	12.5	Trenton	Sept. 1–2, 1781; Sept. 5–8, 1782

TABLE 2   *Encampments of the French Army in New Jersey, 1781–82*

for instance, the New Bridge Landing vicinity, where the British troops encamped on November 25, 1776, may be a potentially revealing spot, while Longbridge Farm, now absorbed into modern Monmouth Junction, is the site of a well-documented American encampment, used two days before the Battle of Monmouth, where archaeological evidence may yet reside in the ground.[29]

One final group of short-term encampment sites, well documented in journals and maps, includes the six locations in New Jersey where General Rochambeau's French army pitched its tents overnight on its march through New Jersey from Newport, Rhode Island, to Yorktown, Virginia, in late August and early September of 1781 and then again on the return trip in early September 1782 (table 2).[30] The placement of these camps in the landscape is depicted with reasonable accuracy in the series of maps produced for Rochambeau by Louis-Alexandre Berthier (fig. 54), and some—the sites at Bullion's Tavern (Liberty Corner) and Somerset Court House (Millstone), and perhaps also at Whippany—certainly have archaeological possibilities that have yet to be systematically probed. Others, like the campsites in Trenton, Princeton, and Pompton, have likely been wholly or partially destroyed by urban development. Most of the camps were occupied for two consecutive nights, since the French army marched in two divisions one day apart, although the stopover at Whippany lasted three days on both the advance and return trip, and the returning army paused at Trenton for four days. The brief duration of these encampments means that they are most likely to be represented by scatters of military artifacts. Evidence of camp structures and hearths may be ephemeral and difficult to recognize in the ground.

All across New Jersey, especially in the zone of conflict in the Piedmont and Inner Coastal Plain, there are countless farmhouses, dwellings in and out of town, ferry houses, taverns, and even workshops and churches where officers and rank and

FIG. 54 *Louis-Alexandre Berthier,* Twenty-first Camp at Whippany, *1781.*
Reproduced in Howard C. Rice Jr. and Anne S. K. Brown, trans. and eds., The American
Campaigns of Rochambeau's Army 1780, 1781, 1782, 1783 *(Princeton, N.J.: Princeton
University Press; and Providence, R.I.: Brown University Press, 1972).*

file of the American, British, and French armies slept and ate, met and planned, guarded and spied, and occasionally engaged in armed conflict. Such places are too numerous to name, many still stand, and the vast majority—surviving or destroyed—may harbor archaeological remains. Linking the archaeology conclusively to the events of the Revolutionary War may not always be feasible (indeed, it usually is not), but even the loosest of physical associations can be worthwhile for property owners and local historians.

In some instances, provocative archaeological data has emerged to bolster appreciation of the role a particular home may have played in the Revolutionary War. In 2000, for example, excavations at Beverwyck in Parsippany–Troy Hills, an estate visited by Washington and several senior American and French officers, have revealed an extraordinarily rich assemblage of eighteenth-century material culture and extensive structural remains of buildings that stood in the 1770s and 1780s. The Zabriskie/Von Steuben House at New Bridge Landing, site of a Washington stopover in September 1780 and the scene of an incident a few months earlier when British troops mistakenly killed several of their own men, has demonstrated that it is surrounded by intact archaeological deposits.[31] Several seasons of excavation at the site of Lord Stirling's "manor" in Basking Ridge, Somerset County, as yet largely unreported, have the potential to yield useful information about the home base of this well-known patriot officer (see fig. 4). A pair of houses owned by the Vanderveer family, one of which still stands and is under restoration, are reputed to have accommodated General Knox and other officers training at the nearby Pluckemin artillery camp. Based on initial survey work, archaeological features and artifacts relating to the Revolutionary War era are anticipated in the grounds surrounding the surviving house, while further evidence of the period was recovered at the other house site in connection with highway intersection improvements.[32]

Battles and Skirmishes

Military confrontations occurred widely over the New Jersey zone of conflict, ranging in scale from minor guerilla actions involving a handful of men and taking only minutes to the set-piece engagement at Monmouth—a grueling fight involving many thousands of troops, extending over more than six hours, and ranging over several square miles of improved agricultural landscape. The latter was one of the largest battles of the war and the one perhaps most reminiscent of near-contemporary European encounters, such as those of the Seven Years' War of 1756–1763. Of greatest historical significance was undoubtedly the first Battle of Trenton, a relatively small-scale affair but one with powerful psychological and strategic consequences for the American cause.[33] Following the immediately subsequent battles at Assunpink Creek and Princeton, the British were forced to abandon their forward positions south of the Raritan and essentially retire to that area of northeastern New Jersey easily dominated from New York City.

Monmouth and Trenton share the distinction of being conflicts initiated by Washington, whereas the majority of the other actions in New Jersey were the result of British initiatives. These include the various American debacles of 1776, such as the loss of Fort Lee in Bergen County; the repulsed Hessian attack on Fort Mercer (Red Bank) in October 1777; and the repeated, though ineffective, British thrusts westward from the "neutral ground" into the Watchungs. The British actions were typified by the officially unsanctioned but de facto–tolerated looting and by the intentional destruction of property, both consistent features of British military operations that did much to alienate otherwise indifferent colonists from the crown.

What can archaeology and historical geography contribute to our understanding of these powerfully dramatic events? Battles are chaotic and essentially ephemeral episodes that make little lasting impression on the landscape. Subsequent evolution of that landscape can make it extremely difficult for the modern observer to comprehend the environment in which the actual events took place. In this regard, it is instructive to compare battlefields of the American Revolution with those of the second great conflict to take place in the United States, the Civil War of 1861–1865.

In the latter case, several factors have combined to make battlefields more visually accessible to the modern eye than those of "four score and seven years" previously. The first of these is the nature of the fighting: Civil War battles frequently took place over several days, permitting the establishment of stable lines of defense that left physical expression in the landscape. Second is the extensive cartographic and documentary record of the engagements, which enables very precise reconstructions to be attempted. Third, and perhaps most significant, is the early appreciation of the physical locations of Civil War battles as hallowed ground that should be preserved in something like their condition at the time of the conflict. This development of a "historic preservation" perspective in the second half of the nineteenth century resulted in the conscious setting aside of considerable tracts of landscape and in attempts to hold them in time and even to re-create the physical environment of the time of the battles.[34]

While the commemorative value of some key sites of Revolutionary War–era conflict along the Champlain-Hudson corridor, notably Ticonderoga, were recognized in the nineteenth century, the battle sites of New Jersey have been less fortunate.[35] Not one of the battles in question lasted longer than a day, and only a handful involved the assault of fortified positions. Maps and written accounts do, of course, survive, Monmouth and Trenton being particularly well served in this respect (fig. 55). But the ahistorical and forward-looking cultural milieu of the early nineteenth century had little time for retrospection and for preserving remnants of a colonial past. It is salutary that even Mount Vernon, home of one of the revered founders of the nation, was saved from demolition only by the private initiative of a group of women. No moves were made by the federal or state government to preserve even this icon.

New Jersey's battlefields were therefore ignored as the landscape filled up and developed. Trenton was transformed from a "pretty village" of half a dozen streets into a major political and industrial center. Princeton's landscape was modified by the abandonment and obliteration of much of the colonial road pattern along which the troops had marched, by the bisection of the battlefield by the Kingston and Princeton Branch Turnpike in 1807, by the expansion of the university and other educational institutions, and by ongoing suburban growth. The Bound Brook battlefield was overwhelmed by changes brought about by alterations to streams and by the arrival of multiple railroad lines, although most of a key bridge and causeway over the mouth of Green Brook do still remain, albeit mostly buried by fill. Other battle sites in the "neutral ground" have suffered similarly. Even Monmouth, still the most rural of the battle sites, presents a picture far removed from the landscape of 1778.

Of the lesser confrontations, even less remains. At Red Bank, the earthen fortifications provide a strong visual reference point, and the Quaker brick house at Han-

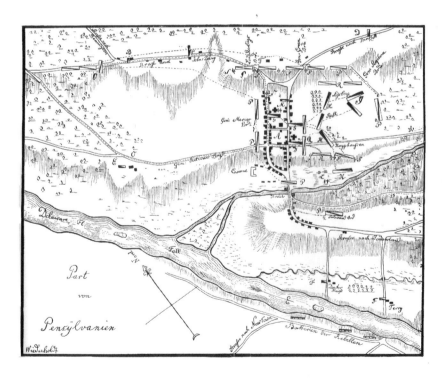

FIG. 55 *Andreas Wiederhold,* Lieutenant Wiederhold's Map of the Battle of Trenton, *1777. Reproduced in William S. Stryker,* The Battles of Trenton and Princeton *(Cambridge: Riverside Press, 1898).*

cock's Bridge in Salem County preserves the physical setting of one of the darker incidents of the war: the massacre of patriot troops during a British raid in March 1778. For the remainder, however, the interested traveler has to make do with historical markers (some of them of questionable accuracy) set incongruously in urban or suburban settings or as isolated and inaccessible signposts beside rural highways.

It is often assumed that battlefields are fertile ground for archaeological investigation, but this is far from the case. In the immediate aftermath of a battle, the landscape would of course have been liberally covered with evidence—corpses, weapons, equipment, and spent ammunition. Little of this material remained in place for long, however. Bodies were commonly removed from the scene of the battle and stripped of clothing and any other usable equipment before burial. Any weapons or other material would be recovered either by the army in control of the field or by the local inhabitants once the armies had moved away. In our own time of almost overwhelming material plenty, it is hard to envisage how very necessary it would have been to recover and reuse anything and everything. Only items well hidden from view would escape these postconflict cleanup operations. Items that did remain had some chance of being preserved in the ground through natural processes, often only to be recovered through agricultural practices and, since World War II, by enthusiasts wielding metal detectors.

There is no question that undisciplined metal detecting, usually characterized as "looting," has resulted in a substantial loss of historical information from battle sites. The key concern is not just that individual items (typically ammunition and military equipment) are lost into private collections or the antiques market. Of greater moment is the loss of context, particularly horizontal spatial information that can provide important insights into the action.

Fortunately, this situation is starting to change as some archaeologists and metal detectorists have begun to find common ground in their desire to understand the history of these events. Nationally, the breakthrough in perception about the utility of metal detecting on battle sites came with a series of studies at the Little Bighorn battlefield in Montana.[36] In New Jersey, the pioneers have been Garry Wheeler Stone of Monmouth Battlefield State Park and Daniel Sivilich and members of the volunteer metal-detecting group BRAVO, who have undertaken informative studies at the Monmouth and Princeton battlefields and other Revolutionary War sites.[37]

The premise of this emerging discipline of battlefield archaeology is that the precise mapping of the locations of military material, particularly ammunition, can provide detailed insights into the progress and movement of the action when used judiciously with the surviving cartographic and narrative sources. At Monmouth, the studies of the movements of two battalions of the British Royal Highlanders have been particularly informative, enabling incidents recorded in the written narrative to be located precisely (fig. 56). An important distinction is drawn in these studies

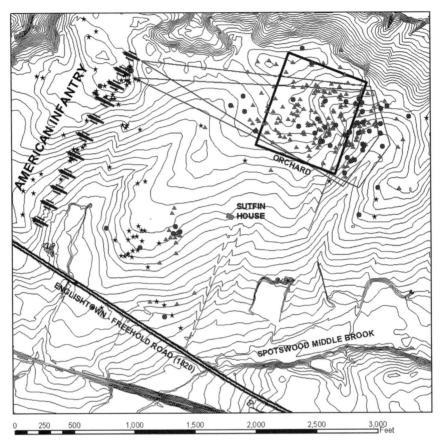

Legend

★   Howitzer Shell Fragments

●   Grape Shot - 2 oz

▲   Canister

FIG. 56 Spatial Distribution of American Artillery Ordnance in the Sutfin Orchard and British Howitzer Shell Fragments on the Perrine Ridge at Monmouth Battlefield State Park. *Courtesy of Daniel M. Sivilich.*

between unfired munitions (termed "drops") and the distorted or fragmentary musket balls or artillery projectiles that have been fired. The drops (typically musket balls) are particularly helpful in locating the positions of troops firing at enemy formations, the cartridges containing the balls having presumably been dropped in the heat of the moment and never recovered. A tight cluster of grapeshot at another location helped pinpoint the location of an American four-pound artillery piece that may possibly have been the cannon so famously kept in action by Molly Pitcher. Concentrations of shell fragments can also provide information about the location of bodies of troops or artillery batteries, and again the research at Monmouth has demonstrated the utility of plotting the locations of this material. Princeton, a much smaller, briefer, and faster-moving battle, has also been subjected to a limited metal detector search that plausibly identified ordnance fired from an American cannon near the Clarke House toward the British advance. Some other battle sites may benefit from the application of these methodologies, although the areas available for study are somewhat limited.

Human remains are a potentially rich source of archaeological information, although investigations must be undertaken with particular sensitivity to cultural traditions and descendants' wishes. Extensive burial grounds have not been identified or investigated at New Jersey battle sites, and in many cases the locations of the burials of those who fell in battle are not known (although one notable exception is the whereabouts of casualties at the Battle of Princeton). Bodies were sometimes placed in temporary graves and later removed to other locations. The most fully investigated burials from the Revolutionary War are those that resulted from the Baylor "massacre," a savage episode that took place on the night of September 27, 1778. Several soldiers of the Third Regiment Light Dragoons of Virginia were outnumbered and unceremoniously killed by a British detachment on a foraging mission from New York. In the late 1960s, a group of six skeletons were encountered, buried in tanning vats. The condition of these remains, including a skull that showed evidence of blunt force trauma, along with some telltale artifacts, such as military buttons, were enough to allow their attribution to the Baylor massacre. One of the burials, through its association with some silver buttons and a silver buckle, was even tentatively identified as being that of Sergeant Isaac Howe Davenport of Dorchester, Massachusetts.[38]

The archaeological evidence from the numerous naval actions on the Delaware River and along the Atlantic coast is generally limited to occasional chance discoveries. The largest quantity of material has come from the Delaware River below Philadelphia. This area was the scene of intense activity in the fall of 1777, as the Royal Navy sought successfully to force a passage up the river past American fortifications, shipping, and water obstructions in order to secure the supply lines for the army occupying the city. Various artifacts have been recovered from the river, including examples of chevau-de-frise placed in the riverbed to block the shipping channels. Fragments of the wreck of the British frigate HMS *Augusta*, which exploded during this campaign, remain at Gloucester Point.[39]

Of more potential are the wrecks of several American vessels, mostly of the Pennsylvania navy, that were deliberately scuttled by the Continentals or sunk by British raiding parties between the fall of 1777 and the spring of 1778. The vessels were hidden in Crosswicks Creek near Bordentown and at other locations on the New Jersey side of the Delaware between Lamberton and Burlington. There are clear indications that some of these wrecks were visible well into the last century, and it is very likely that the remains of some ships are still to be found in the marshes below the falls of the Delaware.[40]

War Matériel

In much the same fashion that the houses and farms of New Jerseyans were co-opted by the war as places of meeting, refuge, and accommodation, so also were forges and furnaces, mills and workshops, and storehouses and taverns frequently sucked into the conflict as actual or potential sources of matériel and provisions. Like the houses and farms, these types of facilities typically display an archaeological record that spans a period longer than the seven war years, making unequivocal attribution of cultural deposits or artifacts to the events of the Revolution almost impossible. Nevertheless, these types of archaeological sites are important to our understanding of the broader context and effects of the Revolutionary War, and in their own way they are as deserving of careful study and sensitive treatment as encampments, fortifications, battlefields, and houses. Mill sites, in particular, tend to leave a strong imprint in the landscape in the form of millponds, dams, raceways, and mill buildings and in conjunction with encampment sites and the historic road network can make intelligible the patterns of military supply in and control over the countryside.

Industrial and commercial sites within the zone of conflict in particular played an important role in the war, notably in southern Somerset, southeastern Hunterdon, Middlesex, Essex, and Bergen counties. For example, beginning in December 1776 and continuing throughout much of 1777, American and British forces vied for control of many of the gristmills, sawmills, fulling mills, and tanneries in central New Jersey. Securing the products of these facilities—flour and other provisions, lumber, wood fuel, cloth, and hides—was often the principal goal, but neither side was beyond destroying buildings and milled goods to prevent its opponent from gaining sustenance from them. William Scudder's gristmill and fulling mill at Mill Berry (modern Aqueduct Mills) on the Millstone River and a pair of tanneries just outside Princeton were burned by the British, while American forces made off with woolen cloth from the fulling mill at Rocky Hill and dumped flour into the North Branch of the Raritan River at Andrew Leake's gristmill to prevent its capture; the British responded by burning this mill to the ground.[41] In archaeological terms, in addition to below-ground structural remains, destruction levels may be recognizable at sites like these, thus allowing a closer connection to documented events.

In the hills of Morris County and northern Somerset and Hunterdon counties, deep within American-controlled territory, and correspondingly in predominantly loyalist Monmouth County, fewer mills and other manufacturing facilities suffered depredation. In these areas, networks of agricultural and industrial processing sites supplied the American, and to a lesser extent, British war efforts. In the North Branch of the Raritan drainage, for example, gristmills owned by John Mehelm, Jonathan Logan, John Taylor, Dr. Oliver Barnet, members of the McDonald and Vanderveer families, and Stephen Hunt were producing flour and feed for American troops in the nearby encampments. Sawmills, fulling mills, tanneries, bark mills, and saltpeter works all operated in the same vicinity, many of them depicted on the maps provided to Washington by Robert Erskine, the products of these establishments being distributed in part certainly to the Continental army.

Of singular importance to both American and British forces were iron- and steel-making sites. Access to these sites in New Jersey was vital to the Continental army's efforts at producing ordnance, artillery carriages, wagon parts, and various types of building materials, including items as mundane as nails. American forces wanted to establish control over the majority of these sites in New Jersey and maintain production, while British forces, with outside supplies of munitions, were more intent on disabling this manufacturing capability. In the New Jersey Highlands, behind American lines in the Morristown area, and farther to the north extending to the New York border, as well as deep in the Pine Barrens of South Jersey, where sources of bog iron were being exploited, there were several iron mines, bloomery forges, fineries, chaferies, and blast furnaces. Other secondary processing facilities, such as plating mills, rolling and slitting mills, and blacksmith shops, which fashioned bar iron and pig iron into finished products, were scattered across the colony, although often nearer to the population centers that provided the market for such products.

Unraveling the contributions of New Jersey's metalworking sites to the American and British war efforts is a complicated task that has received little scholarly attention among historians and archaeologists. Even though labor was scarce and production intermittent, a number of sites both in the Highlands (e.g., the furnaces at Mount Hope, Ringwood, Charlotteburg, and Ringwood; the rolling and slitting mills at Boonton, Andover, and the Union Iron Works in High Bridge) and in the Pine Barrens (e.g., Batsto and Atsion) apparently supplied the Continental army, chiefly in the period 1776–1778.[42] Archaeologically, these sites may leave building foundations and ample trace of their water-powered operations in the rural landscape, along with substantial deposits of slag and other waste materials. The principal difficulty, as with house sites, is recognizing remains and artifacts that are specifically attributable to the Revolutionary War as opposed to a broader continuum of industrial production.

Buried remains of Revolutionary War–era industrial sites also survive in New Jersey's towns, a reminder that urban archaeology can unearth valuable data in the type of heavily developed setting that is all too often written off as being disturbed.

Within 200 feet of the New Jersey statehouse, in the heart of Trenton, lies one of the most significant and best-preserved industrial archaeological resources in the region, a site that was producing iron and steel during the early years of the war (fig. 57). Here, in the sliver of parkland that separates the statehouse from the Old Barracks, massive foundations of a plating mill and steel furnace were found to survive beneath up to 15 feet of later deposits. Exposed during restoration and expansion projects at Thomas Edison State College and the statehouse, these two water-powered facilities were situated on either side of a stream known as Petty's Run, long since placed in a culvert and incorporated into the city's storm sewer system.[43] Benjamin Yard at the plating mill received inquiries from the Continental Congress in Philadelphia in March 1776 as to whether he would make gun barrels for the Continental army, and it seems likely that he did so.[44] The operational status of the nearby steel furnace,

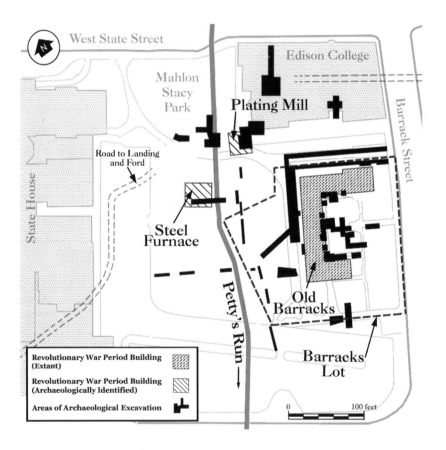

FIG. 57 Revolutionary War Era Features and Archaeological Excavations in the Petty's Run Vicinity in Downtown Trenton. *Hunter Research, Inc.*

originally built by Yard in the mid-1740s, is less clear. The site was partly owned by prominent Philadelphia merchant and suspected loyalist sympathizer John Pemberton from 1772 until 1781, but how frequently the furnace was in blast during the war and for whom steel might have been produced remain uncertain.[45]

A final category of historic site and archaeological resource that merits most careful study in the context of Revolutionary War supply networks comprises the port communities on the Delaware and Raritan rivers and on the Lower Hudson, through which the American and British armies transshipped war matériel and troops. Two of the most revealing programs of archaeological study in New Jersey in recent years have focused on the ports of Lamberton and Raritan Landing, at the head of navigation on the Delaware (serving the Trenton area) and the Raritan (serving New Brunswick and its hinterland), respectively. Both ports represented critical strategic points in the military landscape, Lamberton rather more so for American forces and Raritan Landing rather more so for the British, and both figure sporadically in the documentary record as sites of contention and places where supplies were husbanded. Archaeological monitoring along the Lamberton riverfront at Trenton Landing has produced evidence of storehouses, commercial bake ovens, and a pottery kiln, some of which are considered to have been in use during the war.[46] Excavations at several properties along River Road in Raritan Landing have provided tantalizing remains of the Revolutionary War period, including traces of occupation, conflict, and destruction.[47] The impressive outcome of the investigations in Lamberton and Raritan Landing demonstrates that the archaeological potential of other port communities that were active during the Revolutionary War, for example, Perth Amboy, Salem, Burlington, and Bordentown, should not be left unconsidered, especially since riverfront remains will often be waterlogged and display a high level of preservation.

Geography and Archaeology: Tools for Engagement

The Crossroads of the American Revolution National Heritage Area initiative is helping to usher in a new era of interest in Revolutionary War sites in New Jersey. As this overview demonstrates, archaeological and historical geographical approaches to the New Jersey experience of the war provide both a different perspective and potentially new information on this crucial episode in American and New Jersey history. These final remarks focus on two issues: the value of these approaches as research tools and their role in generating and sustaining public interest in New Jersey's Revolutionary War history.

Historical geography's focus on the physical settings within which historical events and processes took place is one that can undoubtedly enrich our understanding of the American Revolution in New Jersey. As has been outlined in this essay,

the events of 1776–1783 in New Jersey were powerfully influenced by the physical realities of the time. The movements of troops were affected not only by the locations
of roads and rivers but also by the need to protect and control economic resources,
such as farmland, mills, and industrial centers. This perspective is one that in no way
detracts from the wider issues that were at stake in the Revolution but often helps to
make the conflict more explicable at the local and regional levels.

A particular challenge, however, lies in how to incorporate the historical geographer's approach into the current attempts to heighten public awareness of the
Revolutionary War heritage of the Garden State. How, for example, can the eighteenth-century landscape seen by Washington's troops—a landscape of winding dirt
roads, fords, wooden bridges, farms, fences, and woodlots; of mills, taverns, and
churches; of small towns and even smaller villages—be made "real" to a twenty-
first-century population only familiar with multilane highways, blighted cities,
cookie-cutter suburban housing developments, and soulless shopping malls and
whose perception of geography has been noticeably impoverished by the neglect of
this subject in the school curriculum? Why even try? The answer to this last question must surely lie in the importance of place and a sense of time to the human
spirit. Historical geography can truly help people connect with their surroundings.

Two general suggestions may be offered to better embed the historical geography of the Revolutionary War in the New Jersey psyche. One is to make much more
systematic and intentional use, in all levels of education and in historic sites interpretation, of the rich collections of cartographic material that are available: not only
those that survive from the Revolutionary War period itself but also the later maps
of the nineteenth century that document the changes that took place to bring the
present-day landscape into view. The second suggestion is that educators and administrators encourage a much higher level of topographic and geographical awareness
in the many individuals involved in the interpretation of historic sites, landscapes,
and events, so that the physical settings and the events that took place there can be
made more meaningful to the audience.

Archaeology still has much to contribute to the study of the Revolutionary
War in New Jersey. The most exciting recent developments have been in the area of
battlefield and encampment archaeology, where new exploration technologies now
enable extremely ephemeral events and structures to be identified. Although there
has been enormous destruction of Revolutionary War sites in New Jersey over the
last 225 years, in the past half century several research projects and site-specific public archaeology studies performed under the mandate of environmental legislation
have shown that historical evidence survives tenaciously in the ground if it is looked
for carefully enough. Meticulous excavations at Pluckemin, Raritan Landing, and
elsewhere have revealed much about American and British encampment life, and
pioneering work at Monmouth Battlefield is showing how moments in time can be

captured through the recovery, mapping, and careful analysis of the debris of battle. Many other sites await these types of treatment, most notably, perhaps, the extended network of military encampment and supply sites in the hills of Somerset and Morris counties and the immediately surrounding area and the locations of the encampments of the French army that passed through New Jersey in 1781 and 1782.

As a tool for engaging public interest, there is little doubt that archaeology has few rivals among the historical disciplines. Every archaeologist will attest to the enthusiastic response that excavation "open days" or public archaeology programs generate. The state is fortunate in having some of the finest collections of Revolutionary War artifacts in the country, particular those at Morristown National Historical Park, Washington Crossing State Park, Monmouth Battlefield State Park, and the Old Barracks in Trenton. Archaeological endeavors at Revolutionary War sites are a tremendous opportunity to engage the public in the historical process and to demonstrate that our understanding of the past is not only evolutionary but, at times, even revolutionary.

Notes

CROSSROADS OF THE AMERICAN REVOLUTION

1. Philip Vickers Fithian, *Journal and Letters of Philip Vickers Fithian, 1773–1774: A Plantation Tutor of the Old Dominion*, ed. and intro. Hunter Dickinson Farish (Charlottesville, N.C.: Dominion Books, 1968), 160.

2. Lucius Q. C. Elmer, *The Constitution and Government of the Province and State of New Jersey: With Biographical Sketches of the Governors from 1776–1845 and Reminiscences of Bench and Bar during More than a Half Century* (Newark, N.J.: M. R. Dennis, 1872), 61, 71.

3. Leonard Lundin, *Cockpit of the Revolution: The War for Independence in New Jersey* (Princeton, N.J.: Princeton University Press, 1940), 111.

4. William Herbert Mariboe, "The Life of William Franklin, 1731–1813, Pro Rege Et Patria" (Ph.D. diss., University of Pennsylvania, 1962), 444. See also *Documents Relating to the Colonial History of the State of New Jersey (Archives of the State of New Jersey)* 1st ser., 18:565–567 (hereafter cited as *NJA*).

5. Edmund Cody Burnett, *The Continental Congress* (New York: Macmillan, 1941), 125.

6. Jacob Green, *Observations: On the Reconciliation of Great Britain, and the Colonies in Which Are Exhibited Arguments For, and Against, That Measure* (1776; repr., Trenton: New Jersey Historical Association, 1976), 16.

7. Frederick R. Kirkland, ed., "Journal of a Physician on the Expedition against Canada, 1776," *Pennsylvania Magazine of History and Biography* 59 (Oct. 1935): 323–329.

8. Henry P. Johnston, "The Campaign of 1776 Around New York and Brooklyn," *Long Island Historical Society* 3 (1878): 166–170.

9. Douglas Southall Freeman, *George Washington: A Biography* (New York: Scribner, 1951), 4:217.

10. Lundin, *Cockpit of the Revolution*, 144–145; see also Freeman, *George Washington*, 4:278–279.

11. John C. Fitzpatrick, ed., *The Writings of George Washington from the Original Manuscript Sources, 1745–1799*, 39 vols. (Washington, D.C.: U.S. Government Printing Office, 1931–1944), 6:346.

12. Lundin, *Cockpit of the Revolution*, 162–163.

13. Samuel Thornley, ed., *The Journal of Nicholas Cresswell, 1774–1777* (New York: L. MacVeagh, Dial Press, 1924), 176.

14. Mark Edward Lender, *The New Jersey Soldier*, vol. 5 of *New Jersey's Revolutionary Experience* (Trenton: New Jersey Historical Commission, 1975), 17–18.

15. Ibid., 23.

16. Lewis F. Owen, *New Jersey's Revolutionary Struggle*, vol. 6 of *New Jersey's Revolutionary Experience*, 21–22.

17. Mark V. Kwasny, *Washington's Partisan War, 1775–1783* (Kent, Ohio: Kent State University Press,

1996), 214.

18. Ibid., 211.

19. Ibid., 214.

20. Josiah Quincy, ed., *Journals of Samuel Shaw* (Boston: Wm. Crosby and H. P. Nichols, 1847), 74.

21. Joseph H. Jones, ed., *The Life of Ashbel Green, V.D.M.* (New York: R. Carter, 1949), 121.

22. Arthur D. Pierce, *Smugglers Woods: Jaunts and Journeys in Colonial and Revolutionary New Jersey* (New Brunswick, N.J.: Rutgers University Press, 1960), 52.

23. Linda Grant DePauw, *Fortunes of War: New Jersey Women and the American Revolution*, vol. 26 of *New Jersey's Revolutionary Experience*, 24.

24. Ibid., 19.

25. Frances D. Pingeon, *Blacks in the Revolutionary Era*, vol. 14 of *New Jersey's Revolutionary Experience*, 20–21.

26. Lundin, *Cockpit of the Revolution*, 415–416.

27. Owen, *The Revolutionary Struggle in New Jersey*, 29.

28. William Smith, *Historical Memoirs of William Smith, 1778–1783*, ed. W.H.W. Sabine (New York: New York Times, 1971), 438.

29. Howard H. Peckham, ed., *The Toll of Independence: Engagements and Battle Casualties of the American Revolution* (Chicago: University of Chicago Press, 1974), 129.

"THESE WERE TROUBLESOME TIMES INDEED"

The author thanks Paul G. E. Clemens for commenting on an early draft of this essay.

1. Harry J. Carman, ed., *American Husbandry, Containing an Account of the Soil, Climate, Production and Agriculture of the British Colonies in North America and the West Indies . . . by an American* (1939; repr., Port Washington, N.Y.: Kennikat Press, 1964), 110. A contemporary description by a native of New Jersey is Samuel Smith, *The History of the Colony of Nova-Caesaria, or New-Jersey* (Philadelphia, 1765; 1890; repr., Spartanburg, S.C.: Reprint Co., 1975).

2. William Faden, *The Province of New Jersey, Divided into East and West, commonly called The Jerseys*, 1777, Library of Congress. Franklin's population estimate was hampered by the fact that in the 1772 census, assessors in certain counties refused to submit forms (Wm. Franklin to Lord Dartmouth, March 28, 1774, *NJA*, 1st ser., 10:445–446). Modern estimates are Stella H. Sutherland, *Population Distribution in Colonial America* (1936; repr., New York: AMS Press, 1966), 98–99, 109; and Jim Potter, "The Growth of Population in America, 1700–1860," in *Population in History: Essays in Historical Demography*, ed. D. V. Glass and D.E.C. Eversley, 638, table 1a (Chicago: Aldine, 1965). Sutherland points out that the greatest population density was in southern Bergen, Essex, and eastern Middlesex counties, as well as along the Delaware River opposite Philadelphia; the average population density for the entire province was approximately 16 persons/sq. mile (*Population Distribution in Colonial America*, 99, 116.) Potter notes that New Jersey had a very low infant mortality rate, much lower than in contemporary England; also, in 1771–1772, 50 percent of all whites and 45 percent of blacks were under sixteen years old, and males made up slightly more than 52 percent of the total population ("The Growth of Population in America," 655–660). Middle colony population trends are summarized in John J. McCusker and Russell R. Menard, *The Economy of British America, 1607–1789* (Chapel Hill: University of North Carolina Press, 1991), 229. The total population in 1770 of the mainland British colonies (excluding Canada) is estimated at 2,148,076 (*Historical Statistics of the United States: Colonial Times to 1970*, Part 2 [Washington, D.C.: U.S. Government Printing Office, 1975], Series Z 1–19: 1168).

3. On the main road traversing New Jersey, see "A Map of the Road from Trenton to Perth Amboy
. . . 1762," in *New Jersey Road Maps of the Eighteenth Century* (Princeton, N.J.: Friends of the
Princeton University Library, 1981); and Christopher Colles, *A Survey of the Roads of the United
States of America, 1789,* ed. Walter W. Ristow, 154–158 (Cambridge, Mass.: Belknap Press of
Harvard University Press, 1961). Sutherland comments on the dozens of small towns and crossroads villages, especially in central New Jersey, with road networks connecting New York and
Philadelphia (*Population Distribution in Colonial America,* 117). On the transmittal of informa-
tion across the colony, see Larry R. Gerlach, *Prologue to Independence: New Jersey in the Coming of
the American Revolution* (New Brunswick, N.J.: Rutgers University Press, 1976), 32–33, 256, 305,
465n.6. Thomas Doerflinger notes how rumors and price fluctuations were transmitted across
New Jersey "as though the New Brunswick Road were a giant nerve connecting two ganglia" (*A
Vigorous Spirit of Enterprise: Merchants and Economic Development in Revolutionary Philadelphia*
[Chapel Hill: University of North Carolina Press, 1986], 336). Ned C. Landsman points out the
early importance of Scottish entrepreneurs in establishing ferries and building roads across the
colony (*Scotland and Its First American Colony, 1683–1765* [Princeton, N.J.: Princeton University
Press, 1986], 215, 326n.48). The standard survey is Wheaton J. Lane, *From Indian Trail to Iron
Horse: Travel and Transportation in New Jersey, 1620–1860* (Princeton, N.J.: Princeton University
Press, 1939).

4. The phrase is in Franklin to Lord Dartmouth, March 28, 1774, *NJA,* 1st ser., 10:439; the governor
was arguing for a single capital for both divisions. On the colony's early settlement history, social
and ethnic composition, and landholding systems, see Peter O. Wacker, *Land and People: A
Cultural Geography of Preindustrial New Jersey; Origins and Settlement Patterns* (New Brunswick,
N.J.: Rutgers University Press, 1975). On civil disorder, see Brendan McConville, *These Daring
Disturbers of the Public Peace: The Struggle for Property and Power in Early New Jersey* (Ithaca, N.Y.:
Cornell University Press, 1999). References, both contemporary and modern, to the reciprocal relationships between New Jersey and New York and Pennsylvania are legion, but see, for
example, Gerlach, *Prologue to Independence,* xv, 6, 8, 10, 17, 25, 26, 29, 26, 31, 33, 35, 36, 118, 120,
167.

5. Paul G. E. Clemens, "Farming, Planting, and Ranching: The British Colonies," in *Encyclopedia
of the North American Colonies,* ed. Jacob Ernest Cooke et al., 1:686 (New York: Charles Scribner's
Sons, 1993). On the heterogeneity of New Jersey, see also Gerlach, *Prologue to Independence,* xiv,
11–13; and Jack P. Greene, *Pursuits of Happiness: The Social Development of Early Modern British
Colonies and the Formation of American Culture* (Chapel Hill: University of North Carolina Press,
1988), 49, 124, 125, 137. James A. Henretta notes that the Middle colonies were "forced by the
contingencies of history to deal with diversity" (*The Evolution of American Society: An Interdisci-
plinary Analysis* [Lexington, Mass.: D. C. Heath, 1973], 112).

6. The standard survey of the settlement history and cultural landscape of early New Jersey is
Wacker, *Land and People.* The estimated percentages of the various European ethnic stocks are:
English and Welsh (54.2), Scots (3.4), Scots-Irish (6.8), Irish (4.1), Dutch (20.1), German (6.5),
French (3.8), Swedish (1.1); see also Thomas L. Purvis, "The European Origins of New Jersey's
Eighteenth-Century Population," *New Jersey History* 100 (1982): 15–31 (hereafter cited as *NJH*).
Purvis's estimates, which are largely based on 1790 census figures, revise earlier estimates. Lands-
man argues that Purvis underestimates the Scottish population (*Scotland and Its First American
Colony,* 264–274, 339n.7). On the Dutch and German elements, see A. G. Roeber, "'The Origin of
Whatever Is Not English among Us': The Dutch-Speaking and the German-Speaking Peoples
of Colonial British America," in *Strangers within the Realm: Cultural Margins of the First British
Empire,* ed. Bernard Bailyn and Philip D. Morgan, 220–283 (Chapel Hill: University of North
Carolina Press, 1991).

7. Gerlach, *Prologue to Independence,* 13. On Scottish "ethnic trading networks," see Landsman,
Scotland and Its First American Colony, 212–213, 216, 217, 218, 250, 258.

8. On "ethnic others," see Frank Shuffelton, introduction to *A Mixed Race: Ethnicity in Early America*, ed. Frank Shuffelton, 4 (New York: Oxford University Press, 1993). The population estimate of Brotherton is in Franklin to Lord Dartmouth, March 28, 1774, *NJA*, 1st ser., 10:447. On the Lenape (Delawares) during the late colonial period, see Ives Goddard, "Delaware," in *Handbook of North American Indians*, William Sturtevant, gen. ed., vol. 15, *Northeast*, ed. Bruce G. Trigger, 222–223 (Washington, D.C.: Smithsonian Institution, 1978); Gregory Evans Dowd, *The Indians of New Jersey* (Trenton: New Jersey Historical Commission, 1992), 51–61; and Lorraine E. Williams's essay on the Lenape in this volume. On the percentages of slaves colonywide and in each county, see Peter O. Wacker and Paul G. E. Clemens, *Land Use in Early New Jersey: A Historical Geography* (New Brunswick, N.J.: Rutgers University Press, 1992), 100–101, tables 11 and 12; Wacker, *Land and People*, appendixes 1–6, 414–416; and Giles R. Wright's essay in this volume.

9. Jon Butler, *Religion in Colonial America* (New York: Oxford University Press, 2000), 141. Describing New Jersey in 1765, Robert Rogers noted "almost every religious persuasion under heaven; they were like so many jarring elements pent up together" (*A Concise Account of North America* [New York: Johnson Reprint, 1966], 78).

10. An overview is Wallace N. Jamison, *Religion in New Jersey: A Brief History* (Princeton, N.J.: D. Van Nostrand, 1964). More recent general works are Patricia U. Bonomi, *Under the Cope of Heaven: Religion, Society, and Politics in Colonial America* (New York: Oxford University Press, 1986); Jon Butler, *Awash in a Sea of Faith: Christianizing the American People* (Cambridge, Mass.: Harvard University Press, 1990); and Butler, *Religion in Colonial America*. On Anglicans, see Nelson R. Burr, *The Anglican Church in New Jersey* (Philadelphia: Church Historical Society, 1954); on Dutch Reformed, see Randall Balmer, *A Perfect Babel of Confusion: Dutch Religion and English Culture in the Middle Colonies* (New York: Oxford University Press, 1989); on Quakers, see Jean R. Soderlund, *Quakers and Slavery: A Divided Spirit* (Princeton, N.J.: Princeton University Press, 1985). For the distribution of churches and meetinghouses throughout the colony, see relevant maps in Wacker, *Land and People*, 167, 175, 179, 187, 188, 213. John Fea defines "ubiquitarians" as "generic Protestants" who "moved freely among churches, ministers, and meetinghouses, rarely committing to one denomination" ("Rural Religion: Protestant Community and the Moral Improvement of the South Jersey Countryside, 1676–1800" [Ph.D. diss., State University of New York at Stony Brook, 1999], 20, 310, 317). Bonomi defines "indifferent" not as uninterested but instead as "latitudinarian practices" (*Under the Cope of Heaven*, 7, 218–219). The Anglican missionary Uzal Ogden reported in 1771 that in quasi-frontier Sussex County, there were at least a dozen different denominations "and a few deists" ("Copy of a Letter from the Rev. Uzal Ogden," *Proceedings of the New Jersey Historical Society* 4 [1849–1850]: 152–153 [hereafter cited as *PNJHS*]). Jamison notes that most people "appear to have been outside the membership of any church" (*Religion in New Jersey*, 70); Soderlund likewise comments that "probably a large proportion of colonists had no active religious affiliation" (*Quakers and Slavery*, 209); Butler notes that many were bewildered by the diversity (*Religion in Colonial America*, 73). As evidenced by the popularity of almanacs, this religious pluralism was intermingled with a fascination with astrology and the occult (Butler, *Awash in a Sea of Faith*, 67–97).

11. On the general lack of voting alignments along religious lines, see Thomas L. Purvis, *Proprietors, Patronage, and Paper Money: Legislative Politics in New Jersey, 1703–1776* (New Brunswick, N.J.: Rutgers University Press, 1986), 113–114; and Michael Batinski, *The New Jersey Assembly, 1738–1775: The Making of a Legislative Community* (Lanham, Md.: University Press of America, 1987), 92–93. On the "psychology of accommodation" in the Middle colonies, see Greene, *Pursuits of Happiness*, 140–141; and Henretta, *The Evolution of American Society*, 112, 115–116, 124, 166.

12. The phrase is from Philip Vickers Fithian to John Peck, Aug. 12, 1774, Fithian, *Journal and Letters*, 160. On Stirling, see Lundin, *Cockpit of the Revolution*, 21–24, 87–90; and David Paul Nelson, *William Alexander, Lord Stirling* (University: University of Alabama Press, 1987). Stirling's extravagant expenditures and conspicuous consumption ultimately bankrupted him.

13. On the wealthy and the upwardly mobile, see Gordon S. Wood, *The Radicalism of the American Revolution* (New York: Alfred A. Knopf, 1992), 112–113, 118–120. Jackson Turner Main estimates that 10 percent of the white population was wealthy (*The Social Structure of Revolutionary America* [Princeton, N.J.: Princeton University Press, 1973], 276). Gerlach points out the "bewildering web of marriages" among prominent families in New Jersey, New York, and Pennsylvania (*Prologue to Independence*, 31). On Livingston, see Carl E. Prince, *William Livingston: New Jersey's First Governor*, vol. 21 of *New Jersey's Revolutionary Experience*; his revolutionary career is best traced in detail in Carl E. Prince et al., eds., *The Papers of William Livingston*, 5 vols. (Trenton and New Brunswick: New Jersey Historical Commission, 1979–1988) (hereafter cited as *Livingston Papers*), along with the more comprehensive twenty-three-reel microfilm edition that accompanies it. On the process of anglicization and metropolitanization of the elite, see Greene, *Pursuits of Happiness*, 68–69, 174–175; Wood, *The Radicalism of the American Revolution*, 36–40; and Main, *The Social Structure of Revolutionary America*, 215, 217–219.

14. Fithian to Peck, Aug. 12, 1774, Fithian, *Journal and Letters*, 160; Nicholas Collin to his aunt and uncle, July 20, 1771, *Journal and Biography of Nicholas Collin, 1746–1831*, ed. Amandus Johnson, 27 (Philadelphia: New Jersey Society of Pennsylvania, 1936). In comparing his native colony to the more stratified society of Virginia, Fithian noted "The Levil . . . among People of every rank" (*Journal and Letters*, 160). In 1784, a Venezuelan traveler observed that he had not seen "any other place in which the people in general appear happier and on more of an equality than here" (*The New Democracy in America: Travels of Francisco de Miranda in the United States, 1783–84*, trans. Judson P. Wood and ed. John S. Ezell, 73 [Norman: University of Oklahoma Press, 1963]). See also Main, *The Social Structure of Revolutionary America*, 221–222, 223, 226–227.

15. Wood, *The Radicalism of the American Revolution*, 59, 123, 169; Allan Kulikoff, *From British Peasants to Colonial American Farmers* (Chapel Hill: University of North Carolina Press, 2000), 127, 131; Gerlach, *Prologue to Independence*, 13, 15–16; Main, *The Social Structure of Revolutionary America*, 17, 42, 232, 234, 273, 277, 283; and Greene, *Pursuits of Happiness*, 50, 126–127, 188.

16. Daniel Vickers, "The Northern Colonies: Economy and Society, 1600–1775," in *The Cambridge Economic History of the United States*, ed. Stanley L. Engerman and Robert E. Gallman, vol. 1, *The Colonial Era* (Cambridge: Cambridge University Press, 1996), 210. Vickers expanded upon this concept in "Competency and Competition: Economic Culture in Early America," *William and Mary Quarterly*, 3rd ser., 47 (Jan. 1990): 3–29 (hereafter cited as *WMQ*). Greene argues an analogous concept: "the most important element in the emerging British-American culture [was] the conception of America as a place in which free people could pursue their own individual happiness" (*Pursuits of Happiness*, 5). The "colonial American dream" even left its mark on the colony's landscape, e.g., Freehold and Upper Freehold townships in Monmouth County.

17. Kulikoff, *From British Peasants*, 227, 231, 248–249, 252; Clemens, "Farming, Planting, and Ranching," 677–678; Wood, *The Radicalism of the American Revolution*, 43, 49–55; and McCusker and Menard, *The Economy of British America*, 246.

18. Fithian to Peck, Aug. 12, 1774, Fithian, *Journal and Letters*, 160. On the growing scarcity of good land, see Marc Egnal, *New World Economies: The Growth of the Thirteen Colonies and Early Canada* (New York: Oxford University Press, 1998), viii; Bernard Bailyn, *The Peopling of British North America: An Introduction* (New York: Alfred A. Knopf, 1986), 37–38; Main, *The Social Structure of Revolutionary America*, 165, 195; Kulikoff, *From British Peasants*, 127, 129; Henretta, *The Evolution of American Society*, 95; and Wood, *The Radicalism of the American Revolution*, 126. In 1774, Governor Franklin reported that "great Numbers have quit the Colony, & have migrated to Virginia, North Carolina, the Ohio, Missisipi [*sic*], &c." (Franklin to Lord Dartmouth, March 28, 1774, *NJA*, 1st ser., 10:446). Similarly, in 1786 John Rutherford noted "great Emigrations from this State" for various reasons ("Notes on the State of New Jersey . . . 1776 [i.e., 1786]," *PNJHS*, 2nd ser., 1 [1867–1869]: 81). Main notes that "Revolutionary America was a society in flux" in which

"horizontal mobility helped to maintain the very high rate of vertical mobility" (*The Social Structure of Revolutionary America*, 193–194); see also Wood, *The Radicalism of the American Revolution*, 126, 127, 129.

19. Landsman, *Scotland and Its First American Colony*, 196, 214, 218. On tenancy in general, see Kulikoff, *From British Peasants*, 127, 129, 131, 134, 136, 253; Bailyn, *The Peopling of British North America*, 82–85, 157–158n.35, 158–159n.37; Wood, *The Radicalism of the American Revolution*, 55–56, 114; and Greene, *Pursuits of Happiness*, 128. Cottagers contracted to perform seasonal farmwork in exchange for a house and small plot of land.

20. On the poor, see Wood, *The Radicalism of the American Revolution*, 57, 122, 123, 124; Kulikoff, *From British Peasants*, 127, 129, 131, 263; and Henretta, *The Evolution of American Society*, 105. Main refers to a "prestige hierarchy," with the poor, servants, and slaves at the bottom; he also notes that in southwestern New Jersey, the landless made up nearly half of the male population (*The Social Structure of Revolutionary America*, 41, 156, 163, 198). On the transient rural labor force, see Kulikoff, *From British Peasants*, 131, 136, 138; Main, *The Social Structure of Revolutionary America*, 70, 156, 163, 194, 272–273; Henretta, *The Evolution of American Society*, 3, 19, 28, 90, 97, 134, 164; Greene, *Pursuits of Happiness*, 131–133, 187, 189; and Wacker and Clemens, *Land Use*, 10–12, 24, 29. Wacker and Clemens also provide information on wages in the period 1748–1816 (*Land Use*, 104–106, tables 13 and 14). On the employment of blacks, see Graham Russell Hodges, *Slavery and Freedom in the Rural North: African Americans in Monmouth County, New Jersey, 1665–1865* (Madison, Wis.: Madison House, 1997), 43–90; and Soderlund, *Quakers and Slavery*, 55, 65, 69, 70, 74–77, 84.

21. One of the earliest uses of this phrase, which may have been common even by then, is Andrew Burnaby, *Travels Through the Middle Settlements in North-America, in the Years 1759 and 1760* (1775; repr., Ithaca, N.Y.: Great Seal Books, 1960), 73. Similarly, Thomas Pownall, who had served as the colony's lieutenant governor, described in 1754 the well-cultivated plantations along the road from New Brunswick to Trenton: "One rides . . . through a kind of Garden the whole way" (*A Topographical Description of . . . Parts of North America* [London, 1776], republished as *A Topographical Description of the Dominions of the United States of America*, ed. Lois Mulkearn [Pittsburgh: University of Pittsburgh Press, 1949], 109). It is clear that by the late colonial period, the province had earned the reputation as "the Garden of America." See, for example, "Journal of Lord Adam Gordon, 1765," in *Narratives of Colonial America, 1704–1765*, ed. Howard H. Peckham, 266 (Chicago: R. R. Donnelley, 1971); Marquis de Chastellux, *Travels in North America in the Years 1780, 1781, and 1782*, trans. and ed. Howard C. Rice, 1:125 (Chapel Hill: University of North Carolina Press, 1963); and Wood and Ezell, *New Democracy in America*, 72. The descriptions could be influenced, of course, not only by hearsay but also by reading travel literature.

22. On agriculture in eighteenth-century New Jersey, see Wacker and Clemens, *Land Use*; Hubert Schmidt, *Agriculture in New Jersey: A Three-Hundred-Year History* (New Brunswick, N.J.: Rutgers University Press, 1973), 59–104; Carl R. Woodward, *The Development of Agriculture in New Jersey, 1640–1880* (New Brunswick: New Jersey Agricultural Experiment Station, Rutgers University, 1927), 11–63; Clemens, "Farming, Planting, and Ranching," 677–694; and David Steven Cohen, *The Dutch-American Farm* (New York: New York University Press, 1992). A fascinating contemporary account is Carl R. Woodward, ed., *Ploughs and Politics: Charles Read of New Jersey and His Notes on Agriculture, 1715–1774* (New Brunswick, N.J.: Rutgers University Press, 1941). On northern agriculture in general, see Vickers, "Northern Colonies," 219.

23. On by-employments and the household economy, see Wacker and Clemens, *Land Use*, 229–263; McCusker and Menard, *The Economy of British America*, 325, 326, 329; Jacob M. Price, "Reflections on the Economy of Revolutionary America," in *The Economy of Early America: The Revolutionary Period, 1763–1790*, ed. Ronald Hoffman et al., 309, 311, 312 (Charlottesville: University Press of Virginia, 1988); and James A. Henretta, "The War for Independence and American Economic Development," in Hoffman et al., *Economy of Early America*, 58–67.

24. McCusker and Menard point out that "the fully self-sufficient yeoman farmer of colonial America is largely mythical" (*The Economy of British America*, 18). The historiography on self-sufficiency is summarized in T. H. Breen, "An Empire of Goods: The Anglicization of Colonial America, 1690–1776," in *Colonial America: Essays in Politics and Social Development*, 4th ed., ed. Stanley N. Katz et al., 378-384 (New York: McGraw-Hill, 1993). On the "borrowing system" of barter and local exchange, see Kulikoff, *From British Peasants*, 204–205, 219–223, 225.

25. On the international, regional, and local market networks, see James F. Shepherd, "British America and the Atlantic Economy," in Hoffman et al., *Economy of Early America*, 3–44; McCusker and Menard, *The Economy of British America*, 9–12, 60–65, 78–80, 85–87, 197, 277, 282; Vickers, "Northern Colonies," 221–222, 230, 237; Richard L. Bushman, "Markets and Composite Farms in Early America," *WMQ*, 3rd ser., 55 (1998): 351–374; James H. Levitt, *For Want of Trade: Shipping and the New Jersey Ports, 1680–1783* (Newark: New Jersey Historical Society, 1981); Levitt, *New Jersey's Revolutionary Economy*, vol. 9 of *New Jersey's Revolutionary Experience*; Paul G. E. Clemens, *The Uses of Abundance: A History of New Jersey's Economy* (Trenton: New Jersey Historical Commission, 1992), 27, 28, 30; Kulikoff, *From British Peasants*, 205–212, 226; James A. Henretta, "The Transition to Capitalism in America," in *The Transformation of Early American History: Society, Authority, and Ideology*, ed. James A. Henretta, Michael Kammen, and Stanley Katz, 218–238 (New York: Alfred A. Knopf, 1991); and especially Doerflinger, *A Vigorous Spirit*, 74–78, 167. A contemporary summarization of the colony's economy is Wm. Franklin's report to Lord Dartmouth, March 28, 1774, *NJA*, 1st ser., 10:433–454.

   The social, economic, and political ramifications of the "consumer revolution" have been explicated in three important articles by T. H. Breen: "An Empire of Goods"; "Narrative of Commercial Life: Ideology and Commerce on the Eve of the American Revolution," *WMQ*, 3rd ser., 50 (July 1993): 471–501; and "'Baubles of Britain': The American and Consumer Revolutions of the Eighteenth Century," in *Of Consuming Interests: The Style of Life in the Eighteenth Century*, ed. Cary Carson et al., 444–482 (Charlottesville: University Press of Virginia, 1994). See also Carole Shammas, *The Pre-Industrial Consumer in England and America* (Oxford: Clarendon Press, 1990); Henretta, *The Evolution of American Society*, 41–42; and Wood, *The Radicalism of the American Revolution*, 34–35, 135–137, 248–249. Clemens points out a process of the "democratization of wants" in which formerly unaffordable luxuries became "necessaries" for average people ("Material Culture and the Rural Economy: Burlington County, New Jersey, 1760–1820," in Wacker and Clemens, *Land Use*, 288–291).

26. On indebtedness, see Egnal, *New World Economies*, 12–13, 32, 75–76; Kulikoff, *From British Peasants*, 217; McCusker and Menard, *The Economy of British America*, 334–336; Doerflinger, *A Vigorous Spirit*, 137, 171, 181; Main, *The Social Structure of Revolutionary America*, 136, 159–160; Henretta, *The Evolution of American Society*, 138–139, 141–142; and Edward A. Fuhlbruegge, "New Jersey Finances during the American Revolution," *PNJHS* 55 (July 1937): 170–172. The contraction of the economy between 1764 and 1768 is evidenced by the rise in debt cases; see, for example, Court of Common Pleas Minutes, New Jersey State Archives, Trenton, and Court of Common Pleas (loose papers), Monmouth County Archives, Manalapan, N.J.

   There is general agreement among historians and economists regarding the high standard of living in colonial British America. The genesis seems to be Alice Hanson Jones's contention that by 1774, the standard of living in British North America was "probably the highest achieved for the great bulk of the population in any country up to that time" (quoted in McCusker and Menard, *The Economy of British America*, 51). For supporting statements, see Greene, *Pursuits of Happiness*, 182; Egnal, *New World Economies*, 45; Wood, *The Radicalism of the American Revolution*, 4; and Edwin J. Perkins, *The Economy of Colonial America* (New York: Columbia University Press, 1980), 145. Unlike Europe, there was no famine or starvation in America, and colonials had a better diet and nutrition and were consequently several inches taller on average than their counterparts in Britain (Shammas, *Pre-Industrial Consumer*, 5, 121, 133, 145, 148). Daily, weekly, and yearly subsistence estimates are given in Main, *The Social Structure of Revolutionary America*, 115–117. In 1772, ten shillings per week (doubtless a minimum) was considered sufficient for the subsistence of a woman and child (Minutes of the Burlington County Court of Quarter Sessions, New Jersey State Archives.)

27. Gerlach, *Prologue to Independence*, xii–xiii, 19, 24, 25, 33, 37, 247, 313, 358. On the paper money issue, see ibid., 42–52, 70–79; and more generally, Wood, *The Radicalism of the American Revolution*, 248–249. The concerns of New Jersey society in the period 1760–1775—debt, road repairs, building dams, dogs killing sheep—are evidenced in Bernard Bush, comp., *Laws of the Royal Colony of New Jersey*, vols. 4 and 5 (Trenton: Division of Archives and Records Management, New Jersey Department of State, 1977–1986). Wood has pointed out "the localist tendencies of public life"; in general, politics tended to be elitist, personal, paternalistic, even patrimonial (*The Radicalism of the American Revolution*, 78, 80, 86, 87, 89, 92, 245).

28. Pierce, *Smugglers' Woods*, 7–26, 133–134; and Doerflinger, *A Vigorous Spirit*, 19, 181, 193–194. On smuggling and John Hatton, the irascible and eccentric customs collector in the Salem district, see Gerlach, *Prologue to Independence*, 53–61, 397–398n.44, 399n.54. In 1774, Governor Franklin reported that "some smuggling is carried on in this Colony, as well as in every other Part of the British Dominions. On so extensive a Coast, in which there are many Harbours and Inlets, it is next to impossible to Stop it effectually. The Chief Smuggling here, . . . is the Produce of the foreign West India Islands" (Franklin to Lord Dartmouth, March 28, 1774, *NJA*, 1st ser., 10:443–444). There is disagreement among historians regarding the extent of smuggling. Shammas argues that smuggling was "not insignificant" (*Pre-Industrial Consumer*, 65, 74, 80, 82, 83); McCusker and Menard, on the other hand, contend that by the eighteenth century, smuggled goods accounted for a "tiny fraction" of all imports (*The Economy of British America*, 77–78).

    On the riots in Essex and Monmouth counties, see McConville, *These Daring Disturbers*, 239–245; and Gerlach, *Prologue to Independence*, 185–192. McConville speculates that the Monmouth rioters were influenced by Whig ideology. For a contemporary account of grievances in Monmouth, see Anonymous, *Liberty and Property, Without Oppression*, Early American Imprints no. 41951 (n.p., ca. 1769). Wood points out that eighteenth-century riots, which often supported traditional values, were usually purposeful and restrained and that they were also "a means by which ordinary people, usually those most dependent . . . made their power felt temporarily in a political system that was otherwise largely immune to their influence" (*The Radicalism of the American Revolution*, 90).

29. Gerlach, *Prologue to Independence*, 97–100, 131, 132, 133, 136, 139, 141, 159, 167, 196, 206–207, 213, 251.

30. Ibid., 97–99, 123, 129, 132, 133, 136, 139, 141, 196, 206–207, 213, 251, 255, 314; Stockton, quoted in ibid., 107. New Jersey was criticized for its "pacific conduct" regarding the Stamp act (ibid., 422n.12). On the backgrounds of the colony's patriots, see Dennis P. Ryan, *New Jersey's Whigs*, vol. 19 of *New Jersey's Revolutionary Experience*; and John T. Cunningham, *New Jersey's Five Who Signed*, vol. 6 of *New Jersey's Revolutionary Experience*.

31. Doerflinger, *A Vigorous Spirit*, 84. Franklin felt that the claims were "puff'd away in the newspapers" (Franklin to Lord Hillsborough, June 14, 1768, *NJA*, 1st ser., 10:30; see also *NJA*, 1st ser., 26:7, 16). As a show of solidarity with the protest movement, on several occasions students at the College of New Jersey wore homespun at commencement exercises (Gerlach, *Prologue to Independence*, 117, 165, 281).

32. On the effects of the Tea Act, see Breen, "'Baubles of Britain,'" 448. On tea as a ubiquitous beverage, see ibid., 474; and Shammas, *Pre-Industrial Consumer*, 55–56, 63, 76, 111. Shammas observes that "a food riot involving a tax on tea . . . brought on the American Revolution" (*Pre-Industrial Consumer*, 148). On the Tea Act and the Greenwich tea party, see Gerlach, *Prologue to Independence*, 196–202; and Pierce, *Smugglers' Woods*, 118–143. An Essex County young farm

woman commented in 1774: "It seems we have troublesome times a Coming . . . & they say it is tea that caused it So then if they will Quarel about such a trifling thing . . . What must we expect But war" (Jemima Condict diary, quoted in Gerlach, *Prologue to Independence*, 253). In 1775, Cortlandt Skinner felt that although the dispute began over smuggled tea, "now the contest is for dominion" (quoted in ibid., 307–308).

33. The most exhaustive study of events leading up to the outbreak of hostilities found that "the precious few private papers of ranking personages are deafening in their silence on intellectual and philosophical matters" (Gerlach, *Prologue to Independence*, xviii). The classic studies of the effects of ideology on the Revolution are Bernard Bailyn, *The Ideological Origins of the American Revolution* (Cambridge, Mass.: Belknap Press of Harvard University Press, 1967); and Gordon S. Wood, *The Creation of the American Republic, 1776–1787* (New York: W. W. Norton, 1969).

34. Butler, *Religion in Colonial America*, 130. On the ways in which the "ideology of dissent" that was a legacy of the Great Awakening may have influenced the revolutionaries, see Bonomi, *Under the Cope of Heaven*, 9, 161, 186, 208; and Fea, "Rural Religion," 20.

35. On the republicanization of society, see Wood, *The Radicalism of the American Revolution*, 95–101, 110, 169, 174–175, 178–179; he points out that colonial Americans were the "most republican of people in the English-speaking world" (110). On conspiracies, see especially Bailyn, *Ideological Origins*, 94-159.

36. Wood, *The Radicalism of the American Revolution*, 69–73.

37. Gerlach, *Prologue to Independence*, 81, 85, 92, 96, 141, 144–145; Henretta, *The Evolution of American Society*, 136–137; Butler, *Religion in Colonial America*, 123, 130; and Wood, *The Radicalism of the American Revolution*, 169–170. Henretta notes that the effects of the imperial revenue acts were less their intrinsic nature than the fact that they were introduced into the "highly charged atmosphere of a volatile society with a penchant for independence" (*The Evolution of American Society*, 119, 120).

38. Gerlach, *Prologue to Independence*, xi.

39. On the role of committees in New Jersey, see ibid., 225–226, 259–260; and more generally, Richard Buel Jr., "The Committee Movement of 1779 and the Formation of Public Authority in Revolutionary America," in Henretta, Kammen, and Katz, *Transformation of Early American History*, 151–169. On the Continental Association, see Gerlach, *Prologue to Independence*, 225–226, 231–232, 235, 236–237, 248–250, 274–275, 278, 287, 315–316; he notes that by summer 1775, the Association had changed from an instrument of economic coercion to "the political charter of the insurrection" (ibid., 274).

40. "Letter of Thomas Leaming, Jr., to Hon. William Paterson, 1789," *Pennsylvania Magazine of History and Biography* 38 (1914): 116 (hereafter cited as *PMHB*); Leaming was soliciting a federal appointment. One Monmouth County loyalist contended that in 1775, he signed the Continental Association "in consequence of many Threats" (Gilbert Giberson Loyalist Claim, AO 12/15, Public Record Office, Great Britain). On "involuntary allegiance" and "compulsory oath-taking," see Michael Kammen, "The American Revolution as a *Crise de Conscience*: The Case of New York," in *Society, Freedom and Conscience: The Coming of the Revolution in Virginia, Massachusetts, and New York*, ed. Richard M. Jellison, 125–189 (New York: W. W. Norton, 1976).

41. Gerlach, *Prologue to Independence*, 258–260, 270; Gilbert Giberson Loyalist Claim, AO 12/15, Public Record Office, Great Britain. Cf. James Parker and Stephen Skinner accepting appointments as committeemen in order to curb radical excesses (Gerlach, *Prologue to Independence*, 277).

42. Gerlach, *Prologue to Independence*, 239–240, 252, 276–277, 282–283, 354, 452n.47. As one conservative complained, "Those who are not for us are against us is the cry" (ibid., 276). James Kinsey is an example of a Quaker leader of the protest movement who retreated from public life (ibid.,

296). Gerlach identifies Witherspoon as a radical Whig and notes that under his leadership, the College of New Jersey became "a veritable seminary of sedition" (ibid., 274).

43. William Nelson, *The American Tory* (Boston: Northeastern University Press, 1992), 91. Wood points out the importance of local committees in the process of replacing ties to the former royal authority with ties to the new regime (*The Radicalism of the American Revolution*, 213).

44. Quoted in Gerlach, *Prologue to Independence*, 278; for other examples of this commonly expressed fear, see 220, 245, 258. See also the "Pastoral Letter" of the Presbyterian Synod of New York and Philadelphia, May 22, 1775, which was not only read from pulpits throughout the Middle colonies but also printed and distributed (*Records of the Presbyterian Church in the United States of America: Minutes of the General Presbytery and General Synod, 1706–1788* [1904; repr., New York: Arno Press, 1969]), 466); the letter was authored by Rev. John Witherspoon.

45. For petitions submitted to the assembly or to the Provincial Congress opposing independence, see Gerlach, *Prologue to Independence*, 294, 334–335, 473n.82, 485n.45. On the crisis of conscience, see Kammen, "American Revolution." On Cogil (Cowgill), see Wm. Tatem affidavit, no. 0314, Stewart Collection, Savitz Library, Rowan University, Glassboro, N.J.; Cogil was subsequently fined £3 "for seditious words" (Minutes of the Gloucester County Court of Oyer and Terminer, June 20–21, New Jersey State Archives).

46. During June and July, loyalist counterinsurrections broke out in Bergen, Essex, Gloucester, Hunterdon, and Monmouth counties (Gerlach, *Prologue to Independence*, 354). On the counterinsurrections in Monmouth, see David J. Fowler, "Egregious Villains, Wood-Rangers, and London Traders: The Pine Robber Phenomenon in New Jersey during the Revolutionary War" (Ph.D. diss., Rutgers University, 1987), 27–114. On fear of slave uprisings, see Hodges, *Slavery and Freedom*, 94–96.

47. Minutes of the Upper Freehold Baptist Church, March 1777, vol. 1, 1766–1841 (Ac. 2576), Special Collections, Rutgers University Libraries. There are also several entries such as that for March 4, 1776: "nothing done, so few met." Regarding the Baptists, Butler points out that "the war disrupted local congregational life and activity" (*Religion in Colonial America*, 131). Fea likewise notes that the war retarded the denominational growth of Swedish Lutheran churches in south Jersey ("Rural Religion," 19). Other segments of society were also affected: in Burlington County, jurors defaulted and court sessions were disrupted ("August Term 1776—nothing done," Court of Quarter Sessions Minutes, vol. 2, New Jersey State Archives).

48. Paul H. Smith, "The American Loyalists: Notes on Their Organization and Numerical Strength," *WMQ*, 3rd ser., 25 (April 1968): 258. Adams's oft-quoted estimate is referred to in Thomas McKean to Adams, Jan. 1814, *The Works of John Adams*, ed. Charles Francis Adams, 10:87 (1856; repr., Freeport, N.Y.: Books for Libraries Press, 1969). John Shy notes that "beneath the raw irrationality of violence lies motive—some psychic web spun from logic, belief, perception, and emotion that draws people to commit terrible acts and hazard everything they possess" ("Hearts and Minds in the American Revolution: The Case of 'Long Bill' Scott and Peterborough, New Hampshire," in *A People Numerous and Armed: Reflections on the Military Struggle for American Independence* [New York: Oxford University Press, 1976], 165).

49. An estimate of loyalist strength is given in Smith, "American Loyalists," 259–277. On Moody's picaresque wartime career, see *Lieut. James Moody's Narrative of His Exertions and Sufferings in the Cause of Government, since the Year 1776*, 2nd ed. (1783; repr., New York: Arno Press, 1968); and Susan Burgess Shenstone, *So Obstinately Loyal: James Moody, 1744–1809* (Montreal: McGill-Queen's University Press, 2000). Moody's experience bears out the contention that "repressive revolutionary regimes were the decisive factor in loyalist enlistments" (Paul H. Smith, *Loyalists and Redcoats: A Study in British Revolutionary Policy* [Chapel Hill: University of North Carolina Press, 1964], 66).

50. Six years after the war's end, the prominent Quaker merchant and mill owner Richard Waln

lamented that "the radical Evil is the loss of British Community" and also that he was "not without Hopes of seeing Things restored to their old State" (Waln to Joseph Galloway, and Waln to John Warder, both March 29, 1789, Richard Waln Letterbook, Historical Society of Pennsylvania, Philadelphia). General statements regarding the motivations of loyalists can be found in Lundin, *Cockpit of the Revolution*, 70–108; Dennis P. Ryan, *New Jersey's Loyalists*, vol. 20 of *New Jersey's Revolutionary Experience*; Wallace Brown, *The King's Friends* (Providence, R.I.: Brown University Press, 1965); Brown, *The Good Americans* (New York: William Morrow, 1968); Nelson, *The American Tory*; and Robert M. Calhoon, *The Loyalists in Revolutionary America, 1760–1781* (New York: Harcourt Brace Jovanovich, 1973).

51. On the importance of kinship in influencing allegiance, see Dennis P. Ryan, "Six Towns: Continuity and Change in Revolutionary New Jersey, 1770–1792" (Ph.D. diss., New York University, 1974), 75, 143, 144, 155, 162, 173. Gerlach points out that "many communities were genealogically one extended family" (*Prologue to Independence*, 14); similarly, Wood comments that due to intermarrying, come communities were "only enlarged families" that could encompass entire villages or townships (*The Radicalism of the American Revolution*, 44, 48). Henretta argues that within the "complex mosaic of kinship ties" in each settlement, the family was "the first refuge of the individual" (*The Evolution of American Society*, 24, 25). Regarding class, Wallace Brown demonstrates that the typical white male loyalist in New Jersey was a native-born farmer of middling status—much like the typical inhabitant before the war or the typical Whig (*The King's Friends*, 111, 117–119, 121, 160, 161–162, 265, 267).

52. Butler, *Religion in Colonial America*, 121 (he further argues that the Revolution was "a profoundly secular event"); Richard Robins, quoted in "Deposition of William Imlay," April 12, 1777, *Livingston Papers*, 1:304. The idea that the Revolution was a conspiracy fomented by dissatisfied Presbyterians and republicans was a loyalist commonplace; people as diverse as George III and Joseph Cogil of Gloucester County subscribed to it: in 1781, the latter complained "that the Presbyterians were Striving to Get the Rule into thier own hands And that he Never Wold be Subject to a Presbyterian Government" (Wm. Tatem affidavit, no. 0314, Savitz Library, Rowan University). For other examples, see Brown, *The Good Americans*, 132, 223, 253; Doerflinger, *A Vigorous Spirit*, 185, 186, 188, 195, 196, 219, 220, 251; Jamison, *Religion in New Jersey*, 57–58; Wood, *The Radicalism of the American Revolution*, 112; Bonomi, *Under the Cope of Heaven*, 187, 203, 207, 273n.46; and Anne Ousterhout, *A State Divided: Opposition in Pennsylvania to the American Revolution* (New York: Greenwood Press, 1987), 5, 77, 80, 99n.47, 127.

53. Israel Putnam to Wm. Livingston, Feb. 18, 1777 (*Livingston Papers*, 1:241). The Yankee general from Connecticut frankly admitted: "I detest . . . (as Members of Society) the Sect" (*Livingston Papers*, 1:241).

54. The revivalistic *Coetus* faction tended to support the revolution, while the more orthodox *Conferentie* opposed it. See Adrian C. Leiby, *The Revolutionary War in the Hackensack Valley: The Jersey Dutch and the Neutral Ground* (New Brunswick, N.J.: Rutgers University Press, 1980), 19–20, 112–114, 228–231; and Balmer, *Perfect Babel of Confusion*, ix, 149–150, 152.

55. Gerlach, *Prologue to Independence*, 354; cf. Ousterhout, *A State Divided*, 6, 7, 8, 38, 122, 232, 247, 265–266, 305, 309. As in any civil war, there were trimmers and opportunists; for an amusing anecdote regarding the trimming Van Horne family of Bound Brook, see Lundin, *Cockpit of the Revolution*, 251–254.

56. On the Pine Robbers, see Fowler, "Egregious Villains"; on the Highlands gangs, see Leiby, *The Revolutionary War*, 186–199. A general study of revolutionary outlaws is Harry M. Ward, *Between the Lines: Banditti of the American Revolution* (Westport, Conn.: Praeger, 2002). The murder of the Farrs by the notorious Lewis Fenton gang caused an outcry at the time (see Fowler, "Egregious Villains," 163–165, and proclamation offering a reward for Lewis Fenton's apprehension, *Livingston Papers*, 3:161–162).

57. On the Association for Retaliation, see Michael Adelberg, "'A Combination to Trample All Law Underfoot': The Association for Retaliation and the American Revolution in Monmouth County," *NJH* 115 (Fall/Winter 1997): 3–36; and Fowler, "Egregious Villains," 194–197. The Retaliators were headed by David Forman, an inveterate Tory hater who combined civil and military roles; see *American National Biography* (New York: Oxford University Press, 1999), vol. 8, s.v. "Forman, David." On the Board of Associated Loyalists, see Edward H. Tebbenhoff, "The Associated Loyalists: An Aspect of Militant Loyalism," *New-York Historical Society Quarterly* 63 (1979): 115–144; and Fowler, "Egregious Villains," 199–200.

58. There are numerous references to the Huddy incident, which became international in scope; see especially L. Kinvin Wroth, "The Court Martial of Richard Lippincott," in *Sources of American Independence: Selected Manuscripts from the Collections of the William L. Clements Library*, ed. Howard H. Peckham, 2:499–612 (Chicago: University of Chicago Press, 1978); Larry Bowman, "The Court Martial of Captain Richard Lippincott," *NJH* 89 (1971): 23–36; Katherine Mayo, *General Washington's Dilemma* (New York: Harcourt Brace, 1938); and Fowler, "Egregious Villains," 200–203. On the "ethic of individual violent self-defense and self-redress," see Richard Maxwell Brown, *Strain of Violence: Historical Studies of American Violence and Vigilantism* (New York: Oxford University Press, 1975), viii, 238. The ethic of self-redress may be one manifestation of the pervasive code of primal honor, one feature of which was exacting vengeance against family or community enemies; in this sense, it helps explain the crescendo of retributive violence throughout the war (Bertram Wyatt-Brown, *Southern Honor: Ethics and Behavior in the Old South* [New York: Oxford University Press, 1982], 34). Perhaps the ultimate expression of loyalist anger was the placard affixed to Huddy's chest: "Up Goes Huddy For Philip White"; White had died under questionable circumstances while in patriot custody.

59. The phrase is from Calhoon, *The Loyalists*, 368. On the state of protracted siege in parts of New Jersey, see Leiby, *The Revolutionary War*; and Fowler, "Egregious Villains."

60. On black participation in irregular warfare, see Hodges, *Slavery and Freedom*, 91–112; and David Forman to Wm. Livingston, June 9, 1780, *Livingston Papers*, 3:423.

61. Israel Shreve to George Washington, March 28, 1778, quoted in Lundin, *Cockpit of the Revolution*, 376n.12. Cf. Nicholas Collin around the same time: "Everywhere distrust, fear, hatred and abominable selfishness were met with. Parents and children, brothers and sisters, wife and husband, were enemies to one another" (*Journal*, 244–245).

62. Richard Buel, *In Irons: Britain's Naval Supremacy and the American Revolutionary Economy* (New Haven, Conn.: Yale University Press, 1998), 15, 107, 109; Doerflinger, *A Vigorous Spirit*, 205; and Clemens, *The Uses of Abundance*, 28–29.

63. Edward Thomas to Wm. Livingston, June 30, 1776, *Livingston Papers*, 1:59. Cf. Jacob Drake Jr. to Livingston, July 12, 1776: "Our harvest is now Ripe and my men is very uneasey to think that they are Kept hear and luse what must Seport thare children" (*Livingston Papers*, 1:95). On the lure of privateering, see Buel, *In Irons*, 30, 45, 47, 52.

64. On women managing farms, see Kulikoff, *From British Peasants*, 254, 255, 275.

65. On the grain crisis, see Buel, *In Irons*, ix, 6, 14, 17, 18, 19, 24, 47, 49, 52; he notes that New Jersey was a "significant" secondary grain-producing market for the Philadelphia and New York markets (20–21). On army supply and impressment, see E. Wayne Carp, *To Starve the Army at Pleasure: Continental Army Administration and American Political Culture, 1775–1783* (Chapel Hill: University of North Carolina Press, 1984), 64–65, 72, 79, 80, 81, 89, 90, 106, 107, 180; and McCusker and Menard, *The Economy of British America*, 361–362. On the embargo laws, see John D. Cushing, comp., *First Laws of the State of New Jersey* (Wilmington, Del.: Michael Glazier, 1981), 8, 25, 54, 62, 100, 117, 147; Wm. Livingston to the Assembly, Jan. 30, 1777, *Livingston Papers*, 1:204; and Proclamation, Aug. 22, 1778, *Livingston Papers*, 2:421. Cf. Livingston to Geo. Washington, Jan. 12, 1778, on "the boundless avarice of some of our farmers, who would rather

see us engulphed in eternal bondage, than sell their produce at a reasonable price" (*Livingston Papers*, 2:175).

66. Carp, *To Starve the Army*, 72, 77–78, 90, 173, 180; and Buel, *In Irons*, 137–143. On logistics in general, see also Erna Risch, *Supplying Washington's Army* (Washington, D.C.: U.S. Government Printing Office, 1981); and James A. Hutson, *The Logistics of Liberty: American Services of Supply in the Revolutionary War and After* (Newark: University of Delaware Press, 1991).

67. E. James Ferguson, *The Power of the Purse: A History of American Public Finance, 1776-1790* (Chapel Hill: University of North Carolina Press, 1961), 29.

68. Buel, *In Irons*, 45, 122–126; John J. McCusker, *How Much Is That in Real Money? A Historical Commodity Price Index for Use as a Deflator of Money Values in the Economy of the United States* (Worcester, Mass.: American Antiquarian Society, 2001), 76–77, table C–1; Ferguson, *The Power of the Purse*, 29–30; Fuhlbruegge, "New Jersey Finances," 172–173, 175–180. A contemporary depreciation table appears in Cushing, *First Laws*, 245–248. On the British passing counterfeit money, see Lundin, *Cockpit of the Revolution*, 378. On public finance, see also E. James Ferguson et al., eds., *The Papers of Robert Morris, 1781–1784*, 9 vols. (Pittsburgh: University of Pittsburgh Press, 1973–); check the indexes under "New Jersey."

69. Buel, *In Irons*, 129–130. Nicholas Collin noted that many people were ruined by inflation, some "became insane," and the property of minors and widows was "swallowed up by leeches" (*Journal*, 253–254).

70. Carp, *To Starve the Army*, 108–112. On price fluctuations for commodities in the Philadelphia market, which reverberated in New Jersey, see Anne Bezanson, *Prices and Inflation during the American Revolution: Pennsylvania, 1770–1790* (Philadelphia: University of Pennsylvania Press, 1961); and Buel, *In Irons*, 43, 64, 162. In January 1778, commissioners from New Jersey joined those from five other northern states at New Haven, Connecticut, in an ultimately futile attempt to regulate commodity prices and wages (Minutes of the Commissioners to Regulate and Ascertain the Price of Labor, Jan. 15–20, 1778, New Jersey State Archives).

71. Acts passed re "forestalling, regrating, and engrossing" are in Cushing, *First Laws*, 104, 118–119. The terms are defined in *Livingston Papers*, 2:129–130n.7. Because New York and Pennsylvania did not enact price regulations, New Jersey's attempt was ineffective, and the laws were temporarily suspended in 1778 and, finally, in 1780; see Wm. Livingston to Henry Laurens, June 8, 1778, *Livingston Papers*, 2:363–364n.2; and Cushing, *First Laws*, 104. See also Buel, *In Irons*, 24, 137–143; and Carp, *To Starve the Army*, 108–112.

72. Doerflinger notes that the war fostered "new, potentially lucrative investment media" (*A Vigorous Spirit*, 63).

73. On the coastal saltworks, see Harry B. Weiss and Grace M. Weiss, *The Revolutionary Saltworks of the New Jersey Coast* (Trenton, N.J.: Past Times Press, 1959); and Pierce, *Smugglers' Woods*, 225–251. The saltworks suffered from mismanagement, disappointing output, labor problems, extreme weather, "flies & musquetoes in great plenty," and their exposed situation: several were razed or damaged by the British. A firsthand account of the problems, with ample evidence of a premodern work ethic among the laborers, is "Journal of Thomas Hopkins of the Friendship Salt Company, New Jersey, 1780," *PMHB* 42 (1918): 46–61. Two account books of the problem-plagued Pennsylvania State Saltworks near Toms River are at the Historical Society of Pennsylvania.

74. David L. Salay, "The Production of War Material in New Jersey during the Revolutionary War," in *New Jersey in the American Revolution III: Papers Presented at the Seventh Annual New Jersey History Symposium, 1975*, ed. William C. Wright, 8–13 (Trenton: New Jersey Historical Commission, 1976). On exemptions, see Cushing, *First Laws*, 33, 34, 76. Realizing the power of the printed word in disseminating information and propaganda, in December 1777 the legislature

exempted workers at the office of Isaac Collins's *New Jersey Gazette*, the state's first newspaper (Cushing, *First Laws*, 33); see also Wm. Livingston to the Assembly, Sept. 3, 1777, Nov. 26, 1777, and May 29, 1778, *Livingston Papers*, 1:54, 2:345. George Washington initially feared the "evil consequences that would follow a general exemption of all persons concerned in Iron Works" because it favored ironmasters over other occupations (Washington to Richard Henry Lee, April 24, 1777, in Philander Chase et al., eds., *The Papers of George Washington* [Charlottesville: University Press of Virginia, 1999], 9:257).

75. On the iron industry in general, see Charles S. Boyer, *Early Forges and Furnaces in New Jersey* (Philadelphia: University of Pennsylvania Press, 1931); and Arthur D. Pierce, *Iron in the Pines: The Story of New Jersey's Ghost Towns and Bog Iron* (New Brunswick, N.J.: Rutgers University Press, 1957).

76. Thomas M. Doerflinger, "Hibernia Furnace during the Revolution," *NJH* 90 (1972): 102, 104, 106; Salay, "Production of War Material," 13–16; Boyer, *Early Forges*, 28–30, 93–97; and Pierce, *Iron in the Pines*, 122–128. The three partners agreed to invest their 1 percent commission as quartermasters in speculative enterprises; sensitive to accusations of impropriety, Greene remained in the background. The history of the partnership and the problems attendant on ownership and management of the works can be traced in a series of letters from Pettit to Greene in Dennis M. Conrad et al., eds., *The Papers of General Nathanael Greene* (Chapel Hill: University of North Carolina Press, 1983–), 6:122, 149–150, 416; 9:321, 339; 10:150, 354; 11:19, 130; and 12:202, 425, 481. Doerflinger identifies Pettit as one of the "fortune builders" in Revolutionary Philadelphia who was also a leader in the economic resurgence of the 1780s (*A Vigorous Spirit*, 240n.152, 284).

77. Lester J. Cappon et al., eds., *Atlas of Early American History: The Revolutionary Era* (Princeton, N.J.: Princeton University Press, 1976), 105.

78. "Camillus" was one of William Livingston's pseudonyms (*Livingston Papers*, 2:317).

79. Fuhlbruegge, "New Jersey Finances," 186–188. On milling, see Richard W. Hunter, "Patterns of Mill Siting and Materials Processing: A Historical Geography of Water-Powered Industry in Central New Jersey" (Ph.D. diss., Rutgers University, 1999).

80. Price, "Reflections," 318, 321. See also Henretta, "War for Independence," 70, 75, 79, 80. Jeannette P. Nichols notes that "little appeared in print to indicate that the Revolution brought any immediate industrial stimulus" ("The Colonial Industries of New Jersey, 1618–1815," in *New Jersey: A History*, ed. Irving S. Kull, 1:259 [New York: American Historical Society, 1930]).

81. For examples of a privateer bond and instructions, see *NJA*, 2nd ser., 2:40–41; and *Livingston Papers*, 2:415–416, 4:234–236. A brief overview is William James Morgan, "American Privateering in America's War for Independence, 1775–1783," *American Neptune* 36 (April 1976): 79–87.

82. "Letter from Thomas Leaming, Jr., to the Hon. William Paterson, 1789," *PMHB* 38 (1914): 118; see also Pierce, *Smugglers' Woods*, 52. In addition to the Batsto ironworks, the partnership of Nathanael Greene, John Cox, and Charles Pettit also speculated in privateers; see Pettit to Greene, May 5, 1779, March 5–6, 1780, *Greene Papers*, 3:455, 5:439. By 1780, many of the most successful privateers were mere whaleboats; nevertheless, largely due to inflation, a $20,000 bond was required.

83. A modern comprehensive survey of privateering during the Revolutionary War would be welcome; sources are abundant. See William Bell Clark et al., eds., *Naval Documents of the American Revolution*, 10 vols. (Washington, D.C.: U.S. Government Printing Office, 1964–), which unfortunately to date covers only up to 1777, before most of the activity occurred. Owners and bonders of vessels are listed in Charles H. Lincoln, *Naval Records of the American Revolution, 1775–1788* (Washington, D.C.: U.S. Government Printing Office, 1906). References to captures, sittings of the Admiralty court, and vendues appear in *NJA*, 2nd ser., 2–5; check the indexes of the *Livingston Papers* under "Privateering" regarding granting commissions and other mat-

ters. On privateering in New Jersey, see also Pierce, *Smugglers' Woods*, 27–86; and Franklin W. Kemp, *A Nest of Rebel Pirates* (Batsto, N.J.: Batsto Citizens Committee, 1966). The records of New Jersey's Admiralty court are not extant; in fourteen instances, however, cases adjudicated by that court were appealed to the Continental Congress's committees on appeals and Court of Appeals in Cases of Capture; see Revolutionary War Prize Cases, 1776–1787 (M162), U.S. National Archives, reels 3–6, 8, 9, 11. General statements about privateering are in Buel, *In Irons*, 37–38, 42, 91–92, 102–103, 104, 116, 162, 174–177, 221, 297n.7, 13; on loyalist privateers, see ibid., 56–57, 136–137, 164, 189, 217–218. On privateering as a source of income for the new national government, see Ferguson, *The Power of the Purse*, 42.

84. On concerns regarding provisions being sent into New York, see Geo. Washington to Wm. Livingston, April 1, 1777, *Livingston Papers*, 1:290; Livingston to Washington, Aug. 15, 1777, Nov. 22, 1777, Jan. 12, 1778, and Proclamation, Aug. 22, 1778, *Livingston Papers*, 2:34, 120, 176, 422. On the trade between southwestern New Jersey and Philadelphia, see Lundin, *Cockpit of the Revolution*, 374–375; Wm. Livingston to Geo. Washington, Jan. 15, 20, 1778, *Livingston Papers*, 2:187; and Collin, *Journal*, 241, 244–247. On Easter Sunday 1778, Collin was startled by a "terrific cry" near his church as a captured trader was being flogged so severely that he subsequently died (*Journal*, 246).

On laws passed prohibiting contraband trade, see Cushing, *First Laws*, 60, 75, 117, 146, 155, 195, 214, 241, 287, 318, and appendix, 8, 11, 13, 16, 20, 22. On the trade in general, see Lundin, *Cockpit of the Revolution*, 377–378, 407–409; Richard P. McCormick, *Experiment in Independence: New Jersey in the Critical Period, 1781–1789* (New Brunswick, N.J.: Rutgers University Press, 1950), 9–12; Fuhlbruegge, "New Jersey Finances," 181–186; Buel, *In Irons*, 226–227; and Fowler, "Egregious Villains," 204–211, 238–289. As in 1774, patriots entered into associations for the purpose of suppressing the trade; see *New Jersey Gazette*, July 3, 7, 24, and Aug. 7, 21, 1782, regarding meetings at Trenton, Princeton, Nottingham, Chesterfield, and Allentown.

85. See, for example, Minutes of the Burlington County Court of Oyer and Terminer, July 1782; Minutes of the Gloucester County Court of Oyer and Terminer, Feb. 1781; Minutes of the Monmouth County Court of Oyer and Terminer, Jan., May, Nov., 1781, and May 1782, all at the New Jersey State Archives.

86. Writ to apprehend Daniel Taylor et al. (MG 2:63), New Jersey Historical Society, Newark.

87. Presentment re Elizabeth Newell, 1781, Monmouth County Court of Oyer and Terminer; as of Jan. 1783, Newell was apparently still not in custody (Warrant to apprehend Elizabeth Newell, Jan. 29, 1783, Monmouth County Court of Quarter Sessions [loose papers], Monmouth County Archives, Manalapan).

88. Joseph Reed to Wm. Livingston, Nov. 26, Dec. 2–5, 1780, Livingston Papers (microfilm edition), reel 13; Reed to Livingston, Dec. 11, 1780, *Livingston Papers*, 4:105–106; and *NJA*, 2nd ser., 5:132–133, 134. The prominent Whigs were Joseph Ball, former manager and part owner of the strategic Batsto furnace, and Richard Westcott, a militia major. Doerflinger identifies Ball as one of the "fortune builders" in Revolutionary Philadelphia who was also a leader in the economic resurgence of the 1780s (*A Vigorous Spirit*, 240n.152, 284). This incident may be related to the problem of "collusive captures" that emerged toward the end of the war: ship captains would conspire to be captured, then exchanged, only to repeat the process (*NJA*, 2nd ser., 5:458–459).

89. *NJA*, 2nd ser., 5:462.

90. George F. Fort, "An Account of the Capture and Death of the Refugee John Bacon," *PNJHS*, 1st ser., 1 (1845): 151–152; the fact that this account appears in the inaugural issue of the journal indicates that Bacon survived in the remembered history of the state. Governor Livingston's Proclamation, April 14, 1783, is in *Livingston Papers*, 4:516–519. On battle casualties, see Peckham, *The Toll of Independence*, 99. There were doubtless vendettas carried on after hostilities ended, as well as retributive murders, especially in the backcountry areas of the southern states.

91. J.F.D. Smyth, *A Tour in the United States of America* (1784; repr., New York: Arno Press, 1968), 40; Smyth had campaigned in the state during the war. Cf. Dennis Ryan: "No state was so deeply affected by the internal and external convulsions of those years" ("Landholding, Opportunity, and Mobility in Revolutionary New Jersey," *WMQ*, 3rd ser., 36 [1979]: 578). Richard McCormick points out that there were nearly 2,000 claims of damage in Bergen, Essex, Middlesex, Somerset, and Burlington counties; Middlesex had the highest number (655) (*Experiment in Independence*, 20). If the Monmouth County claims were extant—they may never have been compiled—they would increase the total significantly. The distribution of damage claims is depicted graphically in Wacker and Clemens, *Land Use*, 143, map 26. The original damage claims, which were never paid, are at the New Jersey State Archives.

   On the declining moral tone of society, see Buel, *In Irons*, 127–128; and Jamison, *Religion in New Jersey*, 70. John Shy argued that as the war ground on, people became politicized ("The Military Conflict Considered as a Revolutionary War," in *A People Numerous and Armed: Reflections on the Military Struggle for American Independence* [New York: Oxford University Press, 1976]: 198–199). Sung Bok Kim, on the other hand, posited a model in which people became de-politicized ("The Limits of Politicization in the American Revolution: The Experience of Westchester County, New York," *Journal of American History* 80 [Dec. 1993]: 868–889); the situation in Westchester County bore many similarities to that in northeastern New Jersey. Depending on factors of time and place, the wartime experience of New Jersey provides support for both models.

92. Kim argues that in Westchester County, "imperatives of survival" actuated people's behavior ("The Limits of Politicization," 883).

93. On the postwar flood of imports, see Doerflinger, *A Vigorous Spirit*, 242–246; and Buel, *In Irons*, 246–247. The standard study of postwar conditions in the state is McCormick, *Experiment in Independence*. A more general study is Merrill Jensen, *The New Nation: A History of the United States during the Confederation, 1781–1789* (New York: Alfred A. Knopf, 1950). On the postwar mercantile community, see Doerflinger, *A Vigorous Spirit*, 261–266. On the return of the loyalists, see McCormick, *Experiment in Independence*, 25–31. Wood points out that because loyalists "commanded important chains of influence, their removal disrupted colonial society far in excess of their numbers" (*The Radicalism of the American Revolution*, 176). Gilbert Giberson returned to Monmouth County from Canada, but because his family was harassed by neighbors, he relocated to Pennsylvania (Gilbert Giberson Loyalist Claim, AO 12/15, Public Record Office, Great Britain.)

94. The quote is from Ryan, *New Jersey's Whigs*, 20. The process by which liberalism replaced republicanism is discussed in detail in Wood, *The Radicalism of the American Revolution*, 229–270. On the new acquisitive, individualistic "modal personality," see also Henretta, *The Evolution of American Society*, 83, 99, 103; and Greene, *Pursuits of Happiness*, 195.

95. On the sale of loyalist estates, see McCormick, *Experiment in Independence*, 31–33. The phrase is from Ryan, "Landholding, Opportunity, and Mobility," 580.

96. Ryan, "Landholding, Opportunity, and Mobility," 571–592. On the recovery of the former standard of living, see Cathy Matson, "The Revolution, the Constitution, and the New Nation," in *Cambridge Economic History*, 1:401; Doerflinger, *A Vigorous Spirit*, 197, 283, 286–287; and Henretta, *The Evolution of American Society*, 189–190.

NEW JERSEY: RADICAL OR CONSERVATIVE?

1. See, for example, the differences in interpretation between J. Franklin Jameson, *The American Revolution Considered as a Social Movement* (Princeton, N.J.: Princeton University Press, 1926), and Frederick B. Tolles, "The American Revolution Considered as a Social Movement: A Re-

evaluation," *American Historical Review* 60 (1954): 1–12. For a brief introduction to the various interpretations of the Revolution, see George Athan Billias, ed., *The American Revolution: How Revolutionary Was It?* (Fort Worth, Tex.: Holt, Rinehart and Winston, 1990).

2. Carl L. Becker, *The History of Political Parties in the Province of New York 1760–1776* (1909; repr., Madison: University of Wisconsin Press, 1960), 22. For a progressive interpretation of New Jersey in the Revolution, see Lundin, *Cockpit of the Revolution*.

3. Bailyn, *Ideological Origins*; Edmund Morgan, *The Birth of the Republic, 1763–1789* (Chicago: University of Chicago Press, 1956), 156–157.

4. Jesse Lemish, "Jack Tarr in the Streets: Merchant Seamen in the Politics of Revolutionary America," *WMQ*, 3rd ser., 25 (1968): 371–407; Alfred Young, "George Robert Twelves Hewes (1742–1840): A Boston Shoemaker and the Memory of the American Revolution," *WMQ*, 3rd ser., 38 (1981): 561–623; Young, *The Shoemaker and the Tea Party: Memory and the American Revolution* (Boston: Boston Press, 1999). On republicanism, see Robert E. Shalhope, "Toward a Republican Synthesis: The Emergence of an Understanding of Republicanism in American Historiography," *WMQ*, 3rd ser., 29 (1972): 49–80; and Shalhope, "Republicanism and Early American Historiography," *WMQ*, 3rd ser., 39 (1982): 334–356.

5. See David Waldstreicher, *In the Midst of Perpetual Fetes: The Making of American Nationalism, 1776–1820* (Chapel Hill: University of North Carolina Press, 1997); and David W. Conroy, *Public Houses: Drink and the Revolution of Authority in Colonial Massachusetts* (Chapel Hill: University of North Carolina Press, 1995). Reflecting recent concerns of scholars, in spring 2003 the New Jersey State Museum hosted an exhibit and conference titled Caught in the Crossfire: Churches, Taverns and the Revolution.

6. Gordon Wood, *The Creation of the American Republic* (Chapel Hill: University of North Carolina Press, 1969); and Wood, *The Radicalism of the American Revolution*, 5

7. Gerlach, *Prologue to Independence*, 358; John T. Cunningham, *New Jersey: America's Main Road* (Garden City, N.Y.: Doubleday, 1966), 94. See also Donald Kemmerer, *Path to Freedom: The Struggle for Self-Government in Colonial New Jersey, 1703-1776* (Princeton, N.J.: Princeton University Press, 1940), 346; John E. Pomfret, *Colonial New Jersey: A History* (New York: Scribner, 1973), 268–269; and Thomas Fleming, *New Jersey: A Bicentennial History* (New York: W. W. Norton, 1977), 60.

8. For the constitution of 1776, see Julian P. Boyd, ed., *Fundamental Laws and Constitution of New Jersey 1664–1964* (Princeton, N.J.: D. Van Nostrand, 1964), 155–163.

9. See David Alan Bernstein, "New Jersey in the American Revolution: The Establishment of Government amid Civil and Military Disorder, 1770–1781" (Ph.D. diss., Rutgers University, 1970).

10. See Wacker and Clemens, *Land Use*; and Clemens, *The Uses of Abundance*.

11. For information related to the coming of the Revolution in New Jersey, see Gerlach, *Prologue to Independence*.

12. *New York Gazette and Weekly Mercury*, July 1, 1776. See also Cunningham, *New Jersey's Five Who Signed*.

13. For background on royal governor William Franklin, see Willard S. Randall, *A Little Revenge: Benjamin Franklin and His Son* (Boston: Little Brown, 1984); Larry Gerlach, *William Franklin: New Jersey's Last Royal Governor* (Trenton: New Jersey Historical Commission, 1975); Sheila L. Skemp, *William Franklin: Son of a Patriot, Servant of a King* (New York: Oxford University Press, 1990); and Skemp, *Benjamin and William Franklin: Father and Son, Patriot and Loyalist* (Boston: Bedford Books, 1994).

14. The Stamp Act Resolutions are quoted in Larry Gerlach, ed., *New Jersey in the American Revolution, 1763–1783: A Documentary History* (Trenton: New Jersey Historical Commission, 1975),

22–24. Opposition to the Stamp Act appears in Samuel Smith, *The History of the Colony of Nova-Caesaria, or New Jersey* (Burlington, N.J.: printed by James Parker, 1765). See also Carl E. Prince, "Samuel Smith's History of Nova Caesaria," in *The Colonial Legacy: Some Eighteenth Century Commentators*, ed. Lawrence H. Leder, 2:163–180 (New York: Harper and Row, 1971).

15. See Thomas Purvis, "The Origins and Patterns of Agrarian Unrest in New Jersey, 1735-1754," *WMQ*, 3rd ser., 39 (1982): 600–627; McConville, *These Daring Disturbers*; and Larry Gerlach, "Politics and Prerogatives: The Aftermath of the Robbery of the East Jersey Treasury in 1768," *NJH* 90 (1972): 133–168.

16. Charles R. Erdman Jr., *The New Jersey Constitution of 1776* (Princeton, N.J.: Princeton University Press, 1929); Richard J. Connors, *The Constitution of 1776* (Trenton: New Jersey Historical Commission, 1975); and Irwin N. Gertzog, "The Author of New Jersey's 1776 Constitution," *NJH* 110 (1992): 1–19.

17. *Journal of the Votes and Proceedings of the Provincial Convention of New Jersey* (Burlington, N.J.: printed by Isaac Collins, 1776); Maxine N. Lurie, "Envisioning a Republic: New Jersey's 1776 Constitution and Oath of Office," *NJH* 119 (2001): 3–21.

18. John E. O'Connor, *William Paterson: Lawyer and Statesman, 1745–1806* (New Brunswick, N.J.: Rutgers University Press, 1979).

19. Robert F. Williams, "We shall have a Republick established by the end of the week," *New Jersey Lawyer* (Summer 1987): 21–24; Williams, *The New Jersey State Constitution* (New Brunswick, N.J.: Rutgers University Press, 1997), 2; Ruth Bogin, *Abraham Clark and the Quest for Equality in the Revolutionary Era, 1774–1794* (Rutherford, N.J.: Fairleigh Dickinson University Press, 1982), 40.

20. Lurie, "Envisioning a Republic," 6–7, 15–17.

21. Allan Nevins, *The American States during and after the Revolution, 1775–1789* (New York: Macmillan, 1924), 136, 139. Also important in New Jersey is the fact that some delegates were Quakers who appeared willing to accept the constitution only with the reconciliation clause. Quaker authorities had resolved that any support of the Revolutionary governments, even to the extent of using their paper money, was a violation of the Quaker belief in pacifism; the penalty for this was disownment (the equivalent of excommunication, for this involved being read out of Meeting). Thus their willingness to sign at all is remarkable, because it made them participants in the new government. For studies of American Quakers in relation to the Revolution, see Hugh Barbour and J. William Frost, *The Quakers* (New York: Greenwood Press, 1988), 137–151; Jack D. Marietta, *The Reformation of American Quakerism, 1748–1783* (Philadelphia: University of Pennsylvania Press, 1984); William C. Kashatus III, *Conflict and Conviction: A Reappraisal of Quaker Involvement in the American Revolution* (Lantham, Md.: University Press of America, 1990); and Arthur J. Mekeel, *The Relation of the Quakers to the American Revolution* (Washington, D.C.: University Press of America, 1975). For Quakers and the New Jersey Constitution, see Bernstein, "New Jersey in the American Revolution," 70.

22. Two of the others (New Hampshire and South Carolina) also had some reservations, just in case a peaceful solution was found to the dispute with Great Britain. Only Virginia did not hedge. See William Paul Adams, *The First American Constitutions: Republican Ideology and the Making of the State Constitutions in the Revolutionary Era* (Chapel Hill: University of North Carolina Press, 1980), 5.

23. Minutes of Meeting of July 18, 1776, *Journal of the Votes and Proceedings of the Provincial Convention of New Jersey*, 64–65.

24. See William Griffith, *Eumenes; Being a Collection of Papers, Written for the Purpose of Exhibiting Some of the More Prominent Errors and Omissions of the Constitution of New-Jersey . . .* (Trenton, N.J.: printed by G. Craft, 1799).

25. The original text differed slightly in the two versions for the assembly and council. Later, after

the war, the oath was modified (taking out the reference to the king of Great Britain), and legislators continued to sign it until 1844. Copies are in the New Jersey State Archives.

26. It is one of at least ninety such declarations found and discussed by Pauline Maier in *American Scripture: Making the Declaration of Independence* (New York: Alfred A. Knopf, 1997), 47–96.

27. In New Jersey, annual elections (and hence sessions) were provided for under the Concessions of 1665, Concessions of West New Jersey in 1677, and Fundamental Agreements of West New Jersey in 1681, but not under royal government. See Larry R. Gerlach, "Power to the People: Popular Sovereignty, Republicanism, and the Legislature in Revolutionary New Jersey," in *The Development of the New Jersey Legislature from Colonial Times to the Present*, ed. William C. Wright, 7–62 (Trenton: New Jersey Historical Commission, 1976).

28. Ibid., 13.

29. Both the Concessions of West New Jersey in 1677 and the Fundamental Constitutions of East New Jersey in 1683 required juries. A later state court decision would interpret this to mean, by custom, trial by twelve peers (*Holmes v. Walton* [1780]). See Wayne D. Moore, "Written and Unwritten Constitutional Law in the Founding Period: The Early New Jersey Cases," *Constitutional Commentary* 7 (1990): 341-359.

30. Provisions for religious toleration were also included in the Concessions of West New Jersey in 1677, the Fundamental Agreements of West New Jersey in 1681, and the Fundamental Constitutions of East New Jersey in 1683.

31. Wallace N. Jamison, *Religion in New Jersey: A Brief History* (Princeton, N.J.: D. Van Nostrand, 1964).

32. Cynthia Dubin Edelberg, *Jonathan Odell: Loyalist Poet of the American Revolution* (Durham, N.C.: Duke University Press, 1987). For Anglicans and the issue of a bishop, see also Edward J. Cody, *The Religious Issue in Revolutionary New Jersey*, vol. 10 of *New Jersey's Revolutionary War Experience* (Trenton: New Jersey Historical Commission, 1975), 8; Nelson K. Burr, *The Anglican Church in New Jersey* (Philadelphia: Church Historical Society, 1954), 336–372; and Nancy L. Rhoden, *Revolutionary Anglicanism: The Colonial Church of England Clergy during the American Revolution* (New York: New York University Press, 1999).

33. Two out of the three rights mentioned here made it into the Bill of Rights in the 1844 and 1947 constitutions. Only annual elections failed to become a constitutional tradition. Today, New Jersey assembly members are elected every two years, senators every four (except after a census), and governors every four.

34. Gregory Evans Dowd, "Declaration of Independence: War and Inequality in Revolutionary New Jersey, 1776-1815," *NJH* 103 (1985): 47–67, discusses what the Revolution did not change for women, blacks, and Native Americans who lived in New Jersey.

35. Richard P. McCormick, *The History of Voting in New Jersey* (New Brunswick, N.J.: Rutgers University Press, 1953); J. R. Pole, "Suffrage Reform and the American Revolution in New Jersey," *Proceedings of the New Jersey Historical Society* 74 (1956): 173-194.

36. Sophie Drinker, "Votes for Women in Eighteenth-Century New Jersey," *Proceedings of the New Jersey Historical Society* 80 (1962) 31-45; Irwin N. Gertzog, "Female Suffrage in New Jersey, 1790–1807," *Women and Politics* 10 (1990): 47–68.

37. Donald L. Kemmerer, "A History of Paper Money in Colonial New Jersey, 1668–1775," *Proceedings of the New Jersey Historical Society* 74 (1956): 107–144. For the 1780s, see McCormick, *Experiment in Independence*; Mary R. Murrin, *To Save This State from Ruin: New Jersey and the Creation of the United States Constitution, 1776–1789* (Trenton: New Jersey Historical Commission, 1987); and Maxine N. Lurie, "New Jersey Intellectuals and the United States Constitution," *Journal of Rutgers University Libraries* (1987): 65–87. Of course, this particular issue became moot after 1789, when the federal government gained control of currency.

38. See McCormick, *The History of Voting*, 64, where the author states: "for now there was to be no higher authority than the electorate."

39. See, for example, John Cooper in Gerlach, *New Jersey in the American Revolution*; and the arguments of Rev. Jacob Green beginning two years later in David Mitros, ed., *Jacob Green and the Slavery Debate in Revolutionary Morris County, New Jersey* (Morristown, N.J.: Morris County Heritage Commission, 1993).

THE "COCKPIT" RECONSIDERED

1. For example, Lundin, *Cockpit of the Revolution*.

2. Calculating the precise number of battles and skirmishes is probably impossible; not all records of the war have survived, and not all actions were recorded. The count of over 600 (actually 607) engagements or incidents is found in David C. Munn, comp., *Battles and Skirmishes of the American Revolution in New Jersey* (Trenton, N.J.: Department of Environmental Protection, Bureau of Geology and Topography, 1976). Munn counted every military incident and based his tally on detailed archival and local historical sources. The lower figure is from Peckham, *The Toll of Independence*, 125, 141. This is a valuable source and accurate for the engagements reported, but it looks at the national scene and is based on a much narrower examination of New Jersey sources. In yet another count, the National Park Service database of Revolutionary War actions also lists 296 actions in New Jersey (National Park Service, *Crossroads of the American Revolution in New Jersey: Special Resource Study* [Philadelphia: U.S. Department of the Interior, National Park Service, Philadelphia Support Office, 2002], 5). There is no disagreement, however, on the fact that New Jersey was the site of more engagements than any other state. Munn's *Battles and Skirmishes* is the most comprehensive and reliable source, however, and is cited most often in this essay.

3. For overviews of military operations in New Jersey, see Alfred Hoyt Bill, *New Jersey and the Revolutionary War* (Princeton, N.J.: D. Van Nostrand, 1964); and Lewis F. Owen, *The Revolutionary Struggle in New Jersey, 1776–1783* (Trenton: New Jersey Historical Commission, 1975).

4. Washington to John Augustine Washington, Dec. 18, 1776, Fitzpatrick, *The Writings of George Washington*, 6:397–398.

5. Howe was pleased with the campaign; see Ira D. Gruber, *The Howe Brothers and the American Revolution* (New York: Athenaeum, 1972), 148–149; and Troyer Steele Anderson, *The Command of the Howe Brothers during the American Revolution* (New York: Oxford University Press, 1936), 204–209.

6. Howe is quoted at length on this point in Anderson, *The Command of the Howe Brothers*, 206.

7. Mark Edward Lender, "Small Battles Won: New Jersey and the Patriot Military Revival," *New Jersey Heritage* 1 (2002): 33–34.

8. Ibid., 34–35.

9. While he marshaled his forces in Pennsylvania, for example, Washington was able to communicate with civil, militia, and Continental officers in the state. See Washington's detailed letter of December 12, 1776, to New Jersey militia general Philemon Dickinson, then near Trenton (Fitzpatrick, *The Writings of George Washington*, 6:358). Washington sent equally explicit instructions to Continental general William Maxwell at Morristown on December 21, 1776 (ibid., 6:414–416). On December 20, 1776, he also informed the president of Congress that he wanted Maxwell "to harass and annoy the Enemy in their Quarters and cut off their Convoys" (ibid., 6:407).

10. Patriot rank and file did their share of plundering as well but not on a scale approaching British activity. Inventories of damages were tallied under a law of December 1781 (Acts of the . . . General Assembly of the State of New Jersey) and are now in the New Jersey State Archives as "Damages by the British Army, 1776–1782" and "Damages by the American Army, 1776–1782."

11. In his letter to his brother of December 18, 1776, Washington noted that he had wanted to stand at Hackensack or at New Brunswick (Fitzpatrick, *The Writings of George Washington*, 6:398). On December 7, even as his army had begun to cross the Delaware into Pennsylvania, Washington led a column back toward Princeton, pulling back only when intelligence informed him that the British were advancing in strength (ibid., 6:335–336).

12. Washington related his account of the Trenton action in a letter to General Alexander McDougall on December 28, 1776: "I crossed over to Jersey on the Evening of the 25th about nine Miles above Trenton with upwards of 2000 Men and attacked three Regiments of Hessians, consisting of 1500 Men about 8 o'Clock next Morning. Our Men pushed on with such rapidity, that they soon captured four pieces of Cannon out of Six, Surrounded the Enemy, and obliged 30 Officers and 886 privates to lay down their Arms without firing a Shot. Our loss was only two Officers and two or three privates wounded" (ibid., 6:448). The standard history of the battle is William S. Stryker, *The Battles of Trenton and Princeton* (1898; repr., Trenton, N.J.: Old Barracks Association, 2001). For a briefer account that emphasizes the element of chance in the outcome at Trenton, see Mark Edward Lender, "Reversals of Fortune: The Trenton and Princeton Campaign of 1776–1777," *New Jersey Heritage* 1 (2002): 17–29; Trenton casualties are noted on 25.

13. However prosaic and however fixed in legend, there is little evidence that Cornwallis actually used the term. What is certain is his belief that Washington would still be across Assunpink Creek on the morning of January 3. See Don Higginbotham, *The War of American Independence: Military Attitudes, Policies, and Practice, 1763–1789* (New York: Macmillan, 1971), 169; and Stryker, *The Battles of Trenton and Princeton*, 268–269.

14. Washington's account of the Assunpink and Princeton operations is in Washington to the President of Congress, Jan. 5, 1777, Fitzpatrick, *The Writings of George Washington*, 6:467–470.

15. Andrew M. Sherman, *Historic Morristown, New Jersey: The Story of Its First Century* (Morristown, N.J.: Howard Publishing, 1905), 248–249. Records of the actual trial, and a similar Council of Safety proceeding at Morristown, are in *New Jersey v. James Hiss* to *New Jersey v. John Parks*, Morris County Court of Oyer and Terminer, Minutes, Boxed MSS, New Jersey State Library [now in New Jersey State Archives]; Military Record of Captain Moses Estey [copy of original], New Jersey Department of Defense MSS, No. 10304B, New Jersey State Archives. According to available records, these "Tory Continentals" served with records no less distinguished than those of soldiers enlisted under more "patriotic" circumstances. Troop service records are in Revolutionary Veterans File, New Jersey Department of Defense MSS, New Jersey State Archives.

16. Ryan, *New Jersey's Loyalists*, 18–19.

17. On the fate of the Tories, see ibid., 23–26. In February 1776, the same lesson was learned in bloody fashion at Moore's Creek Bridge in North Carolina, an engagement that broke early loyalist activity in the South as decisively as the New Jersey experience did in the North. See Christopher Ward, *The War of the Revolution*, 2 vols. (New York: Macmillan, 1952), 1:663–664.

18. This is not to say that loyalists did not maintain a foothold in New Jersey. They garrisoned Sandy Hook for most of the war, and there was a Tory post on Paulus Hook in modern Jersey City. Unlike the patriot base at Morristown, however, these lodgments never served as secure areas covering civil administration or as depots or encampments for major military formations intended to take and hold territory. The Tory regulars served under Cortlandt Skinner, the last royal attorney general of New Jersey, turned British brigadier. They were tough troops, and they campaigned in theaters from the Middle colonies to the South. After the war, most survivors found new homes in Canada. Their defeat stemmed from no lack of courage. There were the six regiments of Skinner's Greens, so called because of their green uniforms. The Continental army seldom boasted more than three New Jersey regiments. The record of Skinner's regiments is traced in Paul H. Smith, "New Jersey Loyalists and the British 'Provincial' Corps in the War

of Independence," *NJH* 87 (1969): 69–78; and William S. Stryker, *The New Jersey Volunteers in the Revolutionary War* (Trenton, N.J.: Naar, Day and Naar, 1887).

19. A good overview of Morristown as a headquarters and encampment, including its advantageous location, is in Bruce W. Stewart, *Morristown: A Crucible of the American Revolution*, vol. 3 of *New Jersey's Revolutionary Experience*.

20. On iron production, see Salay, "Production of War Material," 13–16. At the time of Washington's arrival, Morristown also had the only powder mill in New Jersey (Fred Bartenstein and Isabel Bartenstein, *A Report on New Jersey's Revolutionary Powder Mill* [Morristown, N.J.: Morris County Historical Society, 1975]).

21. Worthington C. Ford et al., eds., *Journals of the Continental Congress, 1774–1789*, 34 vols (Washington, D.C.: Library of Congress, 1904–1937), 5:762–763.

22. James Kirby Martin and Mark Edward Lender, *A Respectable Army: The Military Origins of the Republic, 1763–1789* (Arlington Heights, Ill.: Harlan Davidson, 1982), 90–92.

23. David C. Munn, comp., *Battles and Skirmishes of the American Revolution in New Jersey* (Trenton: Department of Environmental Protection, Bureau of Geology and Topography, State of New Jersey, ca. 1976), 127–128.

24. Operations to prevent British foraging also served to preserve New Jersey food and forage supplies for patriot forces. In fact, the Americans at Morristown and other points had enough food during 1777.

25. Fitzpatrick, *The Writings of George Washington*, 7:96–97.

26. Johann Ewald, *Diary of the American War: A Hessian Journal*, trans. and ed. Joseph P. Tustin, 55 (New Haven, Conn.: Yale University Press, 1979).

27. Credit for the term goes to Jared C. Lobdell, "Six Generals Gather Forage: The Engagement at Quibbletown, 1777," *NJH* 102 (1984): 35.

28. David Syrett, *Shipping and the American War, 1775–83: A Study of British Transport Organization* (London: University of London, Athlone Press, 1970).

29. Martin and Lender, *A Respectable Army*, 80–81.

30. Accounts of why Howe chose not to march across New Jersey vary; see Gruber, *The Howe Brothers*, 198; and Anderson, *The Command of the Howe Brothers*, 238. For Howe's account, see William Howe, *The Narrative of Lieut. Gen. Sir William Howe in a Committee of the House of Commons . . .*, 2nd ed. (London: printed by H. Baldwin, 1779).

31. For the Philadelphia campaign, see Martin and Lender, *A Respectable Army*, 80–83. Washington used the New Jersey transportation network to reach Philadelphia long before Howe.

32. Washington saw the holding of the river forts as critical. "Gen'l Howe's Situation in Philadelphia will not be the most agreeable; for if his supplies can be stopped by water, it may easily be done by land." He dared to "hope that the acquisition of Philadelphia may instead of his good fortune, prove his [Howe's] ruin" (Fitzpatrick, *The Writings of George Washington*, 9:422–423).

33. For a graphic description of the fight, see Frank H. Stewart, *History of the Battle of Red Bank* (Woodbury, N.J.: Board of Chosen Freeholders of Gloucester County, 1927).

34. The definitive account of the defense of the river forts is John W. Jackson, *The Pennsylvania Navy, 1775–1781: The Defense of the Delaware* (New Brunswick, N.J.: Rutgers University Press, 1974); for a shorter version, see Mark Edward Lender, *The River War: The Fight for the Delaware, 1777* (Trenton: New Jersey Historical Commission, 1979).

35. Although dated, the standard account of the Monmouth campaign remains William S. Stryker, *The Battle of Monmouth*, ed. William Starr Myers (Princeton, N.J.: Princeton University Press, 1927).

36. As a result of poor staff work, for example, a major patriot contingent under General Daniel Morgan, in position on the exposed enemy right and within sound of the guns on June 28, never got into the fight. Redcoat officers were still better at handling large commands in complex operations.

37. Martin and Lender, *A Respectable Army*, 161.

38. The full story of the Pennsylvania and New Jersey mutinies is in Carl Van Doren, *Mutiny in January* (New York: Viking, 1943).

39. "Instructions to Officers to Collect Provisions," Jan. 8, 1780, Fitzpatrick, *The Writings of George Washington*, 17:360–362; Washington to the Magistrates of New Jersey, Jan. 8, 1780, ibid., 17:62–65.

40. On the precise march routes, see National Park Service, *Crossroads of the American Revolution*, 26.

41. This total is tabulated from the chronological list of engagements in Munn, *Battles and Skirmishes*, 132–141.

42. *New Jersey Gazette*, Feb. 3, 1779, *NJA*, 2nd ser., 5:264–265.

43. Munn, *Battles and Skirmishes*, 81; Peckham, *The Toll of Independence*, 55, 69; detail on the skirmishing around Hoppertown is in Leiby, *The Revolutionary War*, 246–251.

44. Thomas Fleming, *The Forgotten Victory: The Battle for New Jersey, 1780* (New York: Reader's Digest Press, 1973). Ewald, the Hessian jaeger captain, thought that the militia was especially effective at Springfield; see his *Diary*, 244–246.

45. Tabulated from the chronological list of engagements or incidents in Munn, *Battles and Skirmishes*, 132–141. Not all of these encounters involved shooting, but the seizure of an enemy vessel driven ashore by weather or run aground was still of military importance.

46. Kemp, *A Nest of Rebel Pirates*, 9, 47–50; *Political Magazine and Parliamentary, Naval, Military, and Literary Journal*, Jan. 1761, 60, quoted in ibid., 103.

47. On loyalist African American combatants, see Pingeon, *Blacks in the Revolutionary Era*, 21–23; for a specific example of a raid involving black loyalists, see Clement Alexander Price, *Freedom Not Far Distant: A Documentary History of Afro-Americans in New Jersey* (Newark: New Jersey Historical Society, 1980), 69.

48. This is the general conclusion of Bernstein, "New Jersey in the American Revolution."

49. Mark Edward Lender, "The Conscripted Line: The Draft in Revolutionary New Jersey," *NJH* 103 (1985): 25.

50. *Votes and Proceedings of the General Assembly of the State of New Jersey*, Aug.–Oct. 1777, 159–160.

51. Stewart, *Morristown*, 23.

52. Quoted in National Park Service, *Crossroads of the American Revolution*, 25.

PICTURING REVOLUTIONARY NEW JERSEY

1. Absolute proof does not exist that the statement was made by Benjamin Franklin, although it has repeatedly been attributed to him. See Alfred M. Heston, *Jersey Waggon Jaunts* (Camden, N.J.: Atlantic County Historical Society, 1926), 2, 310, where the author writes: "In his address [at the Centennial Exhibition in Philadelphia on New Jersey Day, Aug. 24, 1876] Mr. [Abraham] Browning compared New Jersey to an immense barrel, filled with good things to eat and open at both ends, with Pennsylvanians grabbing from one end and the New Yorkers from the other." Heston also notes that in this context, Browning first used the term "Garden State" when referring to New Jersey.

2. See William H. Gerdts Jr., *Painting and Sculpture in New Jersey* (Princeton, N.J.: D. Van Nostrand, 1964), ix, where the author makes it clear that the statement that New Jersey is and was an "artistic desert" is false. The reason, he states, is that not enough attention had been paid to the artists who lived here and contributed to the state's heritage. This situation began to change in 1957 with the mounting of a groundbreaking Newark Museum exhibition, *Early New Jersey Artists: 18th and 19th Centuries.*

3. See Richard P. McCormick, *New Jersey from Colony to State, 1609–1789* (Princeton, N.J.: D. Van Nostrand, 1964), 101.

4. It was not until 1837 in France that Louis Daguerre invented photography. Its general use in America did not occur until the middle of the nineteenth century.

5. Gerdts, *Painting and Sculpture*, 2–7. It is believed that Watson came to the colonies after England's Jacobite Rebellion. He managed to accumulate some wealth by purchasing most of the houses in Perth Amboy and property in New York City. He also is reputed to have been a miser and usurer.

6. William Dunlap, *History of the Rise and Progress of the Arts of Design in the United States,* 2 vols. (New York: George P. Scott, 1834), 1:21. Although today we assume that Dunlap's choice of Watson as the most notable New Jersey artist at the time may be correct, see Gerdts, *Painting and Sculpture*, 2–3, who points out that since both Dunlap and Watson lived in Perth Amboy, perhaps proximity is what influenced Dunlap's choice.

7. For standard sources on Patience Wright, Joseph Wright, and Gilbert Stuart, see Charles Coleman Sellers, *Patience Wright, American Artist and Spy in George III's London* (Middletown, Conn.: Wesleyan University Press, 1976); Monroe H. Fabian, *Joseph Wright: American Artist, 1756–1793* (Washington D.C.: Smithsonian Institution Press, 1985); and Richard McLanathan, *Gilbert Stuart* (New York: Harry N. Abrams, in association with the National Museum of American Art, Smithsonian Institution, 1986).

8. For a discussion of the importance of history painting through the centuries, see Barbara J. Mitnick, "The History of History Painting," in *Picturing History: American Painting: 1770–1930*, ed. William Ayres, 29–43 (New York: Rizzoli International Publications, 1993).

9. Ibid., 31.

10. For information on West, see Allen Staley and Helmut von Erffa, *The Paintings of Benjamin West* (New Haven, Conn.: Yale University Press, 1986); Ann Uhry Abrams, *The Valiant Hero: Benjamin West and Grand-Style History Painting* (Washington, D.C.: Smithsonian Institution Press, 1985); and Dorinda Evans, *Benjamin West and His American Students* (Washington, D.C.: Smithsonian Institution Press, 1980).

11. For Peale, see Charles Coleman Sellers, *Charles Willson Peale* (New York: Charles Scribner's Sons, 1969); and Edgar P. Richardson, Brooke Hindle, and Lillian B. Miller, *Charles Willson Peale and His World* (New York: Harry N. Abrams, 1982).

12. These study excursions to England were necessary, since the only art academies established in America in the eighteenth century did not open their doors until the 1790s. In 1791, Peale began the School for the Fine Arts and, three years later, the Columbianum (or American Academy of Fine Arts), which contained some plaster casts for study. For discussions of these enterprises, see Eliot Clark, *History of the National Academy of Design 1825–1953* (New York: Columbia University Press, 1954), 4; and Richardson, Hindle, and Miller, *Charles Willson Peale*, 87–89. Major portraits painted by Peale during this pre–Revolutionary War period include *The Edward Lloyd Family* (1771, Henry Francis du Pont Winterthur Museum) and the first life portrait of George Washington (1772, Washington and Lee University).

13. See the early biography of Benjamin West by John Galt, *The Life, Studies and Works of Benjamin West, Esquire* (London: T. Cadell and W. Davies, 1820), 48. Also quoted in Staley and Von Erffa, *Paintings of Benjamin West*, 57.

14. See Galt, *The Life, Studies and Works of Benjamin West*, 49–50; Abrams, *The Valiant Hero*, 14; and Mitnick, "The History of History Painting," 29, who quotes Reynolds as follows: "Mr. West has conquered . . . he has treated his subject as it ought to be treated. I retract my objections against the introduction of any other circumstances into historical pictures than those which are requisite and appropriate."

15. Richardson, Hindle, and Miller, *Charles Willson Peale*, 18. Later, on June 17, 1777, he received yet another promotion when he was commissioned as captain of the Fourth Battalion or Regiment of Foot.

16. Evidence of Washington's disdain can be found in the following letter that he wrote on May 21, 1772, to the Reverend Jonathan Boucher: "Inclination having yielded to Importunity, I am now contrary to all expectation under the hands of Mr. Peale; but in so grave—so sullen a mood—and now and then under the influence of Morpheus, when some critical strokes are making, that I fancy the skill of this Gentleman's Pencil, will be hard put to it, in describing to the World what manner of man I am" (Recipient's copy, Henry Ford Museum and Greenfield Village, Dearborn, Mich.). See also David Meschutt, "Life Portraits of George Washington," in *George Washington: American Symbol*, ed. Barbara J. Mitnick, 25–26 (New York: Hudson Hills Press, 1999).

17. Quoted in Mark Thistlethwaite, "The Artist as Interpreter of American History," in *In This Academy: The Pennsylvania Academy of the Fine Arts, 1805–1976* (Philadelphia: Pennsylvania Academy of the Fine Arts, 1976), 107.

18. This work resulted from the fourth sitting Washington gave to Peale; he posed for it between January 20 and February 1, 1779. See Meschutt, "Life Portraits of George Washington," 26, for a discussion of the great popularity of the painting, which encouraged Peale to produce numerous replicas. The accuracy of the pose or location was never in question, for in the true spirit of history painting, the work was and is considered to be a form of mythology, intended to inspire patriotism and nationalism.

19. For basic sources on Trumbull, see John Trumbull, *Autobiography, Reminiscences and Letters of John Trumbull from 1756 to 1841* (New York and London: Wiley and Putnam, 1841); John Hill Morgan, *Paintings by John Trumbull at Yale University* (New Haven, Conn.: Yale University Press, 1926); Helen A. Cooper, *John Trumbull: The Hand and Spirit of a Painter* (New Haven, Conn.: Yale University Art Gallery, 1982); and Irma B. Jaffe, *John Trumbull: Patriot-Artist of the American Revolution* (Boston: New York Graphic Society, 1975).

20. Trumbull, *Autobiography*, 18.

21. Trumbull believed the true date of the commission to be June 28, 1776, but instead, it was dated September 12 of that year. See Trumbull's *Autobiography*, 39–49, for a complete discussion of that period in his life. It is also true that despite his resignation, Trumbull's military career was not over. In August 1778, he carried out a dangerous mission for General John Sullivan in Rhode Island, and he fought against a contingent of German troops.

22. See Jaffee, *John Trumbull*, 79–81. During the same period, Trumbull's father, the governor of Connecticut, had resolved to write a history of the Revolution.

23. Both were completed in 1786 and are in the collection of the Yale University Art Gallery.

24. For Trumbull's Paris period, see Jaffee, *John Trumbull*, 97–122. Trumbull's first version of the *Declaration of Independence* was begun in 1787 and not completed until 1820 (Yale University Art Gallery). Later versions are on display in the Capitol Rotunda in Washington, D.C. (1818), and at the Wadsworth Athenaeum (1832) in Hartford, Conn.

25. See Helen Cooper, *John Trumbull: The Hand and Spirit of a Painter* (New Haven, Conn.: Yale University Press, 1982), 73; and Trumbull, *Autobiography*, 420.

26. See also Jaffe, *John Trumbull*, 151, who makes some interesting comparisons between sections of Trumbull's *Death of Mercer* and Benjamin West's contemporary history paintings. She equates the

composition of Mercer leaning against his fallen horse with Benjamin West's *Edward the Black Prince Crossing the Somme* (1788, Collection of Queen Elizabeth II) and the position of William on horseback with William III in West's *Battle of the Boyne* (1771, presently unlocated). For information on *George Washington at Trenton*, see Jaffe, *John Trumbull*, 315. A third major New Jersey–related Trumbull scene is the portrait *George Washington at Trenton* (1792, Yale University Art Gallery), which Trumbull claimed to have painted from life long after the conclusion of the war.

27. For basic biographical information on Carter, see Glenn B. Opitz, ed., *Mantle Fielding's Dictionary of American Painters, Sculptors and Engravers* (Poughkeepsie, N.Y.: Apollo Book, 1983), 145–146.

28. An exhibition mounted at the Monmouth County Library in October 2001 titled *Searching for Molly Pitcher* further uncovered issues related to the continuing question of her identity and deeds. In fact, little mention was given to Molly Pitcher after the Revolution and for the first half of the nineteenth century; thus it is possible that much of the information available today is based on legend.

29. The most thorough study of the life and work of Leutze is Barbara S. Groseclose, *Emanuel Leutze, 1816–1868: Freedom Is the Only King* (Washington, D.C.: Smithsonian Institution Press for the National Collection of Fine Arts, 1975).

30. For a detailed discussion of Leutze's *Washington Crossing the Delaware*, see ibid., 34–43. The work presently in the collection of the New York Metropolitan Museum of Art is actually Leutze's second version of the subject. The first was damaged in a fire in Germany, subsequently restored by Leutze, and finally destroyed during World War II. In addition to the works of Emanuel Leutze, other American artists also dealt with the subject, for example, Thomas Sully (1783–1872) in his famous *Passage of the Delaware* (1819, Museum of Fine Arts, Boston).

31. *New York Evening Mirror*, Nov. 7, 1851. Also quoted in Ayres, "Preface," *Picturing History*, 17.

32. See Groseclose, *Emanuel Leutze*, 44–46, for a discussion of this work.

33. Ibid., 46.

34. For information on the Centennial celebration and its display of art, see Lillian Miller, "Engines, Marbles and Canvases, the Centennial Exposition of 1876," in *Indiana Historical Society Lectures 1972–73* (Indianapolis: Indiana Historical Society, 1973), 3–29.

35. See Barbara J. Mitnick, "Paintings for the People," in Ayres, *Picturing History*, 157; and Richard G. Wilson, "Presence of the Past," in *The American Renaissance: 1876–1917* (Brooklyn, N.Y.: Brooklyn Museum, 1976), 39–55.

36. For information on Ferris, see Barbara J. Mitnick, *Jean Leon Gerome Ferris: American Painter Historian* (Laurel, Miss.: Lauren Rogers Museum of Art, 1986). From 1900 until his death in 1930, Ferris painted a series of seventy-eight paintings related to events of American history. They were exhibited as a group from 1916 to 1930 at Congress Hall, Philadelphia, and subsequently at the Smithsonian Institution in Washington, D.C. Today they are found in both public and private collections.

37. George Washington to John Augustine Washington, Dec. 18, 1776. For an early source for this quotation, see Jared Sparks, *The Writings of George Washington* (Boston: Russell, Odiorne, and Metcalf and Hilliard, Gray and Co., 1834), 4:231.

38. The groundbreaking work on New Jersey decorative arts during this period is Margaret E. White, *The Decorative Arts of Early New Jersey* (Princeton, N.J.: D. Van Nostrand, 1964).

39. Ibid., 2. The agreement was signed December 7, 1738. See also Mary Harrod Northend, *American Glass* (New York: Tudor Publishing, 1926), 23.

40. See John T. Cunningham, *Made in New Jersey: The Industrial Story of a State* (New Brunswick, N.J.: Rutgers University Press, 1954), 17.

41. White, *The Decorative Arts*, 10.

42. In the late eighteenth century, the Eagle Glass Works also was established at Port Elizabeth, although it appears that the true golden age of glass-making in New Jersey did not begin until about 1840. Nevertheless, the industry owes its establishment in the state to developments begun in the eighteenth century.

43. See Northend, *American Glass*, 30, where the author states that Stanger was eventually absorbed by the Owens Bottle Company of Toledo, Ohio, in 1918.

44. For additional references on glass-making in New Jersey, see Arlene Palmer, *Wistarburgh Glass Works: The Beginning of Jersey Glassmaking—New Jersey 1739–1776* (Alloway, N.J.: Alloway Township Bicentennial Committee, 1976); and, for Glassboro, Robert D. Bole and Edward H. Walton Jr., *The Glassboro Story, 1779–1964* (York, Pa: Maple Press, 1964).

45. White, *The Decorative Arts*, 28.

46. See Edwin Atlee Barber, *Pottery and Porcelain of the United States* (New York: G. P. Putnam's Sons, 1909), 55. Quoted in White, *The Decorative Arts*, 31, from the document of ca. 1690.

47. See White, *The Decorative Arts*, 34–41, 50.

48. For basic information on silver, jewelry, and clock-making in New Jersey, see White, *The Decorative Arts*, 68–89.

49. *Early Furniture Made in New Jersey*, exhibition catalog (Newark, N.J.: Newark Museum, 1958). See also Margaret E. White, "Some Early Furniture Makers of New Jersey," *The Magazine Antiques* 74, no. 4 (October 1958): 322.

50. White, *The Decorative Arts*, 97.

NEW JERSEY ARCHITECTURE

1. Peter Wacker, *Cultural Geography of Eighteenth Century New Jersey*, vol. 4 of *New Jersey's Revolutionary Experience*, 18; Larry Gerlach, *The Road to Revolution*, vol. 7 of *New Jersey's Revolutionary Experience*, 7. The population was estimated to be between 122,000 and 140,000.

2. Thomas Archdeacon, *New Jersey Society in the Revolutionary Era*, vol. 17 of *New Jersey's Revolutionary Experience*, 8. See Wacker, *Land and People*, 164–169, for an analysis of the amalgamation of settlers and their cultural origins.

3. England and Scotland were united in 1707. England conquered Wales in the 1530s, and Ireland did not become part of Britain until 1801.

4. Gerlach, *The Road to Revolution*, 6.

5. Oral Coad, *New Jersey in Travelers' Accounts 1524–1971* (Metuchen, N.J.: Scarecrow Press, 1972), 23, no. 64. Note 64 of this publication excerpts a journal ascribed to Lord Adam Gordon, "Journal of an Officer Who Travelled in America and the West Indies in 1764 and 1765," published in *Travels in the American Colonies* (New York: Macmillan, 1916). See also Coad, *New Jersey in Travelers' Accounts*, 38, no. 107.

6. Miriam V. Studley, *Historic New Jersey through Visitor's Eyes* (Princeton, N.J.: D. Van Nostrand, 1964), 26-27.

7. Thomas Pownall was a royal governor of Massachusetts and lieutenant governor of New Jersey (*A Topographical Description of . . . Parts of North America* [London: J. Almon, 1776]). See also Coad, *New Jersey in Travelers' Accounts*, 18–19, no. 53.

8. Studley, *Historic New Jersey*, 58–59.

9. Archdeacon, *New Jersey Society*, 5–7.

10. National Park Service, National Register of Historic Places Inventory-Nomination Form, Alexander Douglas House, July 1970, State of New Jersey, Historic Preservation Office, Trenton. Although modest in comparison with other Revolutionary War shrines and used only briefly by Washington and his officers, the house was considered important enough to be moved at least three times, beginning in 1871, and "restored" at least once. The house was originally located in the new Kingsbury section of Trenton, which was more distant from the enemy during the Revolution and therefore a more secure place to meet.

11. George De Cou, *Burlington: A Provincial Capital* (Philadelphia: Harris and Partridge, 1945), 33. The author quotes from the journal of a 1679 visit to West Jersey by Dutch Labadists Jasper Dankaerts and Peter Sluyter. The descriptions of these pioneer buildings bear strong similarity to the description of the homes of the earlier New Sweden colony in the lower Delaware. The West Jersey Quakers may have borrowed these building techniques from their Scandinavian neighbors. An elderly resident of the New Sweden colony who was interviewed in the eighteenth century gave a picture of crudely built homes erected by the seventeenth-century pioneers. He recalled that the houses of the first settlers were one small room with a very low doorway heated by a corner chimney of stone, gray sand, or clay. Small holes served as windows and were covered with moveable boards. Clay or moss provided insulation. See Peter Kalm in Studley, *Historic New Jersey*, 43.

12. Bartlett Burleigh James and J. Franklin Jameson, eds., *Journal of Jasper Danckaerts, 1670–1680* (New York: Charles Scribner's Sons, 1913), as cited in Susan Maxman Architects, "Historical Documentation and Strategic Planning Study: The William Trent House," Jan. 1997, 2:A.3-3.

13. Bruce Stewart, *Morristown: A Crucible of the American Revolution*, vol. 3 of *New Jersey's Revolutionary Experience*, 13; Francis Holland, "Historic Structures Report (Part I) Ford Mansion Morristown National Historical Park" (National Park Service, 1959), 4, no. 4.

14. De Cou, *Burlington*, 45–46. De Cou cites Gabriel Thomas, *Account of Pennsylvania and West Jersey* (London: A Baldwin, 1698).

15. Coad, *New Jersey in Travelers' Accounts*, 15, no. 44. See Bampfylde Moore Carew, *The Life and Adventures of Bampfylde-Moore Carew* (London: T. Martin, 1788). The 200 original settlers of Burlington had been drawn primarily from Yorkshire and London and nearby counties. Its regular plan was originally designed to differentiate the parcels divided between the two major groups of proprietors—the Yorkshire part and the London part. The town's physical cohesiveness must have made it seem more "urban" than any other settlement in the colony.

16. Julie Riesenweber, "Order in Domestic Space: House Plans and Room Use in the Vernacular Dwellings of Salem County" (master's thesis, University of Delaware, 1984), 77. Riesenweber notes that the forty-nine original settlers of Fenwick's colony were from London and nearby counties, with a smattering from Gloucester, Norfolk, Nottingham, and Somerset. A few settlers were Welsh and Irish. Most who came to Salem County in 1675 were middle class or of higher economic status (ibid., 7, 31). Hall/parlor plan homes ranged from 400 to 600 square feet. The loft or garret area was sometimes divided by a board partition, which still can be seen in some Salem County houses. See also ibid., 77, 37.

17. A six-bay, two-and-a-half-story addition of 1859 abuts the 1722 structure.

18. Robert Craig, National Park Service, Washington, D.C., National Historic Landmark Nomination Form, 1998, Abel Nicholson House, Elsinboro Township, State of New Jersey, Historic Preservation Office, 12–13.

19. Joseph S. Sickler, *The Old Houses of Salem County* (Salem, N.J.: Sunbeam, 1934), n.p. The Georgian idiom seems to have been used infrequently and with some local modifications. One of the few examples shown by Sickler of the "new" style is the 1737 brick addition to an earlier house by William Mecum. The addition features a stylish pedimented Georgian doorway, cut stone

window surrounds, and a cornice with dentils. Colonel Benjamin Holme used a simpler version of the Georgian plan for his brick house built in 1750.

20. Peter Wacker, "New Jersey's Cultural Landscape before 1800," in *Proceedings of the Second Annual Symposium of the New Jersey Historical Commission, December 5, 1970* (Newark: New Jersey Historical Society, 1971), 47.

21. Ibid., 47. See also Peter Wacker, *The Musconetcong Valley of New Jersey: A Historical Geography* (New Brunswick, N.J.: Rutgers University Press, 1968), 85–86. The "I" House, according to the author, can be found beginning in the late seventeenth century from the Chesapeake Bay (and points south and west) and up through the Delaware Valley. A related house type identified in New Jersey by Wacker is the two-room-deep "English" house, usually thirty feet or more in width (ibid., 87).

22. Thomas Wertenbacker, *The Middle Colonies* (New York: Cooper Square, 1963), 70.

23. Ibid., 153. See also Wacker, "New Jersey's Cultural Landscape," 50–51. The "deep East Jersey cottage," a two-room-deep variant of the East Jersey cottage, is found in areas settled by New Englanders but by the nineteenth century became associated with the Dutch settlements of Bergen County.

24. See Coad, *New Jersey in Travelers' Accounts*, 17, no. 49, for extracts of Peter Kalm's journey from *The America of 1750: Peter Kalm's Travels in North America*, ed. Adolph Benson (New York: Wilson-Erickson, 1937). The comment made by a British officer in 1765 is also noted by Coad (*New Jersey in Travelers' Accounts*, 23, no. 64), who cites an anonymously published journal attributed to Lord Adam Gordon, "Journal of an Officer Who Travelled in America and the West Indies in 1764 and 1765." Also published in *Travels in the American Colonies* (New York: Macmillan, 1916).

25. The "Enlightenment" is an omnibus term applied to the many currents of thought that affected eighteenth-century society in Europe, Britain, and America. According to *The Columbia Encyclopedia*, of overarching concern was that "a rational and scientific approach to religious, social, political and economic issues promoted a secular view of the world and a general sense of progress and perfectibility." With rationality as the guiding principal, Enlightenment thought was expressed in skepticism toward "spiritual and scientific authority, dogmatism, intolerance, censorship and economic and social restraints." The followers of the Enlightenment "sought to discover and to act upon universally valid Principles governing humanity, nature and society." See *The Columbia Encyclopedia*, 6th ed. (New York: Columbia University Press, 2003).

26. According to a 1997 research report on the history of the Trent House, the exact year of its construction cannot be pinpointed, although it seems clear that William Trent had moved to Trenton by 1721. In 1729, his estate was valued at more than 1,100 pounds. A deed of 1729 drawn up by his heirs refers to a "brick dwelling house lately erected by ye said William Trent." See Susan Maxman Architects, "Historic Documentation and Strategic Planning Study; The William Trent House," 2A.3-15.

27. Ibid., 2A.3-19.n.116. A stone "smoak" house was mentioned in 1767 and 1770 advertisements for the property (ibid., 2A.3-35, 36). The comment about the Trent House, cited in the Maxman report, was made by Maryland physician Dr. Alexander Hamilton in his narrative of a 1744 journey. See Albert Bushnell Hart, ed., *Hamilton's Itinerarium* (Saint Louis: W. K. Bixby, 1907).

28. Coad, *New Jersey in Travelers' Accounts*, 18–19, no. 53. See also Pownall, *Topographical Description*. A missionary remarked upon the "thorow" entry in some of the houses he encountered in his travels in New Jersey in the 1750s. See Coad, *New Jersey in Travelers' Accounts*, 16, no. 47, for excerpts from Thomas Thompson, *A Letter from New Jersey, In America, giving Some Account and Description of that Province* (London: printed for M. Cooper, 1756). Reprinted as "A Letter from New Jersey," ed. Fred Shelly, *Proceedings of the New Jersey Historical Society* 74 (1956). Thompson was an Anglican missionary.

29. Low's father was Holland Dutch, and Anthony White's father had served as chief justice of Bermuda. Both men were born in New York.

30. Studley, *Historic New Jersey*, 24.

31. "Preservation Plan for Buccleuch Mansion, New Brunswick NJ." Heritage Studies for Short and Ford Architects, Jan. 1990, 4–6. See also National Park Service, National Register of Historic Places Inventory—Nomination Form, The White House/Buccleuch, New Brunswick, N.J., June 5, 1975, State of New Jersey, Historic Preservation Office. In New Brunswick, a smaller (one-room deep) Georgian house was built by the prosperous tanner Henry Guest in 1760. As with the Low manor, the house is constructed of cut stone on its street elevation, while gable and rear elevations are constructed of fieldstone. See National Park Service, National Register of Historic Places Inventory-Nomination Form, The Henry Guest House, New Brunswick, June 1975. State of New Jersey, Historic Preservation Office. According to Section 7 of this report, the Guest house was moved in 1925 from the corner of Carroll Place and Livingston Avenue to its current location on Livingston Avenue. The house appears to be the subject of an advertisement in 1774 by Henry Guest, who offers for sale "one of the best stone-houses in this province." The ad mentions an adjoining "large and convenient" kitchen and a "good outhouse two stories high." See *New York Gazette; and the Weekly Mercury*, June 27, 1774, in William Nelson and A. Van Doren Honeyman, eds. *Archives of the State of New Jersey*, 1st ser., vol. 29, *Tenth Volume of Extracts from American Newspapers Relating to New Jersey 1773–1774* (Paterson, N.J.: Call Printing, 1917), 404–405. Another example of a fine "in town" Georgian building with streetwise ostentation was constructed about 1765 by Princeton's prosperous tanner Job Stockton, on the town's main thoroughfare. Brick laid in Flemish bond and Georgian fenestration details were used for the principal elevation; the rest of the house was sheathed in clapboard and had only simple openings for windows in the gable ends. See Constance Greiff, "Bainbridge House," in *Princeton History*, vol. 1 (Princeton, N.J.: Princeton Historical Society, 1971).

32. John G. Waite Associates, "Proprietary House: Historic Structures Report," 1996, appendix B. See Annotated List of Documentary Sources and plans compiled by William Pavlovsky, on file in the State of New Jersey, Historic Preservation Office.

33. Holland, "Historic Structures Report," 5. Washington paid for the completion of interior plastering work, which suggests that in 1779, at the time of his arrival, the Ford Mansion still had unfinished punch-list items ("the two rooms above stairs finished at public expense"). Holland cites a 1780 letter written to Mrs. Ford and Washington's records of expenses while commander in chief. The house was described as having a view of some "60 chains." A chain is defined as "a measuring line used in surveying formed of 100 iron rods called links jointed together by eyes at their ends"; a "chain's length: a lineal measure equal to 66 feet or four poles" (*Oxford English Dictionary* [Oxford: Oxford University Press, 1961], 7:247).

34. Holland, "Historic Structures Report," 12. See also Thomas Waterman's description of the Ford Mansion cited by Holland. Waterman oversaw the completion of the National Park Service restoration work on the house in the 1930s after it was given to the federal government by the Washington Association of New Jersey. See also James Elliott Lindsley, *A Certain Splendid House*, rev. ed. (Morristown: Washington Association of New Jersey, 2000); and Barbara J. Mitnick, "The Washington Association of New Jersey," *Catalogue of Antiques and Fine Art* 3, no. 6 (January 2001): 248–249.

35. Johann David Schoepf, *Travels in the Confederation 1783–1784*, ed. Alfred Morrison, 2 vols. (Philadelphia: William J. Campbell, 1911), 2:46. Also quoted in Wacker, *Land and People*, 377. Schoepf was describing Maidenhead (now Lawrenceville). For a recent exhibition dealing with churches as well as taverns in New Jersey in the eighteenth century, see James Turk and Lorraine E. Williams, "Caught in the Crossfire: Churches, Taverns and the Revolution" (Trenton: New Jersey State Museum, 2003).

36. Cody, *The Religious Issue*, 11. According to Cody, Methodists were the last to arrive in the colony and did not appear in significant numbers until the 1760s. According to Peter Wacker, New Jersey Presbyterians were comprised of the former New England Puritan/Congregationalists, Scottish Presbyterians, and Scots-Irish (Ulster Scots); one of the attractions of Presbyterianism was the better political strength afforded by a Presbyterian form of organization. See Wacker, *Land and People*, 174-177.

37. Coad, *New Jersey in Travelers' Accounts*, 16, no. 47. See also Thompson, *Letter from New Jersey*.

38. Coad, *New Jersey in Travelers' Accounts*, 26, no. 72. See also Uzal Ogden Jr., "Copy of a Letter." To the Secretary of the Soc. For the Propagation of the Gospel, July 8, 1771, in *Proceedings of the New Jersey Historical Society* 4 (1849–1850).

39. Coad, *New Jersey in Travelers' Accounts*, 11, no. 34. See Samuel Bownas, *An Account of the Life, Travels and Christian Experiences in the Work of the Ministry of Samuel Bownas* (Philadelphia: William Dunlap, 1759), viii. Preaching, especially by itinerant evangelists, did not require a building. In his 1739–1740 trip to New Jersey, the Methodist preacher George Whitfield reported that he preached to large crowds from a wagon in Maidenhead, in a street in New Brunswick, and in a barn in Basking Ridge. See Coad, *New Jersey in Travelers' Accounts*, 13, no. 37. See also George Whitfield, *George Whitfield's Journals* (London: Banner of Trust, 1960).

40. The original church for St. Mary's (Old St. Mary's) was built in 1703 of brick and is reported to have measured 40 by 33 feet; a steeple was added in 1748 with funds raised from a lottery. The rector reported that the church was in need of repair by 1767, and a western extension and gallery were added in 1769. The building was improved at least three more times in the nineteenth century. See De Cou, *Burlington*, 48, 81–83.

41. William Bassett, *Historic American Buildings Survey of New Jersey* (Newark: New Jersey Historical Society, 1977), Seaville Vicinity Friends Meetinghouse (NJ-74); Friends Meetinghouse, Dover vicinity (NJ-145); and Plainfield Friends Meetinghouse (NJ-142).

42. This rural Baptist meeting was an offshoot of the Middletown Baptist congregation, the first Baptist congregation in the colony. The high center pulpit may indicate an Anglican influence, and although the congregation was "basically Baptist in service and theology, others could worship there" (National Park Service, National Register of Historic Places Inventory-Nomination Form, March 1975. State of New Jersey, Historic Preservation Office, 3, 4, 6).

43. St. Andrew's Episcopal Church in Mount Holly (1742) is shown in an 1806 drawing by architect Benjamin Latrobe as a small, three-bay frame building with a round-headed window (presumably at the east end), a gable roof, and a small, covered porch. At the time Latrobe made the sketch, the building had fallen into disuse due to construction of a new church in 1786. See Edward Carter, John Van Horne, and Charles Brownell, eds., *The Papers of Benjamin Henry Latrobe: The Sketchbooks and Miscellaneous Drawings 1795–1820* (New Haven, Conn.: Yale University Press for the Maryland Historical Society, 1985), sketchbook ix, 242–243. Old St. Mary's Church in Cole's town was the first Anglican church in the vicinity of Moorestown. An old photograph shows a small, three-bay, one-and-a-half-story clapboard building with 12/12 double-hung windows. See George De Cou, *Moorestown and Her Neighbors* (Moorestown, N.J.: News Chronicle, 1952), 89.

44. Most New Jersey Anglicans held allegiance to the crown, and when the war came to New Jersey, the majority of the Church of England's clergy left or went over to enemy lines. For the most part, Anglican Church members were either neutral or Tories. The congregants at Middletown were a notable exception; most were allied with the Revolutionary cause. See Cody, *The Religious Issue*, 19.

45. The brick church was said to be one of the "most architecturally ambitious houses of worship in East Jersey in its day" (National Park Service, National Register of Historic Places Inventory-

Nomination Form, Christ Church, Shrewsbury, April 1995. State of New Jersey, Historic Preservation Office. See Section 7, 2).

46. Ibid. See Section 7 of the nomination for a lengthy discussion of the church's history and architecture. It is said to be the "only wood frame structure by Robert Smith known to exist today" (Section 7, 10) and the "only Colonial building in Monmouth county known to have been designed to any of the five formal orders of architecture" (Section 7, 6). For additional material concerning Smith's design, see information provided by Constance Greiff in the National Register Inventory-Nomination Form file.

47. National Park Service, National Register of Historic Places Inventory-Nomination Form, Christ Episcopal Church, New Brunswick, January 1987. State of New Jersey, Historic Preservation Office, Section 8, 1–3. The eighteenth-century church was taken down in 1852. The tower (struck by lightning in 1803) was rebuilt in 1803 and evidently followed the earlier design. The first organizational meeting for the American Episcopal Church was held in the church in 1784. Christ Church advertised for a qualified individual to "execute and finish" a "spire" for the church in 1774. See William Nelson and A. Van Doren Honeyman, eds., *Archives of the State of New Jersey*, 1st ser., vol. 29, *Tenth Volume of Extracts from American Newspapers Relating to New Jersey 1773–1774* (Paterson, N.J.: Call Printing, 1917).

48. Dennis Ryan, *New Jersey in the American Revolution, 1763–1783: A Chronology* (Trenton: New Jersey Historical Commission, 1975), 16. The meeting is reported in the *New York Journal; or the General Advertiser*, No. 1646, July 21, 1774. The courthouse was not able to accommodate half the number in attendance. See Nelson and Honeyman, *Archives of the State of New Jersey*, 427–428.

49. Cody, *The Religious Issue*, 13–14.

50. Benson, *Peter Kalm's Travels*, 1:123.

51. Rev. Frank R. Symmes, *History of the Old Tennent Church* (Cranbury, N.J.: George Burroughs Printer, 1904), 46. The subscriptions totaled approximately 500 pounds; this was the third church for this congregation and replaced one built twenty years earlier.

52. Ibid., 48–50. As in Anglican churches, social hierarchy was reflected to a degree in the pew rents. The most expensive pews were on either side of the pulpit. See pew diagrams dated 1734 and ca. 1755 in ibid., 39, 49.

53. Wertenbacker, *The Middle Colonies*, 99. The hexagonal form was also used for the first Quaker meetinghouse in Burlington, which was begun in 1683 and finished in 1693. The difficulties in heating such a high-roofed, oddly configured structure may be one of the reasons the form was not used more widely. See De Cou, *Burlington*, 60–61.

54. Wertenbacker, *The Middle Colonies*, 80. The source for the illustration of the church is a ca. 1796 drawing by Archibald Robertson in the collection of the New York Public Library, Manuscript and Archives Division (Emmet no. 2756). Another view of the church is found in Benson, *Peter Kalm's Travels*, opp. 1:122.

55. Wertenbacker, *The Middle Colonies*, 81.

56. The term "ordinary" in the British Isles referred to the provision of food at a regulated price—"an eating house or tavern where public meals are provided at a fixed price; a dining room in such a building" and "a public meal regularly provided at a fixed price in an eating-house or tavern." In the United States, "ordinary" was used more broadly, i.e., "a tavern or inn of any kind." See *Oxford English Dictionary*, 7:187.

57. Walter Van Hoesen, *Early Taverns and Stagecoach Days in New Jersey* (Cranbury, N.J.: Associated University Presses, 1976), 10. The author found 446 "places of public entertainment" noted in the 1784 minutes of the state legislature.

58. Ibid., 61, 131. See also Margaret Hofer, "A Tavern for the Town: Josiah Halstead's Tavern and

Community Life in Eighteenth Century Shrewsbury" (paper prepared for the Monmouth County Historical Association, 1992), 4, 14.

59. The settlements of East Jersey were directed by the assembly to "provide an ordinary," with fines assessed for each month that the decree was not honored. See Van Hoesen, *Early Taverns*, 18.

60. The preamble of the legislative act is quoted by Margaret Hofer, "Taverns and Tavern Life in Central New Jersey" (paper presented to the New Jersey Historical Society, Jan. 13, 1999), 4.

61. Van Hoesen, *Early Taverns*, 42.

62. The Blue Ball, a tavern operated by Josiah Halstead in Shrewsbury, served as a meeting place for the vestry of Christ Church and the Shrewsbury Library Company as well as a court for the justice of the peace from the 1750s through the 1770s. The Norris Tavern (ca. 1763), one of Morristown's two Revolutionary-era taverns, served as a courtroom for the first trial of Benedict Arnold. New Brunswick was an important stop on the stage route from New York to Philadelphia, and its taverns hosted meetings of key civic bodies such as the city council, overseers of the poor, the artillery company, the state medical society, and the Provincial Congress. See Hofer, "Taverns and Tavern Life," 10–11.

63. Stewart, *Morristown*, 6.

64. Advertisement in the *New York Gazette and Weekly Mercury*, Sept. 5, 1774, no. 1195, in Nelson and Honeyman, *Archives of the State of New Jersey*, 471.

65. Van Hoesen, *Early Taverns*, 59–60.

66. See Coad, *New Jersey in Travelers' Accounts*, 38, no. 107, who summarizes an account by Thomas Anburey, *Travels through the Interior Parts of America . . . By an Officer* (London: printed for William Lane, 1791).

67. Benson, *Peter Kalm's Travels*, 1:118–119. New Jersey's Dutch barns are thought to be descended from the great peasant houses of lower Saxony in northern Germany, which combined living quarters, stable, barn, and hayloft in a single dwelling and reflected the need to shelter stock during harsh northern European winters. See Wertenbacker, *The Middle Colonies*, 58–61.

68. Peter Wacker, *The Musconetcong Valley of New Jersey: A Historical Geography* (New Brunswick, N.J.: Rutgers University Press, 1968), 94.

69. Clemens, *The Uses of Abundance*, 27.

70. The summary is taken from "Estimate of the Several Counties in the Province of New Jersey as Valued by the General Assembly September 28, 1751." See Susan Maxman Architects, "Historical Documentation and Strategic Planning Study; The William Trent House," 2:A.3-3. Burlington County's sawmills were valued at twice that of its gristmills. This may reflect inventory on hand rather than the value of the equipment, but the difference is substantial. A history of Burlington claims that sawmill operations preceded grist milling in the county by at least two years, that the first gristmill was established on Olive Mill Creek near Burlington in 1679, and that Stacy Mill at Trenton was established around that time or possibly earlier. It was the custom of millers in Burlington to keep one-tenth of the grain milled as a fee. See De Cou, *Burlington*, 44–45.

71. Susan Maxman Architects, "Historical Documentation and Strategic Planning Study; The William Trent House," 2:A3-3.

72. Wacker, *The Musconetcong Valley*, 119–120.

73. Ibid., 123.

74. Ibid., 103.

75. A bloomery is "the first forge in an iron-works through which the metal passes after having been melted from the ore, and in which it has been made into blooms." A bloom is defined as "an ingot

of iron or steel, or a pile of puddled bars, which has been brought by passing through one set of rolls into the form of a thick bar and left for further rolling when required for use." See *Oxford English Dictionary* 1:934–935.

76. Archdeacon, *New Jersey Society*, 14.

77. Clemens, *The Uses of Abundance*, 28. The author cites an advertisement in the *New York Mercury* of March 5, 1764. At the height of its operations, Hasenclever's stock and equipment were valued at 30,000 pounds. See Archdeacon, *New Jersey Society*, 15.

78. Pierce, *Smuggler's Woods*, 229.

79. Ibid.

CAUGHT IN THE MIDDLE

1. George Washington, "Speech to the Delaware Chiefs," Fitzpatrick, *The Writings of George Washington*, 15:53–56.

2. "George Morgan White Eyes," in Ruth L. Woodward and Wesley Frank Craven, *Princetonians, 1784—1790* (Princeton, N.J.: Princeton University Press, 1991), 442–452.

3. Washington, "Speech to the Delaware Chiefs," 53; "Treaty with the Delawares, 1778," in *Indian Affairs, Laws and Treaties*, ed. Charles J. Kappler, 2:3–5 (Washington, D.C.: United States Government Printing Office, 1904).

4. "Treaty with the Delawares," 2:3.

5. Ibid., 2:5.

6. Charles E. Hunter, "History of the Ohio Valley," in Trigger, *Northeast*, 590.

7. Conrad Weiser, "The Journal of Conrad Weiser, Esqr., Indian Interpreter, to the Ohio," in *Early Western Travels, 1748–1846*, ed. Reuben Gold Thwaites, 21–43 (Cleveland: Arthur H. Clark, 1904).

8. Ibid., 26

9. Anthony F. C. Wallace, *King of the Delawares: Teedyuscung, 1700–1763* (Philadelphia: University of Pennsylvania Press, 1949), 18.

10. *NJA*, 1st ser., 9:174–175.

11. Pierce, *Iron in the Pines*, 31.

12. *NJA*, 1st ser., 9:355–358.

13. Rev. Thomas Brainerd, *The Life of John Brainerd, Missionary to the Indians of New Jersey* (Philadelphia, 1865), 385, quoting John Brainerd.

14. Samuel Thornely, ed., *The Journal of Nicholas Creswell, 1774–1779* (New York: Dial Press, 1924), 106.

15. Ibid., 103.

16. George Washington to Governor George Clinton, May 29, 1778, Fitzpatrick, *The Writings of George Washington* 11:473; Washington to the Board of War, Aug. 3, 1778, ibid., 12:265–266; George Washington, "Journal," June 21, 1754, ibid., 1:88.

17. "George Morgan White Eyes," 443.

18. George Washington to Colonel George Morgan, May 21, 1779, Fitzpatrick, *The Writings of George Washington*, 15:113.

19. R. Pierce Beaver, "Protestant Churches and the Indians," in *Handbook of North American Indians*, William C. Sturtevant, gen. ed., vol. 4, *History of Indian-White Relations*, ed. Wilcomb E. Washburn (Washington, D.C.: Smithsonian Institution, 1988), 433.

20. Mark E. Lender, "The Enlisted Line: The Continental Soldiers of New Jersey" (Ph.D. diss., Rutgers University, 1975). 115; Daughters of the American Revolution, *African American and American Indian Patriots of the American Revolutionary War* (Washington, D.C.: National Society of the DAR, 2001), 127–128. Brainerd, *The Life of John Brainerd*, 316, quoting John Brainerd in 1759.

21. Pierce, *Iron in the Pines*, 34.

22. Edward McM. Larrabee, "Recurrent Themes and Sequences in North American Indian-European Culture Contact," *Transactions of the American Philosophical Society*, n.s., vol. 66, part 7 (Philadelphia: American Philosophical Society, 1976), 17.

MOVING TOWARD BREAKING THE CHAINS

1. William Cooper Nell, *The Colored Patriots of the American Revolution* (Boston: R. F. Wallcut, 1855).

2. See William Wells Brown, *The Negro in the American Revolution: His Heroism and Fidelity* (Boston: Lee Shepard, 1867); George Washington Williams, *A History of the Negro Race in America from 1619 to 1880. Negroes as Slaves, as Soldiers, and as Citizens; Together with a Preliminary Consideration of the Unity of the Human Family, an Historical Sketch of Africa, and an Account of the Negro Governments of Sierra Leone and Liberia* (New York: Putnam and Sons, 1883); Joseph T. Wilson, *The Black Phalanx: A History of the Negro Soldiers of the United States in the Wars of 1775–1812, 1861–65* (Hartford, Conn.: American Publishing, 1887); Benjamin Brawley, *A Social History of the American Negro: Being a History of the Negro Problem in the U.S., Including a History and Study of the Republic of Liberia* (New York: Macmillan, 1921); Luther Porter Jackson, *Virginia Negro Soldiers and Seamen in the Revolutionary War* (Norfolk, Va.: Guide Quality Press, 1944); and Benjamin Quarles, *The Negro in the American Revolution* (Chapel Hill: University of North Carolina Press, 1961). For a discussion of the writings of these historians and other historians of African descent, see Earl E. Thorpe, *The Central Theme of Black History* (Westport, Conn.: Greenwood Press, 1969); and Earl E. Thorpe, *Black Historians: A Critique* (New York: William Morrow, 1971). These studies examined the role of blacks in the war itself. Subsequent scholarship, of which this essay is a part, has examined the broad effects of Revolutionary War sentiment on slavery itself and, even more recently, the nature of northern black life during the era of the war. For a review of some of the recent historical literature—seven books—that deals with the effects of the American Revolution on black life and suggests that the war's effect on manumission in the North was basically "halting and conservative," see Douglas R. Egerton, "Black Independence Struggles and the Tale of Two Revolutions: A Review Essay," *Journal of Southern History* 54, no. 1 (February 1998).

3. Leon F. Litwack, *North of Slavery: The Negro in the Free States, 1790–1860* (Chicago: University of Chicago Press, 1961), 6–7. Regarding Vermont, it was the only state to adopt an antislavery clause in its constitution, which it did in 1777. A breakaway territory claimed by New Hampshire and New York, it was not one of the original thirteen colonies, being admitted to the Union in 1791. Pennsylvania was actually the first state to pass an abolition law, this occurring in 1780.

4. Arthur Zilversmit, *The First Emancipation: The Abolition of Slavery in the North* (Chicago: University of Chicago Press, 1967), 137–138.

5. Edgar J. McManus, *Black Bondage in the North* (Syracuse, N.Y.: Syracuse University Press, 1973), 150–151.

6. For example, see Gary B. Nash and Jean R. Soderlund, *Freedom by Degrees: Emancipation in Pennsylvania and Its Aftermath* (New York: Oxford University Press, 1991). They argue that slavery declined in Philadelphia around the time of the Revolution because of the tendency of slaveholders of a certain class (e.g., master artisans, ship captains, shopkeepers, and taverners—those having one or two slaves) to rid themselves of slaves. Given a fluctuating economy, in the place of slaves they hired wage laborers who could be employed and discharged at will. More affluent

slave owners, in contrast, were inclined to retain their slaves in order to underscore their high social status.

7. Frances D. Pingeon, "Slavery in New Jersey on the Eve of Revolution," in *New Jersey on the American Revolution: Political and Social Conflict*, rev. ed., ed. William C. Wright, 50 (1970; repr., Trenton: New Jersey Historical Commission, 1974).

8. Ibid., 57.

9. Ibid., 58.

10. The years between 1770 and 1810 are identified as the "Revolutionary era" in Peter Colchin, *American Slavery: 1619–1877* (New York: Hill and Wang, 1993), 63; and Ira Berlin, "The Revolution in Black Life," in *The American Revolution: Explorations in the History of American Radicalism*, ed. Alfred F. Young, 351 (De Kalb: Northern Illinois University Press, 1976).

11. For a full discussion of this distinction and its implications for slave life, see Philip D. Morgan, "British Encounters with Africans and African-Americans, circa 1600–1780," in *Strangers within the Realm: Cultural Margins of the First British Empire*, ed. Bernard Bailyn and Philip D. Morgan, 163–219 (Chapel Hill: University of North Carolina Press, 1991).

12. Ira Berlin, *Many Thousands Gone: The First Two Centuries of Slavery in North America* (Cambridge, Mass.: Harvard University Press, 1998), 369, table 1.

13. Benjamin Quarles, "The Revolutionary War as a Black Declaration of Independence," in *Slavery and Freedom in the Age of the American Revolution*, ed. Ira Berlin and Ronald Hoffman, 285 (Charlottesville: United States Capitol Historical Society/University Press of Virginia, 1983).

14. Herbert S. Klein, *The Atlantic Slave Trade* (Cambridge: Cambridge University Press, 1999), 45; Pingeon, *Blacks in the Revolutionary Era*, 14; Berlin, *Many Thousands Gone*, 179.

15. Berlin, *Many Thousands Gone*, 46, 180, 181; Pingeon, "Slavery in New Jersey," 49.

16. The price of twenty pounds for a male slave is provided for Philadelphia by Nash and Soderlund in *Freedom by Degrees*. Given Philadelphia's proximity to New Jersey, it is assumed that a similar price existed in New Jersey for the same period.

17. Zilversmit, *The First Emancipation*, 42.

18. Morgan, "British Encounters with Africans," 161.

19. Gary K. Wolinetz, "New Jersey Slavery and the Law," *Rutgers Law Review*, 50, no. 4 (Summer 1998): 2233.

20. Pingeon, "Slavery in New Jersey," 52.

21. Wolinetz, "New Jersey Slavery," 2236.

22. Henry Scofield Cooley, *A Study of Slavery in New Jersey* (Baltimore: Johns Hopkins University Press, 1896), 42.

23. McManus, *Black Bondage*, 132.

24. Pingeon, *Blacks in the Revolutionary Era*, 19; Herbert Aptheker, *American Negro Slave Revolts* (New York: International, 1943), 201–202.

25. Pingeon, *Blacks in the Revolutionary Era*, 19.

26. Berlin, *Many Thousands Gone*, 184.

27. Quoted in Price, *Freedom Not Far Distant*, 44.

28. Since early census takers failed to differentiate between slaves and free blacks in New Jersey, the figure of 5 percent is a rough estimate based on the 3 percent figure given by Hodges for pre-Revolution Monmouth County in his *Slavery and Freedom*, 64. It is likely that manumissions among Quakers by 1776 would have raised the percentage higher for the entire colony, hence the figure of 400 free blacks, roughly 5 percent of the 8,200 blacks listed for New Jersey

for 1770. Donald R. Wright, *African Americans in the Colonial Era: From African Origins through the American Revolution*, 2nd ed. (Wheeling, Ill.: Harlan Davidson, 2000), 165, also notes that "before 1770 free blacks made up only about 5 percent of the colonial African-American population." Finally, in 1755 in Maryland, one of the few colonies for which a census of the free black population was taken prior to the Revolution, free blacks constituted 4 percent of the total black population. This would also seem to make an estimate of 5 percent for New Jersey reasonable. The figure for Maryland comes from Berlin, "The Revolution in Black Life," 352.

29. For a discussion of these families, see David Steven Cohen, *The Ramapo Mountain People* (New Brunswick, N.J.: Rutgers University Press, 1988), 25–42.

30. Zilversmit, *The First Emancipation*, 14.

31. Cooley, *A Study of Slavery*, 45.

32. For a discussion of the life of Cyrus Bustill, see appendix A, "The Proud Bustills," 145–157, in Lloyd L. Brown, *The Young Paul Robeson: "On My Journey Now"* (Boulder, Colo.: Westview Press, 1997).

33. Zilversmit, *The First Emancipation*, 91–92.

34. The historian Ira Berlin has written considerably on the transformation of Africans into African Americans. See, for example, his "Time, Space, and the Evolution of Afro-American Society on British Mainland North America," *American Historical Review*, 85 (1980): 44–78.

35. Graham Russell Hodges, *Root and Branch: African Americans in New York and East Jersey, 1613–1863* (Chapel Hill: University of North Carolina Press, 1999), 258.

36. For discussion of this incident, see David Steven Cohen, *The Folklore and Folklife of New Jersey* (New Brunswick, N.J.: Rutgers University Press, 1991), 41–42.

37. Quoted in Price, *Freedom Not Far Distant*, 43.

38. Quoted in ibid., 44–45. The historians Shane White and Graham White have contended that the dress and hairstyles of some colonial and antebellum slaves not only perpetuated African cultural traditions but also served as a cultural defense against a dehumanizing system. See Shane White and Graham White, "Slave Hair and African American Culture in the Eighteenth and Nineteenth Centuries," *Journal of Southern History* 61, no. 1 (February 1995): 45–76; and White and White, "Slave Clothing and African-American Culture in the Eighteenth and Nineteenth Centuries," *Past and Present* no. 148 (Aug. 1995): 149–186.

39. Quoted in Price, *Freedom Not Far Distant*, 43.

40. Pingeon, *Blacks in the Revolutionary Era*, 9.

41. Hodges, *Root and Branch*, 86.

42. Discussions of spirit possession range from a focus on Africans, to African Americans, to New World African diaspora peoples in such countries as Haiti, Cuba, and Brazil. Examples include John S. Mbiti, *African Religions and Philosophy* (London: Heinemann, 1970); Robert Farris Thompson, *Flash of the Spirit: African and Afro-American Art and Philosophy* (New York: Random House, 1983); Robert L. Hall, "African Religious Retentions in Florida," in *Africanisms in American Culture*, ed. Joseph E. Holloway (Bloomington: Indiana University Press, 1990); and Maya Deren, *Divine Horsemen: Voodoo Gods of Haiti* (New York: Chelsea House, 1970). Among those who have written extensively on the phenomenon of spirit possession is the social anthropologist Sheila S. Walker. Her writings on this subject include *Ceremonial Spirit Possession in Africa and Afro-America: Forms, Meanings, and Functional Significance for Individuals and Social Groups* (Leiden, Netherlands: E. J. Brill, 1972), and "African Gods in America: The Black Religious Continuum," *Black Scholar* 11, no. 8 (Nov./Dec. 1980): 25–36.

43. The African origins of certain names and words found among black Americans can be found in Lorenzo D. Turner, *Africanisms in the Gullah Dialect* (Ann Arbor: University of Michigan Press,

1947). David Mitros, ed., *Slave Records of Morris County, New Jersey: 1756–1841*, 2nd ed. (Morristown, N.J.: Morris County Heritage Commission, 2002), also proved useful in compiling the list of African and African-sounding names.

44. Hodges, *Root and Branch*, 118.

45. Ibid., 115. The following quotation from Pingeon's *Blacks in the Revolutionary Era*, 16, is also revealing: "Numerous advertisements for runaway slaves described them as possessing fiddles or other musical instruments which, according to their masters, they played with great skill."

46. Hodges, *Root and Branch*, 108–109.

47. An excellent source on how time has been perceived among peoples in Africa and the African diaspora of the New World is Joseph K. Adjaye, ed., *Time in the Black Experience* (Westport, Conn.: Greenwood Press, 1994).

48. Pingeon, "Slavery in New Jersey," 55.

49. Hodges, *Root and Branch*, 159.

50. Ibid.

51. Quoted in Price, *Freedom Not Far Distant*, 46.

52. McManus, *Black Bondage*, 154.

53. The figure of 1,300 black British arms-bearers has been culled from chapters 2, 7, 8, and 9 in Quarles, *The Negro in the American Revolution*. A figure of 1,000 black bearers of arms for the British appears in Mary Francis Berry and John W. Blassingame, *Long Memory: The Black Experience in America* (New York: Oxford University Press, 1982), 297; and James Oliver Horton and Lois E. Horton, *In Hope of Liberty: Culture, Community, and Protest among Northern Free Blacks, 1700–1860* (New York: Oxford University Press, 1997), 62.

54. Hodges, *Root and Branch*, 159.

55. Hodges, *Slavery and Freedom*, 97; see 96–104 for a full discussion of Tye's military exploits.

56. The figure of 5,000 for the number of blacks who bore arms on behalf of the patriot cause is a commonly accepted one. For example, see Quarles, *The Negro in the American Revolution*, ix. See also the standard text, John Hope Franklin and Alfred A. Moss Jr., *From Slavery to Freedom: A History of African Americans*, 7th ed. (New York: McGraw Hill, 1994), 76.

57. Pingeon, *Blacks in the Revolutionary Era*, 21.

58. An entry on Oliver Cromwell appears in Rayford W. Logan and Michael R. Winston, eds., *Dictionary of American Negro Biography* (New York: W. W. Norton, 1982), 142. The oral history interview of Cromwell published in 1852 in the *Burlington (New Jersey) Gazette* appears in Sidney Kaplan, *The Black Presence in the Era of the American Revolution 1770–1800* (Greenwich, Conn.: New York Graphic Society, 1973), 47.

59. Simeon F. Moss, "The Persistence of Slavery and Involuntary Servitude in a Free State (1685–1866)," *Journal of Negro History* 35 (1950): 301–302.

60. Hodges, *Root and Branch*, 141–142. The foremost authorities on Samuel Sutphen are William Schleicher and Susan Winter, whose forthcoming book on Sutphen is reflected in their essay "Patriot and Slave: The Samuel Sutphen Story," *New Jersey Heritage* 1, no. 1 (Winter 2002): 30–43.

61. Peter Williams and Cato are mentioned in Moss, "Persistence of Slavery," 301. For a discussion of the case of Prime, including his petition, see Giles R. Wright, "Prime: Another Resident of Brainbridge House," *Princeton History* no. 10 (1993): 60–66.

62. Berlin, *Many Thousands Gone*, 235.

63. Moss, "Persistence of Slavery," 299; Cooley, *A Study of Slavery*, 23.

64. Hodges, *Root and Branch*, 167–168.

65. McManus, *Black Bondage*, 153

66. Hodges, *Slavery and Freedom*, 115.

67. Cooper's address is printed in its entirety in Gary B. Nash, *Race and Revolution* (Madison, Wis.: Madison House, 1990), 117–131.

68. Moss, "Persistence of Slavery," 292.

69. Cooley, *A Study of Slavery*, 22–23.

70. Wolinetz, "New Jersey Slavery," 2240–2241.

71. Ibid., 2241.

72. Zilversmit, *The First Emancipation*, 188–189.

73. McManus, *Black Bondage*, 173

74. There is some discrepancy as to when New Jersey's first statewide abolition society was organized. The date of 1793 is given in Zilversmit, *The First Emancipation*, 173, and Pingeon, *Blacks in the Revolutionary Era*, 23, while the year 1786 is provided in Cooley, *A Study of Slavery*, 23, and Hodges, *Root and Branch*, 115.

75. Hodges, *Root and Branch*, 167.

76. See Giles R. Wright, *Afro-Americans in New Jersey: A Short History* (Trenton: New Jersey Historical Commission, 1988), 81–82, appendix 3.

77. Zilversmit, *The First Emancipation*, 192.

78. Ibid.

79. Robin Blackburn, *The Overthrow of Colonial Slavery 1776–1848* (London: Verso, 1988), 274.

80. Zilversmit, *The First Emancipation*, 198. Zilversmit notes that while the abandonment clause (section 3 of the 1804 abolition law) was repealed in 1805, the state continued down to 1811 to support some abandoned children because their maintenance had been contracted for prior to the repeal of the abandonment clause.

81. Ibid., 199; Pingeon, *Blacks in the Revolutionary Era*, 26–27.

82. Berlin, *Many Thousands Gone*, 372, table 2.

83. The figure for New Jersey is taken from in Wright, *Afro-Americans in New Jersey*, 80, appendix 2.

84. See ibid.; see also Berlin, *Many Thousands Gone*, 372, table 2.

85. See Wright, *Afro-Americans in New Jersey*, 82, appendix 3.

86. Wolinetz, "New Jersey Slavery," 2242–2243.

87. For a biographical sketch of Richard Allen, see Logan and Winston, *Dictionary of American Negro Biography*, 12–13.

88. Berlin, "The Revolution in Black Life," 359.

89. Ira Berlin, *Generations of Captivity: A History of African-American Slaves* (Cambridge, Mass.: Belknap Press of Harvard University Press, 2003), 102.

"TROUBLESOME TIMES A-COMING"

1. Margaret Morris, *Private Journal Kept during a Portion of the Revolutionary War, for the Amusement of a Sister* (Philadelphia, 1836; repr., New York: Arno Press, 1969), 5–6. Morris's journal is an important and rare civilian account of the period.

2. Margaret Morris to Henry Hill, Oct. 12, 1777, quoted in Patricia A. Beaber, "Margaret Hill Morris," in *Past and Promise, Lives of New Jersey Women*, ed. Joan Burstyn, 32 (Syracuse, N.Y.: Syracuse University Press, 1997).

3. Nancy Woloch, *Women and the American Experience*, 2nd ed. (New York: McGraw-Hill, 1994), 1:64.

4. Joan Hoff-Wilson, "The Illusion of Change: Women and the American Revolution," in *The American Revolution: Explorations in the History of American Radicalism*, ed. Alfred Young, reprinted in Mary Beth Norton and Ruth M. Alexander, eds., *Major Problems in American Women's History*, 2nd ed. (Lexington, Mass.: D. C. Heath, 1996), 85.

5. Jemima Condict Harrison, Diary of Jemima Condict, Oct. 1, 1774, Collection of the New Jersey Historical Society.

6. Biographical information on Elizabeth Franklin and William Franklin is drawn primarily from Larry R. Gerlach, "William Franklin," in *The Governors of New Jersey, 1664–1974*, ed. Paul A. Stellhorn and Michael J. Birkner, 72–76 (Trenton: New Jersey Historical Commission, 1982); and Marylin A. Hulme, "Elizabeth Downes Franklin," in Burstyn, *Past and Promise*, 19–21.

7. Gerlach, *Prologue to Independence*, 332–334.

8. Lundin, *Cockpit of the Revolution*, 221–224. William, freed in October 1778, spent several years working for the loyalist cause in British-held New York before going to England in 1782. He was remarried briefly and died in 1813 in London.

9. Little is written about Susannah Livingston, who emerges largely from the record left by members of her family. The daughter of a wealthy landowning family in New Brunswick, she married William Livingston in 1747, bore thirteen children (several of whom died in childhood), and shared his active political and legal life in New York before the family moved to their estate, Liberty Hall, in Elizabethtown in 1770. William Livingston was a delegate to the First and Second Continental congresses and commanded the North Jersey militia from his headquarters in Elizabethtown before his appointment as governor of the new state of New Jersey in June 1776. Dennis P. Ryan, "William Livingston," in Stellhorn and Birkner, *The Governors of New Jersey*, 77–81.

10. Susannah French Livingston wrote to William Livingston on February 7, 1777: "I have the pleasure to inform you that we are in good health. But our situation is not quite as agreeable as it has been on account of the number of Soldiers that are placed here at this house" (*Livingston Papers*, 1:218–219). Susannah's daughter, Sarah Livingston Jay, lived with her much of the time that her husband, John Jay, was absent on public business. Her daughters, Judith and Susannah, also lived with her. Several historians have assumed that Sukey was the nickname given to Susannah French Livingston by William. Upon closer scrutiny of family correspondence included in the *Livingston Papers*, it is possible that Sukey was the nickname of the Livingston's daughter Susannah, who married John Cleves Symmes in 1794. As the older daughter, it appears that Sukey was the major support of her mother during the war and later of her father after her mother's death. She did not marry until after her father's death.

11. Susannah Livingston to William Livingston, May 30, 1777, *Livingston Papers*, 1:345.

12. Ewald, *Diary*, 22.

13. The common law principle of coverture refers to the status of a married woman considered as under the protection and authority of her husband.

14. Susannah Livingston to William Livingston, Nov. 30, 1777, *Livingston Papers*, 2:126–127; A. Alfred Jones, *The Loyalists of New Jersey* (1927; repr., Bowie, Md.: Heritage Books, 1988), 294.

15. Jones, *The Loyalists of New Jersey*, 65–66. Drummond was the daughter of prosperous Dutch farmers in Bergen County and in 1759 had married Robert Drummond, an influential merchant/shipper in Acquackanonk Landing (now Passaic). The couple had three living children in 1776, ages fourteen, eleven, and two.

16. William W. Scott, *History of Passaic and Its Environs* (New York: Lewis Historical Publishing, 1922), 93; Lorenzo Sabine, *Loyalists of the American Revolution* (Boston: Little, Brown, 1864), 1:387; Leiby, *The Revolutionary War*, 117–118.

17. Ruth M. Keesey, "New Jersey Legislation Concerning Loyalists," *Proceedings of the New Jersey Historical Society* 79, no. 2 (April 1961): 75, 80–81. An estimated 5,000 New Jersey men and women are deemed to have been loyalist, 1,200 having forfeited property under court order. Of all the states, New Jersey ranked fourth in the number of loyalists.

18. Keesey, "New Jersey Legislation," 83–84; Keesey, "Loyalty and Reprisal: The Loyalists of Bergen County, New Jersey and Their Estates," Collections of the Bergen County Historical Society, 1957, Typescript, 106–110n.108.

19. The legal implications of confiscation for wives were complex. Linda Kerber discusses suits brought by the wives of loyalists later trying to reclaim dower rights from the states after their husbands' deaths and by children trying to claim inheritance of mothers' dower rights. See Kerber, *Women of the Republic: Intellect and Ideology in Revolutionary America* (Chapel Hill: University of North Carolina Press, 1980), 123–124.

20. Henry Bischoff, *A Revolutionary Relationship: Theodosia Prevost, Aaron Burr, and the Hermitage* (Ho-Ho-Kus, N.J.: The Friends of the Hermitage, 2004), chs. 1–2. Marcus Prevost was not active in local politics or a leader in local commerce; he was a British military officer on half-pay, gentleman farmer, and slaveholder. Anticipating events to come, he tried unsuccessfully to sell his New Jersey property in 1774. His roots were in England, but Theodosia's were in the colonies, and her relatives, like her neighbors in Hoppertown, differed in their loyalties. Even though the Hermitage is situated on a main route from Paramus to Suffern, New York, where patriot supplies were stored, the estate was apparently not plundered by either British or Continental troops when they passed nearby in December 1776.

21. Theodosia Prevost's husband was posted to Jamaica toward the end of the war and died there in 1781. On July 2, the widow Prevost, at the age of thirty-six, married Aaron Burr Jr., age twenty-six, at the Hermitage. Both governors William Livingston of New Jersey and George Clinton of New York sent congratulations. Shortly thereafter, the Burrs left the Hermitage for Albany, where Aaron continued his legal and political career. Theodosia died in 1794.

22. Late in 1779, the Bergen County authorities served her with an inquisition, causing Prevost to write a letter directly to the legislature, which stalled the matter for a while. Other inquisitions were issued in January 1780, but nothing seems to have come of these.

23. Harriet Stryker-Rodda, "Militia Women of 1780, Monmouth County, New Jersey," *Daughters of the American Revolution Magazine*, April 1979, 309.

24. Holly A. Mayer, *Belonging to the Army: Camp Followers and Community during the American Revolution* (Columbia: University of South Carolina Press, 1996), 122.

25. Ibid., 126. A foot soldier's account of this same scene was somewhat more graphic: "[O]f all specimens of human beings, this group capped the whole. A caravan of wild beasts could bear no comparison with it. . . . Some with two eyes, some with one, and some, I believe with none at all. They 'beggared all description'; their dialect, too, was as confused as their bodily appearance was odd and disgusting. There was the Irish and Scotch brogue, murdered English, flat insipid Dutch and some lingoes which would puzzle a philosopher to tell whether they belonged to this world or some 'undiscovered country'" (Joseph Plumb Martin, *Private Yankee Doodle, Being a Narrative of Some of the Adventures, Dangers and Sufferings of a Revolutionary Soldier*, ed., George F. Scheer, 197–198 [Boston: Little, Brown, 1962]).

26. Sally Stone Forester, "Mary Ludwig Hays McCauley," in Burstyn, *Past and Promise*, 31–32; David G. Martin, *The Story of Molly Pitcher* (Hightstown, N.J.: Longstreet House, 2000), pamphlet.

27. Stryker-Rodda, "Militia Women of 1780," 312.

28. Robert Fridlington, "A 'Diversion' in Newark: A Letter from the New Jersey Continental Line, 1778," *NJH* 105, nos. 1–2 (1987): 77–78.

29. Kerber, *Women of the Republic*, 60–61.

30. John W. Jackson, *Margaret Morris: Her Journal, with Biographical Sketch and Notes* (Philadelphia: George S. MacManus, 1949), 62, 64.

31. Hannah Whitall Smith, *John M. Whitall: The Story of His Life* (Philadelphia: privately printed, 1879), 10–11.

32. Lundin, *Cockpit of the Revolution*, 233–235, 419–421.

33. Patricia Conroy Gray, "Theodosia Johnes Ford," in Burstyn, *Past and Promise*, 18–19.

34. Arthur S. Lefkowitz, *The Long Retreat* (New Brunswick, N.J.: Rutgers University Press, 1998), 99–103. Lefkowitz provides a vivid picture of Washington's army retreating toward Princeton at the beginning of December 1776. It stretched for miles along established roads, as the columns of infantry; mounted officers and troops; cannon; the baggage train of wagons with munitions, equipment, and supplies; civilian settlers; and the wives and children of soldiers, as well as prostitutes, wended their way past farms and homes.

35. Martin, *Private Yankee Doodle*, 96. During the campaign of 1777, Martin found himself waiting for troops to arrive in Mount Holly and noted: "I was a near starved with hunger as ever I wish to be. . . . In the yard and about it was a plenty of geese, turkeys, ducks, and barn-door fowls. . . . I might have taken as many as I pleased, but I took up one only, wrung off its head, dressed and washed it in the stream . . . and stalked into the first house that fell in my way, invited myself into the kitchen, took down the gridiron and put my fowl to cooking upon the coals. The women of the house were all the time going and coming to and from the room. They looked at me but said nothing. . . . When my game was sufficiently broiled, I took it by the hind leg and my exit from the house with as little ceremony as I had made my entrance" (ibid.).

36. Following the lead of Philadelphia women, elite women of Trenton initiated a campaign in 1780 calling for women's financial contributions "for the relief and encouragement of those brave Men. . .who. . .so repeatedly suffered, fought and bled in the cause of virtue and their oppressed county" (William Nelson, ed., *Documents Relating to the Revolutionary History of the State of New Jersey* [Trenton: J. L. Murphy, 1914], 4:486–488); Kerber, *Women of the Republic*, 102–103.

37. Orders given by Generals Cornwallis and Howe upon the invasion in November 1776 prohibited plundering and charged their soldiers with the protection of local people and their property. These orders had little effect. Lundin, *Cockpit of the Revolution*, 172.

38. Ibid., 74. Women came to expect their homes to be sacked upon the appearance of British and Hessian troops. One Hessian officer reported that when he rummaged through one woman's house looking for her patriot husband, "the mistress of the house followed at my heels with three children, and with tears in her eyes continually begged me not to take everything away from her. I assured her that I wanted nothing but her husband, which, however, she did not seem to believe. She gazed in astonishment when I marched off again, leaving her wagons and coach standing" (Ewald, *Diary*, 27).

39. Lundin, *Cockpit of the Revolution*, 429.

40. Sally Stone Forester, "Annetje Van Wagenen Plume," in Burstyn, *Past and Promise*, 35–36.

41. Varnum Lansing Collins, ed., *A Brief Narrative of the Ravages of the British and Hessians at Princeton in 1776–79* (Princeton, N.J.: University Library, 1906), 14–15. In his eyes, the conduct of loyalist troops was far worse than "an Indian War for I Never heard nor read of their [Indians] ravishing of women notwithstanding their cruelty to their captives."

42. Lundin, *Cockpit of the Revolution*, 199; Frank Moore, *Diary of the American Revolution from Newspapers and Original Documents* (New York: Charles Scribner, 1860), 419–422. Early in the war, the Continental Congress appointed a committee to investigate the conduct of the loyalist troops in New Jersey and New York. The committee's report of April 18, 1777, corroborated the Princeton diarist's conclusions.

43. *Papers of the Continental Congress* (M247), Roll 66, Item 53:32, National Archives, quoted in Kerber, *Women of the Republic*, 46.

44. Carla Mulford, ed., *Only for the Eye of a Friend: The Poems of Annis Boudinot Stockton* (Charlottesville: University Press of Virginia, 1995), 24.

45. Ibid., 26–27. As the sister of Elias Boudinot, president of the Continental Congress, Annis Stockton had the connections to bring her close to the workings of the war in New Jersey. Ironically, the Stocktons had been favored friends of colonial governor William and Elizabeth Franklin before William was imprisoned, leading one to suspect Annis must have been especially grieved by the fate of Elizabeth Franklin—though none of her extant poetry deals with their friendship or Elizabeth's death. In his own political leanings, Richard Stockton was slow to espouse the patriot cause, but when he did, he was elected to the Continental Congress. When captured by Tories, however, he signed an oath pledging not to aid the patriot cause and thereafter resigned from Congress and pursued his law career. He died of cancer in 1781. Ibid., 20–21.

46. The ideology of republican motherhood is discussed in some depth by Kerber, *Women of the Republic*, 235. Mothers of the new republic were to be informed and virtuous citizens, assuming, in addition to their traditional domestic responsibilities, the limited political duty of nurturing the concepts of virtuous citizenship in their sons and passing down the concept of republican motherhood to their daughters. Stockton expressed her view of women's role in the new nation in "Lucinda and Aminta, a pastoral, on the capture of Lord Cornwallis and the British army, by General Washington" (lines 161–168), written late in 1781 (*New Jersey Gazette*, Nov. 28, 1781, 2, no. 361 [see Mulford, *Only for the Eye of a Friend*, 111]):

    > And well, my friend, wise nature has assign'd
    > To us such different lots, tis very plain
    > Tho not the sex of men, the same in mind
    > We all are links of the great mystic chain.
    > And sure, to view with reason's mental eye,
    > The harvest rich, of freedom's glorious reign,
    > Must make our bosoms beat with rapturous joy,
    > Since 'tis by us it must descend to men.

47. Annis Boudinot Stockton, "A Poetical Epistle, addressed by a Lady of New Jersey, to her Niece, upon her Marriage, in this City," *Columbian Magazine* 1 (Nov. 1786): 143; Mulford, *Only for the Eye of a Friend*, 35, 135.

48. For scholarship on women's voting rights between 1776 and 1807, see Edward Raymond Turner, "Woman Suffrage in New Jersey, 1790–1807," *Smith College Studies in History* 1 (July 1916): 165–187; Mary Philbrook, "Woman Suffrage in New Jersey prior to 1807," *New Jersey Historical Society Proceedings* 57 (1939): 87–98; J. R. Pole, "The Suffrage in New Jersey, 1790-1807," *New Jersey Historical Society Proceedings* 71 (1953): 39–61; Sophie Drinker, "Votes for Women in 18th Century New Jersey," *New Jersey Historical Society Proceedings* 80 (1962): 31-45; Irwin Gertzog, "Female Suffrage in New Jersey, 1790–1807," *Women and Politics* 10 (1990): 47–58; and Judith A. Klinghoffer and L. Elkis, "'The Petticoat Electors': Women's Suffrage in New Jersey, 1776–1807," *Journal of the Early Republic* 12 (Summer 1992): 159–193.

NEW JERSEY LITERATURE

1. The phrase "Cockpit of the Revolution" was popularized as the title of a book on New Jersey history. See Lundin, *Cockpit of the Revolution*.

2. See Mulford, *Only for the Eye of a Friend*, 13, where the author states that "recent studies of literacy suggest that by the middle to late eighteenth century, most women probably could read in a rudimentary way, even if the only text they read was the Bible. The study of reading always preceded that of writing, and few women were admitted to training in writing."

3. For a brief biographical synopsis of Ashbridge's life and the full text of "Some Account of the Fore-Part of the Life of Elizabeth Ashbridge," the first edition of which was published in Nantwich, England, in 1774, see Nina Baym et al., eds., *The Norton Anthology of American Literature*, 4th ed. (New York: W. W. Norton, 1994), 1:600–621.

4. Carol F. Karlson and Laurie Crumpacker, eds., *The Journal of Esther Edwards Burr 1754–57* (New Haven, Conn.: Yale University Press, 1984). An earlier version is inaccurate and inadequate.

5. All quotations from this and the following paragraph can be found in ibid., 50–79.

6. Ibid., 253–257.

7. Ibid., 256.

8. Printed in *Gazette of the United States*, March 13, 1793, 3. See Mulford, *Only for the Eye of a Friend*, 174–175.

9. Baym et al., *The Norton Anthology*, 600–621.

10. Christine Levenduski, *Peculiar Power: A Quaker Woman Preacher in Eighteenth-Century America* (Washington, D.C.: Smithsonian Institution, 1996).

11. Baym et al., *The Norton Anthology*, 602.

12. Sheila L. Skemp, *William Franklin: Son of a Patriot, Servant of a King* (New York: Oxford University Press, 1990), 269.

13. Epes Sargent, ed., *The Select Works of Benjamin Franklin* (Boston: Phillips, Sampson, 1854), 497–498.

14. Philip M. Marsh, ed., *A Freneau Sampler* (New York: Scarecrow Press, 1963), 21.

15. Ibid., 38–46.

16. Quentin P. Taylor, *The Essential Federalist: A New Reading of the Federalist Papers* (Madison, Wis.: Madison House, 1998), vii.

17. Ibid., x.

18. Herman Melville, *Moby-Dick*, ed. Hershel Parker and Harrison Hayford (New York: Norton, 2002), 73.

19. Eric Foner, ed., *Thomas Paine: Collected Writings* (New York: Library of America, 1995), 91.

20. Ibid., 96–97.

21. Marsh, *A Freneau Sampler*, 136.

22. Phillip P. Moulton, ed., *The Journal and Major Essays of John Woolman*, Library of Protestant Thought (Richmond, Ind.: Friends United Press, 1989), 23.

23. "Civil Disobedience," in *The Essays of Henry D. Thoreau*, ed. Lewis Hyde (New York: North Point Press, 2002), 131.

24. Moulton, *The Journal and Major Essays of John Woolman*, 35.

25. Ibid., 32.

26. Ibid., 29.

27. Sherman Paul, ed., *Walden and Civil Disobedience* (Boston: Riverside, 1960), 223.

28. Moulton, *The Journal and Major Essays of John Woolman*, 32.

29. Ibid., 25.

30. Ibid., 51, 61, 96.

31. Ibid, 95.

HISTORICAL GEOGRAPHY AND ARCHAEOLOGY

1. The state-owned historic sites system managed by the New Jersey Division of Parks and Forestry includes several notable properties that played a key role in the Revolutionary War, e.g., the Old Barracks in Trenton, Princeton Battlefield, Monmouth Battlefield, Washington Crossing, Rockingham, the Wallace House, the Zabriskie/Von Steuben House, and Batsto Furnace.

2. In recent decades, suburban development has encroached upon and continues to pressure key Revolutionary War sites such as Princeton Battlefield and encampments at Valley Forge, Middlebrook, and Pluckemin.

3. Recognition of both the loss of Revolutionary War heritage in New Jersey and the ongoing dilution of the open space that helps to bind historic resources to the cultural landscape lies at the heart of the Crossroads of the American Revolution National Heritage Area initiative outlined in National Park Service, *Crossroads of the American Revolution*.

4. For a summary of books, pamphlets, broadsides, articles, and unpublished compilations relating to the American Revolution in New Jersey, see Donald A. Sinclair and Grace W. Schut, comps., *A Bibliography: The American Revolution and New Jersey* (New Brunswick, N.J.: Special Collections and University Archives, Rutgers University Libraries, 1995). For synthetic overviews of the Revolutionary War in New Jersey, see Lundin, *Cockpit of the Revolution*; Alfred Hoyt Bill, *New Jersey and the Revolutionary War* (Princeton, N.J.: D. Van Nostrand, 1964); and Fleming, *The Forgotten Victory*. For an overview of historic maps relevant to the Revolutionary War period in New Jersey, see John P. Snyder, *The Mapping of New Jersey: The Men and the Art* (New Brunswick, N.J.: Rutgers University Press, 1973), 65–77.

5. Still by far the best general reference on the material culture of colonial America is Ivor Noel Hume, *A Guide to the Artifacts of Colonial America* (New York: Alfred A. Knopf, 1970); more specifically for the Revolutionary War, see George C. Neumann and Frank J. K. Kravic, *Collector's Illustrated Encyclopedia of the American Revolution* (Texarkana, Tex.: Rebel Publishing, 1989).

6. A recent capable summary of military and political events occurring in New Jersey appears in National Park Service, *Crossroads of the American Revolution*, 10–27, 87–92. Other outlines of military actions are given in Munn, *Battles and Skirmishes*; and Mark Edward Lender, *One State in Arms; A Short Military History of New Jersey* (Trenton: New Jersey Historical Commission, 1991).

7. Philadelphia was the least British-occupied of these towns, being under the control of the crown only from October 1777 to June 1778; New York remained under British occupation from its capture in the late summer of 1776 until its evacuation in November 1783; Newark, Elizabethtown, Perth Amboy, New Brunswick, and Raritan Landing were likewise British-controlled for the vast majority of the war years; Burlington, Bordentown, Lamberton, Trenton, Princeton, and Kingston experienced intermittent British occupation between the fall of 1776 and the summer of 1778 but for the most part fell more informally within the American orbit.

8. The King's Highway is followed today by U.S. Route 206 from Trenton to Princeton and by N.J. Route 27 from Princeton to New Brunswick.

9. The British had access to barracks erected during the Seven Years' War (1758–1763) in both Trenton and New Brunswick.

10. Raritan Landing, the primary colonial port on the Raritan River, was located upstream from New Brunswick and was consequently more open to American intervention than New Brunswick; access to Lamberton, a considerable distance up the Delaware, required ships to sail past American-controlled Philadelphia.

11. The British were also no doubt chastened by their experiences on the King's Highway around the time of the Battles of Trenton and Princeton in December 1776/January 1777, when American forces with their superior knowledge of the landscape outmaneuvered them along the main highway corridor on several occasions.

12. Snyder, *The Mapping of New Jersey*, 70–71; Peter J. Guthorn, *American Maps and Map Makers of the Revolution* (Monmouth Beach, N.J.: Philip Freneau Press, 1966); Robert Erskine and Simeon DeWitt, Manuscript Maps, Military Route Maps, 1777–1781 (copies of manuscript maps on file at Washington's Headquarters at Morristown National Historical Park, Morristown, N.J.).

13. Peter J. Guthorn, *British Maps of the American Revolution* (Monmouth Beach, N.J.: Philip Freneau Press, 1966); and Guthorn, *A Collection of Plans, etc. etc. etc. in the Province of New Jersey* (Brielle, N.J.: Portolan Press, 1972).

14. This graphic draws principally on the map "Battles and Skirmishes of the American Revolution in New Jersey," first produced in 1945 by John D. Alden, C.E. historian, New Jersey Society, Sons of the American Revolution, which was revised for the society by D. Stanton Hammond in 1965 and further revised in 1973 by Hammond with Kemble Widmer, New Jersey state geologist and David C. Munn, historical editor, Archives and History Bureau, New Jersey State Library; and maps included in National Park Service, *Crossroads of the American Revolution*.

15. Wacker, *Land and People*, 127, 138, 142.

16. The principal buildings, structures, and sites associated with the Revolutionary War in New Jersey are summarized in National Park Service, *Crossroads of the American Revolution*, 93–98.

17. John L. Cotter, David G. Robert, and Michael Parrington, *The Buried Past: An Archaeological History of Philadelphia* (Philadelphia: University of Pennsylvania Press, 1992), 434–441; Michael Parrington, Helen Schenck, and Jacqueline Thibaut, "The Material World of the Revolutionary War Soldier at Valley Forge," in *The Scope of Historical Archaeology: Essays in Honor of John L. Cotter*, ed. David G. Orr and Daniel G. Crozier, 125–161 (Philadelphia: Temple University Laboratory of Anthropology, 1984).

18. Edward S. Rutsch and Sally Skinner, "Fort Nonsense," *Northeast Historical Archaeology* 2 (1972).

19. Richard Veit, *Digging New Jersey's Past: Historical Archaeology in the Garden State* (New Brunswick, N.J.: Rutgers University Press, 2002), 72–79; Edward S. Rutsch and Kim M. Peters, "Forty Years of Archaeological Research at Morristown National Historical Park, Morristown, New Jersey," *Historical Archaeology* 11 (1977): 15–38; Stanley J. Olsen, "Food Animals of the Continental Army at Valley Forge and Morristown," *American Antiquity* 29 (1964): 506–509.

20. Several investigations of the site of Wayne's brigade encampment have taken place since the mid–1970s, although not all have been formally reported upon. For the first of these studies, see A. A. Boom, "Report on Middlebrook Encampment by the Continental Army during the Middle of 1777 and the Winter of 1778–9," *Somerset County Historical Quarterly* (1975). Draft manuscripts for two subsequent studies in the mid–1970s and early 1980s exist as follows: William Liesenbein, "Report on a Preliminary Archaeological Investigation of the Alleged Site of the 1777 Summer Encampment of Wayne's Brigade at Middlebrook, New Jersey, June 9-July 27, 1974" (Report on file, Department of History, Rutgers University, New Brunswick, N.J., 1974); and Edward S. Rutsch, "Archaeological Investigations for the Elizabethtown Water Company Water Pipeline" (Report on file, New Jersey Historic Preservation Office, New Jersey Depart-

ment of Environmental Protection, Trenton, 1981–1982). A more recent study of Wayne's brigade encampment is Hunter Research Inc., "A Historical and Archaeological Study of Washington Valley Park, East of Middle Brook, Including Part of the Site of Wayne's Brigade Encampment of 1777, Bridgewater Township, Somerset County, New Jersey" (Report on file, New Jersey Historic Preservation Office, 2003).

21. Carl E. Prince, *Middlebrook—The American Eagle's Nest* (Somerville, N.J.: Somerset Press, 1958).

22. For example, Baron Friedrich Von Steuben stayed at the Abraham Staats residence in modern South Bound Brook, and General Nathanael Greene lodged at the Van Veghten house across the river.

23. Possible traces of a Revolutionary War entrenchment reportedly lie close to U.S. Route 22 near Vosseller Avenue, and periodically metal detectorists have unearthed eighteenth-century military artifacts in this general area.

24. Max Schrabisch, "General Knox's Artillery Park, Pluckemin," *Somerset County Historical Quarterly* 6 (1917): 161–168.

25. Veit, *Digging New Jersey's Past*, 64–72; John L. Seidel, "Archaeological Research at the 1778–79 Winter Cantonment of the Continental Army, Pluckemin, New Jersey," *Northeast Historical Archaeology* 12 (1983); and Seidel "The Archaeology of the American Revolution: A Reappraisal and Case Study at the Continental Artillery Cantonment of 1778–1779, Pluckemin, New Jersey" (Ph.D. diss., University of Pennsylvania, 1987).

26. Hunter Research Associates, "Intensive Test Excavations at the Old Barracks, City of Trenton, Mercer County, New Jersey" (Report on file, New Jersey Historic Preservation Office, 1989); Hunter Research, Inc., "Archaeological Investigations at the Old Barracks, Trenton, New Jersey 1994–5: Interior Monitoring and Further Investigation of the Barracks Lot and Parade Ground" (Report on file, New Jersey Historic Preservation Office, 1996).

27. Full publication of the investigation of a British encampment site on the bluffs above Raritan Landing is forthcoming; a provisional assessment was provided in a paper presented to the annual meeting of the Society of Historical Archaeology in Mobile, Alabama, in 2002 by Richard Veit and Robert Wiencek. For British military occupation of Raritan Landing itself, see Jean Howson, Leonard G. Bianchi, and Richard L. Porter, "Pre-Data Recovery Archaeological Investigations at Raritan Landing, N.J. Route 18 Extension Project, Piscataway, Township, Middlesex County, New Jersey" (Report on file, New Jersey Historic Preservation Office, 1995); and Carolyn L. Hartwick and John A. Cavallo, "A Cultural Resource Survey and Archaeological Date Recovery Completed in Connection with the Route 18 Extension and Interim Improvements Project, Piscataway Township, Middlesex County, New Jersey" (Report on file, New Jersey Historic Preservation Office, 1997).

28. Rebecca Yamin, personal communication, 2003; full reporting of the investigation of this site is forthcoming.

29. Several archaeological studies have taken place in the vicinity of the Zabriskie/Steuben House at New Bridge Landing, although deposits and artifacts that are indisputably attributable to the Revolutionary War events of November 1776 have not been identified. See Susan Kardas, "Salvage Excavations at Von Steuben House, River Edge, New Jersey" (Report on file, New Jersey Historic Preservation Office, 1976); Hunter Research, Inc., "Archaeological Investigations in Connection with Exterior Repairs at the Zabriskie/Von Steuben House, Historic New Bridge Landing, River Edge Borough, Bergen County, New Jersey" (Report on file, New Jersey Historic Preservation Office, 2001). The yard of the one surviving house of possible eighteenth-century vintage in the Longbridge Farm vicinity has yielded bayonets of the Revolutionary War period. See Hunter Research, Inc., "Longbridge Farm, South Brunswick, Township, Middlesex County, New Jersey" (Report on file, South Brunswick Township, Middlesex County, New Jersey, 2002).

30. Howard C. Rice Jr. and Anne S. K. Brown, *The American Campaigns of Rochambeau's Army 1780, 1781, 1782, 1783* (Princeton, N.J.: Princeton University Press; Providence, R.I.: Brown University Press, 1972).

31. Barbara C. H. Silber and Wade D. Catts, "The Beverwyck Site. National Register of Historic Places Registration Form" (Report on file, New Jersey Historic Preservation Office, 2001); and Silber and Catts, "'He Has a Very fine Estate': The Beverwyck Site, an 18th-Century Plantation in Northern New Jersey" (paper presented at the annual meeting of the Society for American Archaeology, 2001); Hunter Research, Inc., "Archaeological Investigations in Connection with Exterior Repairs at the Zabriskie/Von Steuben House."

32. Hunter Research, Inc., "Archaeological Data Recovery at the Vanderveer Homestead Site [28So97], Bedminster Township, Somerset County, New Jersey" (Report on file, New Jersey Historic Preservation Office, 1998); and Hunter Research, Inc., "Archaeological Investigations at the Vanderveer/Knox House, Bedminster Township, Somerset County, New Jersey" (Report on file, New Jersey Historic Preservation Office, 1999).

33. Stryker, *The Battles of Trenton and Princeton*; Samuel S. Smith, *The Battle of Trenton* (Monmouth Beach, N.J.: Philip Freneau Press, 1965); William M. Dwyer, *The Day is Ours!* (New York: Viking Press, 1983).

34. Charles R. McGimsey III and Hester A. Davis, "United States of America," in *Approaches to the Archaeological Heritage: A Comparative Study of World Cultural Resource Management Systems*, ed. Henry Cleere, 116–118 (Cambridge: Cambridge University Press, 1984).

35. Edward P. Hamilton, *Fort Ticonderoga; Key to a Continent*, 2nd ed. (New York: Fort Ticonderoga, 1995), 225–230.

36. Douglas D. Scott and Richard A. Fox Jr., *Archaeological Insights into the Custer Battle*, 5th ed. (Norman: University of Oklahoma Press, 1989); Douglas D. Scott, Richard A. Fox Jr., Melissa A. Connor, and Richard Harmon, *Archaeological Perspectives on the Battle of the Little Bighorn* (Norman: University of Oklahoma Press, 1989); Melissa Connor and Douglas D. Scott, "Metal Detector Use in Archaeology: An Introduction," *Historical Archaeology* 32 (1998): 76–85.

37. Daniel M. Sivilich, "Analyzing Musket Balls to Interpret a Revolutionary War Site," *Historical Archaeology* 30 (1996): 101–109; Daniel M. Sivilich and Ralph Phillips, "Cultural Resource Summary Report, Phase 1 Archaeological Surveys Conducted at Princeton Battlefield State Park, 500 Mercer Street, Princeton, New Jersey" (Report on file, New Jersey Historic Preservation Office, 2000); Garry W. Stone and Daniel M. Sivilich, "Archaeology of Molly Hayes and Joseph Plumb Martin," *New Jersey Heritage Magazine* 2 (2003): 30–34.

38. Veit, *Digging New Jersey's Past*, 87–89; Thomas Demarest, "The Baylor Massacre—Some Assorted Notes and Information," *Bergen County History* (1971): 29–94.

39. Samuel S. Smith, *Fight for the Delaware* (Monmouth Beach, N.J.: Philip Freneau Press, 1970); J. Lee Cox, "Phase I Submerged Cultural Resources Investigation, Site Development and Waterfront Park, Gloucester City, Camden County, New Jersey" (Report on file, New Jersey Historic Preservation Office, 2002).

40. Louis Berger and Associates, Inc., "Historic Sites. Trenton Complex Archaeology: Report 12" (Report on file, New Jersey Historic Preservation Office, 1998), 409–461.

41. Hunter, "Patterns of Mill Siting," 602–605.

42. Veit, *Digging New Jersey's Past*, 148–156; Edward Lenik, "Excavations at Charlotteburg Middle Forge," *Bulletin of the Archaeological Society of New Jersey* 30 (1974): 7–10; James A. Mulholland, *A History of Metals in Colonial America* (Birmingham: University of Alabama Press, 1981), 123, 131.

43. Hunter Research, Inc., "Archaeological Investigations at the New Jersey State House, City of Trenton, Mercer County, New Jersey" (Report on file, New Jersey Historic Preservation Office,

1989). A full technical report does not presently exist on the archaeological investigations that were undertaken in 1996 on the site of the Harrow/Yard plating mill in connection with the expansion of Thomas Edison State College.

44. Robert Treat Payne to Benjamin Yard, March 9, 1776 (on file at the Massachusetts Historical Society, Boston).

45. Richard W. Hunter and Richard L. Porter, "American Steel in the Colonial Period: Trenton's Role in a 'Neglected' Industry," *Canal History and Technology Proceedings* 9 (1990): 83–119.

46. A five-volume technical report on archaeological data recovery and monitoring carried out along the South Trenton/Lamberton riverfront between 1998 and 2001 is currently nearing completion. Volume 3 in this series traces the Revolutionary War–era history and archaeology of Lamberton in considerable detail.

47. Technical reports are currently being prepared on the most recent phase of archaeological study at Raritan Landing conducted in connection with improvements to N.J. Route 18; summary information may be found at www.raritanlanding.com; earlier work is outlined in Veit, *Digging New Jersey's Past*, 41–44.

Selected Bibliography

Adams, William Paul. *The First American Constitutions: Republican Ideology and the Making of the State Constitutions in the Revolutionary Era.* Chapel Hill: University of North Carolina Press, 1980.

Archdeacon, Thomas. *New Jersey Society in the Revolutionary Era.* Vol. 17 of *New Jersey's Revolutionary Experience.* Trenton: New Jersey Historical Commission, 1975.

Bailyn, Bernard. *The Ideological Origins of the American Revolution.* Cambridge, Mass.: Belknap Press of Harvard University Press, 1967.

————. *The Peopling of British North America: An Introduction.* New York: Alfred A. Knopf, 1986.

Bassett, William. *Historic American Buildings Survey of New Jersey.* Newark: New Jersey Historical Society, 1977.

Batinski, Michael. *The New Jersey Assembly, 1738–1775: The Making of a Legislative Community.* Lanham, Md.: University Press of America, 1987.

Berlin, Ira, and Ronald Hoffman, eds. *Slavery and Freedom in the Age of the American Revolution.* Charlottesville: United States Capitol Historical Society/University Press of Virginia, 1983.

Buel, Richard. *In Irons: Britain's Naval Supremacy and the American Revolutionary Economy.* New Haven, Conn.: Yale University Press, 1998.

Bill, Alfred Hoyt. *New Jersey and the Revolutionary War.* Princeton, N.J.: D. Van Nostrand, 1964.

Bogin, Ruth. *Abraham Clark and the Quest for Equality in the Revolutionary Era, 1774–1794.* Rutherford, N.J.: Fairleigh Dickinson University Press, 1982.

Boyd, Julian P., ed. *Fundamental Laws and Constitution of New Jersey, 1664–1964.* Princeton, N.J.: D. Van Nostrand, 1964.

Boyer, Charles S. *Early Forges and Furnaces in New Jersey.* Philadelphia: University of Pennsylvania Press, 1931.

Burnett, Edmund Cody. *The Continental Congress.* New York: Macmillan, 1941.

Burr, Nelson R. *The Anglican Church in New Jersey.* Philadelphia: Church Historical Society, 1954.

Burstyn, Joan N., ed. *Past and Promise, Lives of New Jersey Women.* Syracuse, N.Y.: Syracuse University Press, 1997.

Bush, Bernard, comp. *Laws of the Royal Colony of New Jersey.* 5 vols. Trenton: Division of Archives and Records Management, New Jersey Department of State, 1977–1986.

Butler, Jon. *Religion in Colonial America.* New York: Oxford University Press, 2000.

Clemens, Paul G. E. *The Uses of Abundance: A History of New Jersey's Economy.* Trenton: New Jersey Historical Commission, 1992.

Coad, Oral. *New Jersey in Travelers' Accounts, 1524–1971.* Metuchen, N.J.: Scarecrow Press, 1972.

Cody, Edward J.. *The Religious Issue in Revolutionary New Jersey.* Vol. 10 of *New Jersey's Revolutionary War Experience.* Trenton: New Jersey Historical Commission, 1975.

Cohen, David Steven. *The Folklore and Folklife of New Jersey*. New Brunswick, N.J.: Rutgers University Press, 1991.

Collins, Varnum Lansing, ed. *A Brief Narrative of the Ravages of the British and Hessians at Princeton in 1778–79*. Princeton, N.J.: University Library, 1906.

Connors, Richard J. *The Constitution of 1776*. Trenton: New Jersey Historical Commission, 1975.

Cooley, Henry Scofield. *A Study of Slavery in New Jersey*. Baltimore: Johns Hopkins University Press, 1896.

Cunningham, John T. *Made in New Jersey: The Industrial Story of a State*. New Brunswick, N.J.: Rutgers University Press, 1954.

———. *New Jersey: America's Main Road*. Garden City, N.Y.: Doubleday, 1966.

———. *New Jersey's Five Who Signed*. Vol. 6 of *New Jersey's Revolutionary Experience*. Trenton: New Jersey Historical Commission, 1975.

Cushing, John D., comp. *First Laws of the State of New Jersey*. Wilmington, Del.: Michael Glazier, 1981. Facsimile reprint of Peter Wilson, comp. *Acts of the General Assembly of the State of New Jersey*. Trenton, N.J., 1784.

DePauw, Linda Grant. *Fortunes of War: New Jersey Women and the American Revolution*. Vol. 26 of *New Jersey's Revolutionary Experience*. Trenton: New Jersey Historical Commission, 1975.

Dowd, Gregory Evans. "Declaration of Independence: War and Inequality in Revolutionary New Jersey, 1776–1815." *New Jersey History* 103 (1985): 47–67.

———. *The Indians of New Jersey*. Trenton: New Jersey Historical Commission, 1992.

Dwyer, William M. *The Day Is Ours!* New York: Viking Press, 1983.

Elmer, Lucius Q. C. *The Constitution and Government of the Province and State of New Jersey: With Biographical Sketches of the Governors from 1776–1845 and Reminiscences of Bench and Bar during More than a Half Century*. Newark, N.J.: M. R. Dennis, 1872.

Erdman, Charles R., Jr. *The New Jersey Constitution of 1776*. Princeton, N.J.: Princeton University Press, 1929.

Ewald, Johann. *Diary of the American War: A Hessian Journal*. Trans. and ed. Joseph P. Tustin. New Haven, Conn.: Yale University Press, 1979.

Fitzpatrick, John C., ed. *The Writings of George Washington from the Original Manuscript Sources, 1745–1799*. 39 Vols. Washington, D.C.: U.S. Government Printing Office, 1931–1944.

Fleming, Thomas. *The Forgotten Victory: The Battle for New Jersey, 1780*. New York: Reader's Digest Press, 1973.

———. *Liberty! The American Revolution*. New York: Viking Penguin, 1997.

———. *New Jersey: A Bicentennial History*. New York: Norton, 1977.

Foner, Eric, ed. *Thomas Paine: Collected Writings*. New York: Library of America, 1995.

Fowler, David J. "Egregious Villains, Wood Rangers, and London Traders: The Pine Robber Phenomenon in New Jersey during the Revolutionary War." Ph.D. diss., Rutgers University, 1987.

Fuhlbruegge, Edward A. "New Jersey Finances during the American Revolution." *Proceedings of the New Jersey Historical Society* 55 (July 1937): 167–190.

Gerdts, William H., Jr. *Painting and Sculpture in New Jersey*. Princeton, N.J.: D. Van Nostrand, 1964.

Gerlach, Larry R. *Prologue to Independence: New Jersey in the Coming of the American Revolution*. New Brunswick, N.J.: Rutgers University Press, 1976.

———. *The Road to Revolution*. Vol. 7 of *New Jersey's Revolutionary Experience*. Trenton: New Jersey Historical Commission, 1975.

————. *William Franklin: New Jersey's Last Royal Governor.* Trenton: New Jersey Historical Commission, 1975.

————, ed. *New Jersey in the American Revolution, 1763–1783: A Documentary History.* Trenton: New Jersey Historical Commission, 1975.

Gertzog, Irwin. "Female Suffrage in New Jersey, 1790–1807." *Women and Politics* 10 (1990): 47–68.

Green, Jacob. *Observations: On the Reconciliation of Great Britain, and the Colonies in Which Are Exhibited Arguments For, and Against, That Measure,* 1776. Reprint, Trenton: New Jersey Historical Association, 1976.

Greene, Jack P. *Pursuits of Happiness: The Social Development of Early Modern British Colonies and the Formation of American Culture.* Chapel Hill: University of North Carolina Press, 1988.

Groseclose, Barbara S. *Emanuel Leutze, 1816–1868: Freedom Is the Only King.* Washington, D.C.: Smithsonian Institution Press for the National Collection of Fine Arts, 1975.

Henretta, James A., Michael Kammen, and Stanley Katz, eds. *The Transformation of Early American History: Society, Authority, and Ideology.* New York: Alfred A. Knopf, 1991.

Hodges, Graham Russell. *Root and Branch: African Americans in New York and East Jersey, 1613–1863.* Chapel Hill: University of North Carolina Press, 1999.

————. *Slavery and Freedom in the Rural North: African Americans in Monmouth County, New Jersey, 1665–1865.* Madison, Wis.: Madison House, 1997.

Hoffman, Ronald, ed. *The Economy of Early America: The Revolutionary Period, 1763–1790.* Charlottesville: University Press of Virginia, 1988.

Hume, Ivor Noel. *A Guide to the Artifacts of Colonial America.* New York: Alfred A. Knopf, 1970.

Jackson, John W. *Margaret Morris: Her Journal, with Biographical Sketch and Notes.* Philadelphia: George S. MacManus, 1949.

Jaffe, Irma B. *John Trumbull: Patriot-Artist of the American Revolution.* Boston: New York Graphic Society, 1975.

Jamison, Wallace N. *Religion in New Jersey: A Brief History.* Princeton, N.J.: D. Van Nostrand, 1964.

Jones, E. Alfred. *The Loyalists of New Jersey.* 1927. Reprint. Bowie, Md.: Heritage Books, 1988.

Kemmerer, Donald. *Path to Freedom: The Struggle for Self-Government in Colonial New Jersey, 1703–1776.* Princeton, N.J.: Princeton University Press, 1940.

Kulikoff, Allan. *From British Peasants to Colonial American Farmers.* Chapel Hill: University of North Carolina Press, 2000.

Lane, Wheaton J. *From Indian Trail to Iron Horse: Travel and Transportation in New Jersey, 1620–1860.* Princeton, N.J.: Princeton University Press, 1939.

Lefkowitz, Arthur S. *The Long Retreat.* New Brunswick, N.J.: Rutgers University Press, 1998.

Leiby, Adrian C. *The Revolutionary War in the Hackensack Valley: The Jersey Dutch and the Neutral Ground.* New Brunswick, N.J.: Rutgers University Press, 1980.

Lender, Mark Edward. *The New Jersey Soldier.* Vol. 5 of *New Jersey's Revolutionary Experience.* Trenton: New Jersey Historical Commission, 1975.

————. "Reversals of Fortune: The Trenton and Princeton Campaign of 1776–1777." *New Jersey Heritage* 1 (2002): 17–29.

————. "Small Battles Won: New Jersey and the Patriot Military Revival." *New Jersey Heritage* 1 (2002): 33–34.

Levitt, James H. *For Want of Trade: Shipping and the New Jersey Ports, 1680–1763.* Newark: New Jersey Historical Society, 1981.

————. *New Jersey's Revolutionary Economy*. Vol. 9, *New Jersey's Revolutionary Experience*. Trenton: New Jersey Historical Commission, 1975.

Lindsley, James Elliott. *A Certain Splendid House*. Rev. ed. Morristown: Washington Association of New Jersey, 2000.

Lundin, Leonard. *Cockpit of the Revolution: The War for Independence in New Jersey*. Princeton, N.J.: Princeton University Press, 1940.

Lurie, Maxine N. "Envisioning a Republic: New Jersey's 1776 Constitution and Oath of Office." *New Jersey History* 119 (2001): 3–21.

————. "New Jersey Intellectuals and the United States Constitution." *Journal of Rutgers University Libraries* (1987): 65–87.

Main, Jackson Turner. *The Social Structure of Revolutionary America*. Princeton, N.J.: Princeton University Press, 1973.

Martin, James Kirby, and Mark Edward Lender. *A Respectable Army: The Military Origins of the Republic, 1763–1789*. Arlington Heights, Ill.: Harlan Davidson, 1982.

McConville, Brendan. *These Daring Disturbers of the Public Peace: The Struggle for Property and Power in Early New Jersey*. Ithaca, N.Y.: Cornell University Press, 1999.

McCormick, Richard P. *Experiment in Independence: New Jersey in the Critical Period, 1781–1789*. New Brunswick, N.J.: Rutgers University Press, 1950.

————. *New Jersey from Colony to State, 1609–1789*. Princeton, N.J.: D. Van Nostrand, 1964.

McCusker, John J., and Russell R. Menard. *The Economy of British America, 1607–1789*. Chapel Hill: University of North Carolina Press, 1991.

Mitnick, Barbara J. "The History of History Painting." In *Picturing History: American Painting, 1770–1930*, ed. William Ayres. New York: Rizzoli International Publications, 1993.

————. *Jean Leon Gerome Ferris: American Painter Historian*. Laurel, Miss.: Lauren Rogers Museum of Art, 1986.

————. "Paintings for the People: American Popular History Painting, 1875–1930." In *Picturing History: American Painting, 1770–1930*, ed. William Ayres. New York: Rizzoli International Publications, 1993.

————, ed. *George Washington: American Symbol*. New York: Hudson Hills Press, 1999.

Mitnick, Barbara J., and Mark Edward Lender. *George Washington and the Battle of Trenton: The Evolution of an American Image*. Exhibition catalog. Trenton: New Jersey State Museum, 2001.

Mitros, David, ed. *Slave Records of Morris County, New Jersey: 1756–1841*, 2nd ed. Morristown, N.J.: Morris County Heritage Commission, 2002.

Moore, Wayne D. "Written and Unwritten Constitutional Law in the Founding Period: The Early New Jersey Cases." *Constitutional Commentary* 7 (1990): 341–359.

Moulton, Phillip P., ed. *The Journal and Major Essays of John Woolman*. Richmond, Ind.: Friends United Press, 1989.

Mulford, Carla, ed. *Only for the Eye of a Friend: The Poems of Annis Boudinot Stockton*. Charlottesville: University Press of Virginia, 1995.

Munn, David C., comp. *Battles and Skirmishes of the American Revolution in New Jersey*. Trenton: Department of Environmental Protection, Bureau of Geology and Topography, State of New Jersey, 1976.

Murrin, Mary R. *To Save This State from Ruin: New Jersey and the Creation of the United States Constitution, 1776–1789*. Trenton: New Jersey Historical Commission, 1987.

National Park Service. *Crossroads of the American Revolution in New Jersey: Special Resource Study.* Philadelphia: U.S. Department of the Interior, National Park Service, Philadelphia Support Office, 2002.

Nell, William Cooper. *Colored Patriots of the American Revolution.* Boston: R. F. Wallcut, 1855.

Northend, Mary Harrod. *American Glass.* New York: Tudor Publishing, 1926.

Owen, Lewis F. *The Revolutionary Struggle in New Jersey, 1776–1783.* Vol. 6 of *New Jersey's Revolutionary Experience.* Trenton: New Jersey Historical Commission, 1975.

Palmer, Arlene, *Wistarburgh Glass Works: The Beginning of Jersey Glassmaking—New Jersey 1739–1776.* Alloway, N.J.: Alloway Township Bicentennial Committee, 1976.

Pierce, Arthur D. *Iron in the Pines: The Story of New Jersey's Ghost Towns and Bog Iron.* New Brunswick, N.J.: Rutgers University Press, 1957.

———. *Smugglers Woods: Jaunts and Journeys in Colonial and Revolutionary New Jersey.* New Brunswick, N.J.: Rutgers University Press, 1960.

Pingeon, Frances D. *Blacks in the Revolutionary Era.* Vol. 14 of *New Jersey's Revolutionary Experience.* Trenton: New Jersey Historical Commission, 1975.

———. "Slavery in New Jersey on the Eve of Revolution." In *New Jersey in the American Revolution: Political and Social Conflict,* rev. ed., ed. William C. Wright. Trenton: New Jersey Historical Commission, 1974.

Pomfret, John E. *Colonial New Jersey: A History.* New York: Scribner, 1973.

Price, Clement Alexander. *Freedom Not Far Distant: A Documentary History of Afro-Americans in New Jersey.* Newark: New Jersey Historical Society, 1980.

Prince, Carl E. *William Livingston: New Jersey's First Governor.* Vol. 21 of *New Jersey's Revolutionary Experience.* Trenton: New Jersey Historical Commission, 1975.

Prince, Carl E., et al., eds. *The Papers of William Livingston.* 5 vols. Trenton and New Brunswick: New Jersey Historical Commission, 1979–1988.

Purvis, Thomas L. "The European Origins of New Jersey's Eighteen-Century Population." *New Jersey History* 100 (Spring/Summer 1982): 15–31.

———. "The Origins and Patterns of Agrarian Unrest in New Jersey, 1735–1754." *William and Mary Quarterly Journal* 3rd ser., 39 (1982): 600–627.

———. *Proprietors, Patronage, and Paper Money: Legislative Politics in New Jersey, 1703–1776.* New Brunswick, N.J.: Rutgers University Press, 1986.

Quarles, Benjamin. *The Negro in the American Revolution.* Chapel Hill: University of North Carolina Press, 1961.

Rice, Howard C., Jr., and Anne S. K. Brown. *The American Campaigns of Rochambeau's Army, 1780, 1781, 1782, 1783.* Princeton, N.J.: Princeton University Press; Providence, R.I.: Brown University Press, 1972.

Richardson, Edgar P., Brooke Hindle, and Lillian B. Miller. *Charles Willson Peale and His World.* New York: Harry N. Abrams, 1982.

Ryan, Dennis P. *New Jersey in the American Revolution, 1763–1783: A Chronology.* Trenton: New Jersey Historical Commission, 1975.

———. *New Jersey's Loyalists.* Vol. 20 of *New Jersey's Revolutionary Experience.* Trenton: New Jersey Historical Commission, 1975.

———. *New Jersey's Whigs.* Vol. 19 of *New Jersey's Revolutionary Experience.* Trenton: New Jersey Historical Commission, 1975.

Sargent, Epes, ed. *The Select Works of Benjamin Franklin*. Boston: Phillips, Sampson, 1854.

Schmidt, Hubert. *Agriculture in New Jersey: A Three-Hundred-Year History*. New Brunswick, N.J.: Rutgers University Press, 1973.

Sellers, Charles Coleman. *Charles Willson Peale*. New York: Charles Scribner's Sons, 1969.

Sickler, Joseph S. *The Old Houses of Salem County*. Salem, N.J.: Sunbeam, 1934.

Skemp, Sheila L. *William Franklin: Son of a Patriot, Servant of a King*. New York: Oxford University Press, 1990.

Smith, Samuel. *The History of the Colony of Nova-Caesaria, or New-Jersey*. Philadelphia, 1765; 1890. Reprint of 1890 edition. Spartanburg, S.C.: Reprint Co., 1975.

Snyder, John P. *The Mapping of New Jersey: The Men and the Art*. New Brunswick, N.J.: Rutgers University Press, 1973.

Stellhorn, Paul, and Michael J. Birkner, eds. *The Governors of New Jersey, 1664–1974*. Trenton: New Jersey Historical Commission, 1982.

Stewart, Bruce W. *Morristown: A Crucible of the American Revolution*. Vol. 3 of *New Jersey's Revolutionary Experience*. Trenton: New Jersey Historical Commission, 1975.

Stone, Gary W., and Daniel M. Sivilich. "Archaeology of Molly Hayes and Joseph Plumb Martin." *New Jersey Heritage* 2 (2003): 30–34.

Studley, Mirian V. *Historic New Jersey through Visitor's Eyes*. Princeton, N.J.: D. Van Nostrand, 1964.

Stryker, William S. *The Battle of Monmouth*. Ed. William Starr Myers. Princeton, N.J.: Princeton University Press, 1927.

———. *The Battles of Trenton and Princeton*. 1898. Reprint. Trenton, N.J.: Old Barracks Association, 2001.

———. *The New Jersey Volunteers in the Revolutionary War*. Trenton, N.J.: Naar, Day and Naar, 1887.

Trumbull, John. *Autobiography, Reminiscences and Letters of John Trumbull from 1756 to 1841*. New York and London: Wiley and Putnam, 1841.

Van Hoesen, Walter. *Early Taverns and Stagecoach Days in New Jersey*. Cranbury, N.J.: Associated University Presses, 1976.

Veit, Richard. *Digging New Jersey's Past: Historical Archaeology in the Garden State*. New Brunswick, N.J.: Rutgers University Press, 2002.

Wacker, Peter O. *Land and People: A Cultural Geography of Preindustrial New Jersey; Origins and Settlement Patterns*. New Brunswick, N.J.: Rutgers University Press, 1975.

Wacker, Peter O., and Paul G. E. Clemens. *Land Use in Early New Jersey: A Historical Geography*. New Brunswick, N.J.: Rutgers University Press, 1992.

Weiss, Harry B., and Grace Weiss. *The Revolutionary Saltworks of the New Jersey Coast*. Trenton, N.J.: Past Times Press, 1959.

Wertenbacker, Thomas. *The Middle Colonies*. New York: Cooper Square, 1963.

White, Margaret E. *The Decorative Arts of Early New Jersey*. Princeton, N.J.: D. Van Nostrand, 1964.

———. "Some Early Furniture Makers of New Jersey." *The Magazine Antiques* 74, no. 4 (October 1958): 322.

Williams, Robert F. *The New Jersey State Constitution*. New Brunswick, N.J.: Rutgers University Press, 1997.

Wolinetz, Gary K. "New Jersey Slavery and the Law." *Rutgers Law Review* 50, no. 4 (Summer 1998).

Wood, Gordon S. *The Creation of the American Republic, 1776–1787*. New York: W. W. Norton, 1969.

————. *The Radicalism of the American Revolution.* New York: Alfred A. Knopf, 1992.

Woodward, Carl R. *The Development of Agriculture in New Jersey, 1640–1880.* New Brunswick: New Jersey Agricultural Experimentation Station, Rutgers University, 1927.

Wright, Giles R. *Afro-Americans in New Jersey: A Short History.* Trenton: New Jersey Historical Commission, 1988.

Wright, William C., ed. *The Development of the New Jersey Legislature from Colonial Times to the Present.* Trenton: New Jersey Historical Commission, 1976.

————. *New Jersey in the American Revolution III: Papers Presented at the Seventh Annual New Jersey History Symposium, 1975.* Trenton: New Jersey Historical Commission, 1976.

Zilversmit, Arthur. *The First Emancipation: The Abolition of Slavery in the North.* Chicago: University of Chicago Press, 1967.

Notes on Contributors

IAN C. G. BURROW is vice president and a principal archaeologist at Hunter Research, Inc. He has studied several Revolutionary War–era sites in New Jersey, among them the Old Barracks in Trenton, the Pluckemin artillery camp, and the Vanderveer House in Bedminster. He is a fellow of the Society of Antiquaries of London and is the current president of the American Cultural Resource Association.

DELIGHT W. DODYK is a former member of the History Department at Drew University. She currently serves as president of the Board of Trustees of the Women's Project of New Jersey, publisher of the landmark work *Past and Promise: Lives of New Jersey Women* (1990, 1997). Her recent publications include *The Diary of Sarah Reid, a New Jersey Farm Woman* (2001).

THOMAS FLEMING is one of America's most renowned historians of the Revolution. During his almost forty-year career, he has authored numerous works, including *Liberty! The American Revolution,* which accompanied a 1997 six-part television series and was named the best book of the year by the American Revolution Roundtable, and *1776: Year of Illusions* (1975). He is a fellow of the Society of American Historians.

DAVID J. FOWLER is the former director of the David Library of the American Revolution at Washington Crossing, Pennsylvania. His career has been devoted to research, archival studies, and publications, including *Egregious Villains, Wood Rangers, and London Traders: The Pine Robber Phenomenon in New Jersey during the Revolutionary War* (1987).

HARRIETTE C. HAWKINS is the former executive director of the New Jersey Historic Trust. She is an authority on American architectural history and material culture and has lectured widely on issues related to historic preservation and open space. She served as project director for *The Economic Impact of Historic Preservation in New Jersey* (1996).

RICHARD W. HUNTER is the founder and president of Hunter Research, Inc., a firm that specializes in historical and archaeological research and historic preservation. He has studied several Revolutionary War–era sites in New Jersey, among them the Middlebrook Encampments, the Zabriskie/Von Steuben House at New Bridge Landing, and Princeton Battlefield.

He is a past president of Preservation New Jersey, a former member of the state Historic Sites Review Board, and currently vice president of the Trenton Downtown Association.

MARK EDWARD LENDER is a professor of American history and former dean of the Nathan Weiss Graduate College at Kean University. He is a nationally recognized authority on the military aspects of the American Revolution. His New Jersey publications include *The New Jersey Soldier* (1975) and *One State in Arms: A Short Military History of New Jersey* (1991).

MAXINE N. LURIE is an associate professor at Seton Hall University. A distinguished historian of colonial America, she is the foremost authority on the New Jersey Constitution of 1776. In addition to her numerous publications, she recently served as coeditor of the *Encyclopedia of New Jersey* (2004).

BARBARA J. MITNICK is an art historian and adjunct professor of American history painting in the Caspersen School of Graduate Studies at Drew University. Her numerous exhibitions include *Picturing History: American Painting 1770–1930* (1993–1995) and *George Washington: American Symbol* (1999), for which she served as general editor of the accompanying publication. She is the former chair of the Task Force on New Jersey History and the New Jersey Historic Trust.

MERRILL MAGUIRE SKAGGS is Baldwin Professor of the Humanities in Brothers College and the Caspersen School of Graduate Studies at Drew University. She is a recognized authority on American literature and has won several awards for her writing. Her recent publications include *Willa Cather's New York: New Essays on Cather and the City* (2000).

LORRAINE E. WILLIAMS is New Jersey's State archaeologist and curator of Archaeology and Ethnology at the New Jersey State Museum, where she manages the state's nationally-recognized archaeological collections. She has contributed to numerous publications and has curated exhibitions including "Preserving Identity: New Jersey's Indians" (2004) and "Cultures in Competition: Indians and Europeans in Colonial New Jersey" (2002).

GILES R. WRIGHT is an authority on the history of African Americans in New Jersey and director of the Afro-American History Program at the New Jersey Historical Commission. His publications include *Afro-Americans in New Jersey: A Short History* (1988) and *"Steal Away, Steal Away": A Guide to the Underground Railroad in New Jersey* (2002).

Index

ABOUT RIVERGATE BOOKS

From north to south and east to west, New Jersey is a land
of rivers. The State is sandwiched between the Hudson and Delaware
Rivers, with the Raritan, Passaic, and Navesink cutting swaths across it. Rivers
were highly influential in New Jersey's development into a major transportation and
industrial power. In 1766, Rutgers, The State University of New Jersey, was founded as
Queen's College near the banks of the Raritan River in New Brunswick. Rutgers's other
two campuses also lie on or near rivers: Newark (the Passaic) and Camden (the Delaware).
New Jersey is also renowned as a gateway to America. From the millions of immigrants
who came by ship in the nineteenth century to those who arrive today at Newark Liberty
Airport, the State has long represented the land of opportunity to those from other places.
The name Rivergate Books, then, is a fitting one for a regional imprint of Rutgers University
Press. Fulfilling its mandate to serve the people of New Jersey, since 1936 the Press has
published superior books on the State and the surrounding area, from history, recreation,
and popular culture to literature, the environment, and education. Rivergate Books
enhances this long and valued tradition by providing a distinctive name for the
Press's regional book program and reaffirming its commitment to publishing
the best books in this field. With the formation of this new imprint,
Rivergate Books solidifies the Press's dedication to furthering
the interests of a great State and its people.

A NOTE ON THE TYPE

American type designer Carol Twombly's 1989 digital revival of the typefaces
of the esteemed English typecutter William Caslon for the Adobe Corporation is
notable for its faithful reproduction of both the aesthetic details and historical spirit of
Caslon's work, the pinnacle of English Baroque type design and a stalwart of printing and
publishing since its introduction in the mid-eighteenth century. Caslon's type figured
prominently in Revolutionary–era American history: it is the typeface in which the
first printed copies of the Declaration of Independence appeared, and the type
used on the first paper currency issued by the new United States of America.

Designed and composed by Kevin Hanek

Printed and bound by Sheridan Books, Inc.,
Ann Arbor, Michigan